Anglicans and Roman Catholics:
The Search for Unity

Anglicans and Roman Catholics:

The Search for Unity

Edited by

Christopher Hill and E. J. Yarnold SJ

SPCK/CTS

First published in Great Britain 1994 by
The Society for Promoting Christian Knowledge
Holy Trinity Church
Marylebone Road
London NW1 4DU
and the
Incorporated Catholic Truth Society
192 Vauxhall Bridge Road
London SW1V 1PD

British Library Cataloguing-in-Publication Data
A catalogue record for this book is available from
the British Library

ISBN 0-281-04745-6

Typeset by Pioneer Associates, Perthshire
Printed in Great Britain by
The Cromwell Press, Melksham, Wiltshire

Contents

Introduction

Official Comments

Introduction

1

CHRISTOPHER HILL:
The Scope of this Book

This collection of documents about the work of the first
Anglican–Roman Catholic International Commission (ARCIC)
(1969–1981)[1] is not a heroic monument to the triumph of hope
over realism, as some might imagine according to the supposed ebbing of the ecumenical tide. It is rather a milestone on
a journey not yet completed: a milestone, moreover, which the
book's co-editors believe will show that more ground has been
covered than many Anglicans and Roman Catholics realise.

After the final meeting of the first Commission (ARCIC I)
at St George's House, Windsor, in August/September 1981,
the authorities of both churches began to evaluate its Final
Report.[2] Roman Catholic Episcopal Conferences were invited
to respond to the Final Report by the Vatican Secretariat
for Promoting Christian Unity (now the Pontifical Council for
Promoting Christian Unity). The Congregation for the Doctrine
of the Faith pursued an independent first assessment.[3] On
the Anglican side the Anglican Consultative Council sent the

---

[1] For a brief history of which, see the following chapter by my co-editor,
Fr. Edward Yarnold SJ.
[2] For the full text see Chapter 4.
[3] This resulted in the Congregation's *Observations* (1982), for which see
Chapter 5.

3

Final Report to all the Provinces with a view to a world-wide evaluation in preparation for the Lambeth Conference of 1988.

Comments on the work of ARCIC I by critics, friendly or otherwise, had, of course, already been made from the time of the publication of the first Agreed Statement in 1971. Equally, members of the Commission had regularly commended and commented upon each stage of its work. With the Resolutions of the Lambeth Conference (1988) and the Official Response of the Holy See (1991) a further significant stage of evaluation was reached.[4]

The scope of this book is thus to bring together with the text of the Final Report a significant range of official evaluation, comment and explanation. Official comment is carefully distinguished from commendation by members of ARCIC, and outside 'expert opinion' is a third distinct category. Inevitably, the 'pro-ARCIC' sympathies of the co-editors will show! But the book includes criticism as well as praise. In the category of 'expert opinion' we include a 'private' article by Cardinal Josef Ratzinger and an Open Letter by Anglican Evangelicals.[5]

It would have been good to publish more material from elsewhere in the world than the United Kingdom. But the book, including the text of the Final Report of ARCIC I, runs to some 343 pages. Inevitably there have to be limits. The inclusion of material from the Anglican–Roman Catholic Consultation in the USA (ARC–USA) and the document from the French Episcopal Commission for Unity will be seen, however, to be no mere tokenism.[6]

Moreover, on the Roman Catholic side, the practice of publishing the responses from Episcopal Conferences was eventually suspended at Rome's request. This reflects the continuing inner Roman Catholic debate about the authority of National Episcopal Conferences *vis à vis* the central authorities. The positive English and Welsh response was fortunately published before this suspension. Nevertheless, the assessments of all the Episcopal Conferences were collated by the Secretariat/Council for Promoting Christian Unity. They were generally very positive; the English Roman Catholic Bishops' Response is therefore not untypical.[7]

[4] See Chapters 9 and 10.
[5] See Chapters 22 and 23.
[6] See Chapters 15 and 16.
[7] See Chapter 7.

On the Anglican side, nineteen out of twenty-nine Provinces returned synodical or official responses in time for the Lambeth Conference of 1988. The English General Synod report is not untypical in its carefully critical but finally affirming stance.[8] All the Provincial responses received were collated and summarised for the Lambeth Conference by a special international consultation in 1987. These findings were published in the *Emmaus Report* in the same year.[9] In this form they were accessible for the bishops of the Lambeth Conference, who in their turn discerned the consensus of the Anglican Communion on the Final Report of ARCIC.

The actual genesis of this book was more than private enterprise, though the responsibility for the selection of the documents here (re)published remains the responsibility of the editors alone. After the long awaited Vatican Response of 1991, it became clear that all had not been *finally* said. With hindsight, perhaps the designation of the published texts of ARCIC I as 'The Final Report' was less than clear! ARCIC I itself was always quite explicit that more work needed to be done on the central question of authority. Though the Lambeth Conference did not ask for more work on the eucharist and the ordained ministry, the Holy See's Response did – in addition to authority. The second Anglican–Roman Catholic International Commission (ARCIC II) consequently suggested that it might be helpful if a selection of responses were brought together in published form. This book is our response to that invitation. At the same time it commissioned a further clarification on the eucharist and ordained ministry by former members of ARCIC I, which it accepted and endorsed with minor changes. This has in its turn been evaluated in a significant letter from Cardinal Edward Cassidy of the Pontifical Council for Promoting Christian Unity.[10] All this demonstrates that the 'reception' of ecumenical agreements is indeed a continuing process.

Finally, a word about the beginning. The visit of Archbishop Michael Ramsey to Pope Paul VI in Rome and their Common Declaration (1966) are properly regarded as the mandate for official Anglican–Roman Catholic dialogue. The Common Declaration is therefore printed at the conclusion of this

---

[8] See Chapter 8.
[9] Church House Publishing, London, 1987.
[10] See Chapters 17 and 18.

Introduction. In an ideal world the Malta Report, which represented the preliminary work of the Preparatory Commission, would also have been printed at this point. But this has already been published, together with a selection of its papers, in *Anglican–Roman Catholic Dialogue: The Work of the Preparatory Commission.*[11] Readers are referred to this book for this important pre-history.

2

EDWARD YARNOLD:
The History of ARCIC I

There are many points at which one could begin the story of ARCIC. Here we shall take for granted the long pioneering work of the World Council of Churches and the dramatic advance made at the Second Vatican Council, and begin with the historic meeting in Rome of Pope Paul VI and the Archbishop of Canterbury, Michael Ramsey, in 1966, at which the two primates issued a *Common Declaration* inaugurating dialogue between the Roman Catholic Church and the Anglican Communion. The aim expressed was to promote the development of 'respect, esteem and fraternal love' between the two communions in the hope of attaining 'that unity in truth, for which Christ prayed', and 'a restoration of complete communion of faith and sacramental life'. When ARCIC came into existence it customarily described this aim of its founding fathers as that of 'full organic unity'.

[11] eds. A. Clark and C. Davey, Oxford, London, 1974.

The *Declaration* also sketched the method that the Commission was to find so fruitful: there was to be 'a serious dialogue . . . founded on the Gospels and on the ancient common traditions'. In other words, the discussions were to start with what the two Churches held in common and follow where that led rather than reopen old controversies. In support of this strategy the two primates appealed to St Paul: 'Forgetting those things which are behind, and reaching forward unto those things which are before, I press towards the mark for the prize of the high calling of God in Christ Jesus' (Phil. 3.13-14). (Paul VI had already used the same text three years earlier in his first address to the observers from other churches at Vatican II, in support of his promise that 'we are looking towards something new to create, a dream which must become reality'.[1]

One can also find in the *Common Declaration* a general indication of the subjects to be discussed: 'not only theological matters such as Scripture, Tradition and Liturgy, but also matters of practical difficulty felt on either side'. The agenda was worked out in much greater detail by a Joint Preparatory Commission, which was formed with remarkable rapidity and met three times in 1967, completing its report at Malta on 2 January 1968.[2] The Preparatory Commission recommended that there should be established a Permanent Commission

> responsible (in co-operation with the [Roman Catholic] Secretariat for Promoting Christian Unity and the Church of England Council on Foreign Relations in association with the Anglican Executive Officer) for the oversight of Roman Catholic-Anglican relations, and the co-ordination of future work undertaken together by our two Communions (Malta Report, in Final Report, p. 115, para. 21).

In particular, it was recommended that dialogue should focus on intercommunion, the doctrines of the Church, the ministry, and authority, including the 'Petrine primacy' and infallibility. In the event the Commission came increasingly to concentrate on such theological questions, leaving to others the consideration

[1] AAS 55 (1963), pp. 880-1.
[2] The Malta Report is attached to the Final Report as an Appendix. Some of the papers that aided the Preparatory Commission's deliberations are published in *Anglican-Roman Catholic Dialogue: The Work of the Preparatory Commission*, ed. A. C. Clark and C. Davey (London, 1974), see esp. pp.21, 84-106.

of the 'matters of practical difficulty' of which the Pope and the Archbishop spoke.

Between 1970 and 1981 the Permanent Commission met for the first time in January 1970.[3] One of its first actions was to change the word 'Permanent' in its title to 'International', with the consequent acronym ARCIC, as it did not wish to suggest that the separation between the two communions would itself be permanent. Modifying the agenda outlined by the Preparatory Commission, ARCIC came to see that its main task was to discover the extent to which the two Churches shared the same faith concerning the three fundamental but controversial subjects of Eucharist, Ministry and Ordination, and Authority in the Church. The Commission engaged in preliminary work on all three subjects at its first two sessions, held in 1970, at the second of which it worked out provisional drafts on all three doctrines, which, though published in a few ecumenical periodicals,[4] received little public attention. From this point the Commission decided to work on the subjects one by one. The Agreed Statement on *Eucharistic Doctrine* was published in 1971, that on *Ministry and Ordination* in 1973, and *Authority I* in 1977. In 1979 the Commission issued its first *Elucidations*, which formed its response to the comments and questions it had invited on the first two statements. Thereupon, being instructed by Rome and Canterbury to complete its task, the Commission in 1981 submitted to its respective authorities its Final Report, consisting of the matter already published, a second statement on Authority (*Authority II*) and a set of *Elucidations* on *Authority I*, and an Introduction that set out the understanding of the Church underlying all of its thinking.

Thereupon the process of reception began. The Secretariat (now Council) for Christian Unity (CCU) in Rome and the Anglican Consultative Council in Lambeth sent copies to all the bishops of each Church requesting answers to two questions. The first question was whether the Final Report is 'consonant in substance' with the faith of each Church; the second question, however, was put to the two Churches in significantly different forms. Anglicans were asked whether the

---

[3] A summary of the work of each session and a list of members can be found in appendices to the CTS/SPCK edition of the Final Report (1982).

[4] *Theology* (February 1971), *Clergy Review* (February 1971) and *One in Christ* (1971/2–3).

Report 'offers a sufficient basis for taking the next concrete step towards the reconciliation of our Churches grounded in agreement in faith'; Roman Catholics were questioned as to 'the agenda for the next stage of this dialogue'.

The two Churches pursued this process of consultation and decision in their characteristic ways. Each of the twenty-nine provinces of the Anglican Communion, being self-governing, was invited to express its judgement in the form of synodical resolutions. These resolutions were summarized in the *Emmaus Report* ; a position paper that provided information for the General Synod of the Church of England is included (pp. 111–52). In the light of these synodical reactions, the Lambeth Conference, comprising all the diocesan bishops of the world-wide Anglican Communion, adopted a series of resolutions expressing its attitude to the Report, which are also included in this collection (pp. 153–5). The Vatican similarly received responses from many (but not all) episcopal conferences throughout the world, which had been drawn up with the help of the guidance given by the *Observations* of the Congregation of the Doctrine of the Faith (CDF), which were offered in 1982 as the Congregation's 'contribution to the continuation of this dialogue' (see below, pp. 79–91). After considering these episcopal responses, the CDF – in consultation with the CCU – published in 1992 *Response to ARCIC I* as 'the Catholic Church's . . . definitive response' to the Final Report (included below, pp. 156–66).

3
POPE PAUL VI and the ARCHBISHOP OF CANTERBURY (MICHAEL RAMSEY)
The *Common Declaration* (1966)

Rome, Saint Paul Without-the-Walls, 24 March 1966

In this city of Rome, from which Saint Augustine was sent by Saint Gregory to England and there founded the cathedral see of Canterbury, towards which the eyes of all Anglicans now turn as the centre of their Christian Communion, His Holiness Pope Paul VI and His Grace Michael Ramsey, Archbishop of Canterbury, representing the Anglican Communion, have met to exchange fraternal greetings.

At the conclusion of their meeting they give thanks to Almighty God Who by the action of the Holy Spirit has in these latter years created a new atmosphere of Christian fellowship between the Roman Catholic Church and the Churches of the Anglican Communion.

This encounter of the 23 March 1966 marks a new stage in the development of fraternal relations, based upon Christian charity, and of sincere efforts to remove the causes of conflict and to re-establish unity.

In willing obedience to the command of Christ who bade His disciples love one another, they declare that, with His help, they wish to leave in the hands of the God of mercy all that in the past has been opposed to this precept of charity, and that they make their own the mind of the Apostle which he expressed in these words: 'Forgetting those things which are behind, and reaching forth unto those things which are before, I press towards the mark for the prize of the high calling of God in Christ Jesus' (Phil. 3.13–14).

They affirm their desire that all those Christians who belong to these two Communions may be animated by these same sentiments of respect, esteem and fraternal love, and in order to help these develop to the full, they intend to inaugurate between the Roman Catholic Church and the Anglican Communion a serious dialogue which, founded on the Gospels and on the ancient common traditions, may lead to that unity in truth, for which Christ prayed.

The dialogue should include not only theological matters such as Scripture, Tradition and Liturgy, but also matters of practical difficulty felt on either side. His Holiness the Pope and His Grace the Archbishop of Canterbury are, indeed, aware that serious obstacles stand in the way of a restoration of complete communion of faith and sacramental life; nevertheless, they are of one mind in their determination to promote responsible contacts between their Communions in all those spheres of Church life where collaboration is likely to lead to a greater understanding and a deeper charity, and to strive in common to find solutions for all the great problems that face those who believe in Christ in the world of today.

Through such collaboration, by the Grace of God the Father and in the light of the Holy Spirit, may the prayer of Our Lord Jesus Christ for unity among His disciples be brought nearer to fulfilment, and with progress towards unity may there be a strengthening of peace in the world, the peace that only He can grant Who gives 'the peace that passeth all understanding', together with the blessing of Almighty God, Father, Son and Holy Spirit, that it may abide with all men for ever.

† MICHAEL
CANTUARIENSIS

PAULUS PP. VI

4
ARCIC I:
The Final Report (1982)

Preface to the Final Report

The Report which follows is the outcome of work begun at
Gazzada, Italy, on 9 January 1967. A Joint Preparatory Commission met there, in fulfilment of a joint decision by Pope Paul
VI and Archbishop Michael Ramsey, expressed in a *Common
Declaration* during their meeting in Rome in March 1966. Meeting
three times in less than a year, that Commission produced a
Report which registered considerable areas of Roman Catholic
–Anglican agreement, pointed to persisting historical differences and outlined a programme of 'growing together' which
should include, though not be exhausted in, serious dialogue
on these differences. It proclaimed penitence for the past,
thankfulness for the graces of the present, urgency and resolve
for a future in which our common aim would be the restoration of full organic unity.

That Report was endorsed in substance by a letter of Cardinal
Bea in June 1968 and by the Lambeth Conference a few weeks
later. In January 1970 the signatories of the present Report met
first as 'The Anglican–Roman Catholic International Commission'.
Eight members of the Preparatory Commission continued to
serve on the new Commission.

The purpose of this Preface is to explain briefly the aim and
methods of ARCIC as these have matured in the light of our
own experience, of the developments – in some aspects rapid –
within our own Churches in the twelve years of our experience,
in response to criticisms we have received and having regard to
other ecumenical dialogues.

From the beginning we were determined, in accordance
with our mandate, and in the spirit of Phil.3.13, 'forgetting
what lies behind and straining forward to what lies ahead', to

discover each other's faith as it is today and to appeal to history only for enlightenment, not as a way of perpetuating past controversy. In putting this resolve into practice we learned as we progressed. As early as 1970 our preliminary papers on our three main topics link each of them with 'the Church', and this perspective was maintained and is reflected in what follows here: our work is introduced with a statement on the Church, building on the concept of *koinonia*. In the Statement *Eucharistic Doctrine* (Windsor 1971) we went so far as to claim 'substantial agreement' which is consistent with 'a variety of theological approaches within both our communions'. The Preface to our Statement *Ministry and Ordination* (Canterbury 1973) expressed the belief 'that in what we have said here both Anglicans and Roman Catholics will recognize their own faith'.

It was in the first of our two Statements on Authority (*Authority in the Church I,* Venice 1976) that we spoke more fully and revealed a more developed awareness of our aims and methods. Because 'it was precisely in the problem of papal primacy that our historical divisions found their unhappy origin', reference was made to the 'distinction between the ideal and the actual which is important for the reading of our document and for the understanding of the method we have used' (Authority I, Preface). Acknowledging the growing convergence of method and outlook of theologians in our two traditions, we emphasized our avoidance of the emotive language of past polemics and our seeking to pursue *together* that restatement of doctrine which new times and conditions are, as we both recognize, regularly calling for (Authority I, para. 25). In concluding we felt already able to invite our authorities to consider whether our Statements expressed a unity at the level of faith sufficient to call for 'closer sharing . . . in life, worship, and mission'.

Some provisional response to this was forthcoming a few months later in the *Common Declaration* of Pope Paul VI and Archbishop Donald Coggan, made during the latter's visit to Rome in April 1977. Echoing our original statement of intent, 'the restoration of complete communion in faith and sacramental life', Pope and Archbishop declared, 'Our call to this is one with the sublime Christian vocation itself, which is a call to communion' (cf. 1 John 1.3). This passage (*Common Declaration,* paras. 8–9) provides a striking endorsement of a central theme of our Statements, and insists that though our communion remains imperfect it 'stands at the centre of our witness to the world'. 'Our divisions hinder this witness, but they do not close all roads we may travel together.' In other words, the *koinonia* which is the governing concept of what follows here is not a static concept – it demands movement forward, perfecting. We need to accept its implications.

This official encouragement has been echoed by many of our critics. We have seen all of them, encouraging or not, as reflecting the interest aroused by the dialogue and helping us to make ourselves clearer, as we have tried to do in the *Elucidations* (Salisbury 1979 and Windsor 1981).

Paragraph 24 of our Statement *Authority in the Church I* made it clear that, while we had reached a high degree of agreement on 'authority in the Church and in particular on the basic principles of primacy', differences persisted concerning papal authority. A much closer examination of those differences has been our main task since then. The results of that work are embodied in the Statement *Authority in the Church II* (Windsor 1981) which is here presented for the first time. Though much of the material in this Final Report has been published earlier, we are confident that the Report will be read as a whole, and that particular sentences or passages will not be taken out of context.

We believe that growing numbers in both our communions accept that, in the words of the Second Vatican Council's *Decree on Ecumenism*, 'There can be no ecumenism worthy of the name without interior conversion. For it is from newness of attitudes of mind, from self-denial and unstinted love, that desires of unity take their rise and develop in a mature way' (*Unitatis Redintegratio,* para. 7).

It would be wrong, however, to suggest that all the criticisms we have received over the twelve years of our work have been encouraging. We are aware of the limits of our work – that it is a service to the people of God, and needs to find acceptance among them.

But we have as much reason now as ever to echo the concluding lines of the *Common Declaration* of 1977:

to be baptized into Christ is to be baptized into hope – 'and hope does not disappoint us because God's love has been poured into our hearts through the Holy Spirit which has been given us' (Rom. 5.5). Christian hope manifests itself in prayer and action – in prudence but also in courage. We pledge ourselves and exhort the faithful of the Roman Catholic Church and of the Anglican Communion to live and work courageously in this hope of reconciliation and unity in our common Lord.

Introduction

1 Our two communions have been separated for over 400 years. This separation, involving serious doctrinal differences, has been aggravated by theological polemics and mutual intolerance, which have reached into and affected many departments of life. Nevertheless, although our unity has been impaired through separation, it has not been destroyed. Many bonds still unite us: we confess the same faith in the one true God; we have received the same Spirit; we have been baptized with the same baptism; and we preach the same Christ.

2 Controversy between our two communions has centred on the eucharist, on the meaning and function of ordained ministry, and on the nature and exercise of authority in the Church. Although we are not yet in full communion, what the Commission has done has convinced us that substantial agreement on these divisive issues is now possible.

3 In producing these Statements, we have been concerned, not to evade the difficulties, but rather to avoid the controversial language in which they have often been discussed. We have taken seriously the issues that have divided us, and have sought solutions by re-examining our common inheritance, particularly the Scriptures.

4 The subjects which we were required to consider as a result of the Report of the Joint Preparatory Commission all relate to the true nature of the Church. Fundamental to all our Statements is the concept of *koinonia* (communion). In the early Christian tradition, reflection on the experience of *koinonia* opened the way to the understanding of the mystery of the Church. Although '*koinonia*' is never equated with 'Church' in the New Testament, it is the term that most aptly expresses the mystery underlying the various New Testament images of the Church. When, for example, the Church is called the people of the new covenant or the bride of Christ, the context is primarily that of communion. Although such images as the Temple, the

new Jerusalem, or the royal priesthood may carry institutional overtones, their primary purpose is to depict the Church's experience as a partaking in the salvation of Christ. When the Church is described as the body of Christ, the household of God, or the holy nation, the emphasis is upon the relationships among its members as well as upon their relationship with Christ the Head.

5   Union with God in Christ Jesus through the Spirit is the heart of Christian *koinonia*. Among the various ways in which the term *koinonia* is used in different New Testament contexts, we concentrate on that which signifies a relation between persons resulting from their participation in one and the same reality (cf. 1 John 1.3). The Son of God has taken to himself our human nature, and he has sent upon us his Spirit, who makes us so truly members of the body of Christ that we too are able to call God 'Abba, Father' (Rom. 8.15; Gal. 4.6). Moreover, sharing in the same Holy Spirit, whereby we become members of the same body of Christ and adopted children of the same Father, we are also bound to one another in a completely new relationship. *Koinonia* with one another is entailed by our *koinonia* with God in Christ. This is the mystery of the Church.

6   This theme of *koinonia* runs through our Statements. In them we present the eucharist as the effectual sign of *koinonia*, *episcope* as serving the *koinonia*, and primacy as a visible link and focus of *koinonia*.

In the Statement *Eucharistic Doctrine* the eucharist is seen as the sacrament of Christ, by which he builds up and nurtures his people in the *koinonia* of his body. By the eucharist all the baptized are brought into communion with the source of *koinonia*. He is the one who destroyed the walls dividing humanity (Eph. 2.14); he is the one who died to gather into unity all the children of God his Father (cf. John 11.52; 17.20ff).

In the Statement *Ministry and Ordination* it is made clear that *episcope* exists only to serve *koinonia*. The ordained minister presiding at the eucharist is a sign of Christ gathering his people and giving them his body and blood. The Gospel he preaches is the Gospel of unity. Through the ministry of word and sacrament the Holy Spirit is given for the building up of the body of Christ. It is the responsibility of those exercising *episcope* to enable all the people to use the gifts of the Spirit which they have received for the enrichment of the Church's common life. It is also their responsibility to keep the community under the law of Christ in mutual love and in concern for others; for the reconciled community of the Church has been given the ministry of reconciliation (2 Cor. 5.18).

In both Statements on authority the Commission, discussing primacy, sees it as a necessary link between all those exercising *episcope* within the *koinonia*. All ministers of the Gospel need to be in communion with one another, for the one Church is a communion of local churches. They also need to be united in the apostolic faith. Primacy, as a focus within the *koinonia*, is an assurance that what they teach and do is in accord with the faith of the apostles.

7 The Church as *koinonia* requires visible expression because it is intended to be the 'sacrament' of God's saving work. A sacrament is both sign and instrument. The *koinonia* is a sign that God's purpose in Christ is being realized in the world by grace. It is also an instrument for the accomplishment of this purpose, inasmuch as it proclaims the truth of the Gospel and witnesses to it by its life, thus entering more deeply into the mystery of the Kingdom. The community thus announces what it is called to become.

8 The *koinonia* is grounded in the word of God preached, believed and obeyed. Through this word the saving work of God is proclaimed. In the fullness of time this salvation was realized in the person of Jesus, the Word of God incarnate. Jesus prepared his followers to receive through the Holy Spirit the fruit of his death and resurrection, the culmination of his life of obedience, and to become the heralds of salvation. In the New Testament it is clear that the community is established by a baptism inseparable from faith and conversion, that its mission is to proclaim the Gospel of God, and that its common life is sustained by the eucharist. This remains the pattern for the Christian Church. The Church is the community of those reconciled with God and with each other because it is the community of those who believe in Jesus Christ and are justified through God's grace. It is also the reconciling community, because it has been called to bring to all mankind, through the preaching of the Gospel, God's gracious offer of redemption.

9 Christ's will and prayer are that his disciples should be one. Those who have received the same word of God and have been

baptized in the same Spirit cannot, without disobedience, acquiesce in a state of separation. Unity is of the essence of the Church, and since the Church is visible its unity also must be visible. Full visible communion between our two Churches cannot be achieved without mutual recognition of sacraments and ministry, together with the common acceptance of a universal primacy, at one with the episcopal college in the service of the *koinonia*.

Eucharistic Doctrine

Co-Chairmen's Preface

The following Agreed Statement evolved from the thinking and the discussion of the Anglican–Roman Catholic International Commission over the past two years. The result has been a conviction among members of the Commission that we have reached agreement on essential points of eucharistic doctrine. We are equally convinced ourselves that, though no attempt was made to present a fully comprehensive treatment of the subject, nothing essential has been omitted. The document, agreed upon at our third meeting, at Windsor, on 7 September 1971, has been presented to our official authorities, but obviously it cannot be ratified by them until such time as our respective Churches can evaluate its conclusions.

We would want to point out that the members of the Commission who subscribed to this Statement have been officially appointed and come from many countries, representing a wide variety of theological background. Our intention was to reach a consensus at the level of faith, so that all of us might be able to say, within the limits of the Statement: this is the Christian faith of the Eucharist.

September 1971
H. R. McADOO
ALAN C. CLARK

The Statement (1971)

Introduction

1 In the course of the Church's history several traditions have developed in expressing Christian understanding of the

eucharist. (For example, various names have become customary as descriptions of the eucharist: Lord's supper, liturgy, holy mysteries, synaxis, mass, holy communion. The eucharist has become the most universally accepted term.) An important stage in progress towards organic unity is a substantial consensus on the purpose and meaning of the eucharist. Our intention has been to seek a deeper understanding of the reality of the eucharist which is consonant with biblical teaching and with the tradition of our common inheritance, and to express in this document the consensus we have reached.

2 Through the life, death and resurrection of Jesus Christ God has reconciled men to himself, and in Christ he offers unity to all mankind. By his word God calls us into a new relationship with himself as our Father and with one another as his children – a relationship inaugurated by baptism into Christ through the Holy Spirit, nurtured and deepened through the eucharist, and expressed in a confession of one faith and a common life of loving service.

I *The Mystery of the Eucharist*

3 When his people are gathered at the eucharist to commemorate his saving acts for our redemption, Christ makes effective among us the eternal benefits of his victory and elicits and renews our response of faith, thanksgiving and self-surrender. Christ through the Holy Spirit in the eucharist builds up the life of the Church, strengthens its fellowship and furthers its mission. The identity of the Church as the body of Christ is both expressed and effectively proclaimed by its being centred in, and partaking of, his body and blood. In the whole action of the eucharist, and in and by his sacramental presence given through bread and wine, the crucified and risen Lord, according to his promise, offers himself to his people.

4 In the eucharist we proclaim the Lord's death until he comes. Receiving a foretaste of the kingdom to come, we look back with thanksgiving to what Christ has done for us, we greet him present among us, we look forward to his final appearing in the fullness of his kingdom when 'The Son also himself (shall) be subject unto him that put all things under him, that God may be all in all' (1 Cor. 15.28). When we gather around the same table in this communal meal at the invitation of the same Lord and when we 'partake of the one loaf', we are one

in commitment not only to Christ and to one another, but also to the mission of the Church in the world.

II *The Eucharist and the Sacrifice of Christ*

5 Christ's redeeming death and resurrection took place once and for all in history. Christ's death on the cross, the culmination of his whole life of obedience, was the one, perfect and sufficient sacrifice for the sins of the world. There can be no repetition of or addition to what was then accomplished once for all by Christ. Any attempt to express a nexus between the sacrifice of Christ and the eucharist must not obscure this fundamental fact of the Christian faith.[1] Yet God has given the eucharist to his Church as a means through which the atoning work of Christ on the cross is proclaimed and made effective in the life of the Church. The notion of *memorial* as understood in the passover celebration at the time of Christ – i.e. the making effective in the present of an event in the past – has opened the way to a clearer understanding of the relationship between Christ's sacrifice and the eucharist. The eucharistic memorial is no mere calling to mind of a past event or of its significance, but the Church's effectual proclamation of God's mighty acts. Christ instituted the eucharist as a memorial (*anamnesis*) of the totality of God's reconciling action in him. In the eucharistic prayer the church continues to make a perpetual memorial of Christ's death, and his members, united with God and one another, give thanks for all his mercies, entreat the benefits of his passion on behalf of the whole Church, participate in these benefits and enter into the movement of his self-offering.

III *The Presence of Christ*

6 Communion with Christ in the eucharist presupposes his true presence, effectually signified by the bread and wine which, in this mystery, become his body and blood.[2] The real

---

[1] The early Church in expressing the meaning of Christ's death and resurrection often used the language of sacrifice. For the Hebrew *sacrifice* was a traditional means of communication with God. The passover, for example, was a communal meal; the day of atonement was essentially expiatory; and the covenant established communion between God and man.

[2] The word *transubstantiation* is commonly used in the Roman Catholic Church to indicate that God acting in the eucharist effects a change in

presence of his body and blood can, however, only be understood within the context of the redemptive activity whereby he gives himself, and in himself reconciliation, peace and life, to his own. On the one hand, the eucharistic gift springs out of the paschal mystery of Christ's death and resurrection, in which God's saving purpose has already been definitively realized. On the other hand, its purpose is to transmit the life of the crucified and risen Christ to his body, the Church, so that its members may be more fully united with Christ and with one another.

7 Christ is present and active, in various ways, in the entire eucharistic celebration. It is the same Lord who through the proclaimed word invites his people to his table, who through his minister presides at that table, and who gives himself sacramentally in the body and blood of his paschal sacrifice. It is the Lord present at the right hand of the Father, and therefore transcending the sacramental order, who thus offers to his Church, in the eucharistic signs, the special gift of himself.

8 The sacramental body and blood of the Saviour are present as an offering to the believer awaiting his welcome. When this offering is met by faith, a lifegiving encounter results. Through faith Christ's presence – which does not depend on the individual's faith in order to be the Lord's real gift of himself to his Church – becomes no longer just a presence *for* the believer, but also a presence *with* him. Thus, in considering the mystery of the eucharistic presence, we must recognize both the sacramental sign of Christ's presence and the personal relationship between Christ and the faithful which arises from that presence.

9 The Lord's words at the last supper, 'Take and eat; this is my body', do not allow us to dissociate the gift of the presence and the act of sacramental eating. The elements are not mere signs; Christ's body and blood become really present and are really given. But they are really present and given in order that, receiving them, believers may be united in communion with Christ the Lord.

---

the inner reality of the elements. The term should be seen as affirming the *fact* of Christ's presence and of the mysterious and radical change which takes place. In contemporary Roman Catholic theology it is not understood as explaining *how* the change takes place.

10 According to the traditional order of the liturgy the conse-cratory prayer (*anaphora*) leads to the communion of the faithful. Through this prayer of thanksgiving, a word of faith addressed to the Father, the bread and wine become the body and blood of Christ by the action of the Holy Spirit, so that in communion we eat the flesh of Christ and drink his blood.

11 The Lord who thus comes to his people in the power of the Holy Spirit is the Lord of glory. In the eucharistic celebration we anticipate the joys of the age to come. By the transforming action of the Spirit of God, earthly bread and wine become the heavenly manna and the new wine, the eschatological banquet for the new man: elements of the first creation become pledges and first fruits of the new heaven and the new earth.

Conclusion

12 We believe that we have reached substantial agreement on the doctrine of the eucharist. Although we are all conditioned by the traditional ways in which we have expressed and prac-tised our eucharistic faith, we are convinced that if there are any remaining points of disagreement they can be resolved on the principles here established. We acknowledge a variety of theological approaches within both our communions. But we have seen it as our task to find a way of advancing together beyond the doctrinal disagreements of the past. It is our hope that, in view of the agreement which we have reached on eucharistic faith, this doctrine will no longer constitute an obstacle to the unity we seek.

Elucidation (1979)

1 When each of the Agreed Statements was published, the Commission invited and has received comment and criticism. This *Elucidation* is an attempt to expand and explain to those who have responded some points raised in connection with *Eucharistic Doctrine* (Windsor 1971).

Substantial Agreement

2 The Commission was not asked to produce a comprehensive treatise on the eucharist, but only to examine differences which in the controversies of the past divided our two communions.

The aim of the Commission has been to see whether we can today discover substantial agreement in faith on the eucharist. Questions have been asked about the meaning of *substantial* agreement. It means that the document represents not only the judgement of all its members – i.e. it is an agreement – but their unanimous agreement 'on essential matters where it considers that doctrine admits no divergence' (Ministry, para. 17) – i.e. it is a substantial agreement. Members of the Commission are united in their conviction 'that if there are any remaining points of disagreement they can be resolved on the principles here established' (Eucharist, para. 12).

Comments and Criticisms

3 The following comments and criticisms are representative of the many received and are considered by the Commission to be of particular importance.

In spite of the firm assertion made in the Agreed Statement of the 'once for all' nature of Christ's sacrifice, some have still been anxious that the term *anamnesis* may conceal the reintroduction of the theory of a repeated immolation. Others have suspected that the word refers not only to the historical events of salvation but also to an eternal sacrifice in heaven. Others again have doubted whether *anamnesis* sufficiently implies the reality indicated by traditional sacrificial language concerning the eucharist. Moreover, the accuracy and adequacy of the Commission's exegesis of *anamnesis* have been questioned.

Some critics have been unhappy about the realistic language used in this Agreed Statement, and have questioned such words as *become* and *change*. Others have wondered whether the permanence of Christ's eucharistic presence has been sufficiently acknowledged, with a consequent request for a discussion of the reserved sacrament and devotions associated with it. Similarly there have been requests for clarification of the Commission's attitude to receptionism.

4 Behind these criticisms there lies a profound but often unarticulated anxiety that the Commission has been using new theological language which evades unresolved differences. Related to this anxiety is the further question as to the nature of the agreement claimed by the Commission. Does the language of the Commission conceal an ambiguity (either intentional or unintentional) in language which enables members of the two

churches to see their own faith in the Agreed Statement without having in fact reached a genuine consensus?

Anamnesis and Sacrifice

5 The Commission has been criticized for its use of the term *anamnesis*. It chose the word used in New Testament accounts of the institution of the eucharist at the last supper:

> 'Do this as a memorial (*anamnesin*) of me' (1 Cor. 11.24-25; Luke 22.19: JB, NEB).

The word is also to be found in Justin Martyr in the second century. Recalling the last supper he writes:

> 'Jesus, taking bread and having given thanks, said, "Do this for my memorial (*anamnesin*): This is my body"; and like-wise, taking the cup, and giving thanks, he said, "This is my blood"' (*First Apology* 66; cf. *Dialogue with Trypho* 117).

From this time onwards the term is found at the very heart of the eucharistic prayers of both East and West, not only in the institution narrative but also in the prayer which follows and elsewhere: cf. e.g. The Liturgy of St John Chrysostom; Eucharistic Prayer I –The Roman Missal; The Order of the Administration of the Lord's Supper or Holy Communion – The Book of Common Prayer (1662); and Rites A and B of the Church of England Alternative Service Book (1980).

The word is also found in patristic and later theology. The Council of Trent in explaining the relation between the sacri-fice of the cross and the eucharist uses the words *commemoratio* and *memoria* (Session 22, ch. 1); and in the Book of Common Prayer (1662) the Catechism states that the sacrament of the Lord's Supper was ordained 'for the continual *remembrance* of the sacrifice of the death of Christ, and of the benefits which we receive thereby'. The frequent use of the term in contem-porary theology is illustrated by *One Baptism One Eucharist and a Mutually Recognized Ministry* (Faith and Order Commission Paper No. 73), as well as by the *General Instruction on the Roman Missal* (1970).

The Commission believes that the traditional understanding of sacramental reality, in which the once-for-all event of salvation becomes effective in the present through the action of the Holy Spirit, is well expressed by the word *anamnesis*. We accept this use of the word which seems to do full justice to the semitic background. Furthermore it enables us to affirm a strong conviction of sacramental realism and to reject mere symbolism. However the selection of this word by the Commission does not mean that our common eucharistic faith may not be expressed in other terms.

In the exposition of the Christian doctrine of redemption the word *sacrifice* has been used in two intimately associated ways. In the New Testament, sacrificial language refers primarily to the historical events of Christ's saving work for us. The tradition of the Church, as evidenced for example in its liturgies, used similar language to designate in the eucharistic celebration the *anamnesis* of this historical event. Therefore it is possible to say at the same time that there is only one unrepeatable sacrifice in the historical sense, but that the eucharist is a sacrifice in the sacramental sense, provided that it is clear that this is not a repetition of the historical sacrifice.

There is therefore one historical, unrepeatable sacrifice, offered once for all by Christ and accepted once for all by the Father. In the celebration of the memorial, Christ in the Holy Spirit unites his people with himself in a sacramental way so that the Church enters into the movement of his self-offering. In consequence, even though the Church is active in this celebration, this adds nothing to the efficacy of Christ's sacrifice upon the cross, because the action is itself the fruit of this sacrifice. The Church in celebrating the eucharist gives thanks for the gift of Christ's sacrifice and identifies itself with the will of Christ who has offered himself to the Father on behalf of all mankind.

Christ's Presence in the Eucharist

6   Criticism has been evoked by the statement that the bread and wine become the body and blood of Christ in the eucharist (para. 10). The word *become* has been suspected of expressing a materialistic conception of Christ's presence, and this has seemed to some to be confirmed in the footnote on the word *transubstantiation* which also speaks of *change*. It is feared that this suggests that Christ's presence in the eucharist is confined to the elements, and that the Real Presence involves a physical change in them.

In order to respond to these comments the Commission recalls that the Statement affirmed that:

(*a*) It is the glorified Lord himself whom the community of the faithful encounters in the eucharistic celebration through the preaching of the word, in the fellowship of the Lord's supper, in the heart of the believer, and, in a sacramental way, through the gifts of his body and blood, already given on the cross for their salvation.

(*b*) His body and blood are given through the action of the Holy Spirit, appropriating bread and wine so that they become the food of the new creation already inaugurated by the coming of Christ (cf. paras. 7, 10, 11).

Becoming does not here imply material change. Nor does the liturgical use of the word imply that the bread and wine become Christ's body and blood in such a way that in the eucharistic celebration his presence is limited to the consecrated elements. It does not imply that Christ becomes present in the eucharist in the same manner that he was present in his earthly life. It does not imply that this *becoming* follows the physical laws of this world. What is here affirmed is a sacramental presence in which God uses realities of this world to convey the realities of the new creation: bread for this life becomes the bread of eternal life. Before the eucharistic prayer, to the question: 'What is that?', the believer answers: 'It is bread.' After the eucharistic prayer, to the same question he answers: 'It is truly the body of Christ, the Bread of Life.'

In the sacramental order the realities of faith become present in visible and tangible signs, enabling Christians to avail themselves of the fruits of the once-for-all redemption. In the eucharist the human person encounters in faith the person of Christ in his sacramental body and blood. This is the sense in which the community, the body of Christ, by partaking of the sacramental body of the risen Lord, grows into the unity God intends for his Church. The ultimate change intended by God is the transformation of human beings into the likeness of Christ. The bread and wine *become* the sacramental body and blood of Christ in order that the Christian community may *become* more truly what it already is, the body of Christ.

Gift and Reception

7 This transformation into the likeness of Christ requires that the eucharistic gifts be received in faith. In the mystery of the eucharist we discern not one but two complementary movements within an indissoluble unity: Christ giving his body and

blood, and the communicants feeding upon them in their hearts by faith. Some traditions have placed a special emphasis on the association of Christ's presence with the consecrated elements; others have emphasized Christ's presence in the heart of the believer through reception by faith. In the past, acute difficulties have arisen when one or other of these emphases has become almost exclusive. In the opinion of the Commission neither emphasis is incompatible with eucharistic faith, provided that the complementary movement emphasized by the other position is not denied. Eucharistic doctrine must hold together these two movements since in the euchaı ist, the sacrament of the New Covenant, Christ gives himself to his people so that they may receive him through faith.

Reservation

8 The practice of reserving the sacrament for reception after the congregation has dispersed is known to date back to the second century (cf. Justin Martyr, *First Apology*, 65 and 67). In so far as it maintains the complementary movements already referred to (as for example, when communion is taken to the sick) this practice clearly accords with the purpose of the institution of the eucharist. But later there developed a tendency to stress the veneration of Christ's presence in the consecrated elements. In some places this tendency became so pronounced that the original purpose of reservation was in danger of becoming totally obscured. If veneration is wholly dissociated from the eucharistic celebration of the community it contradicts the true doctrine of the eucharist.

Consideration of this question requires clarification of the understanding of the eucharist. Adoration in the celebration of the eucharist is first and foremost offered to the Father. It is to lead us to the Father that Christ unites us to himself through our receiving of his body and blood. The Christ whom we adore in the eucharist is Christ glorifying his Father. The movement of all our adoration is to the Father, through, with, and in Christ, in the power of the Spirit.

The whole eucharistic action is a continuous movement in which Christ offers himself in his sacramental body and blood to his people and in which they receive him in faith and thanksgiving. Consequently communion administered from the reserved sacrament to those unable to attend the eucharistic

celebration is rightly understood as an extension of that celebration. Differences arise between those who would practise
reservation for this reason only, and those who would also
regard it as a means of eucharistic devotion. For the latter, adoration of Christ in the reserved sacrament should be regarded
as an extension of eucharistic worship, even though it does not
include immediate sacramental reception, which remains the
primary purpose of reservation (cf. the Instruction *Eucharisticum
Mysterium*, para. 49, of the Sacred Congregation of Rites (AAS
59, 1967)). Any dissociation of such devotion from this primary
purpose, which is communion in Christ of all his members, is a
distortion in eucharistic practice.

9 In spite of this clarification, others still find any kind of
adoration of Christ in the reserved sacrament unacceptable.
They believe that it is in fact impossible in such a practice truly
to hold together the two movements of which we have spoken:
and that this devotion can hardly fail to produce such an
emphasis upon the association of Christ's sacramental presence
with the consecrated bread and wine as to suggest too static
and localized a presence that disrupts the movement as well as
the balance of the whole eucharistic action (cf. Article 28 of the
Articles of Religion).

   That there can be a divergence in matters of practice and in
theological judgements relating to them, without destroying a
common eucharistic faith, illustrates what we mean by *substantial* agreement. Differences of theology and practice may well
coexist with a real consensus on the essentials of eucharistic
faith – as in fact they do within each of our communions.

Other Issues

10 Concern has been expressed that we have said nothing
about intercommunion, though claiming to have attained a
substantial agreement on eucharistic faith. The reason is that
we are agreed that a responsible judgement on this matter
cannot be made on the basis of this Statement alone, because
intercommunion also involves issues relating to authority and
to the mutual recognition of ministry. There are other important
issues, such as the eschatological dimension of the eucharist
and its relation to contemporary questions of human liberation
and social justice, which we have either not fully developed or
not explicitly treated. These are matters which call for the

common attention of our churches, but they are not a source of division between us and are therefore outside our mandate.

Ministry and Ordination

Co-Chairmen's Preface

At Windsor, in 1971, the Anglican–Roman Catholic International Commission was able to achieve an Agreed Statement on Eucharistic Doctrine. In accordance with the programme adopted at Venice in 1970, we have now, at our meeting in Canterbury in 1973, turned our attention to the doctrine of ministry, specifically to our understanding of the ordained ministry and its place in the life of the Church. The present document is the result of the work of this officially appointed Commission and is offered to our authorities for their consideration. At this stage it remains an agreed statement of the Commission and no more.

We acknowledge with gratitude our debt to the many studies and discussions which have treated the same material. While respecting the different forms that ministry has taken in other traditions, we hope that the clarification of our understanding expressed in the statement will be of service to them also.

We have submitted the statement, therefore, to our authorities and, with their authorization, we publish it as a document of the Commission with a view to its discussion. Even though there may be differences of emphasis within our two traditions, yet we believe that in what we have said here both Anglican and Roman Catholic will recognize their own faith.

September 1973
H. R. McADOO
ALAN C. CLARK

The Statement (1973)

Introduction

1 Our intention has been to seek a deeper understanding of ministry which is consonant with biblical teaching and with the traditions of our common inheritance, and to express in this

document the consensus we have reached.[1] This Statement is not designed to be an exhaustive treatment of ministry. It seeks to express our basic agreement in the doctrinal areas that have been the source of controversy between us, in the wider context of our common convictions about the ministry.

2 Within the Roman Catholic Church and the Anglican Communion there exists a diversity of forms of ministerial service. Of more specific ways of service, while some are undertaken without particular initiative from official authority, others may receive a mandate from ecclesiastical authorities. The ordained ministry can only be rightly understood within this broader context of various ministries, all of which are the work of one and the same Spirit.

I *Ministry in the Life of the Church*

3 The life and self-offering of Christ perfectly express what it is to serve God and man. All Christian ministry, whose purpose is always to build up the community (*koinonia*), flows and takes its shape from this source and model. The communion of men with God (and with each other) requires their reconciliation. This reconciliation, accomplished by the death and resurrection of Jesus Christ, is being realized in the life of the Church through the response of faith. While the Church is still in process of sanctification, its mission is nevertheless to be the instrument by which this reconciliation in Christ is proclaimed, his love manifested, and the means of salvation offered to men.

4 In the early Church the apostles exercised a ministry which remains of fundamental significance for the Church of all ages. It is difficult to deduce, from the New Testament use of 'apostle' for the Twelve, Paul, and others, a precise portrait of an apostle, but two primary features of the original apostolate are clearly discernible: a special relationship with the historical Christ, and a commission from him to the Church and the world (Matt. 28.19; Mark 3.14). All Christian apostolate originates in the sending of the Son by the Father. The Church is apostolic not only because its faith and life must reflect the witness to Jesus Christ given in the early Church by the apostles, but also because it is charged to continue in the apostles'

---

[1] Cf. Eucharist, para. 1, which similarly speaks of a consensus reached with regard to the eucharist.

commission to communicate to the world what it has received. Within the whole history of mankind the Church is to be the community of reconciliation.

5 All ministries are used by the Holy Spirit for the building up of the Church to be this reconciling community for the glory of God and the salvation of men (Eph. 4.11–13). Within the New Testament ministerial actions are varied and functions not precisely defined. Explicit emphasis is given to the proclamation of the word and the preservation of apostolic doctrine, the care of the flock, and the example of Christian living. At least by the time of the Pastoral Epistles and 1 Peter, some ministerial functions are discernible in a more exact form. The evidence suggests that with the growth of the Church the importance of certain functions led to their being located in specific officers of the community. Since the Church is built up by the Holy Spirit primarily but not exclusively through these ministerial functions, some form of recognition and authorization is already required in the New Testament period for those who exercise them in the name of Christ. Here we can see elements which will remain at the heart of what today we call ordination.

6 The New Testament shows that ministerial office played an essential part in the life of the Church in the first century, and we believe that the provision of a ministry of this kind is part of God's design for his people. Normative principles governing the purpose and function of the ministry are already present in the New Testament documents (e.g. Mark 10.43–5; Acts 20.28; 1 Tim. 4.12–16; 1 Pet. 5.1–4). The early churches may well have had considerable diversity in the structure of pastoral ministry, though it is clear that some churches were headed by ministers who were called *episcopoi* and *presbyteroi*. While the first missionary churches were not a loose aggregation of autonomous communities, we have no evidence that 'bishops' and 'presbyters' were appointed everywhere in the primitive period. The terms 'bishop' and 'presbyter' could be applied to the same man or to men with identical or very similar functions. Just as the formation of the canon of the New Testament was a process incomplete until the second half of the second century, so also the full emergence of the threefold ministry of bishop, presbyter, and deacon required a longer period than the apostolic age. Thereafter this threefold structure became universal in the Church.

II *The Ordained Ministry*

7 The Christian community exists to give glory to God through the fulfilment of the Father's purpose. All Christians are called to serve this purpose by their life of prayer and surrender to divine grace, and by their careful attention to the needs of all human beings. They should witness to God's compassion for all mankind and his concern for justice in the affairs of men. They should offer themselves to God in praise and worship, and devote their energies to bringing men into the fellowship of Christ's people, and so under his rule of love. The goal of the ordained ministry is to serve this priesthood of all the faithful. Like any human community the Church requires a focus of leadership and unity, which the Holy Spirit provides in the ordained ministry. This ministry assumes various patterns to meet the varying needs of those whom the Church is seeking to serve, and it is the role of the minister to co-ordinate the activities of the Church's fellowship and to promote what is necessary and useful for the Church's life and mission. He is to discern what is of the Spirit in the diversity of the Church's life and promote its unity.

8 In the New Testament a variety of images is used to describe the functions of this minister. He is servant, both of Christ and of the Church. As herald and ambassador he is an authoritative representative of Christ and proclaims his message of reconciliation. As teacher he explains and applies the word of God to the community. As shepherd he exercises pastoral care and guides the flock. He is a steward who may only provide for the household of God what belongs to Christ. He is to be an example both in holiness and in compassion.

9 An essential element in the ordained ministry is its responsibility for 'oversight' (*episcope*). This responsibility involves fidelity to the apostolic faith, its embodiment in the life of the Church today, and its transmission to the Church of tomorrow. Presbyters are joined with the bishop in his oversight of the church and in the ministry of the word and the sacraments; they are given authority to preside at the eucharist and to pronounce absolution. Deacons, although not so empowered, are associated with bishops and presbyters in the ministry of word and sacrament, and assist in oversight.

10 Since the ordained ministers are ministers of the Gospel, every facet of their oversight is linked with the word of God. In the original mission and witness recorded in Holy Scripture lies the source and ground of their preaching and authority. By the preaching of the word they seek to bring those who are not Christians into the fellowship of Christ. The Christian message needs also to be unfolded to the faithful, in order to deepen their knowledge of God and their response of grateful faith. But a true faith calls for beliefs that are correct and lives that endorse the Gospel. So the ministers have to guide the community and to advise individuals with regard to the implications of commitment to Christ. Because God's concern is not only for the welfare of the Church but also for the whole of creation, they must also lead their communities in the service of humanity. Church and people have continually to be brought under the guidance of the apostolic faith. In all these ways a ministerial vocation implies a responsibility for the word of God supported by constant prayer (cf. Acts 6.4).

11 The part of the ministers in the celebration of the sacraments is one with their responsibility for ministry of the word. In both word and sacrament Christians meet the living Word of God. The responsibility of the ministers in the Christian community involves them in being not only the persons who normally administer baptism, but also those who admit converts to the communion of the faithful and restore those who have fallen away. Authority to pronounce God's forgiveness of sin, given to bishops and presbyters at their ordination, is exercised by them to bring Christians to a closer communion with God and with their fellow men through Christ and to assure them of God's continuing love and mercy.

12 To proclaim reconciliation in Christ and to manifest his reconciling love belong to the continuing mission of the Church. The central act of worship, the eucharist, is the memorial of that reconciliation and nourishes the Church's life for the fulfilment of its mission. Hence it is right that he who has oversight in the church and is the focus of its unity should preside at the celebration of the eucharist. Evidence as early as Ignatius shows that, at least in some churches, the man exercising this oversight presided at the eucharist and no other could do so without his consent (*Letter to the Smyrnaeans*, 8.1).

13 The priestly sacrifice of Jesus was unique, as is also his continuing High Priesthood. Despite the fact that in the New Testament ministers are never called 'priests' (*hiereis*),[2] Christians came to see the priestly role of Christ reflected in these ministers and used priestly terms in describing them. Because the eucharist is the memorial of the sacrifice of Christ, the action of the presiding minister in reciting again the words of Christ at the last supper and distributing to the assembly the holy gifts is seen to stand in a sacramental relation to what Christ himself did in offering his own sacrifice. So our two traditions commonly use priestly terms in speaking about the ordained ministry. Such language does not imply any negation of the once-for-all sacrifice of Christ by any addition or repetition. There is in the eucharist a memorial (*anamnesis*)[3] of the totality of God's reconciling action in Christ, who through his minister presides at the Lord's Supper and gives himself sacramentally. So it is because the eucharist is central in the Church's life that the essential nature of the Christian ministry, however this may be expressed, is most clearly seen in its celebration; for, in the eucharist, thanksgiving is offered to God, the gospel of salvation is proclaimed in word and sacrament, and the community is knit together as one body in Christ. Christian ministers are members of this redeemed community. Not only do they share through baptism in the priesthood of the people of God, but they are – particularly in presiding at the eucharist – representative of the whole Church in the fulfilment of its priestly vocation of self-offering to God as a living sacrifice (Rom. 12.1). Nevertheless their ministry is not an extension of the common Christian priesthood but belongs to another realm of the gifts of the Spirit. It exists to help the Church to be 'a royal priesthood, a holy nation, God's own people, to declare the wonderful deeds of him who called [them] out of darkness into his marvellous light' (1 Pet. 2.9).

III *Vocation and Ordination*

14 Ordination denotes entry into this apostolic and God-given ministry, which serves and signifies the unity of the local

---

[2] In the English language the word 'priest' is used to translate two distinct Greek words, *hiereus* which belongs to the cultic order and *presbyteros* which designates an elder in the community.

[3] Cf. Eucharist, para. 5.

churches in themselves and with one another. Every individual act of ordination is therefore an expression of the continuing apostolicity and catholicity of the whole Church. Just as the original apostles did not choose themselves but were chosen and commissioned by Jesus, so those who are ordained are called by Christ in the Church and through the Church. Not only is their vocation from Christ but their qualification for exercising such a ministry is the gift of the Spirit: 'our sufficiency is from God, who has qualified us to be ministers of a new covenant, not in a written code but in the Spirit' (2 Cor. 3.5–6). This is expressed in ordination, when the bishop prays God to grant the gift of the Holy Spirit and lays hands on the candidate as the outward sign of the gifts bestowed. Because ministry is in and for the community and because ordination is an act in which the whole Church of God is involved, this prayer and laying on of hands take place within the context of the eucharist.

15 In this sacramental act,[4] the gift of God is bestowed upon the ministers, with the promise of divine grace for their work and for their sanctification; the ministry of Christ is presented to them as a model for their own; and the Spirit seals those whom he has chosen and consecrated. Just as Christ has united the Church inseparably with himself, and as God calls all the faithful to lifelong discipleship, so the gifts and calling of God to the ministers are irrevocable. For this reason, ordination is unrepeatable in both our churches.

16 Both presbyters and deacons are ordained by the bishop. In the ordination of a presbyter the presbyters present join the bishop in the laying on of hands, thus signifying the shared nature of the commission entrusted to them. In the ordination of a new bishop, other bishops lay hands on him, as they request the gift of the Spirit for his ministry and receive him into their ministerial fellowship. Because they are entrusted with the oversight of other churches, this participation in his ordination signifies that this new bishop and his church are

[4] Anglican use of the word 'sacrament' with reference to ordination is limited by the distinction drawn in the Thirty-nine Articles (Article 25) between the two 'sacraments of the Gospel' and the 'five commonly called sacraments'. Article 25 does not deny these latter the name 'sacrament', but differentiates between them and the 'two sacraments ordained by Christ' described in the Catechism as 'necessary to salvation' for all men.

within the communion of churches. Moreover, because they are representative of their churches in fidelity to the teaching and mission of the apostles and are members of the episcopal college, their participation also ensures the historical continuity of this church with the apostolic Church and of its bishop with the original apostolic ministry. The communion of the churches in mission, faith, and holiness, through time and space, is thus symbolized and maintained in the bishop. Here are comprised the essential features of what is meant in our two traditions by ordination in the apostolic succession.

Conclusion

17 We are fully aware of the issues raised by the judgement of the Roman Catholic Church on Anglican Orders. The development of the thinking in our two communions regarding the nature of the Church and of the ordained ministry, as represented in our Statement, has, we consider, put these issues in a new context. Agreement on the nature of ministry is prior to the consideration of the mutual recognition of ministries. What we have to say represents the consensus of the Commission on essential matters where it considers that doctrine admits no divergence. It will be clear that we have not yet broached the wide-ranging problems of authority which may arise in any discussion of ministry, nor the question of primacy. We are aware that present understanding of such matters remains an obstacle to the reconciliation of our churches in the one Communion we desire, and the Commission is now turning to the examination of the issues involved. Nevertheless we consider that our consensus, on questions where agreement is indispensable for unity, offers a positive contribution to the reconciliation of our churches and of their ministries.

Elucidation (1979)

Comments and Criticisms

1 After the publication of the Statement *Ministry and Ordination*, the Commission received comments and criticisms, among which it judged the following to be of special concern.

It has been suggested that in the discussion of ministry insufficient attention was given to the priesthood of the whole people of God, so that the document seemed to have too clerical an emphasis. In this connection it has also been said that the distinction between this priesthood of all the faithful and the priesthood of the ordained ministry was not clearly enough explained. Questions have also been raised about the Commission's treatment of the origins and historical development of the ordained ministry and its threefold form; about its comparison of that development with the emergence of the canon of Scripture; and about its views on the place of episcopacy within *episcope* as it is outlined in the Statement (para. 9).

Some have wondered whether the Statement adequately expressed the sacramental nature of the rite of ordination, others whether this aspect has been over-emphasized. The Commission has been asked to consider the implications of the Statement for the question of the ordination of women. There have also been inquiries about the bearing of the Statement upon the problem of recognizing the validity of Anglican Orders.

Priesthood

2 In common Christian usage the term *priesthood* is employed in three distinct ways: the priesthood of Christ, the priesthood of the people of God, the priesthood of the ordained ministry.

The priesthood of Christ is unique. He is our High Priest who has reconciled mankind with the Father. All other priesthood derives from his and is wholly dependent upon it.

The priesthood of the whole people of God (1 Pet. 2.5) is the consequence of incorporation by baptism into Christ. This priesthood of all the faithful (para. 7) is not a matter of disagreement between us. In a document primarily concerned with the ordained ministry, the Commission did not consider it necessary to develop the subject further than it has already done in the Statement. Here the ordained ministry is firmly placed in the context of the ministry of the whole Church and exists for the service of all the faithful.

The Statement (para. 13) explains that the ordained ministry is called priestly principally because it has a particular sacramental relationship with Christ as High Priest. At the eucharist Christ's people do what he commanded in memory of himself and Christ unites them sacramentally with himself in his self-offering. But in this action it is only the ordained minister who presides at the eucharist, in which, in the name of Christ and on behalf of his Church, he recites the narrative of the institution of the Last Supper, and invokes the Holy Spirit upon the gifts.

The word *priesthood* is used by way of analogy when it is applied to the people of God and to the ordained ministry. These are two distinct realities which relate, each in its own way, to the high priesthood of Christ, the unique priesthood of the new covenant, which is their source and model. These considerations should be borne in mind throughout para. 13, and in particular they indicate the significance of the statement that the ordained ministry 'is not an extension of the common Christian priesthood but belongs to another realm of the gifts of the Spirit'.

In this as in other cases the early Church found it necessary for its understanding and exposition of the faith to employ terminology in ways in which it was not used in the New Testament. Today in seeking to give an account of our faith both our communions, in the interpretation of the Scriptures, take cognisance of the Church's growing understanding of Christian truth (cf. Authority I, paras. 2, 3, and 15).

Sacramentality of Ordination

3   The phrase 'in this sacramental act' in para. 15 has caused anxiety on two different counts: that this phrase seems to give the sacrament of ordination the same status as the two 'sacraments of the Gospel'; and that it does not adequately express the full sacramentality of ordination.

Both traditions agree that a sacramental rite is a visible sign through which the grace of God is given by the Holy Spirit in the Church. The rite of ordination is one of these sacramental rites. Those who are ordained by prayer and the laying on of hands receive their ministry from Christ through those designated in the Church to hand it on; together with the office they are given the grace needed for its fulfilment (cf. para. 14). Since New Testament times the Church has required such recognition and authorization for those who are to exercise the principal functions of *episcope* in the name of Christ. This is what both traditions mean by the sacramental rite of ordination.

Both traditions affirm the pre-eminence of baptism and the eucharist as sacraments 'necessary to salvation'. This does not diminish their understanding of the sacramental nature of ordination, as to which there is no significant disagreement between them.

Origins and Development of the Ordained Ministry

4 Our treatment of the origins of the ordained ministry has been criticized. While the evidence leaves ground for differences of interpretation, it is enough for our purpose to recall that, from the beginning of the Christian Church, there existed *episcope* in the community, however its various responsibilities were distributed and described, and whatever the names given to those who exercise it (cf. paras. 8, 9, and especially 6). It is generally agreed that, within the first century, evidence of ordination such as we have described above is provided by the *First Epistle of Clement*, chapters 40–44, commonly dated 95 A.D. Some New Testament passages appear to imply the same conclusion, e.g. Acts 14.23. Early in the second century, the pattern of a threefold ministry centred on episcopacy was already discernible, and probably widely found (cf. the Epistles of Ignatius to the *Ephesians*, 4; *Magnesians*, 13; *Trallians*, 2; *Philadelphians*, 2; *Smyrnaeans*, 8). It was recognized that such ministry must be in continuity not only with the apostolic faith but also with the commission given to the apostles (cf. the *First Epistle of Clement*, 42).

Our intention in drawing a parallel between this emergence of the threefold ministry and the formation of the New Testament canon was to point to comparable processes of gradual development without determining whether the comparison could be carried further (cf. para. 6). The threefold ministry remained universal until the divisions of Western Christianity in the sixteenth century. However, both our communions have retained it.

We both maintain that *episcope* must be exercised by ministers ordained in the apostolic succession (cf. para. 16). Both our communions have retained and remained faithful to the threefold ministry centred on episcopacy as the form in which this *episcope* is to be exercised. Because our task was limited to examining relations between our two communions, we did not enter into the question whether there is any other form in which this *episcope* can be realized.

Ordination of Women

5 Since the publication of the Statement there have been rapid developments with regard to the ordination of women. In those churches of the Anglican Communion where canonical ordinations of women have taken place, the bishops concerned believe that their action implies no departure from the traditional doctrine of the ordained ministry (as expounded, for instance, in the Statement). While the Commission realizes that the ordination of women has created for the Roman Catholic Church a new and grave obstacle to the reconciliation of our communions (cf. Letter of Pope Paul VI to Archbishop Donald Coggan, 23 March 1976, AAS 68), it believes that the principles upon which its doctrinal agreement rests are not affected by such ordinations; for it was concerned with the origin and nature of the ordained ministry and not with the question who can or cannot be ordained. Objections, however substantial, to the ordination of women are of a different kind from objections raised in the past against the validity of Anglican Orders in general.

Anglican Orders

6 In answer to the questions concerning the significance of the Agreed Statements for the mutual recognition of ministry, the Commission has affirmed that a consensus has been reached that places the questions in a new context (cf. para. 17). It believes that our agreement on the essentials of eucharistic faith with regard to the sacramental presence of Christ and the sacrificial dimension of the eucharist, and on the nature and purpose of priesthood, ordination, and apostolic succession, is the new context in which the questions should now be discussed. This calls for a reappraisal of the verdict on Anglican Orders in *Apostolicae Curae* (1896).

Mutual recognition presupposes acceptance of the apostolicity of each other's ministry. The Commission believes that its agreements have demonstrated a consensus in faith on eucharist and ministry which has brought closer the possibility of such acceptance. It hopes that its own conviction will be shared by members of both our communions; but mutual recognition can only be achieved by the decision of our authorities. It has been our mandate to offer to them the basis upon which they may make this decision.

Authority in the Church I

Co-Chairmen's Preface

The Malta Report of the Anglican–Roman Catholic Joint Preparatory Commission (1968) outlined the large measure of agreement in faith which exists between the Roman Catholic Church and the churches of the Anglican Communion (para. 7). It then went on to note three specific areas of doctrinal disagreement. These were listed in the Report as matters for joint investigation. Accordingly the Anglican–Roman Catholic International Commission, proposed by the Report, was recommended to examine jointly 'the question of intercommunion, and the related matters of Church and Ministry', and 'the question of authority, its nature, exercise, and implications'.

To our previous Agreed Statements on the Eucharist (Windsor 1971) and Ministry (Canterbury 1973) we now add an Agreed Statement on Authority in the Church (Venice 1976). The Commission thus submits its work to the authorities who appointed it and, with their permission, offers it to our churches.

The question of authority in the Church has long been recognized as crucial to the growth in unity of the Roman Catholic Church and the churches of the Anglican Communion. It was precisely in the problem of papal primacy that our historical divisions found their unhappy origin. Hence, however significant our consensus on the doctrine of the eucharist and of the ministry, unresolved questions on the nature and exercise of authority in the Church would hinder the growing experience of unity which is the pattern of our present relations.

The present Statement has, we believe, made a significant contribution to the resolution of these questions. Our consensus covers a very wide area; though we have not been able to resolve some of the difficulties of Anglicans concerning Roman Catholic belief relating to the office of the bishop of Rome, we hope and trust that our analysis has placed these problems in a proper perspective.

There is much in the document, as in our other documents, which presents the ideal of the Church as willed by Christ. History shows how the Church has often failed to achieve this ideal. An awareness of this distinction between the ideal and the actual is important both for the reading of the document and for the understanding of the method we have pursued.

The consensus we have reached, if it is to be accepted by our two communities, would have, we insist, important consequences. Common recognition of Roman primacy would bring changes not only to the Anglican Communion but also to the Roman Catholic Church. On both sides the readiness to learn, necessary to the achievement of such a wider *koinonia*, would demand humility and charity. The prospect should be met with faith, not fear. Communion with the see of Rome would bring to the churches of the Anglican Communion not only a wider *koinonia* but also a strengthening of the power to realize its traditional ideal of diversity in unity. Roman Catholics, on their side, would be enriched by the presence of a particular tradition of spirituality and scholarship, the lack of which has deprived the Roman Catholic Church of a precious element in the Christian heritage. The Roman Catholic Church has much to learn from the Anglican synodical tradition of involving the laity in the life and mission of the Church. We are convinced, therefore, that our degree of agreement, which argues for greater communion between our churches, can make a profound contribution to the witness of Christianity in our contemporary society.

It is in this light that we would wish to submit our conclusions to our respective authorities, believing that our work, indebted, as it is, to many sources outside the Commission as well as to its own labours, will be of service not only to ourselves but to Christians of other traditions in our common quest for the unity of Christ's Church.

September 1976
H. R. McADOO
ALAN C. CLARK

The Statement (1976)

Introduction

1 The confession of Christ as Lord is the heart of the Christian faith. To him God has given all authority in heaven and on earth. As Lord of the Church he bestows the Holy

Spirit to create a communion of men with God and with one another. To bring this *koinonia* to perfection is God's eternal purpose. The Church exists to serve the fulfilment of this purpose when God will be all in all.

I *Christian Authority*

2 Through the gift of the Spirit the apostolic community came to recognize in the words and deeds of Jesus the saving activity of God and their mission to proclaim to all men the good news of salvation. Therefore they preached Jesus through whom God has spoken finally to men. Assisted by the Holy Spirit they transmitted what they had heard and seen of the life and words of Jesus and their interpretation of his redemptive work. Consequently the inspired documents in which this is related came to be accepted by the Church as a normative record of the authentic foundation of the faith. To these the Church has recourse for the inspiration of its life and mission; to these the Church refers its teaching and practice. Through these written words the authority of the Word of God is conveyed. Entrusted with these documents, the Christian community is enabled by the Holy Spirit to live out the Gospel and so to be led into all truth. It is therefore given the capacity to assess its faith and life and to speak to the world in the name of Christ. Shared commitment and belief create a common mind in determining how the Gospel should be interpreted and obeyed. By reference to this common faith each person tests the truth of his own belief.

3 The Spirit of the risen Lord, who indwells the Christian community, continues to maintain the people of God in obedience to the Father's will. He safeguards their faithfulness to the revelation of Jesus Christ and equips them for their mission in the world. By this action of the Holy Spirit the authority of the Lord is active in the Church. Through incorporation into Christ and obedience to him Christians are made open to one another and assume mutual obligations. Since the Lordship of Christ is universal, the community also bears a responsibility towards all mankind, which demands participation in all that promotes the good of society and responsiveness to every form of human need. The common life in the body of Christ equips the community and each of its members with what they need

to fulfil this responsibility: they are enabled so to live that the authority of Christ will be mediated through them. This is Christian authority: when Christians so act and speak, men perceive the authoritative word of Christ.

II *Authority in the Church*

4 The Church is a community which consciously seeks to submit to Jesus Christ. By sharing in the life of the Spirit all find within the *koinonia* the means to be faithful to the revelation of their Lord. Some respond more fully to his call; by the inner quality of their life they win a respect which allows them to speak in Christ's name with authority.

5 The Holy Spirit also gives to some individuals and communities special gifts for the benefit of the Church, which entitle them to speak and be heeded (e.g. Eph. 4.11, 12; 1 Cor. 12.4–11).

Among these gifts of the Spirit for the edification of the Church is the *episcope* of the ordained ministry. There are some whom the Holy Spirit commissions through ordination for service to the whole community. They exercise their authority in fulfilling ministerial functions related to 'the apostles' teaching and fellowship, to the breaking of bread and the prayers' (Acts 2.42). This pastoral authority belongs primarily to the bishop, who is responsible for preserving and promoting the integrity of the *koinonia* in order to further the Church's response to the Lordship of Christ and its commitment to mission. Since the bishop has general oversight of the community, he can require the compliance necessary to maintain faith and charity in its daily life. He does not, however, act alone. All those who have ministerial authority must recognize their mutual responsibility and interdependence. This service of the Church, officially entrusted only to ordained ministers, is intrinsic to the Church's structure according to the mandate given by Christ and recognized by the community. This is yet another form of authority.

6 The perception of God's will for his Church does not belong only to the ordained ministry but is shared by all its members. All who live faithfully within the *koinonia* may become sensitive to the leading of the Spirit and be brought towards a deeper understanding of the Gospel and of its implications in

diverse cultures and changing situations. Ordained ministers commissioned to discern these insights and give authoritative expression to them, are part of the community, sharing its quest for understanding the Gospel in obedience to Christ and receptive to the needs and concerns of all.

The community, for its part, must respond to and assess the insights and teaching of the ordained ministers. Through this continuing process of discernment and response, in which the faith is expressed and the Gospel is pastorally applied, the Holy Spirit declares the authority of the Lord Jesus Christ, and the faithful may live freely under the discipline of the Gospel.

7 It is by such means as these that the Holy Spirit keeps the Church under the Lordship of Christ, who, taking full account of human weakness, has promised never to abandon his people. The authorities in the Church cannot adequately reflect Christ's authority because they are still subject to the limitations and sinfulness of human nature. Awareness of this inadequacy is a continual summons to reform.

III *Authority in the Communion of the Churches*

8 The *koinonia* is realized not only in the local Christian communities, but also in the communion of these communities with one another. The unity of local communities under one bishop constitutes what is commonly meant in our two communions by 'a local church', though the expression is sometimes used in other ways. Each local church is rooted in the witness of the apostles and entrusted with the apostolic mission. Faithful to the Gospel, celebrating the one eucharist and dedicated to the service of the same Lord, it is the Church of Christ. In spite of diversities each local church recognizes its own essential features in the others and its true identity with them. The authoritative action and proclamation of the people of God to the world therefore are not simply the responsibilities of each church acting separately, but of all the local churches together. The spiritual gifts of one may be an inspiration to the others. Since each bishop must ensure that the local community is distinctively Christian he has to make it aware of the universal communion of which it is part. The bishop expresses this unity of his church with the others: this is symbolized by the participation of several bishops in his ordination.

9 Ever since the Council of Jerusalem (Acts 15) the churches have realized the need to express and strengthen the *koinonia* by coming together to discuss matters of mutual concern and to meet contemporary challenges. Such gatherings may be either regional or world-wide. Through such meetings the Church, determined to be obedient to Christ and faithful to its vocation, formulates its rule of faith and orders its life. In all these councils, whether of bishops only, or of bishops, clergy, and laity, decisions are authoritative when they express the common faith and mind of the Church. The decisions of what has traditionally been called an 'ecumenical council' are binding upon the whole Church; those of a regional council or synod bind only the churches it represents. Such decrees are to be received by the local churches as expressing the mind of the Church. This exercise of authority, far from being an imposition, is designed to strengthen the life and mission of the local churches and of their members.

10 Early in the history of the Church a function of oversight of the other bishops of their regions was assigned to bishops of prominent sees. Concern to keep the churches faithful to the will of Christ was among the considerations which contributed to this development. This practice has continued to the present day. This form of *episcope* is a service to the Church carried out in co-responsibility with all the bishops of the region; for every bishop receives at ordination both responsibility for his local church and the obligation to maintain it in living awareness and practical service of the other churches. The Church of God is found in each of them and in their *koinonia*.

11 The purpose of *koinonia* is the realization of the will of Christ: 'Father, keep them in thy name, which thou hast given me, that they may be one, even as we are one. . . . so that the world may believe that thou hast sent me' (John 17.11, 21). The bishop of a principal see should seek the fulfilment of this will of Christ in the churches of his region. It is his duty to assist the bishops to promote in their churches right teaching, holiness of life, brotherly unity, and the Church's mission to the world. When he perceives a serious deficiency in the life or mission of one of the churches he is bound, if necessary, to call the local bishop's attention to it and to offer assistance. There will also be occasions when he has to assist other bishops to reach a common mind with regard to their shared needs and

difficulties. Sharing together and active mutual concern are indispensable to the churches' effective witness to Christ.

12 It is within the context of this historical development that the see of Rome, whose prominence was associated with the death there of Peter and Paul, eventually became the principal centre in matters concerning the Church universal.

The importance of the bishop of Rome among his brother bishops, as explained by analogy with the position of Peter among the apostles, was interpreted as Christ's will for his Church.

On the basis of this analogy the First Vatican Council affirmed that this service was necessary to the unity of the whole Church. Far from overriding the authority of the bishops in their own dioceses, this service was explicitly intended to support them in their ministry of oversight. The Second Vatican Council placed this service in the wider context of the shared responsibility of all the bishops. The teaching of these councils shows that communion with the bishop of Rome does not imply submission to an authority which would stifle the distinctive features of the local churches. The purpose of this episcopal function of the bishop of Rome is to promote Christian fellowship in faithfulness to the teaching of the apostles.

The theological interpretation of this primacy and the administrative structures through which it has been exercised have varied considerably through the centuries. Neither theory nor practice, however, has ever fully reflected these ideals. Sometimes functions assumed by the see of Rome were not necessarily linked to the primacy: sometimes the conduct of the occupant of this see has been unworthy of his office: sometimes the image of this office has been obscured by interpretations placed upon it: and sometimes external pressures have made its proper exercise almost impossible. Yet the primacy, rightly understood, implies that the bishop of Rome exercises his oversight in order to guard and promote the faithfulness of all the churches to Christ and one another. Communion with him is intended as a safeguard of the catholicity of each local church, and as a sign of the communion of all the churches.

IV *Authority in Matters of Faith*

13 A local church cannot be truly faithful to Christ if it does not desire to foster universal communion, the embodiment of

that unity for which Christ prayed. This communion is founded on faith in Jesus Christ, the incarnate Son of God, crucified, risen, ascended, and now living through his Spirit in the Church. Every local church must therefore ever seek a deeper understanding and clearer expression of this common faith, both of which are threatened when churches are isolated by division.

14 The Church's purpose in its proclamation is to lead mankind to accept God's saving work in Christ, an acceptance which not only requires intellectual assent but also demands the response of the whole person. In order to clarify and transmit what is believed and to build up and safeguard the Christian life, the Church has found the formulation of creeds, conciliar definitions, and other statements of belief indispensable. But these are always instrumental to the truth which they are intended to convey.

15 The Church's life and work are shaped by its historical origins, by its subsequent experience, and by its endeavour to make the relevance of the Gospel plain to every generation. Through reflection upon the word, through the proclamation of the Gospel, through baptism, through worship, especially the eucharist, the people of God are moved to the living remembrance of Jesus Christ and of the experience and witness of the apostolic community. This remembrance supports and guides them in their search for language which will effectively communicate the meaning of the Gospel.

All generations and cultures must be helped to understand that the good news of salvation is also for them. It is not enough for the Church simply to repeat the original apostolic words. It has also prophetically to translate them in order that the hearers in their situation may understand and respond to them. All such restatement must be consonant with the apostolic witness recorded in the Scriptures; for in this witness the preaching and teaching of ministers, and statements of local and universal councils, have to find their ground and consistency. Although these clarifications are conditioned by the circumstances which prompted them, some of their perceptions may be of lasting value. In this process the Church itself may come to see more clearly the implications of the Gospel. This is why the Church has endorsed certain formulas as authentic expressions of its witness, whose significance transcends the setting in which they were first formulated. This is not to claim that these formulas are the only possible, or even the most exact, way of expressing the faith, or that they can never be improved. Even when a doctrinal definition is regarded by the Christian community as part of its permanent teaching, this does not exclude subsequent restatement. Although the categories of thought and the mode of expression may be superseded, restatement always builds upon, and does not contradict, the truth intended by the original definition.

16 Local councils held from the second century determined the limits of the New Testament, and gave to the Church a canon which has remained normative. The action of a council in making such a decision on so momentous a matter implies an assurance that the Lord himself is present when his people assemble in his name (Matt. 18.20), and that a council may say, 'it has seemed good to the Holy Spirit and to us' (Acts 15.28). The conciliar mode of authority exercised in the matter of the canon has also been applied to questions of discipline and of fundamental doctrine. When decisions (as at Nicaea in 325) affect the entire Church and deal with controverted matters which have been widely and seriously debated, it is important to establish criteria for the recognition and reception of conciliar definitions and disciplinary decisions. A substantial part in the process of reception is played by the subject matter of the definitions and by the response of the faithful. This process is often gradual, as the decisions come to be seen in perspective through the Spirit's continuing guidance of the whole Church.

17 Among the complex historical factors which contributed to the recognition of conciliar decisions considerable weight attached to their confirmation by the principal sees, and in particular by the see of Rome. At an early period other local churches actively sought the support and approbation of the church in Rome; and in course of time the agreement of the Roman see was regarded as necessary to the general acceptance of synodal decisions in major matters of more than regional concern, and also, eventually, to their canonical validity. By their agreement or disagreement the local church of Rome and its bishop fulfilled their responsibility towards other local churches and their bishops for maintaining the whole Church in the truth. In addition the bishop of Rome was also led to intervene in controversies relating to matters of faith – in most

cases in response to appeals made to him, but sometimes on his own initiative.

18 In its mission to proclaim and safeguard the Gospel the Church has the obligation and the competence to make declarations in matters of faith. This mission involves the whole people of God, among whom some may rediscover or perceive more clearly than others certain aspects of the saving truth. At times there result conflict and debate. Customs, accepted positions, beliefs, formulations, and practices, as well as innovations and re-interpretations, may be shown to be inadequate, mistaken, or even inconsistent with the Gospel. When conflict endangers unity or threatens to distort the Gospel the Church must have effective means for resolving it.

In both our traditions the appeal to Scripture, to the creeds, to the Fathers, and to the definitions of the councils of the early Church is regarded as basic and normative.[1] But the bishops have a special responsibility for promoting truth and discerning error, and the interaction of bishop and people in its exercise is a safeguard of Christian life and fidelity. The teaching of the faith and the ordering of life in the Christian community require a daily exercise of this responsibility; but there is no guarantee that those who have an everyday responsibility will – any more than other members – invariably be free from errors of judgement, will never tolerate abuses, and will never distort the truth. Yet, in Christian hope, we are confident that such failures cannot destroy the Church's ability to proclaim the Gospel and to show forth the Christian life; for we believe that Christ will not desert his Church and that the Holy Spirit will lead it into all truth. That is why the Church, in spite of its failures, can be described as indefectible.

V *Conciliar and Primatial Authority*

19 In times of crisis or when fundamental matters of faith are in question, the Church can make judgements, consonant with Scripture, which are authoritative. When the Church meets in ecumenical council its decisions on fundamental matters of faith exclude what is erroneous. Through the Holy Spirit the Church commits itself to these judgements, recognizing that,

---

[1] This is emphasized in the Anglican tradition. Cf. the Lambeth Conferences of 1948 and 1968.

being faithful to Scripture and consistent with Tradition, they are by the same Spirit protected from error. They do not add to the truth but, although not exhaustive, they clarify the Church's understanding of it. In discharging this responsibility bishops share in a special gift of Christ to his Church. Whatever further clarification or interpretation may be propounded by the Church, the truth expressed will always be confessed. This binding authority does not belong to every conciliar decree, but only to those which formulate the central truths of salvation. This authority is ascribed in both our traditions to decisions of the ecumenical councils of the first centuries.[2]

20 The bishops are collectively responsible for defending and interpreting the apostolic faith. The primacy accorded to a bishop implies that, after consulting his fellow bishops, he may speak in their name and express their mind. The recognition of his position by the faithful creates an expectation that on occasion he will take an initiative in speaking for the Church. Primatial statements are only one way by which the Holy Spirit keeps the people of God faithful to the truth of the Gospel.

21 If primacy is to be a genuine expression of *episcope* it will foster the *koinonia* by helping the bishops in their task of apostolic leadership both in their local church and in the Church universal. Primacy fulfils its purpose by helping the churches to listen to one another, to grow in love and unity, and to strive together towards the fullness of Christian life and witness; it respects and promotes Christian freedom and spontaneity; it does not seek uniformity where diversity is legitimate, or centralize administration to the detriment of local churches.

A primate exercises his ministry not in isolation but in collegial association with his brother bishops. His intervention in the affairs of a local church should not be made in such a way as to usurp the responsibility of its bishop.

22 Although primacy and conciliarity are complementary elements of *episcope* it has often happened that one has been emphasized at the expense of the other, even to the point of serious imbalance. When churches have been separated from

---

[2] Since our historical divisions, the Roman Catholic Church has continued the practice of holding general councils of its bishops, some of which it has designated as ecumenical. The churches of the Anglican Communion have developed other forms of conciliarity.

one another, this danger has been increased. The *koinonia* of the churches requires that a proper balance be preserved between the two with the responsible participation of the whole people of God.

23   If God's will for the unity in love and truth of the whole Christian community is to be fulfilled, this general pattern of the complementary primatial and conciliar aspects of *episcope* serving the *koinonia* of the churches needs to be realized at the universal level. The only see which makes any claim to universal primacy and which has exercised and still exercises such *episcope* is the see of Rome, the city where Peter and Paul died.

It seems appropriate that in any future union a universal primacy such as has been described should be held by that see.

VI *Problems and Prospects*

24   What we have written here amounts to a consensus on authority in the Church and, in particular, on the basic principles of primacy. This consensus is of fundamental importance. While it does not wholly resolve all the problems associated with papal primacy, it provides us with a solid basis for confronting them. It is when we move from these basic principles to particular claims of papal primacy and to its exercise that problems arise, the gravity of which will be variously judged:

(*a*)   Claims on behalf of the Roman see as commonly presented in the past have put a greater weight on the Petrine texts (Matt. 16.18, 19; Luke 22.31, 32; John 21.15–17) than they are generally thought to be able to bear. However, many Roman Catholic scholars do not now feel it necessary to stand by former exegesis of these texts in every respect.

(*b*)   The First Vatican Council of 1870 uses the language of 'divine right' of the successors of Peter. This language has no clear interpretation in modern Roman Catholic theology. If it is understood as affirming that the universal primacy of the bishop of Rome is part of God's design for the universal *koinonia* then it need not be a matter of disagreement. But if it were further implied that as long as a church is not in communion with the bishop of Rome, it is regarded by the Roman Catholic Church as less than fully a church, a difficulty would remain: for some this difficulty would be removed by simply restoring communion, but to others the implication would itself be an obstacle to entering into communion with Rome.

(*c*) Anglicans find grave difficulty in the affirmation that the pope can be infallible in his teaching. It must, however, be borne in mind that the doctrine of infallibility[3] is hedged round by very rigorous conditions laid down at the First Vatican Council. These conditions preclude the idea that the pope is an inspired oracle communicating fresh revelation, or that he can speak independently of his fellow bishops and the Church, or on matters not concerning faith or morals. For the Roman Catholic Church the pope's dogmatic definitions, which, fulfilling the criteria of infallibility, are preserved from error, do no more but no less than express the mind of the Church on issues concerning the divine revelation. Even so, special difficulties are created by the recent Marian dogmas, because Anglicans doubt the appropriateness, or even the possibility, of defining them as essential to the faith of believers.

(*d*) The claim that the pope possesses universal immediate jurisdiction, the limits of which are not clearly specified, is a source of anxiety to Anglicans who fear that the way is thus open to its illegitimate or uncontrolled use. Nevertheless, the First Vatican Council intended that the papal primacy should be exercised only to maintain and never to erode the structures of the local churches. The Roman Catholic Church is today seeking to replace the juridical outlook of the nineteenth century by a more pastoral understanding of authority in the Church.

25 In spite of the difficulties just mentioned, we believe that this Statement on Authority in the Church represents a significant convergence with far-reaching consequences. For a considerable period theologians in our two traditions, without compromising their respective allegiances, have worked on common problems with the same methods. In the process they have come to see old problems in new horizons and have experienced a theological convergence which has often taken them by surprise.

In our three Agreed Statements we have endeavoured to get behind the opposed and entrenched positions of past controversies. We have tried to reassess what are the real issues to be resolved. We have often deliberately avoided the vocabulary of past polemics, not with any intention of evading the real

---

[3] 'Infallibility' is a technical term which does not bear precisely the same meaning as the word does in common usage. Its theological sense is seen in paras. 15 and 19 above.

difficulties that provoked them, but because the emotive associations of such language have often obscured the truth. For the
future relations between our churches the doctrinal convergence
which we have experienced offers hope that remaining difficulties
can be resolved.

Conclusion

26 The Malta Report of 1968 envisaged the coming together of
the Roman Catholic Church and the churches of the Anglican
Communion in terms of 'unity by stages'. We have reached
agreements on the doctrines of the eucharist, ministry, and,
apart from the qualifications of para. 24, authority. Doctrinal
agreements reached by theological commissions cannot,
however, by themselves achieve the goal of Christian unity.
Accordingly, we submit our Statements to our respective
authorities to consider whether or not they are judged to
express on these central subjects a unity at the level of faith
which not only justifies but requires action to bring about a
closer sharing between our two communions in life, worship,
and mission.

Elucidation (1981)

Comments and Criticisms

1 After the publication of the first Statement on Authority the
Commission received comments and criticisms. Some of the
questions raised, such as the request for a clarification of the
relation between infallibility and indefectibility, find an answer
in the second Statement on Authority. Another question, concerning our understanding of *koinonia*, is answered in the
Introduction to this Final Report, where we show how the
concept underlies all our Statements.

Behind many reactions to the Statement is a degree of
uneasiness as to whether sufficient attention is paid to the
primary authority of Scripture, with the result that certain
developments are given an authority comparable to that of
Scripture. Serious questions have also been asked about councils and reception, and some commentators have claimed that
what the Statement says about the protection of an ecumenical
council from error is in conflict with Article 21 of the Anglican

Articles of Religion. It has been suggested that the treatment of the place and authority of the laity in the Church is inadequate. There have also been requests for a clarification of the nature of ministerial authority and of jurisdiction. Some questions have been asked about the status of regional primacies – for example, the patriarchal office as exercised in the Eastern churches. Finally, a recurring question has been whether the Commission is suggesting that a universal primacy is a theological necessity simply because one has existed or been claimed.

In what follows the Commission attempts to address itself to these problems and to elucidate the Statement as it bears on each of them. In seeking to answer the criticisms that have been received we have sometimes thought it necessary to go further and to elucidate the basic issues that underlie them. In all that we say we take for granted two fundamental principles – that Christian faith depends on divine revelation and that the Holy Spirit guides the Church in the understanding and transmission of revealed truth.

The Place of Scripture

2 Our documents have been criticized for failing to give an adequate account of the primary authority of Scripture in the Church, thereby making it possible for us to treat certain developments as possessing an authority comparable to that of Scripture itself. Our description of 'the inspired documents . . . as a normative record of the authentic foundation of the faith' (para. 2) has been felt to be an inadequate statement of the truth.

The basis of our approach to Scripture is the affirmation that Christ is God's final word to man – his eternal Word made flesh. He is the culmination of the diverse ways in which God has spoken since the beginning (Heb. 1.1-3). In him God's saving and revealing purpose is fully and definitively realized.

The patriarchs and the prophets received and spoke the word of God in the Spirit. By the power of the same Spirit the Word of God became flesh and accomplished his ministry. At Pentecost the same Spirit was given to the disciples to enable them to recall and interpret what Jesus did and taught, and so to proclaim the Gospel in truth and power.

The person and work of Jesus Christ, preached by the apostles and set forth and interpreted in the New Testament writings, through the inspiration of the Holy Spirit, are the primary norm for Christian faith and life. Jesus, as the Word of God, sums up in himself the whole of God's self-disclosure. The Church's essential task, therefore, in the exercise of its teaching office, is to unfold the full extent and implications of the mystery of Christ, under the guidance of the Spirit of the risen Lord.

No endeavour of the Church to express the truth can add to the revelation already given. Moreover, since the Scriptures are the uniquely inspired witness to divine revelation, the Church's expression of that revelation must be tested by its consonance with Scripture. This does not mean simply repeating the words of Scripture, but also both delving into their deeper significance and unravelling their implications for Christian belief and practice. It is impossible to do this without resorting to current language and thought. Consequently the teaching of the Church will often be expressed in words that are different from the original text of Scripture without being alien to its meaning. For instance, at the First Ecumenical Council the Church felt constrained to speak of the Son of God as 'of one substance with the Father' in order to expound the mystery of Christ. What was understood by the term 'of one substance' at this time was believed to express the content of Christian faith concerning Christ, even though the actual term is never used in the apostolic writings. This combination of permanence in the revealed truth and continuous exploration of its meaning is what is meant by Christian tradition. Some of the results of this reflection, which bear upon essential matters of faith, have come to be recognized as the authentic expression of Christian doctrine and therefore part of the 'deposit of faith'.

Tradition has been viewed in different ways. One approach is primarily concerned never to go beyond the bounds of Scripture. Under the guidance of the Spirit undiscovered riches and truths are sought in the Scriptures in order to illuminate the faith according to the needs of each generation. This is not slavery to the text of Scripture. It is an unfolding of the riches of the original revelation. Another approach, while different, does not necessarily contradict the former. In the conviction that the Holy Spirit is seeking to guide the Church into the fullness of truth, it draws upon everything in human experience and thought which will give to the content of the revelation its fullest expression and widest application. It is primarily concerned with the growth of the seed of God's word from age to age. This does not imply any denial of the uniqueness of the revelation. Because these two attitudes contain differing emphases, conflict may arise, even though in both cases the Church is seeking the fullness of revelation. The seal upon the truthfulness of the conclusions that result from this search will be the reception by the whole Church, since neither approach is immune from the possibility of error.

Councils and Reception

3 The Commission has been said to contradict Article 21 of the Articles of Religion in its affirmation that the decisions of what have traditionally been called ecumenical councils 'exclude what is erroneous'. The Commission is very far from implying that general councils cannot err and is well aware that they 'sometimes have erred'; for example the Councils of Ariminum and of Seleucia of 359 AD. Article 21 in fact affirms that general councils have authority only when their judgements 'may be declared that they be taken out of Holy Scripture'. According to the argument of the Statement also, only those judgements of general councils are guaranteed to 'exclude what is erroneous' or are 'protected from error' which have as their content 'fundamental matters of faith', which 'formulate the central truths of salvation' and which are 'faithful to Scripture and consistent with Tradition'. 'They do not add to the truth but, although not exhaustive, they clarify the Church's understanding of it' (para. 19).

The Commission has also been asked to say whether reception by the whole people of God is part of the process which gives authority to the decisions of ecumenical councils.

By 'reception' we mean the fact that the people of God acknowledge such a decision or statement because they recognize in it the apostolic faith. They accept it because they discern a harmony between what is proposed to them and the *sensus fidelium* of the whole Church. As an example, the creed which we call Nicene has been received by the Church because in it the Church has recognized the apostolic faith. Reception does not create truth nor legitimize the decision: it is the final indication that such a decision has fulfilled the necessary conditions for it to be a true expression of the faith. In this acceptance the whole Church is involved in a continuous process of discernment and response (cf. para. 6).

The Commission therefore avoids two extreme positions. On the one hand it rejects the view that a definition has no authority until it is accepted by the whole Church or even derives its authority solely from that acceptance. Equally, the Commission denies that a council is so evidently self-sufficient that its definitions owe nothing to reception.

The Place of the Laity

4 The Commission has been accused of an over-emphasis upon the ordained ministry to the neglect of the laity.

In guarding and developing communion, every member has a part to play. Baptism gives everyone in the Church the right, and consequently the ability, to carry out his particular function in the body. The recognition of this fundamental right is of great importance. In different ways, even if sometimes hesitantly, our two Churches have sought to integrate in decision-making those who are not ordained.

The reason why the Statement spoke at length about the structure and the exercise of the authority of the ordained ministry was that this was the area where most difficulties appeared to exist. There was no devaluing of the proper and active role of the laity. For instance, we said that the Holy Spirit gives to some individuals and communities special gifts for the benefit of the Church (para. 5), that all the members of the Church share in the discovery of God's will (para. 6), that the *sensus fidelium* is a vital element in the comprehension of God's truth (para. 18), and that all bear witness to God's compassion for mankind and his concern for justice in the world (Ministry, para. 7).

The Authority of the Ordained Ministry

5 We have been asked to clarify the meaning of what some of our critics call 'hierarchical authority' – an expression we did not use. Here we are dealing with a form of authority which is inherent in the visible structure of the Church. By this we mean the authority attached to those ordained to exercise *episcope* in the Church. The Holy Spirit gives to each person power to fulfil his particular function within the body of Christ. Accordingly, those exercising *episcope* receive the grace appropriate to their calling and those for whom it is exercised must recognize and accept their God-given authority.

Both Anglicans and Roman Catholics, however, have criticized the emphasis we placed on a bishop's authority in certain circumstances to require compliance.

The specific oversight of the ordained ministry is exercised and acknowledged when a minister preaches the Gospel, presides at the eucharist, and seeks as pastor to lead the community truly to discern God's word and its relevance to their lives. When this responsibility laid upon a bishop (or other ordained minister under the direction of a bishop) requires him to declare a person to be in error in respect of doctrine or conduct, even to the point of exclusion from eucharistic communion, he is acting for the sake of the integrity of the community's faith and life. Both our communions have always recognized this need for disciplinary action on exceptional occasions as part of the authority given by Christ to his ministers, however difficult it may be in practice to take such action. This is what we meant by saying that the bishop 'can require the compliance necessary to maintain faith and charity in its daily life' (para. 5). At the same time the authority of the ordained minister is not held in isolation, but is shared with other ministers and the rest of the community. All the ministers, whatever their role in the body of Christ, are involved in responsibility for preserving the integrity of the community.

Jurisdiction

6 Critics have asked for clarification on two matters.

First, what do we mean by jurisdiction? We understand jurisdiction as the authority or power (*potestas*) necessary for the effective fulfilment of an office. Its exercise and limits are determined by what that office involves (cf. Authority II, paras. 16–22).

In both our communions we find dioceses comprising a number of parishes, and groups of dioceses at the provincial, national or international level. All of these are under the oversight of a special *episcope* exercised by ministers with a shared responsibility for the overall care of the Church. Every form of jurisdiction given to those exercising such an *episcope* is to serve and strengthen both the *koinonia* in the community and that between different Christian communities.

Secondly, it has been questioned whether we imply that jurisdiction attached to different levels of *episcope* – even within the same order of ministry – is always to be exercised in an identical way. Critics give the example of the relation and possible conflict between metropolitans and local bishops. We believe that the problem is not basically that of jurisdiction but of the complementarity and harmonious working of these differing forms of *episcope* in the one body of Christ. Jurisdiction, being the power necessary for the fulfilment of an office, varies according to the specific functions of each form of *episcope*. That is why the use of this juridical vocabulary does not mean that we attribute to all those exercising *episcope* at different levels exactly the same canonical power (cf. Authority II, para. 16).

Regional Primacy

7 Concern has been voiced that the Commission's treatment of regional primacy is inadequate. In particular, reference has been made to the ancient tradition of patriarchates.

The Commission did not ignore this tradition in its treatment of the origins of primacy (cf. para. 10). It avoided specific terms such as 'metropolitan' and 'patriarch', but in speaking of bishops with a special responsibility of oversight in their regions, the Commission intended to point to the reality behind the historical terms used for this form of episcopal co-responsibility in both east and west. It also pointed to the contemporary development and importance of new forms of regional primacy in both our traditions, e.g. the elective presidencies of Roman Catholic episcopal conferences and certain elective primacies in the Anglican Communion.

Primacy and History

8 It has been alleged that the Commission commends the primacy of the Roman see solely on the basis of history. But the Commission's argument is more than historical (cf. para. 23).

According to Christian doctrine the unity in truth of the Christian community demands visible expression. We agree that such visible expression is the will of God and that the maintenance of visible unity at the universal level includes the *episcope* of a universal primate. This is a doctrinal statement. But the way *episcope* is realized concretely in ecclesial life (the balance fluctuating between conciliarity and primacy) will depend upon contingent historical factors and upon development under the guidance of the Holy Spirit.

Though it is possible to conceive a universal primacy located elsewhere than in the city of Rome, the original witness of Peter and Paul and the continuing exercise of a universal *episcope* by the see of Rome present a unique presumption in its favour (cf. Authority II, paras. 6–9). Therefore, while to locate a universal primacy in the see of Rome is an affirmation at a different level from the assertion of the necessity for a universal primacy, it cannot be dissociated from the providential action of the Holy Spirit.

The design of God through the Holy Spirit has, we believe, been to preserve at once the fruitful diversity within the *koinonia* of local churches and the unity in essentials which must mark the universal *koinonia*. The history of our separation has underlined and continues to underline the necessity for this proper theological balance, which has often been distorted or destroyed by human failings or other historical factors (cf. para. 22).

The Commission does not therefore say that what has evolved historically or what is currently practised by the Roman see is necessarily normative: it maintains only that visible unity requires the realization of a 'general pattern of the complementary primatial and conciliar aspects of *episcope*' in the service of the universal '*koinonia* of the churches' (para. 23). Indeed much Anglican objection has been directed against the manner of the exercise and particular claims of the Roman primacy rather than against universal primacy as such.

Anglicanism has never rejected the principle and practice of primacy. New reflection upon it has been stimulated by the evolving role of the archbishop of Canterbury within the Anglican Communion. The development of this form of primacy arose precisely from the need for a service of unity in the faith in an expanding communion of Churches. It finds expression in the Lambeth Conferences convoked by successive archbishops of Canterbury which originated with requests from overseas provinces for guidance in matters of faith. This illustrates a particular relationship between conciliarity and primacy in the Anglican Communion.

The Commission has already pointed to the possibilities of mutual benefit and reform which should arise from a shared recognition of one universal primacy which does not inhibit conciliarity – a 'prospect (which) should be met with faith, not fear' (Co-Chairmen's Preface). Anglicans sometimes fear the prospect of over-centralization, Roman Catholics the prospect of doctrinal incoherence. Faith, banishing fear, might see simply the prospect of the right balance between a primacy serving the unity and a conciliarity maintaining the just diversity of the *koinonia* of all the churches.

Authority in the Church II

The Statement (1981)

Introduction

1 In our conclusion to our first Statement on Authority in the Church we affirmed that we had reached 'a consensus on authority in the Church and, in particular, on the basic principles of primacy', which we asserted to be of 'fundamental importance' (para. 24). Nevertheless we showed that four outstanding problems related to this subject required further study since, if they remained unresolved, they would appear to constitute serious obstacles to our growing together towards full communion. The four difficulties were the interpretation of the Petrine texts, the meaning of the language of 'divine right', the affirmation of papal infallibility, and the nature of the jurisdiction ascribed to the bishop of Rome as universal primate. After five years of further study we are able to present a fresh appraisal of their weight and implications.

Petrine Texts

2 The position of Peter among the apostles has often been discussed in relation to the importance of the bishop of Rome among the bishops. This requires that we look at the data of the New Testament and what are commonly called the Petrine texts.

3 While explicitly stressing Christ's will to root the Church in the apostolic witness and mandate, the New Testament attributes to Peter a special position among the Twelve. Whether the Petrine texts contain the authentic words of Jesus or not, they witness to an early tradition that Peter already held

this place during Jesus' ministry. Individually the indications may seem to be inconclusive, but taken together they provide a general picture of his prominence. The most important are: the bestowal on Simon of the name Cephas, his being mentioned first among the Twelve and in the smaller circle of the three (Peter, James and John), the faith which enabled him to confess Jesus' Messiahship (Matt. 16.16; Mark 8.29; Luke 9.20; and John 6.69), and the answer of Jesus (Matt. 16.18) in which he is called rock, the charge to strengthen his brethren (Luke 22. 31-32) and to feed the sheep (John 21.16-17) and the special appearance to him of the risen Lord (e.g. Luke 24.34; 1 Cor. 15.5). Although the author of Acts underlined the apostolic authority of Paul in the latter part of his book, he focused in the first part on Peter's leadership. For instance, it is Peter who frequently speaks in the name of the apostolic community (Acts 3.15, 10.41), he is the first to proclaim the Gospel to the Jews and the first to open the Christian community to the Gentiles. Paul seems to have recognized this prominence of Peter among the apostles as well as the importance of James (Gal. 1.18-19). He appears also to have accepted the lead given by Peter at the Council of Jerusalem (Acts 15), even though he was prepared to oppose Peter when he held Peter to be at fault (Gal. 2.11).

4 Responsibility for pastoral leadership was not restricted to Peter. The expression 'binding and loosing', which is used for the explicit commission to Peter in Matt. 16.19, appears again in Matt. 18.18 in the promise made by Christ directly to all the disciples. Similarly the foundation upon which the Church is built is related to Peter in Matt. 16.18 and to the whole apostolic body elsewhere in the New Testament (e.g. Eph. 2.20). Even though Peter was the spokesman at Pentecost, the charge to proclaim the Gospel to all the world had previously been given by the risen Christ to the Eleven (Acts 1.2-8). Although Paul was not among the Twelve, he too was conspicuous for the leadership which he exercised with an authority received from the Lord himself, claiming to share with Peter and others parallel responsibility and apostolic authority (Gal. 2.7-8; 1 Cor. 9.1).

5 In spite of being strongly rebuked by Christ and his dramatic failure in denying him, in the eyes of the New Testament writers Peter holds a position of special importance. This was not due to his own gifts and character although he had been the first to

confess Christ's Messiahship. It was because of his particular
calling by Christ (Luke 6.14; John 21.15–17). Yet while the distinctive features of Peter's ministry are stressed, this ministry is
that of an apostle and does not isolate him from the ministry
of the other apostles. In accordance with the teaching of Jesus
that truly to lead is to serve and not to dominate others (Luke
22.24ff), Peter's role in strengthening the brethren (Luke
22.32) is a leadership of service. Peter, then, serves the Church
by helping it to overcome threats to its unity (e.g. Acts 11.1–18),
even if his weakness may require help or correction, as is clear
from his rebuke by Paul (Gal. 2.11–14). These considerations
help clarify the analogy that has been drawn between the role
of Peter among the apostles and that of the bishop of Rome
among his fellow bishops.

6 The New Testament contains no explicit record of a transmission of Peter's leadership; nor is the transmission of apostolic
authority in general very clear. Furthermore, the Petrine texts
were subjected to differing interpretations as early as the time
of the Church Fathers. Yet the church at Rome, the city in
which Peter and Paul taught and were martyred, came to be
recognized as possessing a unique responsibility among the
churches: its bishop was seen to perform a special service in
relation to the unity of the churches, and in relation to fidelity
to the apostolic inheritance, thus exercising among his fellow
bishops functions analogous to those ascribed to Peter, whose
successor the bishop of Rome was claimed to be (cf. para. 12).

7 Fathers and doctors of the Church gradually came to interpret
the New Testament data as pointing in the same direction. This
interpretation has been questioned, and it has been argued that
it arose from an attempt to legitimize a development which
had already occurred. Yet it is possible to think that a primacy
of the bishop of Rome is not contrary to the New Testament
and is part of God's purpose regarding the Church's unity and
catholicity, while admitting that the New Testament texts offer
no sufficient basis for this.

8 Our two traditions agree that not everything said of the
apostles as the witnesses to the resurrection and saving work of
Christ (Acts 1.21–22) is transmitted to those chosen to continue
their mission. The apostles are the foundations precisely
because they are the unique, commissioned witnesses to the
once-for-all saving work of Christ. Peter's role is never isolated

from that of the apostolic group; what is true of the transmissi-
bility of the mission of the apostolic group is true of Peter as a
member of it. Consequently though the sentence, 'On this rock
I will build my church', is spoken to Peter, this does not imply
that the same words can be applied to the bishop of Rome with
an identical meaning. Even if Peter's role cannot be transmitted
in its totality, however, this does not exclude the continuation
of a ministry of unity guided by the Spirit among those who
continue the apostolic mission.

9 If the leadership of the bishop of Rome has been rejected by
those who thought it was not faithful to the truth of the Gospel
and hence not a true focus of unity, we nevertheless agree that
a universal primacy will be needed in a reunited Church and
should appropriately be the primacy of the bishop of Rome, as
we have specified it (Authority I, para. 23). While the New
Testament taken as a whole shows Peter playing a clear role of
leadership it does not portray the Church's unity and universality
exclusively in terms of Peter. The universal communion of the
churches is a company of believers, united by faith in Christ, by
the preaching of the word, and by participation in the sacraments
assured to them by a pastoral ministry of apostolic order. In a
reunited Church a ministry modelled on the role of Peter will
be a sign and safeguard of such unity.

Jus Divinum

10 The first Statement on Authority poses two questions with
respect to the language of 'divine right' applied by the First
Vatican Council to the Roman primacy: What does the language
actually mean? What implications does it have for the ecclesial
status of non-Roman Catholic communions (Authority I, para
24*b*)? Our purpose is to clarify the Roman Catholic position on
these questions; to suggest a possible Anglican reaction to
the Roman Catholic position; and to attempt a statement of
consensus.

11 The Roman Catholic conviction concerning the place of
the Roman primacy in God's plan for his Church has traditionally
been expressed in the language of *jus divinum* (divine law or
divine right). This term was used by the First Vatican Council
to describe the primacy of the 'successor in the chair of Peter'
whom the Council recognized in the bishop of Rome. The First

Vatican Council used the term *jure divino* to say that this primacy derives from Christ.[1] While there is no universally accepted interpretation of this language, all affirm that it means at
least that this primacy expresses God's purpose for his Church.
Jus divinum in this context need not be taken to imply that the
universal primacy as a permanent institution was directly
founded by Jesus during his life on earth. Neither does the
term mean that the universal primate is a 'source of the
Church' as if Christ's salvation had to be channelled through
him. Rather, he is to be the sign of the visible *koinonia* God
wills for the Church and an instrument through which unity in
diversity is realized. It is to a universal primate thus envisaged
within the collegiality of the bishops and the *koinonia* of the
whole Church that the qualification *jure divino* can be applied.

12 The doctrine that a universal primacy expresses the will of
God does not entail the consequence that a Christian community out of communion with the see of Rome does not belong
to the Church of God. Being in canonical communion with the
bishop of Rome is not among the necessary elements by which
a Christian community is recognized as a church. For example,
the Roman Catholic Church has continued to recognize the
Orthodox churches as churches in spite of division concerning the primacy (Vatican II, *Unitatis Redintegratio*, para. 14).
The Second Vatican Council, while teaching that the Church
of God subsists in the Roman Catholic Church, rejected the
position that the Church of God is co-extensive with the
Roman Catholic Church and is exclusively embodied in that
Church. The Second Vatican Council allows it to be said that a
church out of communion with the Roman see may lack nothing
from the viewpoint of the Roman Catholic Church except that
it does not belong to the visible manifestation of full Christian
communion which is maintained in the Roman Catholic Church
(*Lumen Gentium*, para 8; *Unitatis Redintegratio*, para 13).

13 Relations between our two communions in the past have
not encouraged reflection by Anglicans on the positive significance of the Roman primacy in the life of the universal Church.
Nonetheless, from time to time Anglican theologians have
affirmed that, in changed circumstances, it might be possible
for the churches of the Anglican Communion to recognize the

---

[1] 'ex ipsius Christi Domini institutione seu iure divino' (*Pastor Aeternus*,
ch. 2).

development of the Roman primacy as a gift of divine providence – in other words, as an effect of the guidance of the Holy
Spirit in the Church. Given the above interpretation of the
language of divine right in the First Vatican Council, it is
reasonable to ask whether a gap really exists between the
assertion of a primacy by divine right (*jure divino*) and the
acknowledgement of its emergence by divine providence (*divina
providentia*).

14 Anglicans have commonly supposed that the claim to
divine right for the Roman primacy implied a denial that the
churches of the Anglican Communion are churches. Consequently, they have concluded that any reconciliation with
Rome would require a repudiation of their past history, life
and experience – which in effect would be a betrayal of their
own integrity. However, given recent developments in the
Roman Catholic understanding of the status of other Christian
churches, this particular difficulty may no longer be an obstacle to Anglican acceptance, as God's will for his Church, of a
universal primacy of the bishop of Rome such as has been
described in the first Statement on Authority (para. 23).

15 In the past, Roman Catholic teaching that the bishop of
Rome is universal primate by divine right or law has been
regarded by Anglicans as unacceptable. However, we believe
that the primacy of the bishop of Rome can be affirmed as part
of God's design for the universal *koinonia* in terms which are
compatible with both our traditions. Given such a consensus,
the language of divine right used by the First Vatican Council
need no longer be seen as a matter of disagreement between
us.

Jurisdiction

16 Jurisdiction in the Church may be defined as the authority
or power (*potestas*) necessary for the exercise of an office. In
both our communions it is given for the effective fulfilment of
office and this fact determines its exercise and limits. It varies
according to the specific functions of the *episcope* concerned.
The jurisdictions associated with different levels of *episcope* (e.g.
of primates, metropolitans and diocesan bishops) are not in all
respects identical.

The use of the same juridical terms does not mean that

exactly the same authority is attributed to all those exercising *episcope* at different levels. Where a metropolitan has jurisdiction in his province this jurisdiction is not merely the exercise in a broader context of that exercised by a bishop in his diocese: it is determined by the specific functions which he is required to discharge in relation to his fellow bishops.

17 Each bishop is entrusted with the pastoral authority needed for the exercise of his *episcope*. This authority is both required and limited by the bishop's task of teaching the faith through the proclamation and explanation of the word of God, of providing for the administration of the sacraments in his diocese and of maintaining his church in holiness and truth (cf. Authority I, para. 5). Hence decisions taken by the bishop in performing his task have an authority which the faithful in his diocese have a duty to accept. This authority of the bishop, usually called jurisdiction, involves the responsibility for making and implementing the decisions that are required by his office for the sake of the *koinonia*. It is not the arbitrary power of one man over the freedom of others, but a necessity if the bishop is to serve his flock as its shepherd (cf. Authority: *Elucidation*, para. 5). So too, within the universal *koinonia* and the collegiality of the bishops, the universal primate exercises the jurisdiction necessary for the fulfilment of his functions, the chief of which is to serve the faith and unity of the whole Church.

18 Difficulties have arisen from the attribution of universal, ordinary and immediate jurisdiction to the bishop of Rome by the First Vatican Council. Misunderstanding of these technical terms has aggravated the difficulties. The jurisdiction of the bishop of Rome as universal primate is called ordinary and immediate (i.e. not mediated) because it is inherent in his office; it is called universal simply because it must enable him to serve the unity and harmony of the *koinonia* as a whole and in each of its parts.

The attribution of such jurisdiction to the bishop of Rome is a source of anxiety to Anglicans (Authority I, para. 24*d*) who fear, for example, that he could usurp the rights of a metropolitan in his province or of a bishop in his diocese; that a centralized authority might not always understand local conditions or respect legitimate cultural diversity; that rightful freedom of conscience, thought and action could be imperilled.

19 The universal primate should exercise, and be seen to exercise, his ministry not in isolation but in collegial association with his brother bishops (Authority I, paras. 21 and 23). This in no way reduces his own responsibility on occasion to speak and act for the whole Church. Concern for the universal Church is intrinsic to all episcopal office; a diocesan bishop is helped to make this concern a reality by the universal jurisdiction of the universal primate. But the universal primate is not the source from which diocesan bishops derive their authority, nor does his authority undermine that of the metropolitan or diocesan bishop. Primacy is not an autocratic power over the Church but a service in and to the Church which is a communion in faith and charity of local churches.

20 Although the scope of universal jurisdiction cannot be precisely defined canonically, there are moral limits to its exercise: they derive from the nature of the Church and of the universal primate's pastoral office. By virtue of his jurisdiction, given for the building up of the Church, the universal primate has the right in special cases to intervene in the affairs of a diocese and to receive appeals from the decision of a diocesan bishop. It is because the universal primate, in collegial association with his fellow bishops, has the task of safeguarding the faith and unity of the universal Church that the diocesan bishop is subject to his authority.

21 The purpose of the universal primate's jurisdiction is to enable him to further catholicity as well as unity and to foster and draw together the riches of the diverse traditions of the churches. Collegial and primatial responsibility for preserving the distinctive life of the local churches involves a proper respect for their customs and traditions, provided these do not contradict the faith or disrupt communion. The search for unity and concern for catholicity must not be divorced.

22 Even though these principles concerning the nature of jurisdiction be accepted as in line with the understanding which Anglicans and Roman Catholics share with regard to the Church's structure, there remain specific questions about their practical application in a united Church. Anglicans are entitled to assurance that acknowledgement of the universal primacy of the bishop of Rome would not involve the suppression of theological, liturgical and other traditions which they value or the

imposition of wholly alien traditions. We believe that what has been said above provides grounds for such assurance. In this connection we recall the words of Paul VI in 1970: 'There will be no seeking to lessen the legitimate prestige and the worthy patrimony of piety and usage proper to the Anglican Church . . .'[2]

Infallibility

23 It is Christ himself, the Way, the Truth and the Life, who entrusts the Gospel to us and gives to his Church teaching authority which claims our obedience. The Church as a whole, indwelt by the Spirit according to Christ's promise and looking to the testimony of the prophets, saints and martyrs of every generation, is witness, teacher and guardian of the truth (cf. Authority I, para. 18). The Church is confident that the Holy Spirit will effectually enable it to fulfil its mission so that it will neither lose its essential character nor fail to reach its goal.[3] We are agreed that doctrinal decisions made by legitimate authority must be consonant with the community's faith as grounded in Scripture and interpreted by the mind of the Church, and that no teaching authority can add new revelation to the original apostolic faith (cf. Authority I, paras. 2 and 18). We must then ask whether there is a special ministerial gift of discerning the truth and of teaching bestowed at crucial times on one person to enable him to speak authoritatively in the name of the Church in order to preserve the people of God in the truth.

24 Maintenance in the truth requires that at certain moments the Church can in a matter of essential doctrine make a decisive judgement which becomes part of its permanent witness.[4] Such

---

2 'There will be no seeking to lessen the legitimate prestige and the worthy patrimony of piety and usage proper to the Anglican Church when the Roman Catholic Church – this humble "Servant of the servants of God" – is able to embrace her ever beloved Sister in the one authentic communion of the family of Christ . . .' (AAS 62 (1970), p. 753).

3 This is the meaning of *indefectibility*, a term which does not speak of the Church's lack of defects but confesses that, despite all its many weaknesses and failures, Christ is faithful to his promise that the gates of hell shall not prevail against it.

4 That this is in line with Anglican belief is clear from the Thirty-nine Articles (Article 20): 'The Church hath . . . authority in Controversies of Faith'.

a judgement makes it clear what the truth is, and strengthens the Church's confidence in proclaiming the Gospel. Obvious examples of such judgements are occasions when general councils define the faith. These judgements, by virtue of their foundation in revelation and their appropriateness to the need of the time, express a renewed unity in the truth to which they summon the whole Church.

25 The Church in all its members is involved in such a definition which clarifies and enriches their grasp of the truth. Their active reflection upon the definition in its turn clarifies its significance. Moreover, although it is not through reception by the people of God that a definition first acquires authority, the assent of the faithful is the ultimate indication that the Church's authoritative decision in a matter of faith has been truly preserved from error by the Holy Spirit. The Holy Spirit who maintains the Church in the truth will bring its members to receive the definition as true and to assimilate it if what has been declared genuinely expounds the revelation.

26 The Church exercises teaching authority through various instruments and agencies at various levels (cf. Authority I, paras. 9 and 18–22). When matters of faith are at stake decisions may be made by the Church in universal councils; we are agreed that these are authoritative (cf. Authority I, para. 19). We have also recognized the need in a united Church for a universal primate who, presiding over the *koinonia*, can speak with authority in the name of the Church (cf. Authority I, para. 23). Through both these agencies the Church can make a decisive judgement in matters of faith, and so exclude error.

27 The purpose of this service cannot be to add to the content of revelation, but is to recall and emphasize some important truth; to expound the faith more lucidly; to expose error; to draw out implications not sufficiently recognized; and to show how Christian truth applies to contemporary issues. These statements would be intended to articulate, elucidate or define matters of faith which the community believes at least implicitly. The welfare of the *koinonia* does not require that all the statements of those who speak authoritatively on behalf of the Church should be considered permanent expressions of the truth. But situations may occur where serious divisions of opinion on crucial issues of pastoral urgency call for a more definitive judgement. Any such statement would be intended

as an expression of the mind of the Church, understood not only in the context of its time and place but also in the light of the Church's whole experience and tradition. All such definitions are provoked by specific historical situations and are always made in terms of the understanding and framework of their age (cf. Authority I, para. 15). But in the continuing life of the Church they retain a lasting significance if they are safeguarding the substance of the faith.

The Church's teaching authority is a service to which the faithful look for guidance especially in times of uncertainty; but the assurance of the truthfulness of its teaching rests ultimately rather upon its fidelity to the Gospel than upon the character or office of the person by whom it is expressed. The Church's teaching is proclaimed because it is true; it is not true simply because it has been proclaimed. The value of such authoritative proclamation lies in the guidance that it gives to the faithful. However, neither general councils nor universal primates are invariably preserved from error even in official declarations (cf. Authority Elucidation, para. 3).

28 The Church's judgement is normally given through synodal decision, but at times a primate acting in communion with his fellow bishops may articulate the decision even apart from a synod. Although responsibility for preserving the Church from fundamental error belongs to the whole Church, it may be exercised on its behalf by a universal primate. The exercise of authority in the Church need not have the effect of stifling the freedom of the Spirit to inspire other agencies and individuals. In fact, there have been times in the history of the Church when both councils and universal primates have protected legitimate positions which have been under attack.

29 A service of preserving the Church from error has been performed by the bishop of Rome as universal primate both within and outside the synodal process. The judgement of Leo I, for example, in his letter received by the Council of Chalcedon, helped to maintain a balanced view of the two natures in Christ. This does not mean that other bishops are restricted to a merely consultative role, nor that every statement of the bishop of Rome instantly solves the immediate problem or decides the matter at issue for ever. To be a decisive discernment of the truth, the judgement of the bishop of Rome must satisfy rigorous conditions. He must speak explicitly

as the focus within the *koinonia*; without being under duress from external pressures; having sought to discover the mind of his fellow bishops and of the Church as a whole; and with a clear intention to issue a binding decision upon a matter of faith or morals. Some of these conditions were laid down by the First Vatican Council.[5] When it is plain that all these conditions have been fulfilled, Roman Catholics conclude that the judgement is preserved from error and the proposition true. If the definition proposed for assent were not manifestly a legitimate interpretation of biblical faith and in line with orthodox tradition, Anglicans would think it a duty to reserve the reception of the definition for study and discussion.

30 This approach is illustrated by the reaction of many Anglicans to the Marian definitions, which are the only examples of such dogmas promulgated by the bishop of Rome apart from a synod since the separation of our two communions. Anglicans and Roman Catholics can agree in much of the truth that these two dogmas are designed to affirm. We agree that there can be but one mediator between God and man, Jesus Christ, and reject any interpretation of the role of Mary which obscures this affirmation. We agree in recognizing that Christian understanding of Mary is inseparably linked with the doctrines of Christ and of the Church. We agree in recognizing the grace and unique vocation of Mary, Mother of God Incarnate (*Theotokos*), in observing her festivals, and in according her honour in the communion of saints. We agree that she was prepared by divine grace to be the mother of our Redeemer, by whom she herself was redeemed and received into glory. We further agree in recognizing in Mary a model of holiness, obedience and faith for all Christians. We accept that it is possible to regard her as a prophetic figure of the Church of

---

[5] The phrase 'eiusmodi . . . definitiones ex sese, non autem ex consensu ecclesiae irreformabiles esse': 'such definitions are irreformable by themselves and not by reason of the agreement of the Church' (*Pastor Aeternus*, ch. 4) does not deny the importance of reception of doctrinal statements in the Roman Catholic Church. The phrase was used by the Council to rule out the opinion of those who maintained that such a statement becomes 'irreformable' only subsequently when it is approved by the bishops. The term 'irreformable' means that the truth expressed in the definition can no longer be questioned. 'Irreformable' does not mean that the definition is the Church's last word on the matter and that the definition cannot be restated in other terms.

God before as well as after the Incarnation.[6] Nevertheless the dogmas of the Immaculate Conception and the Assumption raise a special problem for those Anglicans who do not consider that the precise definitions given by these dogmas are sufficiently supported by Scripture. For many Anglicans the teaching authority of the bishop of Rome, independent of a council, is not recommended by the fact that through it these Marian doctrines were proclaimed as dogmas binding on all the faithful. Anglicans would also ask whether, in any future union between our two Churches, they would be required to subscribe to such dogmatic statements. One consequence of our separation has been a tendency for Anglicans and Roman Catholics alike to exaggerate the importance of the Marian dogmas in themselves at the expense of other truths more closely related to the foundation of the Christian faith.

31 In spite of our agreement over the need of a universal primacy in a united Church, Anglicans do not accept the guaranteed possession of such a gift of divine assistance in judgement necessarily attached to the office of the bishop of Rome by virtue of which his formal decisions can be known to be wholly assured before their reception by the faithful. Nevertheless the problem about reception is inherently difficult. It would be incorrect to suggest that in controversies of faith no conciliar or papal definition possesses a right to attentive sympathy and acceptance until it has been examined by every individual Christian and subjected to the scrutiny of his private judgement. We agree that, without a special charism guarding the judgement of the universal primate, the Church would still possess means of receiving and ascertaining the truth of revelation. This is evident in the acknowledged gifts of

[6] The affirmation of the Roman Catholic Church that Mary was conceived without original sin is based on recognition of her unique role within the mystery of the Incarnation. By being thus prepared to be the mother of our Redeemer, she also becomes a sign that the salvation won by Christ was operative among all mankind before his birth. The affirmation that her glory in heaven involves full participation in the fruits of salvation expresses and reinforces our faith that the life of the world to come has already broken into the life of our world. It is the conviction of Roman Catholics that the Marian dogmas formulate a faith consonant with Scripture.

grace and truth in churches not in full communion with the Roman see.

32 Roman Catholic tradition has used the term infallibility to describe guaranteed freedom from fundamental error in judgement.[7] We agree that this is a term applicable unconditionally only to God, and that to use it of a human being, even in highly restricted circumstances, can produce many misunderstandings. That is why in stating our belief in the preservation of the Church from error we have avoided using the term. We also recognize that the ascription to the bishop of Rome of infallibility under certain conditions has tended to lend exaggerated importance to all his statements.

33 We have already been able to agree that conciliarity and primacy are complementary (Authority I, paras. 22–23). We can now together affirm that the Church needs both a multiple, dispersed authority, with which all God's people are actively involved, and also a universal primate as servant and focus of visible unity in truth and love. This does not mean that all differences have been eliminated; but if any Petrine function and office are exercised in the living Church of which a universal primate is called to serve as a visible focus, then it inheres in his office that he should have both a defined teaching responsibility and appropriate gifts of the Spirit to enable him to discharge it.

Contemporary discussions of conciliarity and primacy in both communions indicate that we are not dealing with positions destined to remain static. We suggest that some difficulties will not be wholly resolved until a practical initiative has been taken and our two Churches have lived together more visibly in the one *koinonia*.

Conclusion

This Final Report of the Anglican–Roman Catholic International Commission represents a significant stage in relations between the Anglican Communion and the Roman Catholic

---

[7] In Roman Catholic doctrine, *infallibility* means only the preservation of the judgement from error for the maintenance of the Church in the truth, not positive inspiration or revelation. Moreover the infallibility ascribed to the bishop of Rome is a gift to be, in certain circumstances and under precise conditions, an organ of the infallibility of the Church.

Church. The decision by our respective authorities, made as long ago as 1966, to enter into serious dialogue in order to resolve long-standing issues which have been at the origin of our separation, resulted in our concentration on three main areas of controversy: the doctrine of the eucharist, ministry and ordination, and the nature and exercise of authority in the Church.

This dialogue, however, has been directed not merely to the achievement of doctrinal agreement, which is central to our reconciliation, but to the far greater goal of organic unity. The convergence reflected in our Final Report would appear to call for the establishing of a new relationship between our Churches as a next stage in the journey towards Christian unity.

We understand but do not share the fears of those who think that such Statements constitute a threat to all that is distinctive and true in their own traditions. It is our hope to carry with us in the substance of our agreement not only Roman Catholics and Anglicans but all Christians, and that what we have done may contribute to the visible unity of all the people of God as well as to the reconciliation of our two Churches.

We are well aware of how much we owe to others and of how much we have left others still to do. Our agreement still needs to be tested, but in 1981 it has become abundantly clear that, under the Holy Spirit, our Churches have grown closer together in faith and charity. There are high expectations that significant initiatives will be boldly undertaken to deepen our reconciliation and lead us forward in the quest for the full communion to which we have been committed, in obedience to God, from the beginning of our dialogue.

Official Comments

5

The *Observations* of the Congregation for the Doctrine of the Faith on the Final Report of ARCIC I (1982)

The Co-Chairmen of the Anglican–Roman Catholic International Commission (ARCIC) sent to His Holiness, Pope John Paul II, the Final Report of twelve years of the Commission's work on the questions of Eucharistic doctrine, ministry and ordination, and authority in the Church. At the request of the Holy Father, the Congregation for the Doctrine of the Faith (SCDF) has proceeded with a doctrinal examination of this Report, and its conclusions are set forth in the following observations.

A Overall Evaluation

1 Positive Aspects

The Congregation must first of all give full recognition to the positive aspects of the work accomplished by ARCIC in the course of twelve years of an ecumenical dialogue which is exemplary on several counts. Setting aside a sterile polemical mentality, the partners have engaged in a patient and exacting dialogue in order to overcome doctrinal difficulties which were frankly acknowledged, with a view to restoring full communion between the Catholic Church and the Anglican Communion. This work achieved in common is a singular event in the history of the relations between the two Communions, and is at the same time a notable effort towards reconciliation. Worthy of particular note are:

(i) the quality of the doctrinal rapprochement achieved, in a serious attempt at a converging interpretation of the values considered fundamental by both sides;
(ii) the fact that ARCIC has been attentive to a certain number of observations which the SCDF had previously made about the Windsor, Canterbury, and Venice statements, and has made an effort to respond satisfactorily in two series of *Elucidations* on *Eucharistic Doctrine* and *Ministry and Ordination* (1979) and on *Authority in the Church* (1981).

2 Negative Aspects

The Congregation is obliged nevertheless to point out some negative aspects with regard to the method followed by ARCIC:

(i) The first may be considered a minor point, although it is not without relevance for the document's readers: ARCIC has thought it unnecessary to revise the original statements; rather, it has left their adjustment to two series of elucidations. The result is a lack of harmony and homogeneity which could lead to different readings and to an unwarranted use of the Commission's texts.

The following aspects are more important, for even though they pertain to the method employed, they are not without doctrinal significance.
(ii) The ambiguity of the phrase 'substantial agreement'.

The English adjective could be taken to indicate nothing other than 'real' or 'genuine'. But its translation, at least into languages of Latin origin, as 'substantiel', 'sostanziale' – above all with the connotation of the word in Catholic theology – leads one to read into it a fundamental agreement about points which are truly essential (and one will see below that the SCDF has justified reservations in this regard).

Another source of ambiguity lies in the following fact: a comparison of three texts (Eucharistic Doctrine: *Elucidation*, paras. 2 and 9; *Authority I*, para. 26) shows that the agreement spoken of as 'substantial', while considered by ARCIC to be very extensive, is not yet complete. This does not permit one to know whether, in the eyes of the members of ARCIC, the differences which remain or the things which are missing from the document only deal with secondary points (for example, the structure of liturgical rites, theological opinion, ecclesiastical discipline, spirituality), or whether these are points which truly pertain to the faith. Whatever the case, the Congregation is obliged to observe that sometimes it is the second hypothesis which is verified (for example, Eucharistic adoration, papal primacy, the Marian dogmas), and that it would not be possible here to appeal to the 'hierarchy of truths' of which no.11 of the Decree *Unitatis Redintegratio* (CTS Do 351) of Vatican II speaks (cf. the Declaration *Mysterium Ecclesiae* no.4, para.3).

(iii) The possibility of a twofold interpretation of the texts.

Certain formulations in the Report are not sufficiently explicit and hence can lend themselves to a twofold interpretation, in which both parties can find unchanged the expression of their own position.

This possibility of contrasting and ultimately incompatible readings of formulations which are apparently satisfactory to both sides gives rise to a question about the real consensus of the two Communions, pastors and faithful alike. In effect, if a formulation which has received the agreement of the experts can be diversely interpreted, how could it serve as a basis for reconciliation on the level of church life and practice?

Moreover, when the members of ARCIC speak about 'the consensus we have reached' (cf. Eucharistic Doctrine, para.1), one does not always see clearly whether this means the faith really professed by the two communions in dialogue, or a conviction which the members of the Commission have reached and to which they want to bring their respective coreligionists.

In this regard it would have been useful – in order to evaluate the exact meaning of certain points of agreement – had ARCIC indicated their position in reference to the documents which have contributed significantly to the formation of the Anglican identity (The Thirty-nine Articles of Religion, Book of Common Prayer, Ordinal), in those cases where the assertions of the Final Report seem incompatible with these documents. The failure to take a stand on these texts can give rise to uncertainty about the exact meaning of the agreements reached.

The Congregation finally has to note that, from the Catholic point of view, there remain in the ARCIC Final Report a certain number of difficulties at the level of doctrinal formulations, some of which touch the very substance of the faith.

These difficulties – their description and the reasons for them – will now be listed following the order of the new texts of the Final Report (*Eucharistic Doctrine – Ministry and Ordination: Elucidations* (Salisbury 1979); *Authority II; Authority: Elucidation* (Windsor 1981)).

B Doctrinal Difficulties Noted by the SCDF

I Eucharist (cf. Elucidations, *Salisbury 1979*)

1 Eucharist as Sacrifice

In the *Elucidations,* para. 5, ARCIC has explained the reason for its use of the term *anamnesis* and has recognized as legitimate the specification of *anamnesis* as sacrifice, in reference to the Tradition of the Church and her liturgy. Nevertheless, insofar as this has been the object of controversy in the past, one cannot be satisfied with an explanation open to a reading which does not include an essential aspect of the mystery.

This text says, as does the Windsor Statement (para. 5), 'the Church enters into the movement of [Christ's] self-offering' and the Eucharistic memorial, which consists in 'the making effective in the present of an event in the past', is 'the Church's effectual proclamation of God's mighty acts.' But one still asks oneself what is really meant by the words 'the Church enters into the movement of [Christ's] self-offering' and 'the making effective in the present of an event in the past'. It would have been helpful, in order to permit Catholics to see their faith fully expressed on this point, to make clear that this real presence of the sacrifice of Christ, accomplished by the sacramental words, that is to say by the ministry of the priest saying '*in persona Christi*' the words of the Lord, includes a participation of the Church, the Body of Christ, in the sacrificial act of her Lord, so that she offers sacramentally in him and with him his sacrifice. Moreover, the propitiatory value that Catholic dogma attributes to the Eucharist, which is not mentioned by ARCIC, is precisely that of this sacramental offering (cf. Council of Trent, DS 1743, 1753; John Paul II, Letter *Dominicae Coenae*, no. 8, para. 4, CTS Do 519).

2 Real Presence

One notes with satisfaction that several formulations clearly affirm the real presence of the body and blood of Christ in the sacrament, for example, 'Before the Eucharistic Prayer, to the question: "What is that?", the believer answers: "It is bread." After the Eucharistic Prayer to the same question he answers: "It is truly the body of Christ, the Bread of Life"' (Eucharistic Doctrine: *Elucidation,* para. 6; cf. also Eucharistic Doctrine, paras. 6 and 10).

Certain other formulations, however, especially some of those which attempt to express the realization of this presence, do not seem to indicate adequately what the Church understands by 'transubstantiation' ('the wonderful and unique change of the whole substance of the bread into his body and of the whole substance of the wine into his blood, while only the species of bread and wine remain' – Council of Trent, DS 1652, cf. Paul VI, Encyclical *Mysterium Fidei,* AAS 57 (1965), p. 766) (CTS Do 355).

It is true that the Windsor Statement says in a footnote that this must be seen as 'a mysterious and radical change' effected by 'a change in the inner reality of the elements'. But the same statement speaks in another place (para. 3) of a 'sacramental presence *through bread and wine*', and *Elucidations* (para. 6(b)) says 'His body and blood are given through the action of the Holy Spirit, *appropriating bread and wine* so that they become the food of the new creation.' One also finds the expressions 'the association of Christ's presence with the consecrated elements' (para. 7) and 'the association of Christ's sacramental presence with the consecrated bread and wine' (para. 9). These formulations can be read with the understanding that, after the Eucharistic prayer, the bread and wine remain such in their ontological substance, even while becoming the sacramental mediation of the body and blood of Christ.[1] In the light of these observations, therefore, it seems necessary to say that the substantial agreement which ARCIC so carefully intended to present should receive even further clarification.

---

[1] One may also recall in this regard the Anglican–Lutheran statement of 1972, which reads: 'Both Communions affirm the real presence of Christ in this sacrament, but neither seeks to define precisely how this happens. In the eucharistic action (including consecration) and reception, the bread and wine, while remaining bread and wine, become the means whereby Christ is truly present and gives himself to the communicants' (Report of the Anglican–Lutheran International Conversations 1970–1972, authorized by the Lambeth Conference and the Lutheran World Federation, in *Lutheran World*, vol. XIX (1972), p. 393).

3 Reservation and Adoration of the Eucharist

Elucidations (para. 9) admits the possibility of a divergence not only in the practice of adoration of Christ in the reserved sacrament but also in the 'theological judgements' relating to it. But the adoration rendered to the Blessed Sacrament is the object of a dogmatic definition in the Catholic Church (cf. Council of Trent, DS 1643, 1656). A question could arise here about the current status in the Anglican Communion of the regulation called the 'Black Rubric' of the Book of Common Prayer: '. . . the Sacramental Bread and Wine remain still in their natural substances and therefore may not be adored'.

II *Ministry and Ordination (cf.* Elucidations, *Salisbury 1979)*

1 Ministerial priesthood

Elucidations (para. 12) makes the distinction between the common priesthood of the people of God and the priesthood of the ordained ministry, and makes clear what the priest alone is able to do in the eucharistic action in the following manner: 'it is only the ordained minister who presides at the eucharist, in which, in the name of Christ and on behalf of his Church, he recites the narrative of the institution of the Last Supper, and invokes the Holy Spirit upon the gifts.' But this formulation only means that he is a priest, in the sense of Catholic doctrine, if one understands that through him the Church offers sacramentally the sacrifice of Christ. Moreover, it has been previously observed that the document does not explicitate such a sacramental offering. Because the priestly nature of the ordained minister depends upon the sacrificial character of the Eucharist, lack of clarity on the latter point would render uncertain any real agreement on the former (cf. Council of Trent, DS 1740–1741, 1752, 1764, 1771; John Paul II, Letter *Dominicae Coenae*, no. 8, para. 4 and no. 9, para. 2).

2 Sacramentality of Ordination

ARCIC affirms the sacramental nature of the rite of ordination (para. 13), and further says that 'Those who are ordained . . . receive their ministry from Christ through those designated in the Church to hand it on'. Nevertheless, it does not state clearly enough that it is a tenet of the Church's faith – the possible difficulties of an historical proof notwithstanding – that the sacrament of Holy Orders was instituted by Christ: in effect, note 4 of the Canterbury Statement, which refers to 'The Thirty-nine Articles of Religion' (Article 25), allows one to infer that Anglicans recognize this institution only for the two 'sacraments of the Gospel', that is, Baptism and Eucharist.

It may be noted here that the question bearing on the institution of the sacraments and on the way in which this can be known is intimately linked to the question of the interpretation of Holy Scripture. The fact of institution cannot be considered only within the limits of the certitude arrived at by the historical method; one must take into account the authentic interpretation of the Scriptures which it pertains to the Church to make.

3 Ordination of Women
As ARCIC has noted, since the 1973 Canterbury Statement there have been developments with regard to the ordination of women (cf. *Elucidations*, para. 5). The new canonical regulations which have recently been introduced on this point in some parts of the Anglican Communion, and about which she has been able to speak of a 'slow but steady growth of a consensus of opinion' (cf. Letter of Dr Coggan to Paul VI, 9 July 1975), are formally opposed to the 'common traditions' of the two Communions. Furthermore, the obstacle thus created is of a doctrinal character, since the question whether one can or cannot be ordained is linked to the nature of the sacrament of Holy Orders.[2]

III *Authority in the Church (Statement II, and an* Elucidation, *Windsor 1981)*

1 Interpretation of the Petrine texts of the New Testament
It is necessary to underline the importance of the fact that Anglicans recognize that 'a primacy of the Bishop of Rome is not contrary to the New Testament, and is part of God's

---

[2] In the Declaration *Inter insigniores* (CTS Do 493) of 15 October 1976, one will find the reasons for which the Church does not consider herself authorized to admit women to ordination to the priesthood. It is not a question of socio-cultural reasons, but rather of the 'unbroken tradition throughout the history of the Church, universal in the East and in the West', which must be 'considered to conform to God's plan for his Church' (cf. nos. 1 and 4).

purpose regarding the Church's unity and catholicity' (Authority II, para. 7).

Just as for the institution of the sacraments, however, one should keep in mind that it is not possible for the Church to adopt as the effective norm for reading the Scriptures only what historical criticism maintains, thus allowing the homogeneity of the developments which appear in Tradition to remain in doubt.

From this point of view, what ARCIC writes about the role of Peter ('a special position among the Twelve', para. 3; 'a position of special importance', para. 5) does not measure up to the truth of faith as this has been understood by the Catholic Church, on the basis of the principal Petrine texts of the New Testament (John 1.42; 21.15; Matt. 16.16 – cf. DS 3053), and does not satisfy the requirements of the dogmatic statement of Vatican Council I: 'the apostle Peter . . . received immediately and directly from Jesus Christ our Lord a true and proper primacy of jurisdiction' (Constitution *Pastor Aeternus*, ch. 1, DS 3055).

2 Primacy and Jurisdiction of the Bishop of Rome

In commenting on the '*ius divinum*' used by Vatican Council I in reference to the primacy of the Pope, the successor of Peter, ARCIC says that 'it means at least that this primacy expresses God's purpose for his Church', and that it 'need not be taken to imply that the universal primacy as a permanent institution was directly founded by Jesus during his life on earth' (Authority II, para. 11). In so doing, ARCIC does not respect the exigencies of the word 'institution' in the expression of Vatican Council I 'by the institution of Christ our Lord himself' (Constitution *Pastor Aeternus*, ch. 2, DS 3058), which require that Christ himself provided for the universal primacy.

In this perspective, one should note that ARCIC is not exact in interpreting Vatican Council II when it says that the 'Council allows it to be said that a church out of communion with the Roman See might lack nothing from the viewpoint of the Roman Catholic Church except that it does not belong to the visible manifestation of full Christian communion which is maintained in the Roman Catholic Church' (para. 12). According to Catholic tradition, visible unity is not something extrinsic added to the particular churches, which already would possess and realize in themselves the full essence of the

Church; this unity pertains to the intimate structure of faith, permeating all its elements. For this reason the office of conserving, fostering and expressing this unity in accord with the Lord's will is a constitutive part of the very nature of the Church (cf. John 21.15–19). The power of jurisdiction over all the particular churches, therefore, is intrinsic (i.e. 'iure divino') to this office, not something which belongs to it for human reasons nor in order to respond to historical needs. The Pope's 'full, supreme and universal power over the whole Church, a power which he can always exercise unhindered' (Constitution *Lumen Gentium*, no. 22; cf. *Pastor Aeternus*, DS 3064), which can take different forms according to historical exigencies, can never be lacking.

The ARCIC Report recognizes 'that a universal primacy will be needed in a reunited Church' (Authority II, para. 9) in order to safeguard unity among the particular churches, and that 'in any future union a universal primacy . . . should be held' by the Bishop of Rome (cf. Authority I, para. 23). Such a recognition must be regarded as a significant fact in inter-church relations, but – as noted above – there remain important differences between Anglicans and Catholics concerning the *nature* of this primacy.

3 Infallibility and Indefectibility

One must note first of all that the term indefectibility, which ARCIC uses, is not equivalent to the term retained by the first Vatican Council (cf. Authority I, para. 18).

For ARCIC, the assurance the faithful have of the truth of the teaching of the Church's magisterium, in the last analysis, lies in the fidelity to the Gospel they recognize in it rather than in the authority of the person who expresses it (cf. Authority II, para. 27; Authority: *Elucidation*, para. 3).

The Commission points out in particular a divergence between the two Communions on the following point: 'In spite of our agreement over the need of a universal primacy in a united Church, Anglicans do not accept the guaranteed possession of such a gift of divine assistance in judgement necessarily attached to the office of the Bishop of Rome by virtue of which his formal decision can be known to be wholly assured before their reception by the faithful' (Authority II, para. 31).

As the above references show, agreement between the Anglican understanding of infallibility and the faith professed by Catholics has not yet been reached. ARCIC rightly insists that 'the Church's teaching is proclaimed because it is true; it is not true simply because it has been proclaimed' (Authority II, para. 27). The term 'infallibility', however, refers immediately not to truth but to certitude: for it says that the certitude of the Church about the truth of the Gospel is present without any doubt in the testimony of the successor of St Peter when he exercises his office of 'strengthening his brethren' (Luke 22.32; cf. Constitution *Lumen Gentium*, no. 25; cf. DS 3065, 3074).

Hence one can understand why ARCIC goes on to say that many Anglicans do not accept as dogmas of the Church the definitions of the Immaculate Conception and the Assumption of the Blessed Virgin Mary, whereas for the Catholic Church they are true and authentic dogmas which pertain to the fullness of faith.

4 General Councils

The Windsor *Elucidation* repeats something about which the SCDF has already presented a comment: 'only those judgements of general councils are guaranteed to "exclude what is erroneous" or are "protected from error" which have as their content "fundamental matters of faith" which "formulate the central truths of salvation" . . .' (para. 3). It further accentuates the Venice statement by saying that far from implying that general councils cannot err, 'the Commission . . . is well aware that they "sometimes have erred"' (ibid.).

What is said here about general councils is not exact: the mission which the Church recognizes for the bishops united in council is not limited to 'fundamental matters of faith'; it extends to the entire domain of faith and morals, where they are 'teachers and judges' (cf. Vatican II, Constitution *Lumen Gentium*, no. 25). Moreover, the ARCIC text does not distinguish in the conciliar documents between what is truly defined and the other considerations which are found there.

5 'Reception'

Considering the case of a definition 'ex cathedra' by the Bishop of Rome, the Report (Authority II, para. 29) points out a difference between Catholic doctrine and the Anglican position: 'Roman Catholics conclude that the judgement is preserved from error and the proposition true. If the definition proposed for assent were not manifestly a legitimate interpretation of biblical faith and in line with orthodox tradition, Anglicans would think it a duty to reserve the reception of the definition for study and discussion.'

On the other hand, when ARCIC treats of conciliar definitions and their reception, it speaks as though it had truly arrived at a formula of agreement by avoiding two extremes (*Elucidation*, para. 3). But this formula makes reception by the faithful a factor which must contribute, under the heading of an 'ultimate' or 'final indication', to the recognition of the authority and value of the definition as a genuine expression of the faith (cf. also Authority II, para. 25).

If this is, according to the Report, the role of 'reception', one must say that this theory is not in accord with Catholic teaching as expressed in the Constitution *Pastor Aeternus* of Vatican I, which says: 'the divine Redeemer willed his Church to be endowed (with infallibility) in defining doctrine concerning faith and morals' (DS 3074), nor with the Constitution *Lumen Gentium* of Vatican II, according to which the bishops, assembled in ecumenical council, enjoy this infallibility, and their definitions call for the obedient assent of faith (cf. no. 25).

The Constitution *Dei Verbum* of Vatican II, no. 10, it is true, speaks of 'a remarkable harmony' which is established 'between the bishops and the faithful' in 'maintaining, practising and professing the faith', but it also adds: 'The task of authentically interpreting the word of God, whether written or handed on, has been entrusted exclusively to the living teaching office of the Church, whose authority is exercised in the name of Jesus Christ. This teaching office is not above the word of God, but serves it, teaching only what has been handed on, listening to it devoutly, guarding it scrupulously, and explaining it faithfully by divine commission and with the help of the Holy Spirit; it draws from this one deposit of faith everything which it presents for belief as divinely revealed.'

C Other Points in View of Future Dialogue

1 Apostolic Succession

This question has been at the centre of all ecumenical discussions and lies at the heart of the ecumenical problem; as a result it affects all of the questions treated by ARCIC: the reality of the Eucharist, the sacramentality of the priestly ministry, the nature of the Roman primacy.

The Final Report asserts a consensus on this point (cf. Ministry and Ordination, para. 16), but we may ask whether the text itself provides a sufficient analysis of the question. This is a problem, then, which would deserve to be taken up again, studied more thoroughly, and above all confronted by the facts of church life and practice in the two Communions.

2 Moral Teaching

Quite properly, the dialogue conducted by ARCIC was focused on the three themes which have historically been the object of controversy between Catholics and Anglicans: 'on the eucharist, on the meaning and function of ordained ministry, and on the nature and exercise of authority in the Church' (Introduction to the Final Report, para. 2).

But since the dialogue has as its final objective the restoration of church unity, it will necessarily have to be extended to all the points which constitute an obstacle to the restoration of that unity. Among these points it will be appropriate to give moral teaching an important place.

D Final Remarks

1 On the Agreement Reached in the Final Report of ARCIC

At the conclusion of its doctrinal examination, the SCDF thinks that the Final Report, which represents a notable ecumenical endeavour and a useful basis for further steps on the road to reconciliation between the Catholic Church and the Anglican Communion, does not yet constitute a substantial and explicit agreement on some essential elements of Catholic faith:

(a) because the Report explicitly recognizes that one or another Catholic dogma is not accepted by our Anglican brethren (for example, Eucharistic adoration, infallibility, the Marian dogmas);

(b) because one or another Catholic doctrine is only accepted in part by our Anglican brethren (for example, the primacy of the Bishop of Rome);

(c) because certain formulations in the Report are not

explicit enough to ensure that they exclude interpretations not in harmony with the Catholic faith (for example, that which concerns the Eucharist as sacrifice, the Real Presence, the nature of the priesthood);

(d) because certain affirmations in the Report are inexact and not acceptable as Catholic doctrine (for example, the relationship between the primacy and the structure of the Church, the doctrine of 'reception');

(e) finally because some important aspects of the teaching of the Catholic Church have either not been dealt with or have been only in an indirect way (for example, apostolic succession, the 'regula fidei', moral teaching).

2 On the Next Concrete Step to Be Taken

The SCDF thinks that the results of its examination would recommend:

(a) that the dialogue be continued, since there are sufficient grounds for thinking its continuation will be fruitful;

(b) that it be deepened in regard to the points already addressed where the results are not satisfactory;

(c) that it be extended to new themes, particularly those which are necessary with a view to the restoration of full church unity between the two Communions.

6
Letter by Cardinal J. Ratzinger (Prefect of the Congregation for the Doctrine of the Faith) to Bishop Alan Clark (Roman Catholic Co-Chairman of ARCIC I) (1982)

After twelve years of work together, the Anglican–Roman Catholic International Commission (ARCIC), composed of bishops and theologians appointed by both communions, sent to their respective authorities a final report which sets forth the results obtained, through their theological research and continued prayer, on the important questions of eucharistic doctrine, ministry and ordination, and authority in the Church.

At the request of the Holy Father, the Congregation for the Doctrine of the Faith has studied the ARCIC Final Report and believes that it is an important ecumenical event which constitutes a significant step towards reconciliation between the Anglican Communion and the Catholic Church.

In the same spirit of sincerity that marks the work of ARCIC, and with the desire to contribute to that clarity so indispensable for genuine dialogue, the Congregation must also express its view that it is not yet possible to say that an agreement which is truly substantial has been reached on the totality of the questions studied by the commission.

In effect, as the report itself indicates, there are several points, held as dogmas by the Catholic Church, which are not able to be accepted as such, or are able to be accepted only in part, by our Anglican brethren.

Furthermore, some formulations in the ARCIC report can still give rise to divergent interpretations, while others do not seem able to be easily reconciled with Catholic doctrine. Finally, while recognising that the mixed commission was legitimately limited to essential questions which have been the focus of serious differences between our two communions in the past, one should note that other questions must be examined as well, together and in the same spirit, in order to arrive at a definitive agreement capable of guaranteeing true reconciliation.

This is why, in the judgment of our Congregation, everything should be done to ensure that the dialogue so happily undertaken should continue, that there be further study, especially of the points where the results obtained thus far require it, and that this study be extended to other questions indispensable for the restoration of the ecclesiastical unity willed by Our Lord.

The Congregation for the Doctrine of the Faith, therefore, will send detailed observations about the ARCIC Final Report to all of the episcopal conferences, as its contribution to the continuation of this dialogue.

United with you in prayer that the Holy Spirit may inspire and guide our common efforts so that they all may be perfectly one (John 27.21, 23), I am . . .

Sincerely yours in Christ,
Joseph Card. Ratzinger

7
Response to the Final Report of ARCIC I by the Roman Catholic Bishops' Conference of England and Wales (1985)

A In General

(i) *Background*

1 In their Common Declaration at Canterbury Cathedral, 29 May 1982, Pope John Paul II and the Archbishop of Canterbury joined 'in thanking the members of the Commission for their dedication, scholarship and integrity in a long and demanding task undertaken for the love of Christ and for the unity of the Church'. In formulating this Response to the Final Report of ARCIC I, we, the Bishops' Conference of England and Wales, wish to identify ourselves entirely with these sentiments. Members of the Commission who composed the Final Report were officially appointed for their theological competence and, coming from different countries, represented a wide variety of backgrounds and experience. After twelve years of work and prayer their integrity, dedication and, above all, the remarkable fruit of their dialogue must be fully acknowledged. Such respect for the work of ARCIC I is important for the process of consultation set in motion by the Secretariat for Promoting Christian Unity.

2 In responding to the questions addressed to us by Cardinal Willebrands in his letter of 17 March 1982, this Conference of Bishops is conscious that it does so in the light of considerable discussion and debate of these matters in England and Wales. Already in 1972 we were able to agree with our Theology Commission that 'the Windsor Agreement contains nothing contrary to the Catholic faith', and so commend the document

to the Church in England and Wales for study and discussion. Now, after a number of meetings in which we have been able to study the Final Report as a whole and not merely as a series of separate, unrelated Statements, we respond to the request of Cardinal Willebrands 'to send a considered judgement on the work done, above all as to whether it is consonant in substance with the faith of the Catholic Church concerning the matters discussed' (Sections A and B) and express our views 'on the agenda for the next stage of this dialogue' (Section C).

3 In making this response we are conscious that as the Bishops of England and Wales we bear a special responsibility in this process of consultation which is taking place throughout the universal Church. We acknowledge that the people we serve belong to a 'privileged terrain of ecumenism' (Pope John Paul II, St Peter's Square, 10 June 1982). Our Response will have particular significance in the continuation of this dialogue between our two Communions, especially in this land in which the Anglican Communion finds its centre and where good relations between the Churches have become a matter of common experience. We commend the Final Report as a truly outstanding contribution to this dialogue, and we readily uphold the process undertaken by the Commission as an example of what can be achieved by joint study and of how these studies can be a practical basis for growth in unity.

4 At the outset we wish to state that we recognise in the Final Report much that is an affirmation of our Catholic faith, especially in relation to the true nature of the Church. In our judgement as to how far these statements are in harmony with our faith, we will point out anything which we consider to be inadequate in its treatment or expression. However, we are fully committed to a resolution of these difficulties and offer our response as a contribution to this process.

(ii) *Fundamental Points*

(a) 'Substantial Agreement'
5 The Final Report brings together documents published by ARCIC from 1971–1981. Fundamental to all the work of the Commission was the desire to reach a common understanding of central doctrines for which they used the term 'substantial agreement'. The Final Report claims that differing degrees of

agreement have been achieved by the Commission. The measure of agreement claimed by ARCIC I in relation to the Eucharist and Ministry is that of 'substantial agreement' (Eucharistic Doctrine, para. 12; Ministry and Ordination, para. 17). In the matter of Authority in the Church, the documents claim to have achieved a consensus (Authority I, para. 24) and state that 'substantial agreement on these divisive issues is now possible' (Introduction, para. 2). These claims mean, according to the Final Report, that the documents represent not only an agreement reached between all the members of the Commission, but also an agreement 'on essential matters where it [the Commission] considers that doctrine admits no divergence' (Eucharistic Doctrine: *Elucidation*, para. 2). In coming to a judgement on these claims we wish to underline the importance of reading the Statements in the light of the *Elucidations* and of noting the sequence in which the documents were published in order to avoid unnecessary misunderstandings.

(b) Methodology
6 Since Vatican II it is increasingly recognised that the truth of revelation can be expressed in a variety of ways. The substantial agreement achieved by ARCIC I has been possible because of the particular methodology adopted by the Commission. This has been described as one of its most striking features. It was commended by Pope John Paul II when he said to the members of the Commission: 'Your method has been to go behind the habit of thought and expression born and nourished in enmity and controversy to scrutinise together the great common treasure, to clothe it in a language at once traditional and expressive of the insights of an age which no longer glorifies in strife but seeks to come together in listening to the quiet voice of the Spirit' (Pope John Paul II, Castelgandolfo, 4 September 1980).

7 We too welcome the emergence of this methodology. It is characterised by a joint endeavour to explore our 'common tradition', and achieves an understanding of the context in which concepts arose, how this coloured their meaning and what remains open to further development. It brings about a shared understanding of revelation as expressed in historically conditioned formulae. We commend this methodology, as entailing a serious attempt to develop patterns of thought and

language which give profound and precise expression to our shared faith (cf. *Unitatis Redintegratio*, 11).

8 There remains the delicate and difficult task of specifying the relationship between diverse theologies and the fundamental truths of faith to which Christians must be committed. We acknowledge 'a variety of theological approaches within both our Communions' (Eucharistic Doctrine, para. 12). These approaches need not be mutually exclusive in the expression of truth. Indeed, we perceive that, in our understanding of the Word of God, differing theological expressions often can be complementary. At the same time we are concerned to ensure that the relationship of authoritative formulae to the truths they seek to convey should not be weakened, despite the contingent element in all such formulae.

9 The methodology of the Commission has enabled it to claim a real convergence in doctrine. The Commission has presented this claim to the judgement of the two Churches. An open and continuing dialogue concerning matters of faith, such as the Commission itself conducted, will remain a vital part of the process of coming to this judgement. We pledge ourselves to the strengthening of the atmosphere of trust essential for such dialogue.

(c) *Koinonia*
10 The Introduction to the Final Report states clearly that the concept of *koinonia* is 'fundamental to all our statements' (Introduction, para. 4). In all its work the Commission has indeed demonstrated the richness and potential of this concept. In adopting it as central to an understanding of the Church, the Commission has emphasised that '*koinonia* is grounded in the Word of God preached, believed, and obeyed' (Introduction, para. 8). We welcome this approach to the ecclesiological question. We recognise its biblical roots and we point to the central role it plays in the Dogmatic Constitution of Vatican II, *Lumen Gentium*: 'This Church of Christ is truly present in all legitimate local congregations of the faithful which, united with their pastors, are themselves called Churches in the New Testament. . . . In them the faithful are gathered together by the preaching of the gospel of Christ and the mystery of the Lord's Supper is celebrated, "that by the flesh and blood of the Lord's body the whole brotherhood may

be joined together"' (*Lumen Gentium*, 26). This is an appropriate context for consideration by the Commission of the vital questions covered by their Statements.

11 Emphasis on the local Church has greatly enriched our understanding of the mystery of the presence there of the Church of Christ. It gives rise to certain questions regarding universal primacy as a sign and source of unity in the universal *koinonia* which is the communion of communions. As is stated in the Introduction to the Final Report: 'Full visible communion between our two Churches cannot be achieved without mutual recognition of sacraments and ministry, together with the common acceptance of a universal primacy, at one with the episcopal college in the service of the *koinonia*' (Introduction, para. 9).

B In Particular

12 In each section our Response is threefold.

(a) We wish first of all to acknowledge and appreciate the ground on which the Commission builds up its statements. Though presented here in summary form, this foundation is extensive in its scope and provides a rich context in which to explore the more crucial areas of interest.
(b) It is on these crucial areas that we then focus. Here, especially, we need to judge whether the substantial agreement claimed does in fact match the essential elements of our faith.
(c) Under 'Further Considerations' we indicate points that need or could benefit from further elucidation or expansion.

(i) *Eucharist*

(a) Approach and Perspective
13 The starting point is God's reconciling act in Christ. Here the Church comes into being. 'Christ through the Holy Spirit in the eucharist builds up the life of the Church, strengthens its fellowship and furthers its mission' (Eucharistic Doctrine, para. 3). The mystery of the Eucharist is seen at once to be Christocentric, ecclesial, eschatological, and missionary. The basis laid in the statement gives a very rich and dynamic view of the Eucharist and allows us to explore areas of past controversy with a practical sense of the centrality of the Eucharist in the life of the Church.

(b) Critical Focus

14 *Eucharist as sacrifice* In this statement, the identity of Christ and his Church in offering sacrifice is secured both by the concept of *koinonia*: 'we are his members', and by the use of the notion of memorial (*anamnesis*) in its strong and traditional sense: 'his sacrifice recalled and proclaimed is made effective here and now'. This maintains the uniqueness, the once-and-for-all character, and absolute sufficiency of the historical sacrifice of Jesus and the presence of that unique sacrifice in a sacramental and mysterious manner in the eucharistic celebration (Ministry and Ordination, para. 13). Thus 'we enter into the movement of his [Christ's] self-offering' (Eucharistic Doctrine, para. 5), his self-giving to the Father and his fellow men. This is a true expression of Catholic faith (cf. No. 17 infra).

15 *Real presence* The statement clearly maintains the real and true presence of Christ. The substantial nature of the change of the bread and wine is clearly asserted by the repeated use of the word 'become' as in the statement that 'they become his body and blood', by reference to the transforming action of the Spirit, by use of the language of change in the footnote on transubstantiation, and by the careful description of the role of faith within the individual. In the light of this we accept the statement as an expression of Catholic faith in the real presence.

16 In a number of places the statements about sacrifice and real presence see the Church's celebration as an effective proclamation of God's mighty deeds in Christ. This is a further way in which Catholic faith is affirmed.

(c) Further Considerations

17 What needs to be said more forcibly is that the Eucharist is offered to the Father by the whole Christ, head and members, in the power of the Spirit. The present text, by concentrating on the Eucharist as gift to the Church, gives an emphasis that is too passive in tone.

18 In this treatment of the Eucharist there is also insufficient reference to the resurrection of Christ. Both in contemporary theology and in the Catholic tradition the resurrection is an important and enriching element in the understanding of the Eucharist. Reference to the resurrection as taking place 'once and for all in history' (Eucharistic Doctrine, para. 5) is inadequate both for the understanding of the Lord's passover to the

Father and as a basis for appreciating the celebration of the Eucharist. In the Eucharist we assemble as the Body of Christ, the risen head, and worship through, with and in him. Reference to Calvary is secured by our present union with the risen Lord. The significance of memorial is strengthened by such considerations.

19 The question of reservation and adoration needs to be taken up again. We know that some Anglicans practise reservation. We know that others accord adoration to the sacrament within the celebration. But our unease at the lack of shared appreciation is intensified by the very negative statement, even after elucidations, that 'others still find any kind of adoration of Christ in the reserved sacrament unacceptable' (Eucharistic Doctrine: *Elucidation*, para. 8). The doctrinal implications of this position need to be examined closely. We say this because reservation for Catholics is a sign of Christ's abiding presence in the Church and a much loved focus of devotion.

20 This *Elucidation* goes some way in elaborating the footnote on transubstantiation. Many Catholics were unhappy about the relegation of this point to a footnote, because they felt it was only there that the explicit language of change was used. We do not insist on the language of transubstantiation nor advocate any one theological/philosophical attempt to explain it, but further examination of the notion, begun in this *Elucidation*, is important for the continuing dialogue between the two Churches.

(ii) *Ministry and Ordination*

(a) Approach and Perspective

21 The historical method becomes more evident at this point. The study of the ordained ministry is rightly placed in the context of Christ's ministry, the source of all Christian ministry, and ministry in the total life of the Church. The Church of the apostolic age is seen to be a crucially important period of development, and the complexities of it are recognised. Nevertheless, it is possible to place there the origin and development of the ordained ministry and to see this as part of God's design revealed and put into effect by Christ. Christ is presented as the model of all ministry. Among his people there is a rich diversity of ministry which finds in him its source and

inspiration and is intended to build up the Church as the 'community of reconciliation' (Ministry and Ordination, para. 4). We find in the early sections of the Statement a very good basis for a study of the ordained ministry which takes adequate account of the sources and puts positive content into the notion of Christian ministry.

(b) Critical Focus

22 *Historical development of ordained ministry* That there has been *episcope* ('a focus of leadership and unity') in the Church from the beginning on the strength of a commission to the apostles seems as far as any Catholic needs to go in believing that 'the sacrament of orders was instituted by Christ'. The historical analysis (Ministry and Ordination, paras. 3–6) is brief but impressive. Any possible ambiguity in the phrase 'part of God's design for his people' is removed because that design is explicitly linked to the revelation made by Jesus Christ and disclosed in the gift of the Spirit. Reference to God's design, therefore, includes those structures which are necessary for the Church's fidelity as the body of the risen Lord, among them the emergence of an ordained ministry. In view of that we believe the basis of Catholic faith is here secure.

23 *Ministerial priesthood* Vatican II affirmed that 'though they differ essentially and not only in degree, the common priesthood of the faithful and the ministerial or hierarchical priesthood are none the less ordered one to another; each in its own proper way shares in the one priesthood of Christ' (*Lumen Gentium*, 10). This position is maintained in the Report where both the relationship and distinction are clearly established. Not only do Christian ministers 'share through baptism in the priesthood of the people of God but they are – particularly in presiding at the Eucharist – representative of the whole Church in the fulfilment of its priestly vocation of self-offering to God as a living sacrifice. Nevertheless, their ministry is not an extension of the common Christian priesthood but belongs to another realm of the gifts of the Spirit' (Ministry and Ordination, para. 13). 'The word *priesthood* is used by way of analogy when it is applied to the people of God and to the ordained ministry. These are two distinct realities which relate, each in its own way, to the high priesthood of Christ, the unique priesthood of the new covenant, which is their source and model' (Ministry and Ordination: *Elucidation*, para. 2). We welcome these very clear

statements, as well as that which focuses so well the meaning of this ministerial priesthood when exercised in the celebration of the Eucharist: 'the action of the presiding minister . . . is seen to stand in a sacramental relation to what Christ himself did in offering his own sacrifice' (Ministry and Ordination, para. 13).

24 *Sacramentality of ordination* Here again we approve the position of the Report and have no reservations. The effect of ordination receives abundant testimony and we note especially: 'Not only is their vocation from Christ but their qualification for exercising such a ministry is the gift of the Spirit (cf. 2 Cor. 3.5–6). . . . This is expressed in ordination, when the Bishop prays to God to grant the gift of the Holy Spirit and lays hands on the candidate as the outward sign of the gifts bestowed. . . . In this sacramental act, the gift of God is bestowed upon the ministers . . . , the ministry of Christ is presented to them as a model for their own; and the Spirit seals those whom he has chosen and consecrated . . .the gifts and calling of God to the ministers are irrevocable. For this reason, ordination is unrepeatable in both our Churches' (Ministry and Ordination, paras. 14–15).

(c) Further Considerations

25 On the question of the ordination of women, the Report explains that it is concerned 'with the origin and nature of the ordained ministry and not with the question of who can or cannot be ordained' (Ministry and Ordination: *Elucidation,* para. 5). We do not believe the distinction is as clearcut as the Commission maintains and a problem remains that will have to be taken up. The ordination of women is a fact in the Anglican Communion and already it is regarded as a grave obstacle to the reconciliation of our Churches. For us in England the issue has been further sharpened by the process initiated in the General Synod of the Church of England.

26 In the *Common Declaration* signed by Pope John Paul II and the Archbishop of Canterbury in May 1982, ARCIC II is given the task of continuing the work already begun and 'to examine, especially in the light of our respective judgements on the Final Report, the outstanding doctrinal differences which still separate us, with a view towards their eventual resolution; to study all that hinders the mutual recognition of the ministries of our Communions; and to recommend what practical steps will be necessary when, on the basis of our unity of faith we are able

to proceed with the restoration of full communion'. The Final Report indicates that the question of Anglican Orders is unresolved. 'We are fully aware of the issues raised by the judgement of the Roman Catholic Church on Anglican Orders. The development of the thinking in our two communions regarding the nature of the Church and of the ordained ministry has, we consider, put those issues in a new context' (Ministry and Ordination, para. 17). It is clear that this question must remain on the agenda for our two Churches. Going over the old historical ground may not be a very profitable exercise, but we need to explore the implications of this 'new context'. We must ask whether such an exploration could advance the judgement previously made and whether an agreed act of public convalidation or reconciliation could resolve the present situation. Centring the discussion there, with due discretion and sensitivity, will be a more helpful aim in this ongoing dialogue.

(iii) *Authority in the Church*

(a) Approach and Perspective

27 One of the most outstanding achievements of the Commission is the progress made in tackling the question of authority in the Church, through patient and exacting dialogue. The framework for this understanding has been an appreciation of the dynamic nature of authority in the Church, based on the mandate of Jesus Christ to proclaim his Word. The work of the Holy Spirit is to maintain the Church in unity of faith and to lead it into an ever deeper appreciation of the truth. His presence is a gift to the whole Christian community.

28 Due emphasis is given to the unique role of the ordained minister in the exercise of authority in the Church. This authority is 'a service of the Church, officially entrusted only to ordained ministers, intrinsic to the Church's structure according to the mandate given by Christ and recognised by the community' (Authority I, para. 5). The role of the bishop in the exercise of this authority is clearly recognised by the Report, but care is taken to stress collaboration between all the ordained ministers who share in the mandate of Christ.

29 The historical approach adopted by the Commission to the development of episcopal authority in the Church continues the emphasis on *koinonia* as the keynote of ecclesiology. This

approach does, however, underline some of the difficulties encountered. It is not easy to come to substantial agreement about the nature and exercise of jurisdiction when the record of past centuries includes periods of conflicts and hostilities. We admit the need to reflect constantly on the actual working of jurisdiction in our Church, while upholding its validity and true place. Similarly we wish to recognise the achievement of the Final Report in developing an understanding of the need for both Conciliar and Primatial authority in the elaboration of doctrine from the deposit of faith (Authority I, paras. 15, 16, 17), and in acknowledging some of the balances and tensions between them.

30 This historical approach to episcopal authority leads readily into the question of universal primacy, and gives a helpful framework in which to discuss it. We are pleased to note that the exercise of this authority is seen not only in relation to the episcopal college but also in relation to the faith of the whole Church (Authority I, para. 12 and Authority: *Elucidation*, para. 8).

31 Similarly the question of apostolic succession of the episcopal college and primate is approached in a most encouraging manner, for it is a problem which might seem at first to be intractable. The ordination of a bishop is seen as an authentic expression of the significance of apostolic succession. Speaking of the presence of a number of ordaining bishops, the Final Report says: 'because they are representatives of their churches in fidelity to the teaching and mission of the apostles and are members of the episcopal college, their participation ensures the historical continuity of this church with the apostolic Church and of its bishop with the original apostolic ministry' (Ministry and Ordination, para. 16). The need in the Church for continuity of ministry and therefore of episcopal authority is clearly stated in these documents. Difficulties over agreement about the actual historical exercise of this authority, especially with regard to universal primacy, are approached in such a way as to hold real promise for the future.

(b) Critical Focus

32 *Universal primacy* For us the treatment by the Commission of the role of the universal primate is one of crucial importance, given the history of our two Churches. Therefore, we welcome the statements: 'it seems appropriate that in any

future union a universal primacy such as has been described should be exercised by that see [Rome]' (Authority I, para. 23) and 'if any Petrine function and office are exercised in the living Church of which a universal primate is called to serve as a visible focus, then it inheres in his office that he should have both a defined teaching responsibility and appropriate gifts of the Spirit to enable him to discharge it' (Authority II, para. 33).

33 We believe that although difficulties remain about the concrete expression of this universal primacy, and about the importance attributed to this role in the structure of the Church, the Final Report has provided the firm basis for future substantial agreement in understanding and practice.

34 *Infallibility* It is here that we have to speak of the possibility of substantial agreement rather than its achievement. The statements on Authority go a long way in their evaluation and acceptance of this doctrine. In their consideration of the universal primate, his office, ministry and teaching responsibility, and of 'appropriate gifts of the Spirit to enable him to discharge it' (Authority II, para. 32), they build up the positive groundwork. They recognise that there are times and issues when the Church has to make judgements that are decisive. When the Church commits herself to such judgements in fundamental matters of faith, she is guided by the Spirit and judgements are by the same Spirit protected from error (Authority I, para. 19). A universal council and the universal primate, presiding over the *koinonia* and speaking with authority, are both agencies through which the Church can so act (Authority II, para. 26). Questions that remain seem to relate more to the practical working out of this primacy. How does the universal primate speak out of the faith of the Church? How are the conditions that apply (Authority II, para. 29) to be verified? In what manner does reception of the doctrine complete the process of verification (cf. infra No. 36)? We are convinced that the Commission has come very close to agreement on the central issue and to dispelling the fears that exist. With regard to the former we would hope that agreement can be reached. With regard to the latter we would add that legitimate anxieties have been exaggerated by a history in which disagreement and division have undermined trust. The magisterium is exercised for the strengthening of faith and its infallible exercise brings a certitude that enables the faithful to adhere more

serenely to that faith. There remains the task of clarifying and demonstrating still further the way in which the various instruments of authority in the Church can interact and complement one another without any of them being diminished.

35 *Jurisdiction* If the exercise of authority in the Church is assisted by the Spirit, it needs also to be effective, to be recognised and followed. Canon Law speaks of the power of governance or jurisdiction. The Report deals with this in relation to *episcope* and especially to the way primatial jurisdiction relates to other levels of authority. Jurisdiction is defined as 'the authority or power (*potestas*) necessary for the exercise of an office'. Difficulty is envisaged in this matter, for it is acknowledged to be 'a source of anxiety to Anglicans' when the jurisdiction of the bishop of Rome as universal primate is called universal, ordinary and immediate (Authority II, paras. 16 and 18). The Report gives a fair explanation of jurisdiction and of the scope of the primate's pastoral office. By speaking of the moral limits that arise from the nature of the Church and of that office, it offers on the level of theory an appropriate answer to the anxieties expressed. The specific nature and corresponding functions of each office in the Church are the basis for determining the way in which the jurisdiction attached to each office is to be used for the building up of the Church. Special cases may call for intervention by the primate, but in general he will act in collegial association with his fellow bishops in seeking to serve both the unity and the catholicity of the universal church. Canon Law here speaks of the Roman Pontiff's power as one which 'reinforces and defends the proper, ordinary and immediate power which the Bishops have in the particular churches entrusted to their care' (Canon 333#1). This may not provide all the assurances Anglicans are looking for. We agree with the Report that 'the problem is not basically that of jurisdiction but of the complementarity and harmonious working of these different forms of *episcope* in the one body of Christ' (Authority: *Elucidation*, para. 6).

36 *Reception* The Final Report presents the exercise of authority in the Church with due and balanced emphasis on the reception of teaching. The basis for this emphasis is a clear understanding that doctrinal definitions draw their authority both from the inner truth which they proclaim ('id quod docetur') and from the authority of the person or persons who proclaim them ('a quo docetur'). The response to these two aspects of authority

is by faith and by obedience, and such reception of teaching is the work of the Holy Spirit in the Church. In the Final Report the Commission has sought to express the essential complementarity of both elements in reception.

37 The Final Report also develops the role of reception in the definitive proclamation of teaching. It successfully avoids the extremes of either making reception the criterion of doctrinal truth, or excluding it totally from the conditions needed to be sure that teaching is in accordance with the truth. When the Commission declares 'although it is not through reception by the people of God that a definition first acquires authority, the assent of the faithful is the ultimate indication that the Church's authoritative decision in a matter of faith has been truly preserved from error by the Holy Spirit' (Authority II, para. 25), we believe that its thinking is compatible with Catholic teaching.

38 Reception may indeed be the only grounds for complete assurance that all the conditions for the exercise of infallible magisterium have been present. We would wish to add, however, that in the lived faith of the Church such reception may take some considerable time to emerge.

(c) Further Considerations

39 *Universal primacy* While appreciating the quality of Scriptural scholarship displayed by the Commission in its treatment of the Petrine Texts (Authority II, paras. 2-9), we would question whether such an approach is capable of appreciating the full weight of meaning attributed to these texts by the lived tradition of the Catholic Church. We are convinced that doctrinal formulations emerge from such a lived tradition, and that when approached from within the tradition which has received that doctrine, the development of the teaching can be seen to be rooted in Scripture. The principle of development in our concept of tradition would allow us to claim more for the primacy in that tradition than the Final Report allows. We would wish to see more joint work devoted to this point.

40 We have already expressed our deep appreciation of the historical method as employed by the Commission in its discernment of the faith of the Church. At this point, however, we wish to register a doubt. In its appreciation of the position and role of a universal primate, the Final Report can be interpreted as giving insufficient weight to this primacy as intrinsic to the

nature of the Church. The presence of an actual universal primate we believe to be of necessity to the Church and it is not clear that agreement has been reached on this point. While we share the ideal of universal primacy put forward by the Commission and their concern that the reality has not always measured up to this ideal (Authority I, para. 12), we are anxious lest this distinction be taken too far. We wish to stress the need for an actual and identifiable centre or expression of universality, and to state that a potential openness of the local Church to the universal is not an adequate safeguard of this vital aspect of our understanding of the Church.

41 *Reception* While accepting as sound all that the Commission says about the nature and role of the reception of teaching, we also wish to comment that, in our view, both Communions would benefit from a continuing dialogue on this point. The importance of the reception of teaching is not well understood in the Catholic community and on-going study would help to clarify the differences evident in the treatment of this theme.

42 *Marian doctrine* Examples of the difficulties encountered between our two churches in the exercise of teaching authority are dogmas concerning Mary. On reflection it is clear with regard to the content of teaching about Mary there is a large measure of agreement. We are encouraged by the clear and appropriate devotion given to Mary by many Anglicans. The divergence exists much more in the matter of how some teaching, especially the dogma of the Immaculate Conception, has been authoritatively defined (cf. Authority II, para. 30). These and other matters need further consideration. We are confident that with an increase in our understanding of the nature of the Primate's teaching function in the Church, as well as of the Christological content of Marian dogmas, this divergence could indeed be overcome.

C Recommendations and Conclusions

(i) *Suggestions for Future Agenda*

(a) Church and State

43 It is difficult to comment briefly on the matter of Church/State relationships in so far as these affect the Anglican Communion. For the provinces of that Communion vary greatly

in their relationships with the states in which they live. In England (only) the Church of England is established and the Sovereign is its Supreme Governor. In countries of the Commonwealth which acknowledge the British Sovereign as their Head, the Act of Settlement (establishing the Protestant Succession of the British Crown) remains in force and would need to be repealed. We note that these matters are being kept under review by the English Anglican/Roman Catholic Committee. Many leading members of the Church of England are aware of this 'hurtful anomaly'. Legislative action will be necessary before the state of communion between the two churches is established. We recognise that these matters will have to be given serious consideration nearer the time of unity.

(b) Importance of the Anglican Evangelical Voice

44 We are glad to see that the doctrine of salvation, with particular reference to justification by faith, is central to the work of ARCIC II. In this future dialogue, it is important that the Anglican evangelical voice be heard to great effect. Similarly, priority needs to be given to the various ways in which we are called together by the Word of God. If the initiative, presence and guidance of the Word of God were so presented, not only would it help to overcome some evangelical hesitations, but it would also do full justice to one of the most profound emphases of Vatican II.

45 Further, a strong representation and consideration of Anglican evangelical concerns would secure a more welcome response from other churches which share the evangelical tradition. Bilateral conversations must reach out in many ways to the total Christian community. The achievements of such conversations must be offered as a contribution to the wider ecumenical endeavour and be open to the particular contributions of other Christian churches.

(c) Partnership in Prayer and Action

We wish to endorse, in particular, the spirit of the last sentence of the Final Report: 'We suggest that some difficulties will not be wholly resolved until a practical initiative has been taken and our two Churches have lived together more visibly in one *koinonia*.' It is the widespread experience of many people in our countries that the work of ecumenism must be carried on at all levels and in all the dimensions of Church life. Doctrinal discussions alone are not sufficient. We urge all concerned with the work for Christian unity to press forward in a continuing dialogue of prayer, social action and study. For many this means joint action at local level. This is the essential foundation for the reception of the achievements of ARCIC I and for the eventual more formal expression of the growing sense of the unity which is taking place between our two churches.

(d) Conclusion

47 The words and actions of Pope John Paul II in Canterbury in 1982 introduced a new dimension on the symbolic plane, which presents a challenge we must not fail. We wish to identify ourselves with the Common Declaration signed by him and the Archbishop of Canterbury. In particular we support their hopes and expectations for ARCIC II, and we accept their call to us all:

> While this necessary work of theological clarification continues, it must be accompanied by the zealous work and fervent prayer of Roman Catholics and Anglicans throughout the world as they seek to grow in mutual understanding, fraternal love and common witness to the Gospel. Once more, then, we call on the bishops, clergy and faithful people of both our Communions in every country, diocese and parish in which our faithful live side by side. We urge them all to pray for this work and to adopt every possible means of furthering it through their collaboration in deepening their allegiance to Christ and in witnessing to him before the world. Only by such collaboration and prayer can the memory of the past enmities be healed and our past antagonisms overcome.

8
Church of England Faith and Order Advisory Group on the Final Report of ARCIC I (1985)

Question 1:

We ask whether the Agreed Statements on Eucharistic Doctrine, Ministry and Ordination and Authority in the Church I and II, together with the Elucidations *are consonant in substance with the faith of Anglicans.*

A Eucharist

181 As we have already pointed out, the *Agreed Statement on Eucharistic Doctrine* was presented in 1971 in the conviction that the Commission had 'reached agreement on essential points of eucharistic doctrine', that is in regard to the two central affirmations regarding sacrifice and presence (Co-Chairmen's Preface). Although not setting out to say all that could be said about the eucharist, the report claims to omit nothing essential. The agreement is offered as a consensus 'at the level of faith', so that all might be able to say 'this is the Christian faith of the Eucharist'. In the text itself (Eucharistic Doctrine, para. 12) this is expressed as 'substantial agreement on the doctrine of the eucharist' and is recognized as consonant with 'a variety of theological approaches within both our communions'. In response to criticisms the *Elucidation* makes a less ambitious assertion, more explicitly restricting its scope to the areas of controversy which have divided our two communions in the past. Further, it suggests that 'the document represents not only the judgement of all its members – i.e. it is an agreement – but their unanimous agreement "on essential matters where it considers that the doctrine admits no divergence"' (Eucharistic Doctrine: *Elucidation*, para. 2).

182 In commenting upon the eucharist text we note that
ARCIC has adopted a method different from the one used by
the Faith and Order Commission in the *Lima Text*. The latter
statement is a more comprehensive one on the understanding
of the eucharist, while in the Windsor Statement ARCIC
devotes attention to two main areas of past difference: the
relation of the eucharist to the sacrifice of Christ; and the
presence of Christ in the eucharist. The *Lima Text* provides an
important background against which to set the 'substantial
agreement' reached in the ARCIC statement.

(i) *Eucharist and Sacrifice*

183 The Windsor Statement, like the *Lima Text*, could hardly
have stressed more emphatically that Christ's sacrifice on Calvary
was once-for-all. 'Christ's redeeming death and resurrection
took place once for all in history. . . . There can be no repetition of or addition to what was then accomplished once for all
by Christ' (Eucharistic Doctrine, para. 5). We welcome this
emphasis at the beginning of the discussion of the eucharist
and sacrifice.

184 At the same time the text insists that the atoning work of
Christ is both proclaimed and made effective in the Church in
the present through God's gift of the eucharist. Again, as in
the *Lima Text*, the biblical concept of *anamnesis*, memorial, is
used to describe the relation between the once-for-all sacrifice
of Christ on Calvary and the eucharist. The *Elucidation* of the
Windsor Statement defends the use of *anamnesis* against earlier
criticisms made of it. Although in the past some discussions of
anamnesis have appeared to go too far in the direction of
suggesting either that Calvary is repeated, or that the worshippers,
rather than the Holy Spirit in the Church, make effective the
benefits of Christ's sacrifice through their act of remembering,
we believe that ARCIC is careful to guard against both of these
dangers. As the *Elucidation* emphasizes: 'The Commission
believes that the traditional understanding of sacramental
reality, in which the once-for-all event of salvation becomes
effective in the present through the action of the Holy Spirit, is
well expressed by the word *anamnesis*. . . . it is possible to say at
the same time that there is only one unrepeatable sacrifice in
the historical sense, but that the eucharist is a sacrifice in the
sacramental sense, provided that it is clear that this is not a

repetition of the historical sacrifice' (Eucharistic Doctrine: *Elucidation*, para. 5). And so, the *anamnesis* of the unrepeatable sacrifice is of the risen Lord who, by the Holy Spirit, is present in the here and now of the sacramental action of the Church, with his people. Furthermore, our *anamnesis* takes the form it does because that past event has universal significance and eternal validity. We believe that in using *anamnesis* to describe the eucharistic sacrifice ARCIC is consonant with the faith of Anglicans as witnessed to in our own liturgical texts.

185 It is in the light of the biblical concept of *anamnesis* that we understand the assertion that '[Christ's members] . . . enter into the movement of his self-offering' (Eucharistic Doctrine, para. 5). This phrase has been seen as problematic by some and attention was drawn to it in the earlier response of the Church of England. We understand that the words of the Windsor Statement and the *Elucidation* imply a solidarity of Christ with his Church and the Christians in Christ whereby in our whole Christian life we participate in his self-offering to the Father, sacramentally expressed in the eucharist. This implication is to be welcomed. It stresses that we can make no offering of ourselves (nor even make intercession) apart from Christ, with whom we have been made one in baptism, and who is himself the sole cause of our new standing with God. We think it important to re-affirm our conviction that 'Christ's redeeming death and resurrection took place once and for all in history' (Eucharistic Doctrine, para. 5) and that God graciously regards his death as our death and his risen life as our life. Furthermore, it is in virtue of this that we are called to offer ourselves unreservedly to God through Christ and in the power of the Spirit. Our relation to the Father is grounded in the Son's relationship to his Father and comes to perfection through our union with the Son and his relation to the Father. Christ's action on Calvary is all-sufficient and inclusive and we are drawn into the Son's relation to the Father as God's adopted children. Indeed, it is through baptism that we are incorporated into Christ and are joined with him in his death, resurrection and ascension and therefore with his self-offering to the Father. We do not believe that we make any intercession apart from that which we make in, with and through Christ.

186 Beyond this there are differences of emphasis among Anglicans. On the one hand some stress our offering of ourselves

in terms of grateful response to the once-made vicarious sacrifice of Calvary. They do not thereby exclude participation in the sacrifice of Christ (1 Cor. 10.16), nor do they exclude the intercessory aspect of the eucharist as entreating the merits of Christ's passion on behalf of the whole Church. Others, on the other hand, stress that our offering is possible because it is one with Christ's offering, and understand the eucharist to mean that sacramentally Christ offers himself in his people. The latter do not understand the act of offering as independent of Christ's, and they do not interpret the eucharistic Memorial to be a calling to mind by faithful individuals of an ancient event on the ground of which believers are moved to make an act of self-surrender which is their own. In both emphases the eucharist is both a thanksgiving for Christ's redemptive sacrifice, and a pleading of the Lamb of God who takes away the sin of the world.

187 This offering of ourselves finds its actual liturgical expression in the celebration of the same eucharist which is the effectual proclamation of God's mighty act in Jesus. Just as God accepted Jesus' self-offering on the cross, so he accepts the duty and service of the Church in the eucharist, because of that one and unrepeatable sacrifice. There is, therefore, an irrevocable connection between the once-for-all sacrifice of Christ and the worship of the Church, the eucharist both stemming from and being made effective by Christ's self-offering. It is in this sense that the Church is drawn into the self-offering of Christ.

188 We believe that if the phrase '[Christ's members] . . . enter into the movement of his self-offering' is understood in this way it need not create difficulties for Anglicans, and that it is indeed consonant with biblical thought. Moreover, we should like to draw attention to similar thought expressed in the Roman Catholic–Lutheran dialogue in *The Eucharist*, 1978 (para. 18) and in the Anglican–Reformed dialogue, *God's Reign and Our Unity* (para. 68):

> The Eucharist is a making present of the once-for-all sacrifice of Christ. Joined to Christ in that sacrifice, the Church makes an acceptable offering of itself in thanksgiving to the Father. We therefore invoke the gift of the Spirit from the Father to sanctify both us and the elements of bread and wine, so that in our eating and drinking we may be united with the one sacrifice of Jesus. 'Sanctified by his Spirit, the

Church, through, with and in God's Son Jesus Christ, offers itself to the Father. It thereby becomes a living sacrifice of thanksgiving through which God is publicly praised (World Alliance of Reformed Churches–Roman Catholic Dialogue, Section 81)' (*God's Reign and Our Unity*, para. 68).

Both the Roman Catholic–Lutheran and the Anglican–Reformed dialogues as well as the World Alliance of Reformed Churches –Roman Catholic dialogue, quoted in *God's Reign and Our Unity*, make clear what we understand to be intended in the Windsor Statement and its *Elucidation*.

189 We note that in its discussion of *anamnesis* in relation to the eucharist the emphasis is upon the recalling of the sacrifice of Calvary rather than the total Christ-event from the creation by the Logos to the consummation of the Kingdom. Paragraph 4 has a welcome stress on the eucharistic presence as foretaste of the Kingdom and anticipation of the *parousia*, a theme which is more fully treated in the *Lima Text*. We welcome the balance this provides.

(ii) *Eucharist and the Presence of Christ*

190 When the Windsor Statement was first published in 1971, disquiet was felt by some Anglicans over what the text appeared to them to be saying about the presence of Christ, particularly as that was expressed in the opening sentence of paragraph 6. 'Communion with Christ in the eucharist pre-supposes his true presence, effectually signified by the bread and wine which, in this mystery, become his body and blood' (Eucharistic Doctrine, para. 6). This was not followed by any statement of how the bread and wine became his body and blood: indeed the weight of the text is upon the reality of the presence and not upon the notion of how change takes place. The word *transubstantiation* is not employed in the text but is referred to in an explanatory footnote. 'The term [*transubstantiation*] should be seen as affirming the *fact* of Christ's presence and of the mysterious and radical change which takes place.' In spite of the following assertion that 'in contemporary Roman Catholic theology it is not understood as explaining *how* the change takes place', there were those who were concerned that the use of 'become' and 'radical change' were to be under-stood in a material sense and therefore made it doubtful

whether the Windsor Statement could be described as Anglican teaching. Attention was drawn to this in the official response of the Church of England (*Response by the Church of England to the Agreed Statements by the Anglican–Roman Catholic International Commission*, GS 394).

191   The *Elucidation* has, however, made the intention of the Windsor Statement clear. The *Elucidation* suggests that the statement about 'becoming' must be understood within the context of the Agreed Statement as a whole. Christ's presence in the bread and wine cannot be divorced from the encounter in the whole eucharistic celebration, nor from the action of the Holy Spirit. Here the Windsor Statement echoes what, as we have seen, is emphasized in the *Lima Text*. The *Elucidation* goes further in describing what was intended in the original statement by the use of the word 'become'. It does this first by stating clearly what was not meant:

> *Becoming* does not here imply material change. Nor does the liturgical use of the word imply that the bread and wine become Christ's body and blood in such a way that in the eucharistic celebration his presence is limited to the conse-crated elements. It does not imply that Christ becomes present in the eucharist in the same manner that he was present in his earthly life. It does not imply that this *becoming* follows the physical laws of this world (Eucharistic Doctrine: *Elucidation*, para. 6; cf. *The Lima Text* Eucharist 15).

Rather, 'become' *can* only be understood within the concept of the 'sacramental order'; that is, that order in which the realities of faith, which are real in themselves independently of the existence of the faith of the believer, become present in visible and tangible realities of the earthly order, and are apprehended by faith. It is in the sphere of sacramental realities that we are able to distinguish between two sacramental foci within the framework of the whole eucharist, two moments which are inextricably bound together: the first is when the Lord, whose sacrifice the Church's action recalls, offers himself gratuitously to his people; and the second is when we draw near in faith to accept this gift in communion. Here one emphasis is upon the fact that Christ is really present in the eucharistic elements after the consecration, and the other is on the fact that, when those consecrated elements are given and received, that believing recipient is nourished by Christ himself.

192 In this *Elucidation* we believe that the misgivings of the
earlier official response of the Church of England have been
allayed. Here we find the same necessary balance maintained
as in the *Lima Text*. 'While Christ's real presence in the
eucharist does not depend on the faith of the individual, all
agree that to discern the body and blood of Christ, faith is
required' (*Lima Text* Eucharist 13). As we said in commenting
upon the *Lima Text*, we believe that the two texts are not inconsistent. It is sufficient and faithful to the belief of the Church
through the ages to uphold the real presence of Christ in the
eucharist and his body and blood truly received in the bread
and wine without any further agreement on the mode of that
presence in the elements. As Anglicans, we are glad that, as in
our own liturgical texts, no one theory of change is being set
forward in the Final Report but rather that bread is broken,
wine poured out, in representation of Christ's Paschal sacrifice
and we receive them not as mere bread and wine but as the
body and blood of Christ. Hence we believe that in this ARCIC
is consonant with the faith of Anglicans and with the two principal emphases contained within our tradition.

(iii) *Reservation and Veneration*

193 What is believed about the relation between the presence
of Christ and the eucharistic elements finds its outward expression
in the devotional practices of our churches. Here, as we pointed
out in relation to the *Lima Text*, differences exist both within
the Anglican Church and between our two Communions.
Although the Windsor Statement itself had nothing to say
about either reservation or veneration, the question was raised
by many who read the text. It is discussed at some length in the
Elucidation, where both reservation and veneration are seen as
acceptable only when understood as an extension of the
eucharist itself. Without this linkage there must be a distortion.
There is no disagreement about the proposition that consecration of the elements is for reception in communion, and that
the one we adore in the eucharist is the Saviour himself as he
comes to us in the sacrament of his body and blood. The
difference chiefly lies between those who fear that the link
between consecration and communion is weakened if the
elements are used as vehicles for the adoration of Christ apart
from communion, and those who see the adoration of Christ

(not, of course, of the elements apart from Christ) as an enrichment of their devotion to Christ who comes to us in the eucharist. Thus Roman Catholics and Anglicans agree that consecration is for communion. This was itself said in the Windsor Text: 'the Lord's words at the last supper, "Take and eat; this is my body", do not allow us to dissociate the gift of the presence and the act of sacramental eating'. The Commission's conclusion is that it is possible to accept diverse judgements at this point as well as plurality of practice without any denial of the underlying common doctrinal agreement. We are reminded that the *Lima Text* also upholds a legitimate diversity of practice and piety while pointing to the need to respect the practices of others. Anglicans, in line with the recommendations of the *Lima Text*, require the practice of consuming any of the eucharistic elements not needed for the purpose of communion. Indeed that consumption of the consecrated elements is the rubrical and invariable practice of all Anglicans. It is this which has allowed Anglicans of diverse schools to maintain their unity.

(iv) *Conclusion*

194 In the light of the understandings above we believe that the Windsor Statement together with its *Elucidation* has reached agreement on the two essential points where Anglicans and Roman Catholics have diverged in the past, namely on the relation of the eucharist to the sacrifice of Christ and on the understanding of the presence of Christ in the eucharist. We believe that we can say with the Commission 'this is the Christian faith of the Eucharist'. Moreover we believe the Final Report on the Eucharist to be 'consonant in substance with the faith of Anglicans'.

195 Although we consider with the Commission that nothing essential has been omitted in the areas of controversy, we should nevertheless have liked to have seen emphasized somewhere in the agreement the relationship between the eucharist and the world. This is an important theme throughout the *Lima Text* on the eucharist but is only hinted at in the Windsor Statement: 'the eucharist builds up the life of the Church, strengthens its fellowship and furthers its mission' (Eucharistic Doctrine, para. 3), and also, 'when we gather round the same table . . . and when we "partake of the one loaf", we are one in commitment not only to Christ and to one another, but also to the

mission of the Church in the world' (Eucharistic Doctrine, para. 4). The eucharist is not simply the meal of the faithful in which Anglicans and Roman Catholics hope one day to share. The eucharist is the feast where the Church may acknowledge the signs of renewal already at work in the world, where, united with Christ in a sacramental way, it prays for the world and is the centre from which Christians go out renewed by the power of the Spirit to act as servants of reconciliation in a broken and divided world. Although we believe the Commission is right to suggest that Anglicans and Roman Catholics would not be divided on this, nevertheless we should like to have seen greater emphasis upon it in the text. Concern for the world cannot be an optional extra in our understanding of the eucharist, but rightly belongs as an integral part of our common belief. As such it deserves expression in any statement of agreement on the eucharist made by our two churches.

B Ministry

196 The *Agreed Statement on Ministry and Ordination* was presented in 1973 in the conviction that the Statement was not 'designed to be an exhaustive treatment of ministry' but that 'it seeks to express our basic agreement in the doctrinal areas that have been the source of controversy between us, in the wider context of our common convictions about the ministry' (Ministry and Ordination, para. 1). Further, in their conclusion to the Statement the Commission says, 'what we have to say represents the consensus of the Commission on essential matters where it considers that doctrine admits no divergence' (Ministry and Ordination, para. 17). And at the end of the *Elucidation* of the Canterbury Statement they add their belief that the agreements recorded have 'demonstrated a consensus in faith on eucharist and ministry' (Ministry and Ordination: *Elucidation*, para. 6). We note that, as in the case of the Windsor Statement, ARCIC did not attempt a comprehensive statement on ministry, but concentrated on areas which have been the subjects of controversy.

(i) *Ministry in the Church*

197 The Canterbury Statement makes clear that the ordained ministry is related both to the ministry of Christ, 'the source and model . . . from which all ministry flows and takes its

shape', and also to the ministry of the whole people of God (Ministry and Ordination, para. 3). Although we should like to have had the subject of the ministry of the whole people of God developed at greater length, we recognize that more is added in Authority I, when the role of the laity in expressing the *sensus fidelium* is treated. In general what is said about the relation between the ministry of Christ, the ministry of the whole people of God and the ordained ministry is close to the *Lima Text* and to the 1938 *Doctrine Report*.

(ii) *Apostolic Ministry*

198   Paragraph 4 treats of the concept of apostolic ministry pointing to two discernible features of the original apostolate: 'a special relationship with the historical Christ, and a commission from him to the Church and the world' (Ministry and Ordination, para. 4). We should like to have seen the 'relationship with the historical Christ' amplified to include witnessing to the resurrection (Acts 1.22) since this both unites the two elements of the apostolic function and explains the inclusion of Paul as an Apostle. At the same time the two features listed are not exhaustive. The guardianship of doctrine or apostolic truth is already a feature of apostolic authority in the New Testament (Ministry and Ordination, para. 5). And the most significant description of the earliest church is that 'they devoted themselves to the apostles' *didache* and *koinonia*, to the breaking of bread and prayers' (Acts 2.42). In one sense, as the Canterbury Statement implies, the Apostles are unique and unrepeatable. In another, their function was communicable and there are those within the Church who continue to have a special responsibility for the apostolic ministry and who symbolize and maintain the apostolicity which belongs to the whole Church. This is developed further in the section on Vocation and Ordination where succession is seen, as in the *Lima Text*, as succession in fidelity to the teaching and mission of the Apostles. Nevertheless, the participation in the ordination of a new bishop by bishops who are 'representative of their churches in fidelity to the teaching and mission of the Apostles' marks the continuity of the newly-ordained bishop with the apostolic Church. It also signifies the continuity of the bishop with the apostolic ministry. Succession is in the faithful witness to the apostolic teaching and mission and this is signified

and maintained in the person of the bishop. Again the Canterbury Statement's view of apostolicity and apostolic succession is very close indeed to that which the *Lima Text* points and we believe is consonant with the faith of Anglicans.

(iii) *The Threefold Order of Ministry*

199 Paragraphs 5 and 6 of the Canterbury Statement consider how with the growth of the Church 'the importance of certain functions led to their being located in specific officers of the community', officers who were given 'some form of recognition and authorization' (Ministry and Ordination, para. 5). What the Commission had to say about the earliest records is important not only for Roman Catholics and Anglicans but for all those churches seeking the reconciliation of ministries. Although the New Testament shows that 'ministerial office played an essential part in the life of the Church in the first century', there is, however, no blueprint for ministry which can be extracted from the New Testament, for that record only gives evidence of diversity and lack of definition. However, 'just as the formation of the Canon of the New Testament was a process incomplete until the second half of the second century, so also the full emergence of the threefold ministry of bishop, presbyter and deacon required a longer period than the apostolic age. Thereafter this threefold structure became universal in the Church' (Ministry and Ordination, para. 6). In commenting upon this passage in the earlier paper, *Response of the Church of England*, GS 394, the Faith and Order Advisory Group registered some unease. What, for example, are we to make of the likening of the emergence of a threefold order to the emergence of the Canon? Does this imply that such an order is binding on the Church in the same way as the Canon is binding? Further is the reference to the universality of the threefold structure meant to be construed as 'unchurching those ecclesial bodies which do not have a threefold ministry'? It appears from the *Elucidation* that the intention of the Canterbury Statement was to draw a parallel between the emergence of the threefold ministry and the Canon in order to point to a comparable process of gradual development 'without determining whether the comparison could be carried further'. What is more, when it declares the threefold structure as becoming universal, ARCIC indicates that it remained universal

until the divisions of Western Christianity in the sixteenth century. Thus we understand the Commission to be saying that the threefold ministry cannot be read back into Scripture, but that it developed from the New Testament period under the guidance of the Holy Spirit and is of God. Further, there is nothing in the text which could involve us in invalidating the ministries of others. Neither does the text imply that the threefold form of ministry is necessarily destined for ever and is never open to development under God. Nevertheless our two Communions have both maintained this pattern, and we recall the challenge of the *Lima Text* that such a pattern 'may serve today as an expression of the unity we seek and also as a means for achieving it' (*Lima Text*, Ministry 22).

200   The fact that both Anglicans and Roman Catholics are committed to a threefold pattern of ministry makes it all the more disappointing that there is no confession from both our churches that the development of the office of deacon has not yet reached its fulfilment, and that there is so little said about either the theology or practice of a diaconate.

201   In addition we should have welcomed a fuller treatment in the Canterbury Statement of the theology of episcopacy taking up and developing the important pointers that are there in paragraphs 9 and 16. The bishop, the one to whom the oversight of the Church is entrusted, is the one who signifies and maintains 'the communion of the churches in mission, faith and holiness, through time and space' (Ministry and Ordination, para. 16). A joint statement on the theology of episcopacy by Anglicans and Roman Catholics might have helped to commend episcopacy to the non-episcopal churches in the move towards unity.

202   Further, we should have liked to have seen a fuller treatment of what the Commission understood about episcopacy and collegiality. There are two possible emphases: the one on a college of bishops of which a priest becomes a member when he is consecrated a bishop; the other on a group of ordained ministers and laity who with their bishop act collegially. ARCIC never makes clear, either in the statement on ministry or in the statement on authority, how they understand the bishop in relation to collegiality. Both understandings, we believe, would present challenges to our Anglican understanding and practice of collegiality.

(iv) *The Priesthood of the Ordained Ministry*

203 In paragraph 13 the Canterbury Statement develops the consensus of the Commission on the priesthood of the ordained ministry. They share with the *Lima Text* the view that the priesthood of the ordained ministry is related both to the priesthood of Christ and to the priesthood of the whole people of God (*Lima Text*, Eucharist 17). The *Elucidation* clarifies the three distinct ways in which the term 'priest' is used in a passage similar to that of GS 281 which we quoted above:

> The priesthood of Christ is unique. He is our High Priest who has reconciled mankind with the Father. All other priesthood derives from his and is wholly dependent upon it. The priesthood of the whole people of God (1 Peter 2.5) is the consequence of incorporation by baptism into Christ (Ministry and Ordination: *Elucidation*, para. 2).

The *Elucidation* also recognizes that any use of the term *priesthood* is 'by way of analogy when it is applied to the people of God and to the ordained ministry'. The statement further asserts that the term 'priest' came to be used of the ordained ministry because, in the celebration of the eucharist as the memorial of Christ's sacrifice, Christians saw Christ's priesthood reflected in the one who presided.

204 Recent Church of England documents (e.g. Anglican–Methodist Unity Commission, *The Scheme*, pp. 24f; *Response by the Church of England*, GS 394, paras. 31–3) have drawn attention to divergent views concerning the priesthood of the ordained ministry currently held within the Church of England. We believe, however, that all Anglicans could accept the concept of that priesthood expounded in the *Lima Text* and expressed by ARCIC in the latter part of paragraph 13: 'Christian ministers are members of this redeemed community. Not only do they share through baptism in the priesthood of the people of God, but they are – particularly in presiding at the eucharist – representative of the whole Church in the fulfilment of its priestly vocation of self-offering to God as a living sacrifice (Romans 12.1)'. In this sense we all accept the use of the term 'priest' for the one who presides at the eucharist, though many would welcome the proposal of the Anglican–Methodist Ordinal (already reflected in the Roman Catholic Ordinal, and those of the United Churches of North and South India) that the use of

the New Testament term 'presbyter' would avoid much popular confusion.

205 Some, believing that in the eucharist all the faithful are united with Christ sacramentally in his self-offering and so share in his royal priesthood, welcome the further suggestion of the Canterbury Statement that there is a sense in which the minister who presides, and only that minister, acts in a priestly way in 'reciting again the words of Christ at the Last Supper and distributing . . . the holy gifts', thereby relating in a different way to the priesthood of Christ. They see this view reflected in the later statement that the ministry of the ordained is not an extension of the common Christian priesthood but belongs to another realm of the gifts of the Spirit. While other Anglicans have criticized this statement – its meaning is far from clear – all would accept some distinction between the common priest-hood and the priesthood of the ordained ministry in the sense that the latter is not simply a delegation 'from below'. In the words of the Lutheran–Roman Catholic International Report *The Ministry in the Church* 'it cannot be derived from the congregation . . . it is not an enhancement of the common priesthood and the minister as such is not a Christian to a greater degree'. Anglicans would say that just as in the Ministry of the Word the ordained minister speaks to the congregation in the name of God, so 'as celebrant he is more than the people's representative. In taking, breaking and consecrating he acts in Christ's name and in the name not only of the particular congregation but of the Holy Catholic Church down the ages' (A. M. Ramsey, *Why the Priest?*). But the common priesthood and the ministerial priesthood are nonetheless interrelated. The minister, though not the delegate of the congregation, does act in its name and focuses thereby their offering of worship. Indeed, many Anglicans understand the differences between the common priesthood and the ministerial priest-hood in terms of the latter's representative function, especially within the liturgy. We also prefer the formulation in the *Elucidation* which avoids an isolated stress on the recitation of the Words of Institution. In the Ministry *Elucidation* (para. 2) it is there made clear that the ordained minister, who presides at the eucharist, recites the Institution narrative and invokes the Holy Spirit in the name of Christ and on behalf of his Church. In considering ARCIC's careful justification of the priestly language common to our two traditions all Anglicans should

be reassured by the Commission's repeated affirmation that 'the priestly sacrifice of Jesus was unique, as is also his continuing High Priesthood' (Ministry and Ordination, para. 13).

206 We believe that the consensus on the priesthood of the ordained ministry registered by the Commission in the Canterbury Statement and as explicated in the *Elucidation*, is compatible with the faith of Anglicans. Furthermore we reckon that what is said here is very close to what is expressed in the Anglican–Methodist *Ordinal* and although it goes further than the *Lima Text* it does not contradict the direction of that text.

207 We should like to have seen included in the Canterbury Statement more emphasis upon the intimate relationship between the royal priesthood of the Church and the priesthood of the ordained ministry. Priestly language is appropriately used of ordained ministers because they preside at the eucharist, and also because they represent and focus the priestly ministry of the people of God.

(v) *Lay Celebration*

208 We note that the Commission is quite clear that the one who has oversight in the Church, namely the bishop, and the presbyters who are joined with him in that oversight, should preside at the celebration of the eucharist. As we suggested in our discussion of the *Lima Text*, this is faithful to the understanding and practice of the Church of England.

(vi) *Women and the Ordained Ministry*

209 After the completion of the Canterbury Statement developments in the Anglican Communion resulted in certain Provinces ordaining women to the priesthood. The *Elucidation*, commenting upon this, argues that although such a move presented a 'grave obstacle' to the reconciliation of our two communions, nevertheless the principles upon which ARCIC's doctrinal argument rests are not affected by such ordination. The Statement was 'concerned with the origin and nature of the ordained ministry and not with the question of who can or cannot be ordained'. The present debate in the Church of England on the ordination of women illustrates the need to decide whether the ordination of women to the priesthood

represents a fundamental change in doctrine or only a matter of discipline to be determined by individual provinces or dioceses. There are those who agree that the consensus of the Canterbury Statement is not affected by this question. Others would hold that this is not the case, and that as the priesthood of the ordained ministry is related both to the priesthood of Christ and the priesthood of the whole people of God, it is imperative that any agreement on ministry should make clear that the priesthood must be open to women as well as men, even if certain regions of the world for cultural and other reasons do not find it appropriate to ordain women to the priesthood.

(vii) *Conclusion*

210 We believe that the Canterbury Statement together with the important clarifications in the *Elucidation* does substantially reflect the Church of England's view on ministry and ordination as conveyed in our own liturgical documents. We agree that we can recognize our own faith in the text; it is consonant with the faith of Anglicans. We recognize, as the Commission itself stated, that it is not an exhaustive treatment of ministry and there are matters which we look forward to exploring together in the future. In particular, a deeper understanding of the ministry of the whole people of God; a more detailed explication of the theology of the episcopate and diaconate and the exercise of collegiality; and a clarification of how we may live together while holding different views on the ordination of women to the priesthood. We recognize also that the Church's ministry is not only carried out by individuals but is exercised through structures. The theology of ministry set out in the Canterbury Statement is bound up closely with the development of this subject in *Authority I* in its treatment of conciliarity and primacy.

211 However, we consider that on the formerly divisive issues, including the understanding of ministry and priesthood, the Canterbury Statement represents substantial agreement. We share ARCIC's view that it provides a significantly new context in which to view *Apostolicae Curae*, and provides a firm basis upon which to move towards the reconciliation of our two ministries.

C Authority I and II

(i) *Introduction*

212 The two statements on Authority in the Final Report deal with sensitive issues of a different order from those on eucharist and ministry. Whereas the eucharist and the three-fold ministry have been a constant feature of both Roman Catholic and Anglican experience, the rejection of Roman Catholic jurisdiction has since the sixteenth century been a distinguishing feature of Anglicanism. The statements on Authority in effect ask the critical question whether being out of communion with the Roman see is an accidental and contingent fact of Anglican history or of the very substance of the Anglican understanding of the nature of the Church. The statements face us with the question of whether the doctrine of the Church and in particular the nature and exercise of authority in the Church can be so stated that Roman Catholics and Anglicans can together affirm a common faith.

213 In their Preface to *Authority I*, the Venice Statement, the Co-Chairmen express 'a belief that the Commission has made a significant contribution' to the unresolved questions on the nature and exercise of authority in the Church. They further describe this as consensus covering a wide area and setting a proper perspective for the difficulties Anglicans felt about Roman Catholic belief about the office of the bishop of Rome. In spite of difficulties the Commission believe their statement on Authority in the Church represents 'a significant convergence with far-reaching consequences' (Authority I, para. 25), and suggest even consensus on 'authority in the Church and in particular on the basic principle of primacy' (Authority I, para. 24).

(ii) *Authority, Scripture and Tradition*

214 The primary authority for all Christians is seen by ARCIC as Jesus Christ himself (Authority I, para. 1). The basic apostolic witness to the Gospel of God's saving activity in Jesus Christ is given in Holy Scripture, which is 'a normative record of the authentic foundation of faith' to which 'the Church has recourse for the inspiration of its life and mission', writings inspired by the Holy Spirit to which 'the Church refers its

teaching and practice' (Authority I, para. 2). In the *Elucidation* to *Authority I*, ARCIC comments on the presuppositions about the relationship between Scripture and Tradition, and in a paragraph which is both frank and eirenic sets out the crux of the question at issue (Authority: *Elucidation*, para. 2). On the one hand, Scripture comes from the living proclamation of the Church; and the formation of the Canon takes place within the experience of the Church's worship and is the product of it. On the other hand, the Church has always treated Holy Scripture as the criterion or norm for the post-apostolic Church; and the development in the interpretation of the original datum of divine revelation is a continuing process through which Tradition comes to be formed. 'It is not enough for the Church simply to repeat the original apostolic words. It has also prophetically to translate them. . . . All such re-statements must be consonant with the apostolic witness recorded in the Scriptures' (Authority I, para. 15). Accordingly, while ARCIC plainly gives primacy to the authority of Scripture, the Commission has not argued for Scripture being the sole and exclusive source of guidance. (Their handling of this question is in line with Richard Hooker's admonition to 'take great heed lest, in attributing unto Scripture more than it can have, the incredibility of that do cause even those things which indeed it hath to be less reverently esteemed'.) Although the Commission can hardly be held guilty, as they have been accused, of failing to give account of the primacy of Scripture, there still lie behind their reports questions about the authority and interpretation of Scripture, about the significance of the closing of the Canon, and about the dynamic nature of Tradition. These are questions which in the future Anglicans and Roman Catholics will need to explore together.

(iii) *The Nature of Authority*

215 The Commission cannot have been unaware of the difficulties of speaking at all about authority within a secular social climate where all forms of authority are under constant question. Criticism and challenge are features of modern 'pluralistic' societies. Generalizations about the modern world are not easy to make, but there is nevertheless a new social context in which authority is exercised. It affects the theology and practice of all the churches; authority becomes more accountable as it is more

widely questioned. The influence of the eighteenth century Enlightenment with its exhortation to think everything out for oneself, and the political theory of liberal democracy, generate an atmosphere of hesitation about commending beliefs or practices on the grounds that they pertain to the tradition of a community from time immemorial; and in the twentieth century, after more than two centuries of independent critical and historical study of the Bible, Christian appeals to sacred texts are at least as liable to provoke critical dissent as is the invocation of community tradition. Nevertheless, ARCIC has taken for granted that the community of faith is called into being by God to mediate the faith to the individual, and that to follow Jesus Christ is indeed to be set under authority. Between Roman Catholics and Anglicans it is taken to be common ground that authority is intrinsic to the gospel.

216 Any understanding of authority in the Church lies ultimately in the biblical doctrine of God. The authority of the Church, as the introduction to *Authority I* affirms, is derived from the authority of Christ given to the Church. The Church is the body that mediates not her own authority but that which she receives from her Lord. 'This is Christian authority: when Christians so act and speak, men perceive the authoritative word of Christ' (Authority I, para. 3). We believe that had the Commission drawn out at the outset some of the characteristics which belong to Christ's own authority, these might have permeated and strengthened all that followed. Amongst such characteristics we would emphasize the doctrine of God as at once powerful and yet giving his children freedom to challenge him; of God who in Christ took the form of a servant and suffered, thereby demonstrating power as of the powerless in worldly terms (it is the power of the crucified that is lodged in the Church); and of God whose authority is exercised in enabling his creatures to respond freely. Any exercise of authority in the Church must be informed both by an understanding of the nature and being of God as revealed in Christ crucified and risen, and also by an acknowledgement of the fact that Christ's authority is mediated through the authorities of the Church which are 'subject to the limitations and sinfulness of human nature' (Authority I, para. 7).

(iv) *Authority and Communion*

217 Although we should like the Commission to have drawn out more the characteristics of Christ's own exercise of authority as a model for the exercise of authority in the Church, we recognize the importance of ARCIC's understanding of the Church as 'communion' for its understanding of the nature and exercise of authority. The unity of the fellowship of the Church which exists across time and space is the gift of God to his Church. Because the members of this visible communion are frail and imperfect, they also need ordered structures to assure the proclamation of the word and the celebration of the sacraments of grace.

218 The Final Report uses the term *koinonia*, 'communion', to talk about the Church (cf. paras. 255–60 below). This biblical term speaks of the coming together in the fellowship of God and humanity. It seems likely that the Commission used the word because it lays primary emphasis on personal and communal relationships rather than on the more juridical categories of mediaeval and later theology. To speak of the Church as *koinonia* is to underline its character as the visible sign of an inward spiritual grace.

219 But in the context of ARCIC's exploration of authority, the term also suggests that the present divisions of the churches entrenched in juridical forms, need to be transcended as separated Christians together converge towards the fullness and universality which is in Christ (see Eph. 4.13). In the Final Report (Authority I, paras. 8–13) the use of *koinonia* not only expresses the general truth that, in the common life of the body of Christ, Christians are always members of one another. It also brings out a point of weight for the ecumenical dialogue: namely, that a local church,[1] both in a particular congregation and in the family of a diocese (or a regional group of churches) needs to be open to the universal dimension of the Church if authenticity, balance and fullness are to be

---

[1] In the documents of Vatican II, 'local church' and more often 'particular church' refer either to a single episcopal community or to a regional group of churches. The Reformed tradition, along with popular usage, uses the term 'local church' to refer to a particular congregation. The Anglican–Reformed statement, *God's Reign and Our Unity* (para. 111) discusses various ways in which the term is used.

experienced and preserved. As we have seen, the whole Church is involved in every eucharistic celebration. Openness to catholicity is fundamental to the life of each particular church if it is to realize its true being and if it is to maintain the fullness of faith. On the one hand, a plurality of theological interpretations, of forms of worship, and even of disciplinary rules, is or ought to be a source of richness. On the other hand, the diversities need to be held together in unity if centrifugal forces are not to become disruptive, whether in faith or order. The specific problems in conversations about unity between Anglicans and Roman Catholics arise as soon as the questions are put: (a) By what organs in this visible communion is the authenticity of eucharistic fellowship in unity and truth to be safeguarded? (b) Whether and where, among the diversity of ministries God has given to his people, we may discern a means of rendering concrete the unity and universality which should be apparent in every community which meets to celebrate the eucharist? These are not questions which press upon Anglicans only when in dialogue with Roman Catholics; but in this setting they have a peculiar sharpness.

(v) *Conciliar and Primatial Authority*

220 The principal questions unravelled in the two statements on authority concern the relation between conciliar and primatial structures of authority. The thought of the Commission proceeds from the oversight of the ordained ministry, focused in the bishop as president of the eucharistic community, to the coming together of bishops in council at a regional level; then to the emergence of specially prominent sees with a wider canonical jurisdiction (such as the patriarchates among Orthodox churches – see Authority I: *Eludication*, para. 7); and finally to the role assigned in the long history of the Church to the bishops of Rome, where St Peter and St Paul taught and died. At each stage of the argument conciliarity and primatial leadership are linked. Accordingly the Commission moves from the local to the universal. The Church as here envisaged is not a structure in which all authority flows from the 'top' downwards. The text clearly states the principle of subsidiarity, namely that nothing ought to be done at a higher level than is necessary. In the Church of Christ, it is insisted, authority is for service and not domination. At each stage in the unfolding of the picture

of authority in the Church, the exercise of pastoral oversight is linked to service for the building up of the fellowship of Christ's Church.

221 ARCIC is clearly aware that the picture of conciliar and primatial authority they have outlined is an ideal one, and that during the course of history the actual exercise of authority in the Church has at many times failed to reflect this ideal. In their preface to the first statement on authority the Co-Chairmen write: 'An awareness of this distinction between the ideal and the actual is important both for the reading of the document and for the understanding of the method we have pursued' [see above p. 42]. Thus ARCIC does not claim that the actual exercise of authority has always adequately embodied the authority of the Lord of the Church, who is the crucified Christ. Nor do the statements suggest that either the conciliar Anglican model or the primatial Roman model, in the past or even the present, offers an actuality to be regarded with complacency. But in the view of ARCIC abuses should not destroy a proper use. Therefore, whatever the human failures of practice or of vision, there remains the need for structures which can serve the visible unity and universality which are of the very essence of the Church. The conciliar pattern often shows a structure of authority so dispersed and diffused that diversity is more apparent than unity, and action to remedy acknowledged faults can be slow and ineffective. The primatial pattern is liable to be centralized to the point where form and order may seem to be prized more than vitality, criticism and the risks of freedom; but it can often have the advantage that necessary and difficult decisions are easier to take and to implement. Controversy, tension and conflict have in fact always marked the life of the Church. They need not always be regarded as a sign of ill-health in the body, provided that the position under critical attack is not integral to the essential teaching or ethic of the Church.

222 To propose to bring together a diffused and dispersed conciliar pattern with a more centralized primatial structure is to presuppose that there is a mutual recognition of the respective virtues of each pattern. The recent stress in Roman Catholic statements on 'collegiality' (i.e. the sharing of the episcopate with the bishop of Rome in the guiding of the Church) and the development of synodical life in the Roman Catholic

Communion indicate some movement in the direction of decentralization. The present situation is that in practice authority in the Roman Catholic Church is more dispersed and more 'local' than it has been. At the same time in the Anglican Communion there is the acceptance of the canonical principle of primacy, both at the level of metropolitical authority in provinces and at the level of the presidential role assigned by consensus to the Archbishop of Canterbury. The essential difference lies not in the notion of primacy operating at various levels, but in the content of practical leadership and power which Roman Catholics attribute to the see of Rome in teaching and, above all, in jurisdiction, together with their affirmation that such a power is necessary and proper to the Church.

223 ARCIC has approached primacy in conjunction with the concepts of conciliarity which Roman Catholics and Anglicans share. Synods, at which local churches have been and are represented by their bishops and often (even in ancient and mediaeval times) by others as well, have found their charter in the apostolic council at Jerusalem (Acts 15) and the Lord's promise that where two or three have met in his name, he is present in their midst (Matt. 18.20). From the apostolic age onwards the Church experienced serious conflicts of interpretation of the apostolic faith, and through the medium of synods found it possible to make decisions on the authentic forms of doctrine or practice. In making such judgements, synods understood their declarations or 'dogmas' to be consonant with or taken out of Scripture even when, as at Nicaea in 325 or at Chalcedon in 451, they found it impossible merely to repeat the words of the Scripture if grave heresy was to be excluded. Moreover, later councils frequently clarified the statements of earlier councils and corrected the balance of what had come to be seen as a one-sided or partial reaction. At particularly difficult periods of controversy, history has seen the phenomenon of conflicting parties producing opposing councils; and so 'among the complex historical factors which contributed to the recognition of conciliar decisions considerable weight attached to their confirmation by the principal sees, and in particular by the see of Rome' (Authority I, para. 17). The act of confirmation and assent played a material role in the general acceptance (which was in no case immediate) of the ancient ecumenical councils of the undivided Church at which, in some degree, both western and eastern delegates

took decisions together or in consultation. These councils occurred at times of crisis when fundamental matters were believed to be in question. The Orthodox Churches give special honour to the first seven ecumenical councils, all held in the Greek world, to which the West also assented. Anglicans share the general judgement of the Roman Catholic and Orthodox Churches, and also the mainstream churches of the Reformation, that the ancient ecumenical councils decided wisely and were enabled by the guidance of the Holy Spirit to exclude erroneous and misleading doctrines. Some Anglican theologians have attached an exceptional weight to the judgements of the first four ecumenical councils (Nicaea 325; Constantinople 381; Ephesus 431; Chalcedon 451). Not all councils which at the time claimed the title 'ecumenical' have been received as authoritative, i.e. as making decisions irreversibly and beneficially correcting the Church's course. The possibility of errors or inadequacies, recognized in Article 21 of the Articles of Religion ('General councils . . . may err, and sometimes have erred') is checked by the Church's process of reception, of which, together with the judgement of the faithful, the confirmation and assent by the bishops of leading sees constitute a part.

(vi) *Reception, the* Sensus Fidelium *and the Role of the Laity*

224 'Theology justifies and history demonstrates that the ultimate authority and right of collective action lie with the whole body of the Church and that the co-operation of clergy and laity in church government and discipline belongs to the true idea of the Church' (*The Convocations and the Laity*, CA 1240, CIB, 1958, para. 1, p. 15). It is of course easier to make statements about lay involvement and dispersed authority than to define the precise relation and interdependence of the lay and ordained. Nevertheless ARCIC puts the matter very positively: 'The perception of God's will for his Church does not only belong to the ordained ministry but is shared by all its members' (Authority I, para. 6). The interpretation of the gospel in diverse cultures and changing situations is a responsibility laid on the whole Church, not merely on its ordained ministers. Moreover ARCIC sees the whole community as both responding to and assessing the teaching of the ordained ministry (Authority I, para. 6). The *sensus fidelium* is a vital element in the compre-

hension and declaration of God's truth (Authority I, para. 18). Such language implies that lay participation in the realm of authority is not simply confined to the participation of a few lay people in synodical bodies. There is an interconnection between the role of a trained, spiritually formed and participating laity and the vernacular use of Scripture and the preaching of the word in liturgy. In the context of a discussion of teaching authority in the Church, ARCIC writes: 'The Church in all its members is involved in . . . a definition which clarifies and enriches their grasp of the truth. Their active reflection upon the definition in its turn clarifies its significance. Moreover, although it is not through reception by the people of God that a definition first acquires authority, the assent of the faithful is the ultimate indication that the Church's authoritative decision in a matter of faith has been truly preserved from error by the Holy Spirit. The Holy Spirit who maintains the Church in the truth will bring its members to receive the definition as true and to assimilate it if what has been declared genuinely expounds the revelation' (Authority II, para. 25). All Anglicans should welcome this emphasis, while also recognizing the inherent difficulty of speaking about the reception of authoritative teaching by the whole people of God whilst the Churches remain divided.

225 ARCIC comments further on the crucial concept of reception: 'By "reception" we mean the fact that the people of God acknowledge such a decision or statement because they recognize in it the apostolic faith. They accept it because they discern a harmony between what is proposed to them and the *sensus fidelium* of the whole Church. As an example, the creed which we call Nicene has been received by the Church because in it the Church has recognized the apostolic faith. Reception does not create truth nor legitimize the decision: it is the final indication that such a decision has fulfilled the necessary conditions for it to be a true expression of the faith. In this acceptance the whole Church is involved in a continuous process of discernment and response'. The Commission adds that it avoids two extreme positions. 'On the one hand it rejects the view that a definition has no authority until it is accepted by the whole Church or even derives its authority solely from that acceptance. Equally, the Commission denies that a council is so evidently self-sufficient that its definitions owe nothing to reception' (Authority: *Elucidation*, para. 3).

226 The process whereby the Canon of the New Testament was established (a process not complete before the middle of the fourth century) provides an illuminating analogy. The process was not one whereby apostolic authority was conferred on certain books; rather apostolic authority was recognized as inhering in them. But it was also a process of discrimination involving a critical judgement on the part of the faithful as to whether certain books, though claiming apostolic authority, could in fact be recognized as possessing it. One of the criteria was whether the teaching these books embodied was in accord with the fullness of the apostolic faith as the Church had received it and believed it.

227 We believe that the Commission's statements on reception are soundly based, and fully in line with characteristically Anglican ways of thinking about authority and the active part played by the body of the faithful. At the same time it is also characteristically Anglican to understand a special responsibility for the safeguarding of unity and truth as resting on the episcopate (cf. the description of the office of a bishop in the ASB, *Ordination of a Bishop*, p. 388). As a chief pastor a bishop shares with his fellow bishops a special responsibility to maintain and further the unity of the Church, to uphold its discipline and to guard its faith. As representatives of the living teaching office of the Church, bishops have laid on them the task of authentically interpreting the Word of God, in which role their task is to speak in the name of Christ himself. Their teaching office is therefore never above the Word of God or independent of it, but is a service for upholding the truth of the gospel. It would not, therefore, be consistent with Anglican forms for the ordination of bishops to doubt that the commission entrusted to bishops (and therefore also the gift of God proportionate to the task) includes the care for true doctrine and the proclamation of that to the faithful. And the proper response to the Word of God is obedience. Hence it would be misleading, as ARCIC observes (Authority II, para. 31), to suggest that in controversies of faith no definition, whether by council or primate, possesses a right to attentive sympathy and acceptance until it has been examined by every individual Christian and subjected to his or her private judgement. Such a suggestion would make nonsense of the proposition that the Church has authority in matters of faith.

228 A balanced statement of the true doctrine of reception is inherently difficult, and the manner in which it is handled by ARCIC, we consider, well protects the Anglican position in the matter, while granting that a fully satisfactory formula is not easy to achieve. In relation to the teaching office of the bishop of Rome, ARCIC points out that, if his judgement is to express a decisive discernment of the truth, it must satisfy rigorous conditions: 'He must speak explicitly as the focus within the *koinonia*; without being under duress from external pressures; having sought to discover the mind of his fellow bishops and of the Church as a whole; and with a clear intention to issue a binding decision upon a matter of faith or morals'. ARCIC continues: 'When it is plain that all these conditions have been fulfilled, Roman Catholics conclude that the judgement is preserved from error and the proposition true. If the definition proposed for assent were not manifestly a legitimate interpretation of biblical faith and in line with orthodox tradition, Anglicans would think it a duty to reserve the reception of the definition for study and discussion' (Authority II, para. 29). This language, 'legitimate' and 'in line with tradition', illustrates the Commission's avoidance (see para. 211 above) of the proposition that Scripture is the exclusive and sole source of guidance. At the same time Anglicans ask that the teaching office of the Church shall be seen to be drawing upon the deposit of faith and scrupulously proclaiming only what has been handed on.

229 ARCIC is consistent with this position when in a statement agreed by the whole Commission it is said: 'Neither general councils nor universal primates are invariably preserved from error even in official declarations' (Authority II, para. 27). In a sentence which is consistent with the general view of the Commission (see Authority II, paras. 25, 27) it is said: 'Anglicans do not accept the guaranteed possession of such a gift of divine assistance in judgement necessarily attached to the office of the bishop of Rome by virtue of which his formal decisions can be known to be wholly assured before their reception by the faithful' (Authority II, para. 31). This does not imply an understanding of reception widely distinct from that assented to by the Roman Catholic members of ARCIC (though we may note the *Observations* of the Sacred Congregation for the Doctrine of the Faith record dissent on this point) and is easy to reconcile with the historical facts referred to above (see para. 223 above), namely that the general acknowledgement of the ancient

ecumenical councils to which Rome and the West assented was not immediate and in some cases took considerable time. In other words, reception by the faithful is a continuing process of assimilation which is also a critical appropriation and interpretation.

230 It is important that Anglicans should maintain their position on this point for three reasons in particular. First, there is the matter of historical precedent. If it took three centuries for the Canon of the New Testament to be finally received, and half a century for the Council of Nicaea, should we expect any papal utterances to be accepted overnight? ARCIC mentions the reception of the so-called Tome of Leo by the Council of Chalcedon (Authority II, para. 29) but does not make it sufficiently clear that this Council accepted it as an authoritative statement of faith only after careful examination. Secondly, Anglicans are not alone in believing that there is no office or institution in the Church which can claim the power to make statements whose preservation from fundamental error the Church may be sure of before their reception by the whole Church. The Orthodox Churches are as committed to the doctrine of the Church's infallibility as is the Roman Catholic Church, but they equally affirm that the power of such utterance is a gift of the Holy Spirit which, when given, demands recognition and cannot be presumed upon beforehand in virtue of office. And thirdly, it is surely of theological significance that the dogmas which are particularly in question, those of 1854, 1870 and 1950, are precisely those which have been proclaimed within a deeply broken Church.

231 So, while welcoming what the Commission says generally about reception of conciliar statements, particularly what is said in paragraph 25 of *Authority II*, we would agree with the Anglican members of the Commission that the papal statements ought no less to be subject to the same process of reception even when they are made after conciliar consultation. However, we note with gratitude the Commission's own judgement on this matter that 'contemporary discussions of conciliarity and primacy in both communions indicate that we are not dealing with positions destined to remain static'.

(vii) *Dialogue and Dissent*

232 The absence from Anglican experience for more than four hundred years of a universal primacy invested with even a qualified and conditional sovereignty in teaching and in juris- diction makes Anglicans inclined to understand decision-making by authority in terms of a developing dialogue, including criticism and response, rather than as a monologue. We should have welcomed it if ARCIC had been able to say something about the openness of authority to constructive critical conversation. We can freely acknowledge that Anglicans easily convey the impression that in their view nothing of fundamental dogma is ever really decided, and that comprehensiveness has no defin- able bounds. However both Anglicans and Roman Catholics have come to be sensitive to the fear that ecclesiastical authority may stifle challenge and silence criticism. Anglicans, whilst they are aware of the Lord's warning against offending the weak (Matt. 18.6), naturally think that it is often the duty of authority not to bring debate to a speedy conclusion but rather to ensure that legitimate options in interpretation are kept open and even protected. Respect for the principle, dear to Augustine and Hooker, that reason is a great gift of God for discerning religious truth entails the recognition that people of reason may disagree deeply and yet remain in communion. It would have been specially helpful to Anglican readers if ARCIC had been able to illuminate an issue which is equally a question for both Roman Catholics and Anglicans. But the problem is sharpened in the ecumenical discussion by the ways in which the Roman curia commonly exercises a juridical discipline over the explorations of its more adventurous dogmatic and moral theologians, whereas in the Anglican communion authority intervenes, if at all, both at a point which appears to many Roman Catholics to be late in the day, and in a manner which is less than incisive. This last point is in part a reflection of the Anglican assumption that Church teaching is well known through liturgy, worship and pastoral care.

(viii) *Papal Primacy*

233 The questions discussed so far are problems common to both Anglicans and Roman Catholics, which would press upon

our attention apart from the specific issues of Roman primacy which, for many readers in the ARCIC Final Report, has been the one great issue. Anglicans are accustomed to thinking of authority as diffused through many media by which God guides the Church and protects his people from error. A unique and supreme place is occupied by the Bible, accessible to every one of the faithful, together with the apostolic creed and the rule of faith for its interpretation, within the universal communion which Christ intended his Church to be. Of this communion a common baptism and shared eucharist are effectual signs; the episcopal ministry is the sign and instrument of unity and continuity in time and space. Within this order of bishops, doing for us something of what the apostles did for the first Christians, should there be a primatial focus?

234 We now turn to this question, remembering that ARCIC treats Roman primacy as a presidency within the universal episcopate, and not apart from it. Anglicans and Roman Catholics are at one in their understanding of the episcopate as a ministry involving not only oversight of each local church but also a care for the universal communion of which each church is a part (Authority I, para. 8). ARCIC sees the office of universal primate as a special and particular case of this care for universal communion which is proper to the episcopal office itself. The question to be settled is: what is the theological basis for affirming this primacy to be a Petrine office necessary to the true fulness of the Church's being, endowed with a responsibility for uniquely authoritative teaching at the highest level for all Christian people, and for the exercise of discipline and order throughout the universal Church?

235 In response to criticisms, including those of GS 394, that their argument for universal primacy centred at Rome was historical and not doctrinal, the Commission claim in the *Elucidation* that their statement is 'more than historical'. Their argument proceeds in three stages:

(i) According to Christian doctrine the unity in truth of the Christian community demands visible expression.
(ii) Maintenance of that visible unity at the universal level includes the *episcope* of a universal primate, as well as universal conciliarity.
(iii) Historically and contingently there is a strong presumption that the Holy Spirit has led the Church to locate a universal primacy in the see of Rome.

236   ARCIC begins from the agreed premise that unity is of the essence of the Church, and that unity in truth within the Christian fellowship requires visible expressions. In the family of the diocese the focus of unity is found not in an institution as much as in the person of the bishop; in the province in the archbishop or metropolitan. Is there one bishop acknowledged as president of the episcopal college, whose office and care it is to be a sign of the universality and unity of the whole Church? The Roman Catholic answer points to the Church of Rome, where Gentile Christianity found its capital city, where the ancient churches looked for leadership, especially in conflicts with heresy, and to which disciplinary appeals from provincial decisions came to be referred. ARCIC remarks that the church of Rome was exercising leadership long before anyone is known to have sought to justify this authority by quoting Petrine texts from the New Testament. (The First Epistle of Clement shows this in operation already.) Nevertheless, from the mid-third century onwards, the theme of succession to Peter became increasingly prominent. The New Testament certainly portrays Peter as having a special position of leadership and authority among the apostles, and in various places speaks of a commission which he received from the Lord. For ARCIC, however, there is no simple transfer of Petrine authority to his successors, whether in the universal episcopate or in the particular see of Rome. 'The New Testament contains no explicit record of a transmission of Peter's leadership; nor is the transmission of apostolic authority in general very clear' (Authority II, para. 6). As witnesses of the 'once-for-all saving work of Christ' the apostles are unique. But the apostles are not an authority for the Church only in the sense that they provide good historical testimony for the gospel events. The communities which came into being in consequence of their mission began to look to the apostolic Church as a source of legitimacy. The continuing tradition and life of the Church necessitates an answer to the question: Who speaks in the name of the apostles now? The Church of the second century answered this question, first in terms of personal ministerial succession, then in terms of the apostolic faith in the creed, and finally in the formation of the New Testament Canon.

237   ARCIC's treatment of Roman primacy proceeds inductively rather than by deduction from proof-texts. It sees the primacy, like episcopacy in general, as a development which the Church has needed and which answers the question: Where and how

can the unity and universality of the Church have visible expression? In the continuing interaction between the living tradition of the Church's life and the text of the New Testament, the Church rightly looks for principles, analogies, guidelines for its present situation, and cannot always find a clear-cut text to answer the problems arising at much later times. As the ancient Church grew in numbers and geographical extent, the need was increasingly felt to find a centre of gravity located in the churches believed to be of apostolic foundation. Where might the churches of the second century better look for leadership than to the great church of Rome, where an unquestioned community tradition knew that Peter and Paul had once taught and died? ARCIC understands the relevance to Roman authority of Peter's leadership among the apostles in terms of an analogy. Modern Roman Catholic scholars and theologians make little or no attempt to use words from the New Testament in the old way as simple proof-texts, as if there existed a straight line from 'Thou art Peter and on this rock I will build my church' to the ideology of Gregory VII or Boniface VIII or even Vatican I. The question is rather whether, if the Church of Christ is to be a visible communion with a sign of universality and unity, we need a comparable leadership, a Petrine office, exercising a presidency of love and an authority of service to unity.

238 Anglicans will find no difficulty in agreeing that the unity of the Church ought to be visible nor that oversight of some kind ought to be exercised at a universal level. Whether and to what extent this includes the exercise of oversight by a single person is another question. ARCIC's argument provides the framework for a theological justification. It is based on three assertions: that pastoral authority belongs primarily to the bishop (Authority I, para. 5); that pastoral authority belongs to the bishop of a principal see (Authority I, para. 11) and that Rome became the principal centre in matters concerning the Church universal (Authority I, para. 12). These three assertions require fuller treatment if the unease expressed in GS 394 is to be dispelled, namely that the case for a universal primacy, and a primacy centred on Rome, has been assumed rather than made.

239 ARCIC makes no special attempt to trace back the primacy of the bishop of Rome (nor, for that matter, the threefold ministry) to an immediate institution by the Jesus of history.

ARCIC appears to have seen the emergence of Roman primacy in the early Church as a development, like monepiscopacy or the baptismal creed, which the churches of the second and third centuries found themselves needing. The evidence of history points to a development in which the bishops of Rome found themselves called to exercise a pastoral responsibility which other churches expected them to fulfil. After the emperors became Christian, the bishops of Rome particularly helped to preserve the Church's freedom from total domination by the secular power.

240 Appeals to the working of divine providence in history are open to more than one interpretation. ARCIC notes that 'from time to time Anglican theologians have affirmed that, in changed circumstances, it might be possible for the churches of the Anglican Communion to recognize the development of the Roman primacy as a gift of divine providence – in other words, as an effect of the guidance of the Holy Spirit in the Church' (Authority II, para. 13). There would be a difficulty here if the argument were to be that the empirical history of the papacy is so remarkable that an unprejudiced mind would be bound to regard it as a sign of providence. One would then feel bound to ask how a concept of primacy, as an element in an ecclesiology which ARCIC acknowledges to be a statement of an ideal, can be justified on the basis of an actuality which ARCIC freely concedes to have been marked by instances of grave failure. If a description of an actual development is regarded as providential, then that development and not some similar but distinct ideal ought to become prescriptive. Moreover, some would feel that if the argument is to proceed on the basis of historical providence, more evidence must be provided that this development is in accordance with the inner and essential character of the Christian faith. ARCIC's commendation of the Petrine office does not depend on the exemplary behaviour of every bishop of Rome or the perfect functioning of the papacy in every age, any more than Anglicans would think that a commendation of episcopacy needs to depend on the invariably perfect exercise of the episcopal office. The root question is whether in the visible communion of the universal Church on earth, believers, congregations and dioceses are given a bond of universal communion, a sign and instrument for the manifestation of the Church's wholeness. The consequent question is whether this sign of universality and unity has, or

has not, already been given to the Church in the Roman see. It may of course be observed that such arguments appear more readily compelling to those who already possess the ministry in question, be it episcopacy or papacy, than to those who do not.

241 The Commission is clear that to accept a universal prima-cy as 'the sign of the visible *koinonia* God wills for the Church and an instrument through which unity in diversity is realized' (Authority II, para. 11) would not mean for Anglicans a denial that the Churches of the Anglican Communion are and have been Churches. This is made quite clear in the course of the Commission's treatment of *ius divinum* (Authority II, paras. 10–15). There would be for Anglicans no 'repudiation of their past history, life and experience' – which, as the Commission says, would in effect be a betrayal of their own integrity. In other words Anglicans do not believe that communion with the see of Rome is the sole touchstone of catholicity and ecclesiality.

242 While many agree on the value of a universal primate as a sign of the visible fellowship of the Church, and even upon the Roman primatial office as the obvious candidate for such a primatial see, the question of what special responsibilities and duties such a person should have for keeping unity in truth and ordering all things in love is a more difficult matter. (We need also to consider what is said in other dialogues, such as the Anglican–Orthodox and Anglican–Reformed dialogue, about a universal sign of unity and continuity.)

(ix) *Infallibility*

243 The Final Report affirms that the term 'infallibility' is 'applicable unconditionally only to God, and that to use it of a human being, even in highly restricted circumstances, can produce many misunderstandings' (Authority II, para. 32). Yet it is not only the term that is difficult. Discussion of the reliability of the teaching office in the Church and of the main-tenance of the Church in the truth brings ARCIC to a problem in Anglican–Roman Catholic relations which many in both Communions would expect to constitute an insuperable obsta-cle. ARCIC strips the subject of a number of myths, and Anglicans can be grateful for the clearcut statement (Authority I, para. 19) that in Roman Catholic as in Anglican understanding of teaching authority there is no power to create new truths or

to add to the faith; definitions by councils or primates clarify and safeguard, but do not innovate. Furthermore it is noted that in Roman Catholic doctrine, 'infallibility means only the preservation of the judgement from error for the maintenance of the Church in the truth, not positive inspiration or revelation' (Authority II, para. 32, n. 7). Such language goes far to meet fears. Nevertheless no formal claim is made that on this difficult subject a full and unqualified agreement has been reached. It is enough to say that if the careful analysis of the intricate question at issue is accepted as a broadly correct account, the size of the problem has been unquestionably reduced. The area of surviving unclarity (which seems an apter word than 'disagreement' between 'positions') appears now to be a matter for discussion in the context of growing rapprochement. If teaching office in the Church is understood along the lines proposed in the ARCIC text, then we see a less formidable obstacle to consensus in this sphere than appears in the Roman claim to universal, immediate, and ordinary jurisdiction; a claim that creates obstacles of a different order of magnitude.

244 There is a reason for gratitude that the Roman Catholic members of ARCIC were evidently willing and able to enter into the conciliar framework instinctive to Anglican minds, so that all the Commission perceived the two prime difficulties to lie in the nature of 'reception' (see above, paras. 224-31) and in any language which tends to set the bishop of Rome apart from the episcopate in general, or indeed from the universal Church. In effect, the declaration of Vatican I, that in *ex cathedra* definitions on faith and morals the Pope can speak with that reliability with which Christ has endowed the entire Church, is very exactly interpreted by ARCIC as an expression of conciliarity; that is to say, the bishop of Rome is then a privileged instance of the faithful witness to Christian truth which is borne by all true Christians. Anglicans also acknowledge, as we have seen, that there is a special responsibility on the shoulders of bishops. The mind of the Church as a whole, after thorough consultation, together with the study of Scripture and orthodox tradition, may in certain circumstances and conditions be rightly articulated by one bishop.

245 ARCIC agreed (Authority II, para. 23 and n. 3) that the force of the confused and confusing term 'infallibility' used in relation to an actual organ of church teaching is distinct, even

if inseparable from the wider term 'indefectibility'. The latter term is accurately defined as having no reference to lack of faults in the empirical Church, but rather as a shorthand term for the assertion of faith that, despite weaknesses and failures, the Holy Spirit will enable the Church neither to lose its essential character nor to fail to reach its goal. The term has an eschatological content, pointing beyond present distress to the final triumph of God, but also implying confidence that through the Church, even as it now is, the Kingdom is in process of realization.

246 ARCIC evidently implies that 'infallibility' in the Church's teaching office is not reducible to indefectibility. Furthermore, the organs of the Church's authoritative teaching are plainly concrete. Thus 'the Church's judgement is normally given through synodal decision, but at times a primate acting in communion with his fellow bishops may articulate the decision even apart from a synod. Although responsibility for preserving the Church from fundamental error belongs to the whole Church, it may be exercised on its behalf by a universal primate' (Authority II, para. 28). Accordingly it is noted that 'in Roman Catholic doctrine . . . the infallibility ascribed to the bishop of Rome is a gift to be, in certain circumstances and under precise conditions, an organ of the infallibility of the Church' (Authority II, para. 32, n. 7). ARCIC therefore in effect denies that the bishop of Rome, even when it is claimed that he is acting in virtue of special privilege as president of the universal episcopate, acts wholly on his own in any other than a juridical sense. This obviously does not imply that the bishop of Rome, or indeed any bishop, may take no initiative or may act only as a mere spokesman for words put into his mouth by others; and we think that those who have understood ARCIC to mean this are misconstruing the text. Nevertheless, it is agreed that no doctrine first becomes a doctrine of the faith by virtue of being defined by a council or primate; for the scope of definition cannot extend beyond the deposit of divine revelation and the clarification and safeguarding of its implications. 'The Church's teaching is proclaimed because it is true; it is not true simply because it has been proclaimed' (Authority II, para. 27).

247 Teaching authority in the Church is a topic that has been the subject of considerable Roman Catholic debate in recent

years. We can readily understand that the Anglican members of ARCIC may not always have been clear about the exact shape of the Roman Catholic doctrine, particularly in relation to 'infallibility', since more than one view has been current. For example the Roman Congregation for the Doctrine of the Faith (*Observations* B.III.3) has criticized the view of the Roman Catholic members of ARCIC by insisting that infallibility 'refers immediately not to truth but to certitude'. This seems to say that the concept of 'infallibility' is concerned with the psychological problem of assurance about truth rather than with doctrinal truth itself. This point may illustrate the fact of diversity of view on the Roman Catholic side. The interpretation here sponsored by the Congregation seems to diminish rather than to increase the divide from Anglican understanding of the relation of teaching authority to the sacred tradition of faith.

(x) *Jurisdiction*

248 We turn now to the question of jurisdiction. It is important to note that ARCIC's discussion of papal jurisdiction is set within the context of episcopal jurisdiction in general. 'Jurisdiction in the Church may be defined as the authority or power (*potestas*) necessary for the exercise of an office. In both our Communions it is given for the effective fulfilment of office and this fact determines its exercise and limits' (Authority II, para. 16). On papal jurisdiction, ARCIC says much that we find both important and attractive; 'it is not the arbitrary power of one man over the freedom of others'; it 'is to serve the faith and unity of the whole Church' (Authority II, para. 17); it is to be exercised 'not in isolation but in collegial association with his brother bishops'; 'primacy is not an autocratic power over the Church but a service in and to the Church which is a communion in faith and charity of local churches' (Authority II, para. 19); 'there are moral limits to its exercise' (Authority II, para. 20) and moreover 'collegial and primatial responsibility for preserving the distinctive life of the local churches involves a proper respect for their customs and traditions' (Authority II, para. 21).

249 Nevertheless we believe that consideration of universal oversight should be developed in closer connexion with an emphasis on the right and sometimes duty of the community to engage in critical discussion of decisions on faith and morals.

The process of reception can never be purely passive. Also, we should like the text to have given more stress to the right of local churches to discover a proper diversity of expression in thought and life – something we believe to be in accord with the diversity recorded in the New Testament. The Commission asserts that 'Anglicans are entitled to assurance that acknowledgement of the universal primacy of the bishop of Rome would not involve the suppression of theological, liturgical and other traditions which they value or the imposition of wholly alien traditions' (Authority II, para. 22). There is perhaps an inevitable lack of specificity here. Some will be alarmed by the history of suppression of local rites and theologies within the Roman Catholic Communion during the last two hundred years; others will be encouraged by the degree of autonomy allowed in recent years to local bishops and episcopal conferences. The anxieties of those who remain sceptical will not be allayed by reference to the sensitive words of Paul VI in 1970: 'There will be no seeking to lessen the legitimate prestige and worthy patrimony of piety and usage proper to the Anglican Church . . .' We believe, together with the Commission, that what is said about universal jurisdiction needs to be held together with the role of the people of God in the reception of decisions made by the universal primate, even when they are arrived at after conciliar consultation. Only when such insights are sufficiently developed in relation to the exercise of primatial authority will fears be overcome and its benefits be acknowledged.

250   There is another area of concern, related to the 'attribution of universal, ordinary and immediate jurisdiction to the bishop of Rome by the First Vatican Council'. As the Final Report says, this is 'a source of anxiety to Anglicans who fear that the way is thus open to its illegitimate or uncontrolled use' (Authority I, para. 24 (d), Authority II, para. 18). It is one thing to acknowledge the personal primacy of the bishop of Rome, together with his duty to intervene when the unity of Christian communion is in peril. It is another thing to accept the degree of centralization of Church government which still appears to be associated with it. Anglicans could not be happy with an interpretation of jurisdiction which saw the proper autonomy of local bishops and churches as a matter of delegation or concession from central authority, rather than as a matter of inherent right.

(xi) *Conclusion*

251 We recognize and are thankful for the important achieve-ments of this statement on Authority in the Church. We believe the work of ARCIC provides an important stepping stone on the way to realizing unity between our two communions. While not providing answers, the text does offer 'a significant contri-bution' to the unresolved questions on the nature and experience of authority in the Church. While not registering the same substantial agreement as is registered in the eucharist or even the ministry text, we agree that it does mark 'a significant con-vergence with far-reaching consequences'. The reservations we have expressed are intended to help further joint study on the way towards consensus. We believe that the Commission is right in encouraging us to think that a greater degree of agreement can be reached by building upon these statements. At the same time we would wish to emphasize the importance of the discus-sion that needs to go on about the organs by which, under God, an all too human Church is preserved from fundamental error, and enabled despite all weaknesses and human failings to be the vehicle of the gospel of forgiveness and new life. It would be one thing for Anglicans to say 'yes' to the universal primacy of the bishop of Rome as the person who particularly signifies the unity and universality of the Church and to acknowledge his special responsibilities for maintaining unity in the truth and ordering things in love; it would be quite another to agree to infallibility without the understanding of reception as we have described it.

252 It is, however, important for Anglicans not only to put questions to our Roman Catholic partners but also to hear those questions which the texts put to us. The most pressing question put by ARCIC to Anglicans, who confess their faith in 'one, holy, catholic and apostolic Church' is, how is the unity and catholicity of the Church to be manifested? And if, as we maintain, the exercise of authority and discipline is a necessary part of the Church's existence, what form or forms of authority should serve the manifestation of this unity and catholicity? We cannot be concerned only with the deposits left behind by the exercise of authority in times past, the Scripture, the first ancient General Councils. The question is, through what persons or institutions is Christ's authority now mediated in the universal Church?

253 The question of universal authority raised by ARCIC faces us inescapably with the question of authority in the Anglican Communion. We ought not to take refuge behind the 'legal' autonomy of each national church or province in order to evade the theological question of our coherence as a Communion. The work of ARCIC as well as Anglican practice suggests that the coherence is to be manifested both in personal (episcopal and primatial) and in conciliar forms. It is not a matter of creating some new 'central' authority, by delegation or transference of power from national churches conceived as 'sovereign', but of recognizing the authority inherent by virtue of ordination in the bishops and primates, whereby they can act together, in consultation with the laity, on behalf of their churches. Having recognized that inherent authority it is our task to discover structures through which the authority can be most adequately expressed and acknowledged.

254 Finally, Anglicans need to give critical attention to the role played in the Church of England, both past and present, by state authority. The Co-Chairmen of ARCIC refer to the problem of papal authority as lying at the source of our divisions. They might also have raised the matter of royal authority. Ought we not to think carefully about the nature of the authority attaching to the General Synod? There is need to distinguish between the authority that it derives from Parliament through the Enabling Act and subsequent Measures, and the inherent authority that it has as a combined meeting of the two Provincial Synods of Canterbury and York (which are older than Parliament) together with representatives of the laity of the two provinces. There is need to consider the relation between decisions of a representative church body and reception by the Church in this context. There is need also to consider the limitations of decisions taken by parts, smaller or greater, of the universal Church. Further, the control exercised by royal authority over appointments and canonical legislation in the Church of England should be examined in comparison with similar forms of state control over churches in other lands.

D The Introduction to the Final Report

255 Finally, in responding to the Final Report, we wish to acknowledge the importance of the introductory section on the nature of the Church. This provides a significant ecclesiological

framework for what is said about the eucharist, the ministry and authority in the Church. The concept of *koinonia* we believe is an important one and not just one model among many New Testament models that might have been selected. *Koinonia* is not so much a model of the Church as a fundamental quality of the life of the Church manifested and experienced at all levels of the Church's life. As the report suggests, the eucharist is the effectual sign of *koinonia*, *episcope* serves the *koinonia* and primacy is the visible link and focus of *koinonia* (Introduction, para. 6). The use of *koinonia* raises the problem, which we have noted in other places, of the distinction between the ideal and the actual.

256 Among the strengths of the concept of *koinonia* is that it enables ARCIC to reflect the polarity to be found in the New Testament between the use of the word 'church' as referring to the universal Church and its use in referring to local churches. ARCIC refuses to see either local churches as mere subdivisions of the universal Church or the universal Church as no more than the sum total of local churches. 'The *koinonia* is realized not only in the local Christian communities but also in the communion of these communities with one another' (Authority I, para. 8). The fellowship of the local church is expressed in its eucharistic life, which is served by the *episcope* of the ordained ministry. The fellowship of the wider church is served by regional councils and primates. The fellowship of the universal Church is served by the episcopate as a whole and is focused in the universal primate. *Koinonia* is seen as both the goal and the way, the riches and depths of which all will be unfolded only as the journey progresses. As this is worked out, there emerges a picture, admittedly incomplete, of what unity and diversity might mean in a united Church. There is a double emphasis: both on the need for Catholic unity focused in structures and persons transcending the local, and on the need for a proper local diversity which must never be stifled.

257 The ecclesiology of ARCIC may be seen as essentially biblical and patristic in inspiration. The ecclesiological self-understanding of the early Church is to be discerned not in explicit theological reflection or systematic statement from that period, but by observation of the way in which the churches actually lived and functioned. What emerges from the Final Report is a more balanced ecclesiology which accords closely,

we consider, with the vision of the Church expressed in much recent theological writing. One of its merits is that it moves away from the juridical emphasis which is characteristic of the ecclesiology of the mediaeval and post-mediaeval periods.

258 According to this picture, the nature of the Church is more adequately and accurately grasped by attending primarily to its quality as a participation in the divine life rather than to its juridical structure. The Church is thus primarily to be seen as the eucharistic fellowship in which the visible and the invisible are joined, with the ordained ministry responsible for the building up of the eucharistic community. Each church understands itself as a particular manifestation of the one universal Church. For this reason, each local church requires structures to maintain and serve its communion with each other church. The communion of the churches is served by the communion of their pastors with each other. Thus there have emerged structures of conciliarity and primacy. Their task is to hold in the communion the local communions by maintaining their fellowship in faith and love. The task of the universal primate is to be the centre of this universal communion.

259 A question needing to be asked is whether, in developing an ecclesiology of this kind rather than trying simply to bring together the ecclesiologies mainly associated with Roman Catholic and Protestant traditions, ARCIC is pointing towards an ecclesiology which properly comprehends the particular emphases of the divided traditions. In this ecclesiology each local church is a complete eucharistic fellowship, entrusted with the tradition of the Gospel. But it belongs to the completeness of each local church that it remains in communion with its sister churches. This communion is built on a unity in faith and love which is so maintained through collegial and synodical structures that the universality of the catholic Church receives a visible manifestation as a communion of communions at every level.

260 We look forward to work developing the ecclesiological insights of the Final Report, which will help us to deepen our understanding of the goal to which we are moving, and thus also of the appropriate steps to take on the way to that goal.

9
The 1988 Lambeth Conference: Resolution 8 and Explanatory Note regarding ARCIC I

The bishops at the 1988 Lambeth Conference had before them a report which collated the responses of the Provinces to ARCIC – the *Emmaus Report* (ACC/Church House Publishing, 1987). The bishops passed the following Resolution at the Lambeth Conference:

This Conference:

1. Recognises the Agreed Statements of ARCIC I on *Eucharistic Doctrine, Ministry and Ordination,* and their *Elucidations,* as consonant in substance with the faith of Anglicans and believes that this agreement offers a sufficient basis for taking the next step forward towards the reconciliation of our Churches grounded in agreement in faith.

2. Welcomes the assurance that, within an understanding of the Church as communion, ARCIC II is to explore further the particular issues of the reconciliation of ministries; the ordination of women; moral questions; and continuing questions of authority, including the relation of Scripture to the Church's developing Tradition and the role of the laity in decision-making within the Church.

3. Welcomes *Authority in the Church (I* and *II)* together with the *Elucidation,* as a firm basis for the direction and agenda of the continuing dialogue on authority and wishes to encourage ARCIC II to continue to explore the basis in Scripture and Tradition of the concept of a universal primacy, in conjunction with collegiality, as an instrument of unity, the character of such a primacy in practice, and to draw upon the experience of other Christian Churches in exercising primacy, collegiality and conciliarity.

4. In welcoming the fact that the ordination of women is to form part of the agenda of ARCIC II, recognises the serious responsibility this places upon us to weigh the possible implications of action on this matter for the unity of the Anglican Communion and for the universal Church.

5. Warmly welcomes the first Report of ARCIC II, *Salvation and the Church* (1987), as a timely and significant contribution to the understanding of the Churches' doctrine of salvation and commends this Agreed Statement about the heart of Christian faith to the Provinces for study and reflection.

Explanatory Note

This Conference has received the official responses to the Final Report of the Anglican–Roman Catholic International Commission (ARCIC I) from the member Provinces of the Anglican Communion. We note the considerable measure of consensus and convergence which the Agreed Statements represent. We wish to record our grateful thanks to Almighty God for the very significant advances in understanding and unity thereby expressed.

In considering the Final Report, the Conference bore two questions in mind:

(i) Are the Agreed Statements consonant with Anglican faith?

(ii) If so, do they enable us to take further steps forward?

Eucharistic Doctrine

The Provinces gave a clear 'yes' to the Statement on *Eucharistic Doctrine*. Comments have been made that the style and language used in the statement are inappropriate for certain cultures. Some Provinces asked for clarification about the meaning of *anamnesis* and bread and wine 'becoming' the body and blood of Christ. But no Province rejected the Statement and many were extremely positive.

While we recognise that there are hurts to be healed and doubts to be overcome, we encourage Anglicans to look forward with the new hope which the Holy Spirit is giving to the Church as we move away from past mistrust, division and polarisation.

While we respect the continuing anxieties of some Anglicans in the area of 'sacrifice' and 'presence', they do not appear to reflect the common mind of the Provincial responses, in which it was generally felt that the *Elucidation* of *Eucharistic Doctrine* was a helpful clarification and reassurance. Both are areas of 'mystery' which ultimately defy definition. But the Agreed Statement on the Eucharist *sufficiently* expresses Anglican understanding.

Ministry and Ordination

Again, the Provinces gave a clear 'yes' to the Statement on *Ministry and Ordination*. The language and style have, however, been a difficulty for some Provinces, especially in the Far East. Wider representation has also been called for from Africa. Though this has now been partially remedied in ARCIC II, there is still currently no representation from Latin America, a subcontinent with very large Roman Catholic populations.

An ambivalent reply came from one Province which has traditionally experienced a difficult relationship with the Roman Catholic Church. This seems to reflect the need for developing deeper links of trust and friendship as ecumenical dialogue goes forward.

While some Provinces asked for a clarification of 'priesthood' the majority believed this had been dealt with sufficiently – together with the doctrine of the eucharist – to give grounds for hope for a fresh appraisal of each other's ministries and thus to further the reconciliation of ministries and growth towards full communion.

Authority in the Church

The responses from the Provinces to the two Statements on *Authority in the Church* were generally positive.

Questions were, however, raised about a number of matters, especially primacy, jurisdiction and infallibility, collegiality, and the role of the laity. Nevertheless, it was generally felt that *Authority in the Church* (*I* and *II*), together with the *Elucidation*, give us real grounds for believing that fuller agreement can be reached, and that they set out helpfully the direction and agenda of the way forward.

10
The Official Roman Catholic Response to the Final Report of ARCIC I (1991)

General Evaluation

1 The Catholic Church gives a warm welcome to the Final Report of ARCIC I and expresses its gratitude to the members of the International Commission responsible for drawing up this document. The Report is a result of an in-depth study of certain questions of faith by partners in dialogue and witnesses to the achievement of points of convergence and even of agreement which many would not have thought possible before the Commission began its work. As such, it constitutes a significant milestone not only in relations between the Catholic Church and the Anglican Communion but in the ecumenical movement as a whole.

2 The Catholic Church judges, however, that it is not yet possible to state that substantial agreement has been reached on all the questions studied by the Commission. There still remain between Anglicans and Catholics important differences regarding essential matters of Catholic doctrine.

3 The following Explanatory Note is intended to give a de-tailed summary of the areas where differences or ambiguities remain which seriously hinder the restoration of full communion in faith and in the sacramental life. This Note is the fruit of a close collaboration between the Congregation for the Doctrine of the Faith and the Pontifical Council for Promoting Christian Unity, which is directly responsible for the dialogue – a dialogue which, as is well known, continues within the framework of ARCIC II.

4 It is the Catholic Church's hope that its definitive response to the results achieved by ARCIC I will serve as an impetus to further study, in the same fraternal spirit that has characterized this dialogue in the past, of the points of divergence remaining,

as well as of those other questions which must be taken into account if the unity willed by Christ for his disciples is to be restored.

Explanatory Note

5 Before setting forth for further study those areas of the Final Report which do not satisfy fully certain elements of Catholic doctrine and which thereby prevent our speaking of the attainment of substantial agreement, it seems only right and just to mention some other areas in which notable progress has been achieved by those responsible for the redaction of the Report. The members of the Commission have obviously given a great deal of time, prayer, and reflection to the themes which they were asked to study together and they are owed an expression of gratitude and appreciation for the manner in which they carried out their mandate.

6 It is in respect of *Eucharistic Doctrine* that the members of the Commission were able to achieve the most notable progress toward a consensus. Together they affirm 'that the eucharist is a sacrifice in the sacramental sense, provided that it is clear that this is not a repetition of the historical sacrifice' (Eucharistic Doctrine: *Elucidation*, para. 5); and areas of agreement are also evident in respect of the real presence of Christ: 'Before the eucharistic prayer, to the question "What is that?", the believer answers: "It is bread". After the eucharistic prayer, to the same question he answers: "It is truly the body of Christ, the Bread of Life"' (Eucharistic Doctrine: *Elucidation*, para. 6). The Catholic Church rejoices that such common affirmations have become possible. Still, as will be indicated further on, it looks for certain clarifications which will assure that these affirmations are understood in a way that conforms to Catholic doctrine.

7 With regard to *Ministry and Ordination*, the distinction between the priesthood common to all the baptized and the ordained priesthood is explicitly acknowledged: 'These are two distinct realities which relate, each in its own way, to the high priesthood of Christ' (Ministry and Ordination: *Elucidation*, para. 2). The ordained ministry 'is not an extension of the common Christian priesthood but belongs to another realm of the gifts of the Spirit' (Ministry and Ordination, para. 13). Ordination is described as a 'sacramental act' (Ministry and

Ordination, para. 15) and the ordained ministry as being an essential element of the Church: 'The New Testament shows that ministerial office played an essential part in the life of the Church in the first century, and we believe that the provision of a ministry of this kind is part of God's design for his people' (Ministry and Ordination, para. 6). Moreover, 'it is only the ordained minister who presides at the eucharist' (Ministry and Ordination: *Elucidation*, para. 2). These are all matters of significant consensus and of particular importance for the future development of Anglican–Roman Catholic dialogue.

8 On both the eucharist and the ordained ministry, the *sacramental* understanding of the Church is affirmed, to the exclusion of any purely 'congregational' presentation of Christianity. The members of the Commission are seen as speaking together out of a continuum of faith and practice which has its roots in the New Testament and has developed under the guidance of the Holy Spirit throughout Christian history.

9 When it comes to the question of *Authority in the Church*, it must be noted that the Final Report makes no claim to substantial agreement. The most that has been achieved is a certain convergence, which is but a first step along the path that seeks consensus as a prelude to unity. Yet even in this respect, there are certain signs of convergence that do indeed open the way to further progress in the future. As the Congregation for the Doctrine of the Faith pointed out in its *Observations* of 1982 on the Final Report: 'It is necessary to underline the importance of the fact that Anglicans recognize that a "primacy of the Bishop of Rome is not contrary to the New Testament, and is a part of God's purpose regarding the Church's unity and catholicity"' (cf. Authority II, para. 7). If this is taken with the statement made by His Grace Archbishop Runcie during his visit to Pope John Paul II in 1989 and with reference to infallibility in *Authority II*, para. 29, then one can rejoice in the fact that centuries of antagonism have given way to reasoned dialogue and theological reflection undertaken together.

10 Despite these very consoling areas of agreement or convergence on questions that are of great importance for the faith of the Catholic Church, it seems clear that there are still other areas that are essential to Catholic doctrine on which complete agreement or even at times convergence has eluded the Anglican–Roman Catholic Commission.

11 In fact, the Report itself acknowledges that there are such matters, and this is particularly true in respect of the Catholic dogma of Papal Infallibility, to which reference has just been made. In the section *Authority in the Church II*, it is stated that 'In spite of our agreement over the need for a universal primacy in a united Church, Anglicans do not accept the guaranteed possession of such a gift of divine assistance in judgement necessarily attached to the office of the bishop of Rome by virtue of which his formal decisions can be known to be wholly assured before their reception by the faithful' (para. 31).

12 The Final Report recalls the conditions set down for an infallible definition by the First Vatican Council, but goes on to give a different understanding of this question on the part of Catholics and Anglicans: 'When it is plain that all these conditions have been fulfilled, Roman Catholics conclude that the judgement is preserved from error and the proposition true. If the definition proposed for assent were not manifestly a legitimate interpretation of biblical faith and in line with orthodox tradition, Anglicans would think it a duty to reserve the reception of the definition for study and discussion' (Authority II, para. 29).

13 Similarly, the Commission has not been able to record any real consensus on the Marian dogmas. For while *Authority in the Church II*, para. 30, indicates that 'Anglicans and Roman Catholics can agree in much of the truth that the dogmas of the Immaculate Conception and Assumption are designed to affirm', under the same heading it is stated: 'The dogmas of the Immaculate Conception and the Assumption raise a special problem for those Anglicans who do not consider that the precise definitions given by these dogmas are sufficiently supported by Scripture. For many Anglicans the teaching authority of the bishop of Rome, independent of a council, is not recommended by the fact that through it these Marian doctrines were proclaimed as dogmas binding on all the faithful. Anglicans would also ask whether, in any future union between our two Churches, they would be required to subscribe to such dogmatic statements'.

14 This statement and several others in the Final Report illustrate the need for much further study to be done in respect of the petrine ministry in the Church. The following quotations from the Final Report, while reflecting the more positive approach of Anglicans in recent times in this connection, also

illustrate the reservations that still exist on the part of the Anglican community:

> Much Anglican objection has been directed against the manner of the exercise and particular claims of the Roman primacy rather than against universal primacy as such (Authority: *Elucidation*, para. 8).

> Relations between our two communions in the past have not encouraged reflection by Anglicans on the positive significance of the Roman primacy in the life of the universal Church. Nonetheless, from time to time Anglican theologians have affirmed that, in changed circumstances, it might be possible for the churches of the Anglican Communion to recognize the development of the Roman primacy as a gift of divine providence – in other words, as an effect of the guidance of the Holy Spirit in the Church (Authority II, para. 13).

> In spite of our agreement over the need for a universal primacy in a united Church, Anglicans do not accept the guaranteed possession of such a gift of divine assistance in judgement necessarily attached to the office of the bishop of Rome by virtue of which his formal decisions can be known to be wholly assured before their reception by the faithful (Authority II, para. 31).

15 With regard to the magisterial authority of the Church, there is a very positive presentation in *Authority in the Church II*, paras. 24–7. We read in fact that 'at certain moments the Church can in a matter of essential doctrine make a decisive judgement which becomes part of its permanent witness. . . . The purpose of this service cannot be to add to the content of revelation, but to recall and emphasize some important truth'. A clear statement is made, moreover, in *Authority in the Church: Elucidation*, para. 3, to the effect that reception of a defined truth by the People of God 'does not create truth nor legitimize the decision'. But as has just been noted with regard to the primacy, it would seem that elsewhere the Final Report sees the 'assent of the faithful' as required for the recognition that a doctrinal decision of the Pope or of an Ecumenical Council is immune from error (Authority II, paras. 27 and 31). For the Catholic Church, the certain knowledge of any defined truth is not guaranteed by the reception of the faithful that

such is in conformity with Scripture and Tradition, but by the authoritative definition itself on the part of the authentic teachers.

16 Dealing with the authority of the Ecumenical Councils (Authority II, para. 3), ARCIC I describes the scope of doctrinal definitions by the Councils as being concerned with 'fundamental doctrines' or 'central truths of salvation'. The Catholic Church believes that the Councils or the Pope, even when acting alone, are able to teach, if necessary in a definitive way, within the range of all truth revealed by God.

17 A further point of difficulty emerges in the position taken regarding the relationship of the ecclesial character of a Christian community and its incorporation into Catholic communion through union with the See of Rome. With references to *Lumen Gentium* no. 8 and *Unitatis Redintegratio* no. 13, which are not fully accurate, the Report states: 'The Second Vatican Council allows it to be said that a church out of communion with the Roman see may lack nothing from the viewpoint of the Roman Catholic Church except that it does not belong to the visible manifestation of full Christian communion which is maintained in the Roman Catholic Church' (Authority II, para. 12). It is the teaching of the Second Vatican Council that a church outside of communion with the Roman Pontiff lacks more than just the visible manifestation of unity with the Church of Christ which subsists in the Roman Catholic Church.

18 The manner in which ARCIC I writes in respect of the role of Peter among the twelve – 'a special position' (Authority II, para. 3), 'a position of special importance' (Authority II, para. 5) – does not express the fullness of the Catholic faith in this regard. The dogmatic definition of the First Vatican Council declares that the primacy of the Bishop of Rome belongs to the divine structure of the Church; the Bishop of Rome inherits the primacy from Peter who received it 'immediately and directly' from Christ (DS 3055; cf. *Lumen Gentium* no. 22). From a Catholic viewpoint, it is not possible then to accept the interpretation given in *Authority in the Church II* concerning the *Jus divinum* of the First Vatican Council, namely that it 'need not be taken to imply that the universal primacy as a permanent institution was directly founded by Jesus during his life on earth' (para. 11). The Catholic Church sees rather in the primacy of the successors of Peter something positively

intended by God and deriving from the will and institution of Jesus Christ.

19 As is obvious, despite considerable convergence in this regard, full agreement on the nature and the significance of the Roman primacy has not been reached. As Pope John Paul II pointed out during his visit to the World Council of Churches on June 12, 1984, the petrine ministry must be discussed 'in all frankness and friendship', because of the importance of this from the Catholic point of view and the difficulty that it poses for other Christians.

20 It is clear, as already affirmed, that on the questions of Eucharist and the Ordained Ministry, greater progress has been made. There are, however, certain statements and formulations in respect of these doctrines that would need greater clarification from the Catholic point of view.

21 With regard to the Eucharist the faith of the Catholic Church would be even more clearly reflected in the Final Report if the following points were to be explicitly affirmed:

> that in the Eucharist, the Church, doing what Christ commanded his Apostles to do at the Last Supper, makes present the sacrifice of Calvary. This would complete, without contradicting it, the statement made in the Final Report, affirming that the Eucharist does not repeat the sacrifice of Christ, nor add to it (Eucharistic Doctrine, para. 5, *Elucidation*, para. 5);

> that the sacrifice of Christ is made present with all its effects, thus affirming the propitiatory nature of the eucharistic sacrifice, which can be applied also to the deceased. For Catholics 'the whole Church' must include the dead. The prayer for the dead is to be found in all the Canons of the Mass, and the propitiatory character of the Mass as the sacrifice of Christ that may be offered for the living and the dead, including a particular dead person, is part of the Catholic faith.

22 The affirmations that the Eucharist is 'the Lord's real gift of himself to his Church' (Eucharistic Doctrine, para. 8) and that the bread and wine 'become' the body and blood of Christ (Eucharistic Doctrine: *Elucidation*, para. 6) can certainly be interpreted in conformity with Catholic faith. They are insufficient, however, to remove all ambiguity regarding the mode of the real presence which is due to a substantial change in the

elements. The Catholic Church holds that Christ in the Eucharist makes himself present sacramentally and substantially when under the species of bread and wine these earthly realities are changed into the reality of his Body and Blood, Soul and Divinity.

23 On the question of the reservation of the Eucharist, the statement that there are those who 'find any kind of adoration of Christ in the reserved sacrament unacceptable' (Eucharistic Doctrine: *Elucidation*, para. 9), creates concern from the Roman Catholic point of view. This section of *Eucharistic Doctrine*: *Elucidation*, seeks to allay any such doubts, but one remains with the conviction that this is an area in which real consensus between Anglicans and Roman Catholics is lacking.

24 Similarly, in respect of the Ordained Ministry, the Final Report would be helped if the following were made clearer:

that only a validly ordained priest can be the minister who, in the person of Christ, brings into being the sacrament of the Eucharist. He not only recites the narrative of the institution of the Last Supper, pronouncing the words of consecration and imploring the Father to send the Holy Spirit to effect through them the transformation of the gifts, but in so doing offers sacramentally the redemptive sacrifice of Christ;

that it was Christ himself who instituted the sacrament of Orders as the rite which confers the priesthood of the New Covenant. This would complete the significant statement made in *Ministry and Ordination*, para. 13, that in the Eucharist the ordained minister 'is seen to stand in sacramental relation to what Christ himself did in offering his own sacrifice'. This clarification would seem all the more important in view of the fact that the ARCIC document does not refer to the *character* of priestly ordination which implies a configuration to the priesthood of Christ. The character of priestly ordination is central to the Catholic understanding of the distinction between the ministerial priesthood and the common priesthood of the baptized. It is moreover important for the recognition of Holy Orders as a sacrament instituted by Christ, and not therefore a simple ecclesiastical institution.

25 The Commission itself has, in *Ministry and Ordination*: *Elucidation*, para. 5, referred to the developments within the

Anglican Communion after the setting up of ARCIC I, in connection with the ordination of women. The Final Report states that the members of the Commission believe 'that the principles upon which its doctrinal agreement rests are not affected by such ordinations; for it was concerned with the origin and nature of the ordained ministry and not with the question who can or who cannot be ordained'. The view of the Catholic Church in this matter has been expressed in an exchange of correspondence with the Archbishop of Canterbury, in which it is made clear that the question of the subject of ordination is linked with the nature of the sacrament of Holy Orders. Differences in this connection must therefore affect the agreement reached on *Ministry and Ordination*.

26 The question of Apostolic Succession is not dealt with directly in the Final Report of ARCIC I, but it is referred to in *Ministry and Ordination*, para. 16, and in *Ministry and Ordination*: *Elucidation*, para. 4. The essential features of 'what is meant in our two traditions by ordination in the apostolic succession' are set down in *Ministry and Ordination*, para. 16, and the statement is made that 'because they [the ordaining bishops] are entrusted with the oversight of other churches, this participation in his ordination signifies that this new bishop and his church are within the communion of churches. Moreover, because they are representatives of their churches in fidelity to the teaching and mission of the apostles and are members of the episcopal college, their participation also ensures the historical continuity of this church with the apostolic Church and of its bishop with the original apostolic ministry'.

27 These statements stand in need of further clarification from the Catholic perspective. The Catholic Church recognizes in the apostolic succession both an unbroken line of episcopal ordination from Christ through the apostles down through the centuries to the bishops of today and an uninterrupted continuity in Christian doctrine from Christ to those today who teach in union with the College of Bishops and its head, the Successor of Peter. As *Lumen Gentium* 20 affirms, the unbroken lines of episcopal succession and apostolic teaching stand in causal relationship to each other: 'Among those various ministries which, as tradition witnesses, were exercised in the Church from the earliest times, the chief place belongs to the office of those who, appointed to the episcopate in a sequence running back to the beginning, are the ones who pass on the

apostolic seed. Thus, as Saint Irenaeus testifies, through those who were appointed bishops by the apostles, and through their successors down to our own time, the apostolic tradition is manifested and preserved throughout the world'. This question, then, lies at the very heart of the ecumenical discussion and touches vitally all the themes dealt with by ARCIC I: the reality of the Eucharist, the sacramentality of the ministerial priesthood, the nature of the Roman Primacy.

28 A final word seems necessary in relation to the attitude of the Final Report to the interpretation of Scripture in so far as the role of tradition is concerned. It is true that this subject was not treated specifically by the Commission, yet there are statements made which cannot be allowed to pass without comment in this reply. As is well known, the Catholic doctrine affirms that the historical–critical method is not sufficient for the interpretation of Scripture. Such interpretation cannot be separated from the living Tradition of the Church which receives the message of Scripture. The Final Report seems to ignore this when dealing with the interpretation of the petrine texts of the New Testament, for it states that they 'do not offer sufficient basis' on which to establish the primacy of the Bishop of Rome. In the same way, the Final Report introduces with reference to the infallible judgements of the Bishop of Rome the need for such decisions to be 'manifestly a legitimate interpretation of biblical faith and in line with orthodox tradition' (Authority II, para. 29).

29 Certainly, there is need, then, for further study concerning Scripture, Tradition, and the Magisterium and their interrelationship since, according to Catholic teaching, Christ has given to his Church full authority to continue, with the uninterrupted and efficacious assistance of the Holy Spirit, 'to preserve this word of God faithfully, explain it and make it more widely known' (*Dei Verbum*, 9–10).

Conclusion

30 The above observations are not intended in any way to diminish appreciation for the important work done by ARCIC I, but rather to illustrate areas within the matters dealt with by the Final Report about which further clarification or study is required before it can be said that the Statements made in the

Final Report correspond fully to Catholic doctrine on the Eucharist and on Ordained Ministry.

31 The quite remarkable progress that has been made in respect of Authority in the Church indicates just how essential this question is for the future of Roman Catholic–Anglican dialogue.

32 The value of any consensus reached in regard to other matters will to a large extent depend on the authority of the body which eventually endorses them.

33 The objection may be made that this reply does not sufficiently follow the ecumenical method, by which agreement is sought step by step, rather than in full agreement at the first attempt. It must, however, be remembered that the Roman Catholic Church was asked to give a clear answer to the question: are the agreements contained in this Report consonant with the faith of the Catholic Church? What was asked for was not a simple evaluation of an ecumenical study, but an official response as to the identity of the various statements with the faith of the Church.

34 It is sincerely hoped that this reply will contribute to the continued dialogue between Anglicans and Catholics in the spirit of the Common Declaration made between Pope John Paul II and Archbishop Robert Runcie during the visit of the latter to Rome in 1989. There it is stated: 'We here solemnly recommit ourselves and those we represent to the restoration of visible unity and full ecclesial communion in the confidence that to seek anything else would be to betray Our Lord's intention for the unity of his people'.*

* [The Response was originally published with unnumbered paragraphs. We have added them as they were published in *Catholic International* and *Origins* for convenience.]

11
Roman Catholic Bishops' Conference of England and Wales: Statement on the Roman Catholic Official Response (1991)

The Bishops of England and Wales welcome and have carefully studied the Response of the Holy See to the Final Report of ARCIC I, and reiterate their gratitude and support for the members of the International Commission. It is fully agreed that the Report represents a 'significant milestone' in Anglican–Catholic relations and in the ecumenical movement as a whole. Whilst in the words of the Response 'it is not yet possible to state that substantial agreement has been reached on all the questions studied by the Commission', we wish to record our appreciation of the remarkable convergence and agreement that have been achieved.

Clearly more work needs to be done, as ARCIC itself acknowledged. Clarifications are rightly asked for which touch all the three Statements, particularly regarding the subject of Authority where, indeed, the Commission did not claim 'substantial agreement'.

We note the encouragement given to the Commission by the present Holy Father in 1980 when he described its method as 'going behind the habit of thought and expression, born and nourished in enmity and controversy, to scrutinise *together* the great common treasure'.

The Response raises this question of 'ecumenical method' and we recognise that this is of great importance for the success of ecumenical dialogue. The ARCIC dialogue enables our two communities to question each other as to their belief with a view to achieving agreement at the level of faith. It is our conviction that these dialogues must be accompanied by an ever deepening communion of faith and life.

We commend the Response for careful study by all who are concerned with Anglican–Roman Catholic relations. As Bishops of England and Wales, we commit ourselves to continue the work for the restoration of full communion between the Roman Catholic Church and the Anglican Communion.

12
Comments of the Archbishop of Canterbury (George Carey) on the Official Roman Catholic Response (1991)

Today I have received from Cardinal Edward Cassidy of the Pontifical Council for Promoting Christian Unity, on behalf of His Holiness Pope John Paul II, the Response from the Roman Catholic Church to the Final Report of the Anglican–Roman Catholic International Commission of September 1981. It is now my intention to offer the Response to the churches of the Anglican Communion for study, reflection and comment along with this personal reflection.

Roman Catholics and Anglicans alike will appreciate that this Response is another significant step along the road towards the visible unity of the Church which is our Lord's will. The dialogue between our two Communions began in 1967 following a joint decision by Pope Paul VI and Archbishop Michael Ramsey during their meeting at Rome in March 1966. The succeeding years of serious dialogue have been a pilgrimage of repentance for the alienation of the past, of joy for the mutual rediscovery of our common heritage of faith and of thanksgiving for the progress made. In this journey together we have been sustained by the resolution expressed in the Report of the Joint Preparatory Commission and repeated in the Preface to the Final Report which called for: 'a resolve for a future in which our common aim would be the restoration of full organic unity'. This same resolve was echoed in the final words of the conclusion which talked of: 'high expectations that significant initiatives will be boldly undertaken to deepen our reconciliation and lead us forward in the quest for the full communion to which we have been committed, in obedience to God, from the beginning of our dialogue'.

I appreciate the care and the time taken in the formulation of this Response which is an indication of the seriousness with which the Roman Catholic Church regards the fruits of the first Anglican–Roman Catholic International Commission. I welcome the tone and warmth of the Response which affirms the very considerable agreement which has been achieved especially in the areas of the Eucharist and Ministry and on Ordination. The Response recognises that the degree of doctrinal unity that this represents is the bedrock for our mutual confidence that further progress is possible. For that reason the criticisms which are offered may be seen as a constructive evaluation by the Roman Catholic Church of the Final Report offered in a spirit of love. In that same spirit I offer a personal reflection on this Response.

Both Communions were asked the same question: 'Are the agreements contained in the Final Report consonant with the faith of the Roman Catholic Church/Anglican Communion?' At the 1988 Lambeth Conference it was my privilege to present the Final Report on behalf of the Primates and to move the related motion which was overwhelmingly carried. We recognised that not everything in the Report was expressed in the terms, language, thought-forms and even theology of the 39 Articles and the Book of Common Prayer. Nevertheless we believed that the documents on the Eucharist and on Ministry and Ordination were 'consonant' with the faith of the Church as expressed within the Anglican Communion. In the case of the Roman Catholic Response, however, the question to our two Communions appears to have been understood instead as asking: 'Is the Final Report *identical* with the teachings of the Roman Catholic Church?' The argument of the Response suggests that a difference in methodology may have led to this approach. If either Communion requires that the other conforms to its own theological formulations, further progress will be hazardous. Humility is required of both Communions so that, having distanced themselves from some of the more polarised language and theological formulations of the past, they may discover new possibilities through the Spirit of God. These possibilities remain open to us since the Response itself is part of a dialogue which must be continued and developed.

I am encouraged that the Roman Catholic Church like the Anglican Communion remains unreservedly committed to the pursuit of unity in faith and in common life.

13
An Extract from Pope John Paul II's Address to a Group of English Roman Catholic Bishops (1992)

There is one further aspect of your ministry to which I would briefly refer. It is the important question of ecumenism and the need to place the difficulties encountered along the path to Christian unity within the general context of changed and much improved ecumenical relations. A number of recent events, including the publication of the *Official Response to the ARCIC I Final Report,* have shown that it is possible to go to the heart of the serious differences between divided Christians and still persevere in a fraternal and progressive dialogue. The significance of the *Response* lies not only in its furtherance of the theological dialogue, important though this is, but especially in the fact that the Catholic Church and the Anglican

Communion are speaking to each other at the level of what may be called a truly ecclesial dialogue. It is precisely at this level that, eventually and with God's grace, substantial moves towards unity of faith and visible ecclesial unity will take place. The question of 'ecumenical method' should also be seen in this light. I look forward to the forthcoming visit of His Grace Archbishop Carey as an opportunity to discuss together the course which future discussion on ecumenical relations with the Anglican Communion might take.

Ecumenism of course is not solely a matter for the highest Church authorities. It also involves a dialogue of life at the level of exchanges and co-operation between believers at every level. It is heartening to know that such organizations as Churches Together in England, CYTUN in Wales and the Council of Churches for Britain and Ireland are producing good results. May God continue to inspire all Christians in England and Wales with sentiments of evangelical love, mutual trust and respect for one another, for the sake of an ever more effective witness to God's word and service of Christ's saving mission.

14
French Roman Catholic Episcopal Commission for Christian Unity: Concerning the Holy See's Response to the Final Report of ARCIC I (1992)

At the invitation of the Roman Secretariat for Unity, the French Episcopal Conference, along with others elsewhere, gave its opinion on the Final Report of ARCIC I, and took part

in the process of discernment by formulating some general
and specific remarks on the texts comprising the Final Report.
In the spring of 1985 our answer was published, along with
that of the English and Welsh bishops, a few months after it
was sent to Rome, in *Documentation catholique* (DC) 1902 (1–15
September, 1985), pp. 867–82.[1]

We have read in the same publication (2043 (2 February
1992), pp. 111–15) a reply which was sent together with a letter
from Cardinal Edward Idris Cassidy, the President of the
Pontifical Council for Promoting Christian Unity, addressed to
the current Co-Chairmen of ARCIC II. Among other things it
said:

> Over the past few years there has been wide consultation
> within the Catholic Church on this document and on the
> official response to be given in respect of its conclusions.
> The preparation of this response was finally entrusted by
> Pope John Paul II to the Congregation for the Doctrine of
> the Faith which had issued the first official Catholic reaction
> to the Report in 1982, and the Congregation has had a
> determining role in drawing up the formal reply which I am
> now forwarding to you.[2]

We regard ourselves as included under the phrase 'countries
where large communities of Catholics and Anglicans live along-
side one another' either permanently or seasonally. Bearing in
mind then the comments made by the English and Welsh bishops
and by ourselves in 1985, we wish to express our reactions to
the Holy See's recent Response, in the compilation of which
the Congregation for the Doctrine of the Faith has played a
'determining role'. We have an added reason for wishing to do
this because our Anglican–Roman Catholic committees in the
United Kingdom and France have published with the approval
of the episcopal conferences of the two countries a modest
joint publication entitled *Twinnings and Exchanges, Jumelages et
Echanges* (CTS, London, 1990).

---

[1] The English Text of the English and Welsh Response was published by
the Catholic Truth Society, London, 1985, and in *One in Christ*, 1985/2
(see Chapter 7); the English translation of the Response from France in
One in Christ, 1985/4.

[2] The English text is taken from *The Pontifical Council for Promoting
Christian Unity Information Service* (IS), 82 (1993/1), p. 47.

The General Evaluation and the Conclusion of the Holy See's Response

We were pleased to note the 'warm welcome' and the 'gratitude' which the Response of December 1991 expressed towards the members of ARCIC I and towards the 'points of convergence and even of agreement' which their efforts have achieved. We are glad to read that the Final Report 'constitutes a significant milestone' in Catholic–Anglican relations and also 'in the ecumenical movement as a whole'.

We note the wish expressed that the Report will 'serve as an impetus to further study', and the sincere hope that it will 'contribute to the continued dialogue between Anglicans and Roman Catholics in the spirit of the Common Declaration made between Pope John Paul II and Archbishop Robert Runcie' at Rome in 1989.

We regret however that the final Response seems to take no notice of the important comments expressed in 1985 in the replies of the Episcopal Conference of England and Wales and our own Conference, even if we too accompanied our remarks with the invitation to pass beyond the stages already reached of *substantial agreement* on the eucharist and ministry, *fundamental consensus* on authority in the Church and primacy, and *convergences* on the primacy and infallibility of the pope. These distinctions were made by the Final Report of ARCIC I, although the Holy See's Response seems to suspect the Commission of stating that 'substantial agreement has been reached on *all* the questions studied by the Commission'. The Final Report however laid no claim either to that or to a complete correspondence with Catholic doctrine, as the *Observations* of the Congregation for the Doctrine of the Faith, dated March 1982 and published on 5 May of the same year (cf. *Documentation catholique* 1830 (1982), pp. 507–14 and 531)[3] were quick to recall.

It is no business of ours to pass judgment on the final version published by the Holy See of its response to ARCIC I's final document, but we would like to express some observations on this 'definitive response to the results achieved by ARCIC I', because we are astonished at the demands for an identity of formulations in an age when we live in a society which has become conscious of its multicultural character.

---

[3] The English version of the *Observations* was published by the CTS, London, in 1982 (see Chapter 5).

*Can One Judge 'Results' without Reference
to the Objectives?*

In the *Common Declaration* of 24 March 1966, which is the foundation document of Catholic–Anglican dialogue, Pope Paul VI and Archbishop Ramsey declared their intention to 'inaugurate between the Roman Catholic Church and the Anglican Communion a serious dialogue . . . founded on the Gospels and on the ancient common traditions, . . . and to strive in common to find solutions for all the great problems that face those who believe in Christ in the world today' (DC 1469 (1966), cols. 681–4).[4] This led to the Malta Report of 3 January 1968, which defined the agenda for ARCIC I on eucharist, ministry and authority in the Church.

Towards the end of ARCIC I's work John Paul II confirmed the joint commission's mandate in the following terms:

> Your method has been to go behind the habit of thought and expression born and nourished in enmity and controversy, to scrutinise together the great common treasure, to clothe it in a language at once traditional and expressive of the insights of an age which no longer glories in strife but seeks to come together in listening to the quiet voice of the Spirit (Castelgandolfo, 4 September 1980).

In the same sense, Cardinal Josef Ratzinger has on several occasions, at least as early as 1976 (*Proche-Orient chrétien* 26 (1976), pp. 214–15), and again in *The Tablet* of 26 October 1991, stated what he wrote in 1982: 'Rome must not require more from the East with respect to the doctrine of primacy than had been formulated and was lived during the first millennium' (cf. *Principles of Catholic Theology*, Ignatius Press, San Francisco, 1987, p. 199). That does not amount, he added in reference to Anglicans, to 'the denial of the existence of the universal Church in the second millennium'.

Even with this important qualification, in assessing an understanding between Anglicans and Catholics who had been commissioned to found their dialogue on 'common traditions' and 'to scrutinise together the great common treasure', one cannot insist that the views expressed will be identical with the formulations of councils which took place after the separation without any participation on the Anglican side.

[4] Original English text in the Final Report (CTS/SPCK, London, 1982), p. 118 (see Chapter 3).

The Legitimate Terms of Reference
of Ecumenical Dialogue

In our French reply of 1985 (DC 1902 (1985), pp. 867-8)[5] we attempted to formulate these terms of reference as follows:

> We think that theological research is needed to clarify both the link with and the distance from the confessional documents of each Church which new convergence texts and ecumenical agreements have to maintain. Two approaches seem quite excluded: neither confession may demand from the other a literal adoption of official documents which were drawn up during the time of separation. This would *a priori* remove every possibility from the ecumenical dialogue undertaken. Secondly, neither Church can speak or take action today with full responsibility unless it verifies that what it is now saying is in harmony with what it judges to be irrevocable in its past attitudes. The special fruitfulness of the ecumenical dialogue is to bring to expression in a new and truly reconciled language all the aspects of the truth of faith which are contained in the traditions of each Church – aspects which have often been expressed from one-sided, polemical and ultimately negative viewpoints. Greater fidelity to the Gospel asks from each dialogue partner an attitude of conversion in the way it speaks, both in what it has said and in what it has not said.
>
> On the Catholic side we think this could be said: the Catholic Church owes it to itself as well as to its dialogue partners to sharpen up its conciliar and dogmatic hermeneutic, so as to avoid investing with irreformable character documents not intended to be used at that level. Whenever such an intention is clearly recognised, it is nowadays understood to refer to the positive sense of the decisions in question. However, the Catholic Church admits that the way in which some truths have been expressed was not only not the best way possible and remains open to improvement, on account of the inevitable historical and cultural conditioning in which it came about, but was also sometimes formulated from a one-sided view of the truth concerned, particularly as a result of the polemics of the time. It therefore needs to be integrated into a broader and better balanced problematic so as to become acceptable to our dialogue partners. The

[5] English translation in *One in Christ*, 1985/4, pp. 331-2.

ecumenical dialogue is a place in which the Catholic Church is seeking this fuller expression. Once it has recognised ecumenical 'agreed statements', they will constitute an officially valid interpretation of earlier documents. It is to this interpretation alone that our dialogue partners will be obliged to subscribe within the framework of rediscovered communion.[6]

The Unity of Faith and Expressions of Faith

The importance John XXIII attached to the directive which he formulated in his opening address at Vatican II is well known; he commented on it in his homily of 4 November 1962, for the feast of St Charles Borromeo, the fourth anniversary of his own enthronement as Bishop of Rome, and also in his reply to Cardinal Tisserant's address on 23 December 1962: '. . . authentic doctrine . . . should be studied and expounded through the methods of research and through the literary forms of modern thought. The substance of the ancient doctrine of the deposit of faith is one thing, and the way in which it is presented is another.'[7]

---

[6] Cf. *Mysterium Ecclesiae*, a Declaration of the Congregation for the Doctrine of the Faith, 24 June 1973 (*Vatican Council II: More Post Conciliar Documents*, ed. A. Flannery (Fowler Wright, Leominster, 1982), pp. 433–4):

> In view of the above, it must be stated that the dogmatic formulas of the Church's Magisterium were from the very beginning suitable for communicating revealed truth, and that as they are they remain for ever suitable for communicating this truth to those who interpret them correctly. It does not however follow that every one of the formulas has always been or will always be so to the same extent. For this reason theologians seek to define exactly the intention of teaching proper to the various formulas, and in carrying out this work they are of considerable assistance to the living Magisterium of the Church, to which they remain subordinated. For this reason also it often happens that ancient dogmatic formulas and others closely connected with them remain living and fruitful in the habitual usage of the Church, but with suitable expository and explanatory additions that maintain and clarify their original meaning. In addition, it has sometimes happened that in this habitual usage of the Church certain of these formulas gave way to new expressions which, proposed and approved by the sacred Magisterium, presented more clearly or more completely the same meaning.

[7] Translation taken from *The Documents of Vatican II*, ed. W. Abbott and J. Gallagher (Geoffrey Chapman, London, 1966), p. 715.

The Council was to echo the expression in its statement of the relationship between theology and culture: 'aliud est ipsum depositum Fidei seu veritates, aliud modus secundum quem enuntiantur' ('the deposit or truths of faith is one thing, and the manner in which they are expressed is another') (*Gaudium et Spes* 62.2). The Decree on Ecumenism states: 'si quae . . . in doctrinae enuntiandae modo – qui ab ipso deposito fidei sedulo distingui debet – minus accurate servata fuerint, opportuno tempore recte debiteque instaurentur' ('if . . . in the formulation of doctrine – which must be carefully distinguished from the deposit of faith itself – anything has been preserved that is not completely accurate, it should be appropriately rectified at the proper moment') (*Unitatis Redintegratio* 6). Moreover section 17 of the same decree was to repeat the same statement explicitly in claiming a legitimate diversity in the 'theological formulation of doctrines' with regard to the East and the West.

Pope Paul VI, on his first visit to Constantinople to meet Patriarch Athenagoras I at the Phanar on 25 July 1967, recalled in this connection three important events of the fourth and fifth centuries which reveal the primacy which unity of faith was granted over expressions of faith:

> In the light of our love for Christ and of our brotherly love, we perceive even more clearly the profound identity of our faith, and the points on which we still differ must not prevent us from seeing this profound unity. And here, too, charity must come to our aid, as it helped Hilary and Athanasius to recognize the sameness of the faith underlying the differences of the vocabulary at a time when serious disagreements were creating divisions among Christian bishops. Did not pastoral love prompt St Basil, in his defence of the true faith in the Holy Spirit, to refrain from using certain terms which, accurate though they were, could have given rise to scandal in one part of the Christian people? And did not St Cyril of Alexandria consent in 433 to abandon his beautiful formulation of theology in the interests of making peace with John of Antioch, once he had satisfied himself that in spite of divergent modes of expression, the faith was identical? (*Tomos Agapis* no. 46 (172)) (English text in IS (1967/3), p. 10).

Some years later Paul VI, and then John Paul II, signed common christological professions of faith, avoiding the use of the

Chalcedonian formula of the two natures, with the Syrian Orthodox Patriarch of Antioch (DC 1600 (1972), p. 48), with the Coptic Pope Shenouda III (DC 1633 (1973), pp. 510–16), and with the new Syrian Patriarch of Antioch Zakka I Iwas (DC 1880 (1984), pp. 822–6).[8]

Following the 1974 Synod of Bishops on evangelisation, Paul VI stated in *Evangelii Nuntiandi* 63: 'The individual Churches . . . have the task of assimilating the essence of the Gospel message and of transposing it, without the slightest betrayal of its essential truth, into the language that these particular people understand, then of proclaiming it in this language. The transposition has to be done with the discernment, seriousness, respect and competence which the matter calls for in the field of liturgical expression, and in the areas of catechesis, theological formulation, secondary ecclesial structures, and ministries. And the word "language" should be understood here less in the semantic or literary sense than in the sense which one may call anthropological and cultural.'

It was in the light of these acts and declarations of the Council and the Successor of Peter that our Episcopal Conference and, we believe, the Episcopal Conference of England and Wales expressed in 1982 their evaluation and their remarks, both critical and constructive, on the Final Report on ARCIC I. We do not find the same climate in the Explanatory Note of the Holy See's Response of 1991.

It seems to us that, for the authors of the Response, conformity to the faith means to express oneself in terms which are identical with the expressions of faith of the Catholic Church as they have been formulated after the Councils of Trent and Vatican I. In saying this, we have in mind the Response's comments on 'propitiatory sacrifice', 'substantial change', the phrase '*subsistit in*' as used in *Lumen Gentium* 8 and *Unitatis Redintegratio* 4, the 'priestly character', etc.

In our opinion the synthesis of eucharistic theology given by the instruction *Eucharisticum Mysterium* of 25 May 1967, John Paul II's letter for Maundy Thursday 1980, and the theological document of the Lourdes International Congress of 1981, *Jesus Christ, bread broken for a new world*, translate Catholic eucharistic doctrine more ecumenically than the argument contained in the Response to ARCIC I's Final Report.

[8] English versions of these three professions of faith are given in IS, 16 (1972), p. 5; 22 (1973), p. 9; 55 (1984), pp. 61–3.

Cardinal Willebrands's address on 'The meaning of "*subsistit in*" in the ecclesiology of communion' seems to us to take the fundamental choices of Vatican II into account better than the references made to the expression in the Response and better than certain interpretations offered by minimalist theologians.[9]

We agree unreservedly with the words of the Episcopal Conference of England and Wales in 1985:

> In making this response we are conscious that as the Bishops of England and Wales we bear a special responsibility in this process of consultation which is taking place throughout the universal Church. . . . Our Response will have particular significance in the continuation of this dialogue between our two Communions, especially in this land in which the Anglican Communion finds its centre and where good relations between the churches have become a matter of common experience. We commend the Final Report as a truly outstanding contribution to this dialogue, and we readily uphold the process undertaken by the Commission as an example of what can be achieved by joint study and of how these studies can be a practical basis for growth in unity.[10]

We are in total agreement, too, with the Conference of England and Wales when, after referring to ARCIC I's methodology, which John Paul II had praised in his address at Castelgandolfo on 4 September 1980 which we have quoted above, they added:

> We too welcome the emergence of this methodology. It is characterised by a joint endeavour to explore our 'common tradition', and achieves an understanding of the context in which concepts arose, how this coloured their meaning and what remains open to further development. It brings about a shared understanding of revelation as expressed in historically conditioned formulae. We commend this methodology, as entailing a serious attempt to develop patterns of thought

[9] The French version of Cardinal Willebrands's speech is contained in DC 1953 (1988), pp. 35–41. The English text is printed in *Origins*, 17/2, 28 May 1987, pp. 27–33.

[10] English text in the Bishops' Conference of England and Wales, *Response to the Final Report of ARCIC I* (CTS and Catholic Media Office, London, 1985), n. 3; also in *One in Christ*, 1985/2 (see Chapter 7).

and language which give profound and precise expression to our shared faith (cf. *Unitatis Redintegratio* 11).[11]

Ecumenical Method, Dysfunction and Suspended Questions

The Holy See's Response shows awareness of the fact that its method could provoke comment. In its Conclusion, it remarks: 'The objection may be made that this reply does not sufficiently follow the ecumenical method, by which agreement is sought step by step, rather than in full agreement at the first attempt.'[12] It seems to us, however, that there are other comments that can be made regarding this 'definitive Response'.

We would like to propose three:

1 *The relationship between episcopal conferences and the Congregation for the Doctrine of the Faith.*

At the time of the publication of ARCIC I's Final Report, before the episcopal conferences and their doctrinal commissions could make any study of the document, the Congregation saw fit to send to the presidents of episcopal conferences and to publish for the faithful its markedly one-sided *Observations*, expressing 'the hope that the bishops will be willing to give them careful consideration' (letter of 2 April 1982).

The account we have given of the replies made by the French and English episcopal conferences to the Vatican department which then went by the name of 'Secretariat for Christian Unity' suffices to show that the episcopates most directly concerned were unable to adopt the observations which had been publicly sent to them. The 'definitive Response' which has recently appeared, ten years after ARCIC I's Final Report was sent to Rome, seems completely to ignore the replies of the episcopal conferences which have been made public. Is this a healthy exercise of the collegiality and the ecclesiology of communion which form 'the central and fundamental concept' of Vatican II?

2 *The relations between the Pontifical Council for the Promotion of Christian Unity and the Congregation for the Doctrine of the Faith.*

In an official letter to the Co-Chairmen of ARCIC II dated 13 July 1985, Cardinal Willebrands, the then President of the Secretariat for Christian Unity, wrote:

[11] *Response to the Final Report of ARCIC I*, n. 7 [chap. 7].
[12] IS, 82/1 (1993), p. 51 [chap 10].

We look forward to the voicing of the consensus of the Anglican Communion when the bishops of that Communion gather for the Lambeth Conference in 1988. . . . If at the end of this process of evaluation the Anglican Communion as such is able to state formally that it professes the same faith . . . concerning the Eucharist and the Ordained Ministry, the Roman Catholic Church would acknowledge the possibility that in the context of such a profession of faith the texts of the Ordinal might no longer retain that *'nativa indoles'* [native character] which was at the basis of Pope Leo [XIII]'s judgment. . . . In that case such a profession of faith could open the way to a new consideration of the Ordinal . . . a consideration which could lead to a new evaluation by the Catholic Church of the sufficiency of these Anglican rites as far as concerns future ordinations.[13]

On 6 August 1988, Dr Runcie, who as Archbishop of Canterbury presided over the Lambeth Conference comprising the bishops of the twenty-nine provinces of the Anglican Communion, in a letter addressed to the Holy Father stated clearly:

The Conference went on to consider the responses of 23 autonomous Provinces to the Final Report of . . . ARCIC I. One of the most important tasks of the Conference was to pronounce the consensus of the Anglican Communion on the Agreed Statements of the dialogue established by our predecessors in 1966. The Bishops, by a very large majority, recognized the ARCIC Agreed Statements on the eucharist and the ordained ministry as 'consonant in substance with the faith of Anglicans'. On authority the Agreed Statements were welcomed as a 'firm basis' for the future dialogue.[14]

The Lambeth resolution also affirmed that 'this agreement offers a sufficient basis for taking the next step forward towards the reconciliation of our Churches grounded in agreement of faith'.[15]

---

[13] English text in *Anglican Orders–a New Context* (CTS, London, 1986).
[14] English text in IS, 70 (1989/2), p. 60.
[15] The original text is printed in *The Truth Shall make you Free: The Lambeth Conference 1988, The Reports, Resolutions and Pastoral Letters from the Bishops* (Anglican Consultative Council, London, 1988), p. 210.

Replying to this letter on 8 December 1988, the Holy Father observed:

> I would first of all acknowledge the signs of openness to fuller communion with the Catholic Church which were evident at several points in the [Lambeth] Conference, not least in your opening address and in the resolutions on the Final Report of ARCIC I. At the same time . . . the Lambeth Conference's treatment of the question of women's ordination has created a new and perplexing situation for the members of the Second Anglican/Roman Catholic International Commission to whom, in 1982, we gave the mandate of studying 'all that hinders the mutual recognition of the ministries of our Communions'. The ordination of women to the priesthood . . . appears to pre-empt this study and effectively block the path to the mutual recognition of ministries. . . . It would seem that the discussion of women's ordination in the Anglican Communion has not taken sufficiently into account the ecumenical and ecclesiological dimensions of the question. . . . It is urgent that this aspect be given much greater attention in order to prevent a serious erosion of the degree of communion between us.[16]

Thus the problem of re-establishing communion between Catholics and Anglicans is complex, but why does the Holy See's 'definitive Response' make no mention of these two major contributions to the difficult journey, namely the letter of the President of the Secretariat for Unity, and the Lambeth Conference's resolution on the eucharist and ordained ministry?

The Apostolic Constitution *Pastor Bonus* (28 June 1988) made provision for the role of the Congregation for the Doctrine of the Faith (nn. 48–54) and the functions of the Pontifical Council for the Promotion of the Unity of Christians (nn. 135–8) (DC 1969 (1988), p. 908; 1970 (1988), p. 975). The two departments came together for a joint session from 30 January to 1 February 1989. Addressing them on 1 February, John Paul II made the following statement:

> Each of the two Departments has its own specific area of competence. . . . Therefore, collaboration between these two Departments is necessary every time the matter in hand requires it. Indeed, there must be perfect harmony of effort

---

[16] English text in IS, 70 (1989/2), p. 60.

every time ecumenical dialogue takes up doctrinal questions, and every time subjects having an ecumenical implication are treated within the Catholic Church.[17]

Why is it necessary to give episcopal conferences the impression that there is a one-way traffic in collaboration and harmony?

3 *The official statements of the Holy Father and the documents of the Congregation for the Doctrine of the Faith.*

Paul VI and John Paul II have made many declarations and interventions, and taken many initiatives, to promote, encourage and stimulate the Catholic Church's progress towards the visible unity of Christians, and all of them tend in the same direction. 'Irreversible', 'inescapable demand', 'pastoral priority'. . . . One could quote a wealth of similar expressions used by the Holy Father in the most official documents, on his apostolic journeys, and in audiences given to all the churches and Christian communities.

The slow pace of the magisterial acts of 'reception' of the innumerable ecumenical statements of agreement, consensus or convergence and the reservations which accompany the acts of reciprocal recognition sometimes cause us to doubt the ecumenical openness and commitment which John Paul II emphatically reaffirmed to the Roman Curia on 28 June 1985:

> I must reaffirm that the Catholic Church is committed to the ecumenical movement with an irrevocable decision, and it desires to contribute to it with all its possibilities. For me, the Bishop of Rome, that constitutes one of the pastoral priorities. It is an obligation which I have to carry out in a particular way, precisely by virtue of the pastoral responsibility which pertains to me. This movement is stirred by the Holy Spirit, and I consider myself to be profoundly responsible in its regard.[18]

Moreover, we wish the last paragraph of the Conclusion of the Holy See's Response to ARCIC I's Final Report to carry its full force:

> It is sincerely hoped that this reply will contribute to the continued dialogue between Anglicans and Catholics in the

---

[17] English text in IS, 70 (1989/2), p. 57.
[18] English text in IS, 59 (1985/3–4), pp. 5–6.

spirit of the Common Declaration made between Pope John
Paul II and Archbishop Robert Runcie during the visit of the
latter to Rome in 1989. There it is stated: 'We here solemnly
recommit ourselves and those we represent to the restoration of visible unity and full ecclesial communion in the
confidence that to seek anything else would be to betray
Our Lord's intention for the unity of his people.'[19]

15

An Extract from an Account of a Meeting between Pope John Paul II and the Archbishop of Canterbury (George Carey) (1992)

On 25 May 1992 the Archbishop of Canterbury, the Most Revd
George Leonard Carey, was welcomed by Pope John Paul II in
the Biblioteca Privata for their first meeting.

In visiting the Holy See, Archbishop Carey followed in the
footsteps of his four immediate predecessors. Especially important was the visit of Archbishop Michael Ramsey to Pope Paul
VI in 1966, which marked a decisive turning point in Anglican–
Roman Catholic relations. It was at that meeting that the
Anglican–Roman Catholic International Commission (ARCIC)
was founded. The last visit of an Archbishop of Canterbury to
the Pope was in October 1989 when Archbishop Robert Runcie
returned the visit made to Canterbury by the Pope John Paul II
in 1982.

---

[19] English text in IS, 82 (1993/1), p. 51.

The Pope and the Archbishop of Canterbury stressed their commitment to the search for fuller communion between Anglicans and Roman Catholics that was first made in 1966 by Pope Paul VI and Archbishop Ramsey. In that context they also spoke together of some of the complex and exacting issues that figure in the present dialogue between the Catholic Church and the Anglican Communion.

ARCIC I

The Holy Father and the Archbishop spoke about the Catholic response to the Final Report of ARCIC I. The Archbishop was assured by the Holy Father that although the response was not able to endorse the claim of ARCIC I to have reached *substantial agreement* between Anglicans and Roman Catholics on the Eucharist and the Ordained Ministry, that judgment should not be interpreted as putting a brake on the dialogue. Rather, the response which described the Final Report as a 'milestone' in Anglican–Roman Catholic relations should be seen as a stimulus to the resolution of outstanding differences.

Pope John Paul II and Archbishop Carey emphasised their commitment to the process of dialogue which is to be pursued both at the theological level and in the framework of exchanges and cooperation between the believers at all levels.

The Pope and the Archbishop spoke of the question of the ordination of women to the priesthood. The Archbishop expressed his conviction that this development is a possible and proper development of the doctrine of the ordained ministry. The Holy Father reiterated what has already been said to Archbishop Carey's predecessors, that this development constitutes a decision which the Church does not see itself entitled to authorise, and which constitutes a grave obstacle to the whole process of Anglican–Roman Catholic reconciliation. It was agreed, however, that there must be further study of the ecclesial and ecumenical aspects of this question.

16
Anglican–Roman Catholic Consultation in the United States: Agreed Statement on the Lambeth and Vatican Responses to ARCIC I (1992)

Introduction

1 With the issuance of the Anglican–Roman Catholic International Commission's Final Report in 1982, a new context was established for Anglican–Roman Catholic dialogue, a context shaped in large measure by the invitation for response and reception that accompanied the Final Report. Now that responses have been given by both churches, the context has changed again. We of ARC-USA understand this context to be one of continuing study and reception, which we look forward to with hope that further clarifications of the issues addressed by this dialogue at every level will deepen the unity that we already share and bring us closer to that full unity that the Lord intends for his people.

2 In this country, our two churches have been in productive dialogue since 1965. During that time, ARC-USA has issued eight major documents and four texts that were reactions to three Agreed Statements of ARCIC.[1] It is from this experience that we face the new context. While looking forward in hope, we also recognize among ourselves a range of assessments concerning the import and implications of the two churches' responses to the Final Report. Nevertheless, we find ourselves both encouraged and challenged by this new context, and we

---

[1] George Tavard, a member of both ARCIC I and ARC-USA from the beginning, has written a helpful historical reflection on ARC-USA's work. We look forward to its publication soon.

hope to stir up in the members of our churches the same sense of encouragement and challenge.

3 Therefore, in this document we will indicate a number of points in the responses that we find both significant and of concern, and we will set forth our own understanding of the path forward in this new context.

Status of the Responses

4 On March 24, 1966, Pope Paul VI and Archbishop of Canterbury Michael Ramsey met in Rome and signed a Common Agreement, declaring their intention 'to inaugurate between the Roman Catholic Church and the Anglican Communion a serious dialogue which, founded on the Gospels and on the ancient common traditions, may lead to that unity in truth, for which Christ prayed.'[2] Following the 1968 Malta Report of the Joint Preparatory Commission, the Anglican–Roman Catholic International Commission (ARCIC I) met for the first time in 1970. In 1982, ARCIC I issued its Final Report, which includes three Agreed Statements, two *Elucidations*, a further Statement on *Authority in the Church*, and an introduction to the Church as *koinonia*.

5 In issuing the Final Report, ARCIC I hoped to help 'begin a process of extensive prayer, reflection, and study that will represent a marked advance towards the goal of organic union between the Roman Catholic Church and the Anglican Communion.'[3]

6 Even as ARCIC II began its work on salvation and the nature of the Church, the Anglican Communion and Roman Catholic Church each began its own process of study and response to the Final Report of ARCIC I.

---

[2] The Common Declaration by Pope Paul VI and the Archbishop of Canterbury, March 24, 1966, in *Called to Full Unity: Documents on Anglican–Roman Catholic Relations 1966–1983*, ed. Joseph W. Witmer and J. Robert Wright (United States Catholic Conference, Washington, 1986), p. 3.

[3] Herbert J. Ryan, 'Foreword to the American Edition,' Anglican–Roman Catholic International Commission, *The Final Report* (Forward Movement Press/United States Catholic Conference, Cincinnati/Washington, 1982), p. vi.

7 In the Anglican Communion, in preparation for the Lambeth Conference of 1988, the Anglican Consultative Council[4] asked each Province to consider

> Whether the Agreed Statements on Eucharistic Doctrine, Ministry and Ordination, and Authority in the Church (I and II), together with Elucidations, are consonant in substance with the faith of Anglicans and whether the Final Report offers a sufficient basis for taking the next concrete step towards the reconciliation of our Churches grounded in agreement in faith.[5]

The formal synodical responses of 19 out of 29 Provinces were summarized and discussed in the *Emmaus Report*, issued in 1987. The Lambeth Conference, meeting the next year, responded to the Final Report by a resolution in which the Conference

> Recognizes the Agreed Statements of ARCIC I on *Eucharistic Doctrine, Ministry and Ordination*, and their *Elucidations*, as consonant in substance with the faith of Anglicans and believes that this agreement offers a sufficient basis for taking the next step forward. . . . Welcomes *Authority in the Church (I* and *II)* together with the *Elucidation*, as a firm basis for the direction and agenda of the continuing dialogue on authority . . .[6]

8 We note here that the authority of the Lambeth Response for Anglicans is not entirely clear. This point arises out of a statement printed in the 1988 Lambeth Conference proceedings (p. 9, n. 1). This statement, which is similar to statements found in Lambeth proceedings since 1888, says that 'Resolutions passed by a Lambeth Conference do not have legislative authority in any Province, until they have been approved by the provincial synod of the Province.' At the same time, however, the *Emmaus Report* emphasizes that, 'Though there can be no question of a legislative or juridical decision, there are moments when the Lambeth Conferences have discerned,

---

[4] The Anglican Consultative Council was created after the 1968 Lambeth Conference to provide Communion-wide continuity of consultation and guidance on policy; it has neither legislative nor jurisdictional powers.

[5] *Emmaus Report: A Report of the Anglican Ecumenical Consultation* (Forward Movement Press, Cincinnati, 1987 [Church House Publishing, 1987]), p. 44.

[6] Resolution 8, The Lambeth Conference 1988, published in *The Truth Shall Make You Free* (Church House Publishing, London, 1988), pp. 210–12 [chap. 9].

articulated and formed the common mind of the Anglican Communion on important matters of faith and morals. . . . In the end the bishops have a special responsibility for guarding and promoting the apostolic faith, a responsibility which is theirs by ordination and office.'[7] The Lambeth Conference of 1988 did recognize 'the Agreed Statements of ARCIC I on *Eucharistic Doctrine, Ministry and Ordination,* and their *Elucidations,* as consonant in substance with the faith of Anglicans and believes that this agreement offers a sufficient basis for taking the next step forward towards the reconciliation of our Churches grounded in agreement in faith.'[8]

9 The December 1991 document from the Vatican is the official response of the Roman Catholic Church to the Final Report. It is described as 'the fruit of close collaboration between the Congregation for the Doctrine of the Faith and the Pontifical Council for Promoting Christian Unity.'[9] Since the Apostolic Constitution of 1988, *Pastor Bonus,* the Congregation for the Doctrine of the Faith has had final responsibility in matters of faith and doctrine.

10 When the Final Report was issued in 1982, Cardinal Willebrands, then president of the Secretariat for Promoting Christian Unity, also asked Roman Catholic episcopal conferences to evaluate the Final Report. He asked for careful study and considered judgment, and requested that the replies of the conference address the question of 'whether it [the Final Report] is consonant in substance with the faith of the Catholic Church concerning matters discussed.'[10]

11 Since a number of these evaluations were never published and none is cited in the Vatican Response, it is hard to determine how much influence these evaluations had on the December 1991 text. The Vatican Response, however, would still be the official position of the Roman Catholic Church concerning the Final Report,[11] even in the unlikely case that the conference evaluations were not used at all.

---

7 *Emmaus Report,* p. 73, cf. Lambeth Conference 1978. Resolution 13.
8 Lambeth Conference 1988, Resolution 8.
9 Vatican Response to ARCIC Final Report in *Origins,* vol. 21, p. 443.
10 US National Conference of Catholic Bishops, *Evaluation of the ARCIC Final Report,* published in *Origins,* vol. 14, p. 409.
11 Report of the Catholic Theological Society of America Committee on the Profession of Faith and the Oath of Fidelity, April 15, 1990, pp. 51–2.

12 Where the Lambeth Response found 'consonance in substance on the Eucharist and Ministry and Ordination,' the
Vatican Response judged 'that it is not yet possible to state that
substantial agreement has been reached on all the questions
studied' by ARCIC I, athough the Vatican Response considers
the Final Report a 'significant milestone not only in relations
between the Catholic Church and the Anglican Communion
but in the ecumenical movement as a whole.'[12]

13 ARCIC I itself claimed only 'a high degree of agreement'
on authority. With this, both the Lambeth Response and the
Vatican Response seem to concur. Lambeth found ARCIC I's
Authority in the Church I and *II*, together with the *Elucidation*, 'a
firm basis for the direction and continuing dialogue on authority,'[13] while the Vatican said that 'the most that has been
achieved is a certain convergence, which is but a first step
along the path that seeks consensus as a prelude to unity.'[14]

14 The Vatican Response does not close off discussion of the
issues in the Final Report. On the contrary, it encourages
further study and clarification (cf. para. 30). Its authors hope
that the Response itself will contribute to the dialogue that is
leading to '"the restoration of visible unity and full ecclesial
communion"' (para. 34).

15 Accordingly, the Final Report constitutes both resource
and agenda in the Anglican–Roman Catholic relationship.
Together with the responses to it, the Final Report clarifies
certain questions and poses certain challenges that seem to
mark where the next steps must be taken in our journey
together.

The Search for a Common Language

16 ARCIC I's method was to engage in serious dialogue on
'persisting historical differences' in order to contribute to the
'growing together' of the two churches (Preface). Therefore,
ARCIC I was

> concerned, not to evade the difficulties, but rather to avoid
> the controversial language in which they have often been

[12] *Origins*, vol. 21, p. 441.
[13] See note 6.
[14] *Origins*, vol. 21, p. 443.

discussed. We have taken seriously the issues that have divided us, and have sought solutions by re-examining our common inheritance, particularly the Scriptures (Introduction, para. 3).

This method was approvingly summarized by John Paul II in his address to the Commission:

> Your method has been to go behind the habit of thought and expression born and nourished in enmity and controversy, to scrutinize together the great common treasure, to clothe it in a language at once traditional and expressive of the insights of an age which no longer glories in strife but seeks to come together in listening to the quiet voice of the Spirit.[15]

17 The Vatican Response, however, does not allude to ARCIC I's method. It perceives ambiguities in the language of the Final Report. Thus, it calls for certain clarifications to ensure that 'affirmations are understood in a way that conforms to Catholic doctrine [of the Eucharist]' (para. 6). Likewise, it calls for clarification of statements on ordained ministry in the Final Report. The Vatican Response seems to urge that clarification be given through the use of language that is closer to and even identical with traditional Roman Catholic theological formulations. (For example, the Response identifies a number of points it would like to have 'explicitly affirmed.' One of these is 'the propitiatory character of the Mass as the sacrifice of Christ.' The Response also asks that clarification be given on a number of matters, and cites 'the fact that the ARCIC document does not refer to the character of priestly ordination which implies a configuration to the priesthood of Christ.')[16]

18 If an Agreed Statement does not employ the traditional language of one or both churches, does it thereby fail to express adequately the faith of those churches? Some commentators have pointed to the obstacle to ecumenical progress created by one church's demanding adherence to its own formulation. It seems to us that the Vatican Response calls us to more painstaking study of the criteria by which each church should evaluate the language of Agreed Statements.

---

[15] *One in Christ* 16, 341.
[16] Vatican Response in *Origins*, vol. 21, p. 445.

The Issue of Substantial Agreement

19 The use of phrases such as *substantial agreement, substantial identity,* and *consonant in substance* in the Final Report and in the Vatican Response to it has been widely criticized as ambiguous. *Substantial* and *in substance* can mean either 'in very large part' or 'fundamental, basic.' In addition, the term *substantial* carries overtones from various historical theological controversies and from its use in scholastic theology.

20 The Resolution that makes up the brief Lambeth Response to ARCIC I 'Recognizes the Agreed Statements of ARCIC I on *Eucharistic Doctrine, Ministry and Ordination,* and their *Elucidations,* as consonant in substance with the faith of Anglicans . . .'[17] In formulating this reply, the Lambeth Response seems to have taken 'consonance in substance' in a broader sense as meaning something like 'compatibility.' Thus, while the overall evaluation of the Lambeth Conference was positive, it also reported 'continuing anxieties' regarding Eucharistic sacrifice and presence as well as, on *Ministry and Ordination,* requests 'for a clarification of "priesthood."' As E. J. Yarnold has remarked: 'The point seems to be that a statement is consonant with Anglican faith if it can be said to fall within the legitimate range of Anglican comprehensiveness, though individual Anglicans would be under no obligation to subscribe to it themselves.'[18]

21 The Vatican Response, on the other hand, seems to have taken 'consonance in substance' as meaning full and complete identity: 'What was asked for was not a simple evaluation of an ecumenical study, but an official response as to the identity of the various statements with the faith of the church' (para. 33). From this perspective, the Vatican Response must be understood, then, as claiming that ARCIC I failed to reach agreement on basic issues.

22 The main criterion for judgment used by the churches – consonance in substance with the faith – was identically stated. But, as we have noted here, the meaning of this phrase varies between the two churches. We suggest, then, that beyond the ambiguity in the term *substantial* there exists a much larger

[17] See note 5.
[18] *The Tablet,* December 7, 1991, p. 1525.

issue, which lies in the assumption that everyone knows what substantial (in the sense of 'fundamental') agreement would look like and how it might be expressed.

The Issue of Doctrinal Language

23 The intrinsic problem is the complex question of doctrinal language. How does one express the faith of the Church? This is, of course, a question with a long history of controversy.

24 What is meant by 'the faith of the Church'? For members of the Anglican and Roman Catholic communities, the tendency may be to assume, without very much hesitation, that the faith of the Church is identical with the official pronouncements of the community, however these pronouncements may be framed. But the fact is that the faith of the women and men who make up our communities is never simply the same as the words of our doctrinal formulae, liturgical forms, and catechetical statements. In Roman Catholic theology, a distinction has long been made between the *fides implicita* of the members of the Church and magisterial doctrinal statements. What must always be kept in mind is that the saving faith of the Church is the concrete faith of the people of God, which the official formulations of the faith are intended to support.

25 Yet two further questions arise: first, how does one know what the faith of any person or any group is, save through that faith's expression in word and deed? Second, by what processes and on what grounds have the words of councils, popes, bishops, and theologians come to be accepted as more authoritative than the words of any other believer or group of believers?

26 The first of these questions cannot be answered by appealing to the words of prayer rather than the words of doctrine, for at least as many differences exist in the devotional styles and practices of various believers as in their verbal expressions of faith. The *lex orandi* does not circumvent the question of adequacy of expression that confronts the *lex credendi*.

27 The second question is not simply another way of raising the issue of magisterial authority. The problem to which it points is that the words of official doctrinal and liturgical formulae, as well as the faith statements of any individual or

community, all fall short of the mysteries that they seek to express. At best, when Christians seek to articulate the faith of the Church, we deal with degrees of inadequacy.

28 Certainly in our communities we live and pray together in the assumption that there is an agreement which, despite the differences in the ways we express our faith both in words and in practices, is substantial. But how do we know that? We pray the creed together Sunday after Sunday, and as we recite the words of the creed, we assume that the persons surrounding us intend substantially the same as we do. But on what grounds do we make this assumption?

29 The Vatican Response's use of the language of official Roman Catholic formulae to test whether agreement has been reached on the substance of faith seems at odds with the practice employed in other ecumenical conversations. For example, few would argue against the statement that the doctrines of the Trinity and the Incarnation are the central articles of the Christian creed and that those articles have received normative expression in the formulae of the first four ecumenical councils.

30 Nevertheless, the Roman Catholic Church has been willing to join in a common declaration of faith which deliberately avoids conciliar language that has proven controversial. One such declaration was deemed sufficient to permit some sacramental sharing between the Roman Catholic and the Syrian Orthodox churches. In their 1984 declaration, Pope John Paul II and Patriarch Zakka I appeal to the council of Nicaea, and then affirm:

> The confusion and schisms that occurred between their Churches in the later centuries, [the Pope and the Patriarch] realize today, in no way affect or touch the substance of their faith, since these arose only because of differences in terminology and culture and in the various formulae adopted by different theological schools to express the same matter.[19]

Here the substance of faith is distinguished from culturally determined terminology and the formulae of theological

---

[19] 'Towards a Fully Unanimous Gospel Witness,' Common Declaration by Pope John Paul II and Patriarch Zakka I of Antioch, June 23, 1984, *Catholic International*, vol. 2, no. 14 (July 15–31, 1991), pp. 662–3.

schools, including terminology and formulae worked out and adopted by one of the first four ecumenical councils.

31 From this example, it is apparent that the Roman Catholic Church has found it possible to affirm 'substantial agreement' without agreement on specific doctrinal formulae, even when those formulae are as hallowed as the Chalcedonian formula. This common declaration does not indicate how the 'substance' of faith is to be discerned when even the formula of Chalcedon is judged a matter of 'terminology and culture.'

32 This question raises the issue of doctrinal language. If, indeed, thought is dependent upon language and experience is dependent upon thought, then it is highly problematic to claim that one can distinguish the substance of faith from the culturally determined language of its expression.[20] How does one discern the substance beneath the words save through the words? It is a mistake to assume that when one speaks of the mysteries of faith, one can refer beyond the various attempts to speak about those mysteries to the mysteries themselves as if they are simply 'there' and available for inspection.

33 One way of dealing with this puzzle of doctrinal language is to accept orthopraxies as the test of orthodoxy; that is, to recognize that doctrines are expressions of the communal life of the Church and that shared life may make differing doctrinal formulae intelligible and reveal them to be compatible and even identical in intent. But such an interpretation means that attempts to share life must precede or at least accompany attempts to compare doctrinal statements. It might even suggest that shared sacramental life must precede or at least accompany attempts to compare doctrines on sacraments.

34 In any case, the very different understandings of 'substantial agreement' in the Lambeth and Vatican Responses to the Final Report raise important questions on the understanding of doctrine and the hermeneutics of doctrinal language at work in the dialogues. These questions lie beneath any assumption that the substance of faith is readily available for consultation

---

[20] This problem is foreshadowed in John XXIII's opening speech to the Second Vatican Council: 'The substance of the ancient doctrine of the deposit of faith is one thing, and the way in which it is presented is another.' Quoted in Francis A. Sullivan, 'The Vatican Response to ARCIC I,' *Bulletin/Centro Pro Unione*, p. 39 [chap. 24].

as the criterion of doctrinal language.These questions must be addressed in the future by our two churches.

The Challenge of Reception in the New Context

35 We understand that the importance of the process of reception was not fully realized in 1966 when Archbishop Ramsey and Pope Paul VI established the Anglican–Roman Catholic dialogue. How were the Commission's agreements to be fully accepted or rejected by each church? As has been noted above, the Anglican Communion has produced a response of its bishops gathered at the Lambeth Conference of 1988 but while the bishops have 'a special responsibility for guarding and promoting the apostolic faith their response is not a legislative or juridical decision.'[21] The dependence of the Roman Catholic Church's response on prior consultations of bishops' conferences remains unclear. We ask whether texts such as the Final Report require new procedures of reception that more adequately reflect our affirmation of the real but imperfect communion in which we already live.

36 The sparse documentation style of the Vatican and Lambeth Responses has also complicated the process of receiving them. While the Vatican Response is longer and more detailed, neither Response contains adequate reference to the materials upon which the Responses build. With further documentation, the bases for the judgments expressed would be easier to discern. To this extent, the contribution of the Responses to the dialogue could be made more effective than it currently is. We hope that future responses from our two churches will provide the material needed to facilitate understanding, appreciation, and acceptance of their judgments.

37 ARCIC I said

> we are convinced that if there are any remaining points of disagreement they can be resolved on the principles here established. We acknowledge a variety of theological approaches within both our communions. But we have seen it as our task to find a way of advancing together beyond the doctrinal disagreements of the past (Eucharistic Doctrine, para. 12).

[21] *Emmaus Report*, p. 73.

We take this to indicate that ARCIC I claims 'substantial agreement' in the sense that, whatever differences may remain on the issues explored in the Final Report, they would not today provoke division between our two churches. Hence, they cannot warrant our continuing division.

38 Thus, we take our two churches' different judgments on whether 'substantial agreement' has been reached as both encouragement and challenge: encouragement, in that both Responses rejoice in the notable progress that has been achieved; challenge, in that we are confronted with our willingness to stay divided over matters that would not initiate a division. This reality places in front of us our need for continuous repentance of our willingness to be divided, and continuous conversion toward the unity Christ offers us with one another, which is a mirror of his own unity with the Father.

17
ARCIC II: Requested Clarifications on Eucharist and Ministry (1993)

In this paper we seek to answer the queries raised in the 1991 Response of the Holy See to the Final Report of ARCIC (1982) concerning the Eucharist and the Ordained Ministry. We are encouraged by what is said in the Response that this may 'serve as an impetus to further study'.

The Commission was inspired by two official statements of the Roman Catholic Church. The first came from the address by Pope John XXIII at the opening of the Second Vatican Council, when he said: 'The substance of the ancient doctrine of the deposit of faith is one thing, and the way in which it is presented is another.'[1] The second statement is paragraph 17 of *Unitatis Redintegratio* which, in speaking of East and West, includes the words, '. . . sometimes one tradition has come nearer than the other to an apt appreciation of certain aspects of a revealed mystery, or has experienced them in a clearer manner. As a result, these various theological formulations are often to be considered as complementary rather than conflicting.' This concept has been endorsed by *The Catechism of the Catholic Church* (1992), which affirms that when the Church 'puts down her roots in a variety of cultural, social and human terrains, she takes on different external expressions and appearances in each part of the world. The rich variety of ecclesiastical disciplines, liturgical rites and theological and spiritual heritage proper to the local churches, in harmony among themselves, shows with greater clarity the catholicity of the undivided Church.' In our study of Eucharist and Ministry we discovered beneath a diversity of expressions and practice a profound underlying harmony. This harmony is not broken when an element of the truth is more strongly affirmed in one tradition than in another, in which nevertheless it is not denied. Such is especially the case with eucharistic adoration, as we shall later show.

Eucharist

The Response to the Final Report, whilst approving the main thrust of the statement on *Eucharistic Doctrine*, asks for clarification concerning the following points:

> (a) the essential link of the eucharistic Memorial with the *once-for-all* sacrifice of Calvary which it makes sacramentally present;
> (b) 'the propitiatory nature of the eucharistic sacrifice, which can be applied also to the deceased'. The Response stressed the fact that 'for Catholics the whole Church must include the dead'. It appears to want reassurance that the Anglican Communion shares the same view;

[1] This quotation is from Pope John XXIII's Italian text. However, the official Latin text in translation reads, 'For the deposit of faith, or the truths which are contained in our venerable doctrine, are one thing, and the way in which they are expressed is another, with, however, the same sense and meaning.'

(c) certitude that Christ is present sacramentally and substantially when 'under the species of bread and wine these earthly realities are changed into the reality of his Body and Blood, Soul and Divinity';

(d) the adoration of Christ in the reserved sacrament.

The Response of the Holy See states that the Catholic Church rejoices because the members of the Commission were able to affirm together 'that the eucharist is a sacrifice in the sacramental sense, provided that it is clear that this is not a repetition of the historical sacrifice'. In the mind of the Commission the making present, effective and accessible of the unique historic sacrifice of Christ does not entail a repetition of it. In the light of this the Commission affirms that the belief that the eucharist is truly a sacrifice, but in a sacramental way, is part of the eucharistic faith of both our communions. As has been stated in the *Elucidation* on *Eucharistic Doctrine*, para 5: 'The Commission believes that the traditional understanding of sacramental reality, in which the once-for-all event of salvation becomes effective in the present through the action of the Holy Spirit, is well expressed by the word *anamnesis*. We accept this use of the word which seems to do full justice to the semitic background. Furthermore it enables us to affirm a strong conviction of sacramental realism and to reject mere symbolism.'

When we speak of the death of Christ on Calvary as a sacrifice, we are using a term to help explain the nature of Christ's self-offering, a term which is not exhaustive of the significance of that self-offering. However, it has become normative for the Christian tradition because of its intimate relation with the unique propitiatory character of the death of Christ. This theme of propitiatory sacrifice is clearly emphasised in the classical eucharistic liturgies of the churches of the Anglican Communion (e.g. the English Book of Common Prayer, 1662), where the words immediately preceding the *Sursum Corda* have always included 1 John 2.1, 2, 'If anyone sin, we have an advocate with the Father, Jesus Christ the righteous, and he is the propitiation for our sins'. So the Prayer of Consecration begins:

Almighty God, our heavenly Father, who of thy tender mercy didst give thine only Son Jesus Christ to suffer death upon the Cross for our redemption; who made there (by his one oblation of himself once offered) a full, perfect, and sufficient sacrifice, oblation, and satisfaction, for the sins of the whole world; and did institute, and in his holy Gospel command us to continue, a perpetual memory of that his precious death, until his coming again . . .

Similarly, the propitiatory dimension of the eucharist is explicit in the Final Report when it says that through the eucharist 'the atoning work of Christ on the cross is proclaimed and made effective' and the Church continues to 'entreat the benefits of his passion on behalf of the whole Church'. This is precisely what is affirmed at the heart of the eucharistic action in both classical and contemporary Anglican liturgies (e.g. The Book of Common Prayer, 1662):

O Lord and heavenly Father, we thy humble servants entirely desire thy fatherly goodness mercifully to accept this our sacrifice of praise and thanksgiving, most humbly beseeching thee to grant, that by the merits and death of thy Son Jesus Christ, and through faith in his blood, we and *all thy whole Church* may obtain remission of our sins, and all other benefits of his passion.[2]

'All thy whole Church' must be understood in the light of the article in the Nicene Creed which precedes it, 'I believe in the one holy catholic and apostolic church . . . in the resurrection of the dead and the life of the world to come'. For this reason commemoration of the faithful departed has continued to be part of the intercessions in Anglican eucharistic liturgies past and present (compare also the liturgical provision for a eucharist at a Funeral and in the Commemoration of the Faithful Departed in the Alternative Service Book, 1980, of the Church of England, pp. 328ff and 936f).

---

[2] A nuanced example of propitiatory language in association with the eucharist is found in the writings of the seventeenth century Anglican divine, Jeremy Taylor: 'It follows then that the celebration of this sacrifice be, in its proportion, an instrument of applying the proper sacrifice to all the purposes for which it was first designed. It is ministerially, and by application, an instrument propitiatory: it is eucharistical, it is an homage and an act of adoration: and it is impetratory, and obtains for us and for the whole church, all the benefits of the sacrifice, which is now celebrated and applied; that is, as this rite is the remembrance and ministerial celebration of Christ's sacrifice, so it is destined to do honour to God . . . to beg pardon, blessings, and supply of all our needs' (*Discourse* XIX 4).

The Holy See's Response gladly recognises our agreement with regard to the real presence of Christ: 'Before the eucharistic prayer, to the question "What is that?", the believer answers: "It is bread". After the eucharistic prayer, to the same question he answers: "It is truly the body of Christ, the Bread of Life".' It also acknowledges that, 'The affirmations that the Eucharist is "the Lord's real gift of himself to his Church" (Eucharistic Doctrine, para. 8), and that bread and wine "become" the body and blood of Christ (Eucharistic Doctrine: *Elucidation*, para. 6) can certainly be interpreted in conformity with Catholic faith'. It only asks for some clarification to remove any ambiguity regarding the mode of the real presence. The Response speaks of the earthly realities of bread and wine being changed into 'the reality of his Body and Blood, Soul and Divinity'. In its preparatory work the Commission examined with care the definition of the Council of Trent (DS 1642, 1652), repeated in the *Catechism of the Catholic Church* (1992) (no. 1376). Though the Council of Trent states that the soul and divinity of Christ are present with his body and blood in the eucharist, it does not speak of the conversion of the earthly realities of bread and wine into the Soul and Divinity of Christ (DS 1651). The presence of the Soul is by natural *concomitantia* and the Divinity by virtue of the hypostatic union. The Response speaks of a 'substantial' presence of Christ, maintaining that this is the result of a substantial change in the elements. By its footnote on transubstantiation the Commission made clear that it was in no way dismissing the belief that 'God, acting in the eucharist, effects a change in the inner reality of the elements' and that a mysterious and radical change takes place. Paul VI in *Mysterium Fidei* (AAS 57, 1965) did not deny the legitimacy of fresh ways of expressing this change even by using new words, provided that they kept and reflected what transubstantiation was intended to express. This has been our method of approach. In several places the Final Report indicates its belief in the presence of the living Christ truly and really in the elements. Even if the word 'transubstantiation' only occurs in a footnote, the Final Report wished to express what the Council of Trent, as evident from its discussions, clearly intended by the use of the term.

Reservation of the Blessed Sacrament is practised in both our churches for communion of the sick, the dying and the absent. The fear expressed in the Response that a real consensus between Anglicans and Roman Catholics is lacking concerning the adoration of Christ's sacramental presence requires careful analysis. Differences in practice do not necessarily imply differences in doctrine, as can be seen in the case of East and West. The difficulty is not with reservation of the sacrament but with the devotions associated with it which have grown up in the Western Church since the twelfth century outside the liturgical celebration of the eucharist. To this day these devotions are not practised in the Eastern Churches, just as they had not been during the Church's first thousand years. Nevertheless, the belief concerning Christ's presence has been and remains the same in East and West. Obviously the distinction between faith and practice is especially pertinent here. We recognised the fact that some Anglicans find difficulty with these devotional practices because it is feared that they obscure the true goal of the sacrament. However, the strong affirmation that 'the Christ whom we adore in the eucharist is Christ glorifying his Father' (Eucharistic Doctrine: *Elucidation*, para. 8) clearly shows that in the opinion of the authors of the document there need be no denial of Christ's presence even for those who are reluctant to endorse the devotional practices associated with the adoration of Christ's sacramental presence. Provision for the reservation of the Sacrament is found within the Anglican Church according to pastoral circumstances. In the Church of England, for example, this is regulated by the faculty jurisdiction of the diocesan bishop.

The 1662 Book of Common Prayer authoritatively expresses the historic Anglican teaching that the consecrated elements are to be treated with reverence. After communion the rubric instructs the minister to 'return to the Lord's Table, and reverently place upon it what remaineth of the consecrated Elements, covering the same with a fair linen cloth'. A further rubric states that 'the Priest . . . shall, immediately after the Blessing, reverently eat and drink the same.' Such reverence remains the Anglican attitude (cf. the collect provided for the Thanksgiving for the Institution of Holy Communion, Alternative Service Book 1980, p. 920):

> Almighty and heavenly Father, we thank you that in this wonderful sacrament you have given us the memorial of the passion of your Son Jesus Christ. Grant us so to reverence the sacred mysteries of his body and blood, that we may

know within ourselves and show forth in our lives the fruits of his redemption; who is alive and reigns with you and the Holy Spirit, one God, now and for ever.

Ministry and Ordination

The Holy See's Response acknowledged that 'significant consensus' has been achieved with regard to *Ministry and Ordination*. Encouraged by this we seek to give the requested clarifications.

Concerning the Ordained Ministry the Response asks ARCIC to make clearer the following affirmations:

(a) only a validly ordained priest, acting 'in the person of Christ', can be the minister offering 'sacramentally the redemptive sacrifice of Christ' in the Eucharist;

(b) the institution of the sacrament of orders, which confers the priesthood of the New Covenant, comes from Christ. Orders are not 'a simple ecclesiastical institution';

(c) the 'character of priestly ordination implies a configuration to the priesthood of Christ';

(d) the apostolic succession in which the unbroken lines of episcopal succession and apostolic teaching stand in causal relationship to each other.

Crucial to the ARCIC agreement is the recognition that the ordained ministry is an essential element of the Church and that it is only the episcopally ordained priest who presides at the eucharist (Ministry and Ordination: *Elucidation*, para. 2). In several instances the Final Report states that the celebration of the eucharist is the sacramental memorial of the once-for-all self-offering of Christ on the cross to his Father (as described above). In the celebration of the eucharistic memorial, the self-offering of Christ is made present. The community, gathered around the ordained minister who presides in Christ's name at the celebration, enters into communion with this self-offering. In reciting the narrative of the institution, in praying the Father to send the Holy Spirit to effect the transformation of the gifts and through them of the faithful, in distributing these holy gifts to the assembly, the presiding minister stands in a special sacramental relation to what Christ himself did at the Last Supper, pointing to his redemptive sacrifice on the cross. Together with the assembly, but exercising his own specific ecclesial function, the one who presides is thus the minister of the sacramental self-offering of Christ.

The Response seeks the amplification and completion of that part of the Final Report which we have just clarified by affirming that Christ himself instituted the sacrament of Orders. Concerning ordained ministers the Final Report states, 'Not only is their vocation from Christ but their qualification for exercising such a ministry is the gift of the Spirit' (Ministry and Ordination, para. 14), received in and through the Church. In this way they carry on the commission given to the apostles by Jesus in person. After the resurrection the Holy Spirit conferred upon the apostolic group what was necessary for the accomplishment of their commission. They in turn were led by the Lord to choose collaborators and successors who, through the laying on of hands, were endowed with the same gift of God for ministry in the Church.

Thus the sacramental ministry is something positively intended by God and derives from the will and institution of Jesus Christ. This does not necessarily imply a direct and explicit action by Jesus in the course of his earthly life. A distinction needs to be drawn between what Jesus is recorded as saying and doing, and his implicit intentions which may not have received explicit formulation till after the Resurrection, either in words of the risen Lord himself or through his Holy Spirit instructing the primitive community: 'All this I have spoken while still with you. But the Counsellor, the Holy Spirit, whom the Father will send in my name, will teach you all things and will remind you of everything I have said to you' (John 14.25, 26).

The Final Report had no intention of excluding the notion of sacramental 'character', which is found in official Anglican documents (e.g. the Canon Law of the Church of England, c.1.2). The Commission believed it to be more constructive to retain the idea without the use of a term which has sometimes been misconstrued. The Final Report emphasises the Spirit's seal and the irrevocability of the gifts and calling of God of ministers. This is the meaning of 'character' as described by Augustine, assumed in the Council of Trent (DS 1767, 1774) and taught in the *Catechism of the Catholic Church* (1992) (1582). Thus the Final Report states:

In this sacramental act, the gift of God is bestowed upon the ministers, with the promise of divine grace for their work and for their sanctification; the ministry of Christ is presented to them as a model for their own; and the Spirit seals those whom he has chosen and consecrated. Just as Christ has united the Church inseparably with himself, and as God calls all the faithful to lifelong discipleship, so the gifts and calling of God to the ministers are irrevocable. For this reason, ordination is unrepeatable in both our churches (Ministry and Ordination, para. 15).

Anglicans and Roman Catholics agree that the communion of the churches in the apostolic tradition involves not only all the existing churches of today but also those of the past, extending back to the first apostolic community. This communion is rooted in the apostolic faith and mission, but it involves far more than this. The sacramentality of the Church requires a sacramental continuity, expressed especially in the eucharist, celebrated in communion with the bishop: 'The communion of the churches in mission, faith, and holiness, through time and space, is thus symbolized and maintained in the bishop' (Ministry and Ordination, para. 16).

The prime function of the episcopal ministry is to safeguard the continuity of the local churches with the apostolic Church in its faith, teaching and mission. Thus each episcopal ordination is part of a successive line which links the bishops of today with the apostolic ministry. We believe that this is precisely what *Lumen Gentium* wanted to express:

Among those various ministries which, as tradition witnesses, were exercised in the Church from the earliest times, the chief place belongs to the office (*munus*) of those who, appointed to the episcopate in a sequence running back to the beginning, are the ones who pass on the apostolic seed. Thus, as Saint Irenaeus testifies, through those who were appointed bishops by the apostles, and through their successors down to our own time, the apostolic tradition is manifested and preserved throughout the world (*Lumen Gentium*, 20).[3]

The Commission stated that its concern was the origin and

---

[3] Inter varia illa ministeria quae inde a primis temporibus in ecclesia exercentur, teste traditione, praecipuum locum tenet munus illorum qui, in episcopatum constituti, per successionem ab initio decurrentem, apostolici seminis traduces habent: Ita, ut testatur S. Irenaeus, per eos qui ab apostolis instituti sunt episcopi et successores eorum usque ad nos, traditio apostolica in toto mundo manifestatur et custoditur.

nature of the ordained ministry, not the question of who can or cannot be ordained (Ministry and Ordination: *Elucidation*, para. 5). However, the Response maintains that the Ordination of Women affects the Final Report's claim to have reached substantial agreement on *Ministry and Ordination*. We are confronted with an issue that involves far more than the question of ministry as such. It raises profound questions of ecclesiology and authority in relation to Tradition. This subject is part of the mandate entrusted to ARCIC II.

18
Letter by Cardinal E. Cassidy (President of the Pontifical Council for the Unity of Christians) to the Co-Chairmen of ARCIC II (1994)

Bishop Mark Santer,
Bishop of Birmingham;

Bishop Cormac Murphy-O'Connor,
Bishop of Arundel and Brighton

On 4 September 1993, you sent me a document containing 'Clarifications of certain aspects of the Agreed Statements on Eucharist and Ministry' which had been submitted to and approved by the ARCIC II meeting taking place in Venice at that time.

This document has been examined by the appropriate dicasteries of the Holy See and I am now in a position to assure you that the said clarifications have indeed thrown new light on the questions concerning Eucharist and Ministry in the Final Report of ARCIC I for which further study had been requested.

The Pontifical Council for Promoting Christian Unity is therefore most grateful to the members of ARCIC II, and to those from ARCIC I who prepared these clarifications. The agreement reached on Eucharist and Ministry by ARCIC I is thus greatly strengthened and no further study would seem to be required at this stage.

There is one observation that I should like to bring to your notice in this connection. It concerns the question of *Reservation of the Blessed Sacrament*, and in particular the comparison which is made on page 202 of the 'Clarifications' between the practice of the Orthodox Churches (and the Catholic Churches of Eastern Rite) and that of the Anglican Communion. Orthodox and Eastern-rite Catholics have a very clear and uniform practice concerning the reservation of the Blessed Sacrament. While there are differences in respect to devotions connected with the Reserved Sacrament, adoration of the Reserved Sacrament is normal for both Orthodox and Greek–Catholics. The 'Clarifications' do not seem to make clear that this can be said unreservedly and uniformly for Anglicans. In fact the 'Clarifications' state that 'provision for the reservation of the Sacrament is found within the Anglican Church *according to pastoral circumstances*' and that 'in the Church of England, for example, this is regulated by the faculty jurisdiction of the diocesan bishop'. It seems important to stress that the Response of the Holy See to the Final Report was concerned not with the question of devotions associated with Christ's presence in the Reserved Sacrament, but with the implications of diverse Anglican practice regarding Reservation itself and attitudes towards the Reserved Sacrament.

The remarkable consensus reached up to now on the themes dealt with by ARCIC I will only be able to be seen in its full light and importance as the work of ARCIC II proceeds. This would appear to be particularly the case in respect of the study of the questions still open in relation to the third part of the Final Report of ARCIC I, dealing with Authority in the Church. It would seem urgent, then, that this question be taken up as soon as possible by ARCIC II.

With the expression of my deep esteem and kind personal greetings,

Yours sincerely in the Lord,
Edward Card. Cassidy

Comments by Members of ARCIC

19
HENRY CHADWICK:
Unfinished Business (1992)

When Christian communities come to suspend communion with each other, they grow apart, and the longer the separation lasts, the harder reconciliation may become. They gradually develop a distinct ethos and express their faith in different terms. If their parting originated in bad temper, they normally frown on interconfessional marriages, one side will normally refuse recognition to the orders of the other, and both parties hold distorted images of the belief and practice of the other side.

These unpleasantnesses occurred in ancient times between those who accepted the definition of the Council of Chalcedon and those who found its wording, in one preposition, objectionable. Between Chalcedonian and pre-Chalcedonian Churches relations are much improved, but have still some way to go to restored communion. Similarly, between the Orthodox Churches of the East (which now have an extensive diaspora in the West) and the Roman Catholic Church, a millennium of discussion has at some moments come remarkably close to peace and communion; but then the tide of success has receded, and the good will is easily replaced by mutual recrimination, each side holding the other at fault for the disillusionment and failure.

The Vatican's response of 1991 to the Final Report of the first Anglican–Roman Catholic International Commission (ARCIC I) has, at least for a considerable number of students, appeared to be pouring tepid water on a dialogue which had been widely acknowledged, even by some in the Curia, to represent remarkable and genuine progress, going far beyond merely verbal similarity. When the Final Report appeared, initially anxious readers had been astonished and gratified to find that the agreed statements did not depend on foggy or subtle ambiguities, but incisively articulated the essence of the matter as shared doctrine. There is now perhaps a danger that, as with the ups and downs of conversation with the Orthodox, disappointment may take over, each side thinking the other party's will at fault for the 'failure', if that is what it really is (a matter far from clear as yet), or even ready to charge the other party with failing to grasp the nature of real ecumenism.

The Vatican verdict nowhere says or implies that the ARCIC report is dissonant from official Roman Catholic teaching in such a sense that a bishop or priest using this text for catechetical purposes is being instructed to cease from doing anything so hazardous. What is being said is that the language is not identical with that familiar from the definitions of Trent or Vatican I, and that in consequence some few concepts associated by the Vatican with a generalised Protestantism (and not mentioned directly by ARCIC) have not been expressly excluded. For the Vatican, therefore, ARCIC's account of the articles of faith examined is not so much wrong as less than full.

The point about language is not a new one to surviving members of ARCIC I; for the commission explicitly and consciously sought to avoid terms that carry a heavy polemical load of association.

ARCIC's programme was defined by Pope Paul VI and Archbishop Michael Ramsey in 1966; the ground principle should be to work together towards making united affirmations on the basis of 'the gospels and the ancient common traditions'. Members of ARCIC I were themselves taken aback to discover how wide and profound was the resulting area of shared discourse. Question and answer, with no holds barred, elicited something that St Athanasius knew in the fourth century, namely that Christians using different terms (in Athanasius' time contradictory terms) could actually mean the same thing. The commission was heartened when in 1980 Pope John Paul was understood to approve the method of going behind habits of thought and expression born and nourished in enmity and controversy. ARCIC endeavoured with considerable, if not

invariable, success, to avoid emotionally charged language. The
commission, the Pope said, was writing for an age which no
longer glories in strife but seeks to come together in listening
to the quiet voice of the Spirit.

On the elements of eucharistic belief ARCIC felt it had
reached 'substantial agreement', a phrase St Anselm of Canterbury used when dissenting from Cardinal Humbert's opinion
that the Greek eucharist using leavened bread is invalid. The
Congregation for the Doctrine of the Faith, in its observations
of 1982, found ambiguity in the phrase. Though the analysis of
the nature of the ambiguity was not very illuminating and even
misrepresented ARCIC, it was perhaps a natural and defensible
fear on the congregation's part that the unwary might think
that matters not mentioned in ARCIC's eucharistic statement
were unimportant. It was far from the mind of ARCIC, however,
to suppose that eucharistic adoration, for example, is a matter
of indifference, or that everything of significance had been said
in the statement. The commission was going back to first
principles in Scripture and sacred tradition and asking what is
done in the eucharistic action. In that respect its agreement
was far-reaching enough to provide a foundation on which
remaining questions of disagreement, inherited from different
community traditions, ought in time to find a fraternal resolution.

If so much could be said together, there seemed good hope
that even more would be agreed as the two Communions
learnt to trust each other better. The ARCIC members had
quickly discovered how deeply their partners in dialogue loved
God and his Church. If they shared so much at the deepest
level of faith, could they avoid hoping that in due time, by
God's grace, language would be given for expressing this
sharing? For to love God and keep his commandments is
intimately linked with love of God's children (1 John 5.2).

That 'substantial agreement' is a phrase troubled by ambiguity is obviously correct. Whether one thinks that on eucharistic
doctrine ARCIC achieved such agreement depends on the way
in which one defines 'substantial'. For the Vatican it means
everything of any importance, and in the terms defined by the
teaching authority. An agreement on primary principles must
fail to satisfy so tight a definition of substantial.

The Vatican verdict offers a series of points, not all equally
momentous and load-bearing, but matters on which it feels
unease with the ARCIC report – in some instances because of

what is not said rather than because of what the report actually contains. The verdict's repetitions could suggest to a literary critic that the Roman text emerged from a conflation of independent drafts; but if so, the composers of those drafts were writing for an authority which they understood to feel distrust of ARCIC.

Not that the Vatican has in the least set out to rubbish the Final Report as incompatible with the Catholic faith – a judgement that would necessarily have been highly critical of, and humiliating for, the eminent and passionately loyal Catholic theologians responsible for much of the document's making. But one does not need to read much between the lines to see that there is a disturbing underlying assumption common to many of the points raised, namely: if nine reasonably literate Anglicans, standing in a tradition shaped mainly by Augustine and Hooker but above all by the Book of Common Prayer, could sign so deeply Catholic a document without one dissenting squeak, there must be some clever ambiguities or at the very least some discreet silences to make possible this surprising fact.

It is not as if the Anglican team was packed with Anglo-Catholics. The Final Report does not easily fit the Vatican's image of Anglicanism, nor that familiar Roman Catholic hope that the Anglicans will turn out to be ordinary common-or-garden Protestants in the end. There are moments in the Vatican verdict when what is under fire is not what ARCIC has set out but what some in the Curia think some Anglicans might be able to say if the Final Report alone were taken to be sufficient. Therefore there is a kind of search for unidentified submarines below the surface of apparently tranquil waters.

The principal issues now being raised by the Vatican verdict can perhaps be fairly summarised in terms of relatively few significant questions. Among these questions, two are of massive importance but are not thereby necessarily and inherently contentious between Canterbury and Rome.

In the first place, a recurrent theme in the verdict is that, for the Anglicans in ARCIC, the truth of an ecclesiastical definition primarily hangs on the content being consonant with Scripture and accepted sacred tradition, and therefore more on the content than on the organs of authority through which the definition has been proclaimed or is now proposed; whereas, for a Catholic of Roman obedience, the truth of a definition depends less on the *content* and more on the primate or the general council *by whom* the definition is given.

At the back of this contrast lies an old problem which, for Anglican theologians of the seventeenth and eighteenth centuries, turned on the question of 'fundamentals'. Are the fundamentals those defined by the Church, or is the true Church identified by the fundamentals (Word, dominical sacraments, Creed, visible continuity of ministry)? There will not be the easiest of conversations between those who think the essentials are constitutive of the Church and those who think that the essentials are those proposed for acceptance by the Church through its organs of definition. Nevertheless the antithesis becomes uncomfortable to the point of misstatement when made too absolute. ARCIC sought to keep both aspects together: 'The Church's teaching is proclaimed because it is true; it is not true simply because it has been proclaimed' (Authority II, para. 27).

The ARCIC report unreservedly supported the idea that the Church needs organs of authority to guide the faithful, and expressly recognised that 'a service of preserving the Church from error has been performed by the bishop of Rome as universal primate both within and outside the synodal process' (Authority II, para. 29), Leo I being an instance. But it goes without saying that ARCIC did not think the Church a body liable to limitless error and apostasy which can be held in the truth by no other organ than the see of Peter and vicar of Christ.

The Vatican feels distinctly uncomfortable, with repeated emphasis, when ARCIC notes an Anglican concern that dogmatic definitions be 'manifestly a legitimate interpretation of biblical faith and in line with orthodox tradition'. That looks like too qualified an acceptance of the primatial teaching office. However, not only Anglican readers will be disturbed or even alarmed at the implication, if it is indeed fairly deduced, that there is no conceivable limit on what the papal teaching office may think fit to define. The 1983 Code of Canon Law (749, 3) happily requires 'manifest demonstration' as a condition prerequisite for infallible definition, and that may encourage the hope of a gap less wide than is now being suggested.

It has been widely supposed by careful readers that in 'unpacking' papal infallibility the second of the two ARCIC documents on Authority made real progress – obviously far more than with universal papal jurisdiction, where ARCIC's language is considerably more diffident. Nevertheless, the Vatican verdict picks out the treatment of Mariology as if it were the crucial test of Roman teaching authority. And it is no doubt true that Anglicans, invited to justify a positive evaluation of Roman teaching authority, would be more likely to start from such highly significant actions as papal ratifications of general councils rather than from truths that look secondary in the sense of being dependent and derived.

The problem of relating theological content with the defining organ of definition easily comes to beset the discussion of the Marian dogmas of the Immaculate Conception and the Assumption. Here the Vatican verdict is spectacularly negative, acknowledging no reality to the degree of consensus which ARCIC's careful statement sought to articulate. Admittedly, the ARCIC paragraph includes a sentence that men of peace may well regret, to the effect that 'for many Anglicans, the teaching authority of the bishop of Rome, independent of a council, is not recommended by the fact that through it these Marian doctrines were proclaimed as dogmas binding on all the faithful'. That style of wording may have conveyed an impression of aversion or even scorn when what is being queried is definability *de fide*, with the platitude that high office may suffer diminution of respect if authority is invoked to impose what is not manifestly necessary for full saving faith.

That in devotion and practice the honour of Mary is unduly neglected by many Anglicans is not an issue in this debate. Nor are extravagances elsewhere. But it could have been a step forward rather than backward if the Vatican had felt able to acknowledge that in cold fact there is no real controversy between Rome and Canterbury that the mother of our Redeemer was prepared (like Jeremiah) from the first moment of her being for her divine calling of forming and shaping our Lord's humanity; moreover, that whatever the precise honour bestowed upon her in the communion of saints it is congruous with the honour bestowed on her on earth.

That I take to be close to the heart of the matter in the two Marian affirmations, and the fairly minuscule argument concerns the appropriateness and, some would add, the possibility of giving a very exact answer to the questions 'Did Mary feel the pull of human sinfulness?' and 'What precise form does her heavenly glory take?' The definitions of 1854 and 1950 provide answers to questions that had earlier been in controversy within the Catholic tradition. That of 1854 needs careful statement if one is not to prejudice the solidarity of Mary with the rest of humanity and to impinge on the theologically basic fact that she belongs to the creaturely order. The Vatican verdict is little concerned with these questions of content, and seems to place the truth of the doctrines less in what they say than in the papal right to define them.

Except between Franciscans and Dominicans, the Marian doctrines were not a cause of ecclesiastical division at the time of the Reformation. Of Mary's festivals, that on 8 December is firmly in the calendar of the Book of Common Prayer. The Vatican verdict cannot be faulted in thinking the matter merits further study. But Canterbury and Rome are not out of communion with one another because in dogma they disagree about Mary. Because they are separated, they talk as if dogma about Mary is causative of division, thereby obscuring the fact that the most potent reason for their division is that they are divided.

The second grand question which, in the eyes of the authors of the Vatican text, separates Canterbury from Rome is the way of evaluating historical evidence at points where history impinges upon dogmatic affirmations. For instance, the Anglican–Roman Catholic International Commission (ARCIC) did not think it either necessary or correct to assert that the Petrine texts of the New Testament are in themselves a sufficient historical foundation for asserting that Jesus intended to found the papacy. That the role of St Peter in the apostolic age offers strong encouragement to the idea that the Church needs a Petrine office to be an effective bond of unity and universality is a far less controversial proposition, and while grounded in good historical evidence is more than a merely historical statement.

A related issue is whether we are bound to say, in direct and simple terms, that Jesus instituted the sacrament of ordination. There is good reason to believe that he commissioned the apostles whose title – 'the sent' – presupposes just that; moreover, that they commissioned successors in local communities who, in time, would commission a further group of ministers with pastoral oversight. If that is what is meant, there is not too much to dispute about. The Vatican verdict, however, quotes the Second Vatican Council on the unbroken linear succession of ordinations as being constitutive of apostolic succession, and conveys the impression that, since the Council settled the matter, further consideration of history is happily irrelevant. Anglicans will not be the only theologians to be anxious at that impression.

There is, of course, no doubt about the continuity of the Christian communities in which the early pastors exercised oversight – *episkope* – and the first epistle of Clement offers striking testimony to ministerial succession as a visible sign of continuity and authenticity (not to mention the accepted responsibilities of the Roman Church for other communities). It is, moreover, not an issue between Canterbury and Rome that history by itself has no method making possible the establishment of norms for the belief and life of the Church. The resurrection of Christ is affirmed on more than historical grounds, but is not deficient in a historical basis.

The question the Vatican has raised is entirely proper, only it is not one which presses on only one party to the discussion. Neither side (if side is the right term) can complacently feel thankful that, if there happens to be a leaky timber, at least it is up at the other end of the ship.

There is an appeal to history in the position that the Church's tradition offers insufficient authority for the ordination of women to the priesthood. ARCIC was concerned to state accurately the nature of the priestly office and of ordination. The question of who is eligible for ordination seemed to the commission a derived and secondary (not insignificant) matter in comparison with its primary task. The Vatican verdict is sure that belief in even the possibility of priesthood for women must presuppose a different and un-Catholic concept of the very nature of the sacrament of order. This position is supported by a reference to the correspondence exchanged between the Vatican and Archbishop Runcie. Any who, like the present writer, found both sides of that correspondence in some degree obscure may feel disappointment here. There would have been a good opportunity for a concise and lucid statement to clarify what the difference is.

Perhaps this is an area where again there is an antithesis between content and defining organ of authority. One can meet thoughtful Roman Catholics who think women could be priests if the pope were so to decide but not otherwise. Likewise there are Anglicans who think women could be priests, given an ecumenical consensus, or at least mutual respect for a liturgical and disciplinary diversity, like that in the case of clerical celibacy (or even the *Filioque* clause added to the Nicene Creed by the Latin Church?). In both Communions, others want to discern clear theological principle, decisive whether for or against. In this matter the organ of authority is easier to identify than the theological argument.

That is not to say that authority is not moved by reasons, or that no serious theological considerations contribute to hesitations about the priesting of women. Beyond all controversy, no one could want doubt to threaten the power of the sacraments to assure communicants of being thereby incorporate in Christ's mystical body. Among the theological themes that make for hesitation, first importance seems naturally to go not to the symbolic role of the presiding celebrant at the Eucharist, acting in Christ's name and person, but to the point that the Lord, who was surely not imprisoned in the social conventions of his time, did not commission women among the apostles, and that this has been a determinant of Catholic tradition through two millennia. The utilitarian argument that priesting women has awkward consequences for the internal harmony of the community and for ecumenical relations, especially with the Orthodox, depends on the practical effects of these other two considerations – 2,000 years of tradition and the celebrant's symbolic role. Western theology unlike Eastern Orthodoxy likes tradition to be supported. Though the argument from unchanging practice through 2,000 years may have to be qualified by the reflection that tradition is not now felt to be so absolute by the present generation which has seen vast changes, the point still looks a lot stronger than consideration of symbolism inherent in the celebrant's maleness.

It will astonish a number of students to discover that the Vatican verdict directly links the maleness of the priestly office with the concept of 'character' in ordination: the argument used is that ordination assimilates the priest to the character of Christ, and therefore makes it necessary for the priest and Christ to be of the same sex. ARCIC wished its work to be reasonably clear to laity and therefore did not use the technical word 'character', preferring instead to express the idea of indelibility more accessibly with the phrase 'seal of the Spirit'. The bold and striking exposition of character in the Vatican's verdict goes much further than anything formally defined, but will be understood by those who know their way about the later medieval schoolmen.

ARCIC expresses the essential elements of what the Vatican verdict seems to be looking for in the proposition that 'the action of the presiding minister' in the Eucharist 'stands in a sacramental relation to what Christ himself did in offering his own sacrifice'. It will repay study to examine what is required by the Vatican verdict in addition to all this if due assurance is to be given. It may be proper to recall that ARCIC was not writing an exhaustive treatise on sacramental theory, but concentrating upon matters believed to be points of abrasion and disagreement. Character in ordination has not hitherto been one of these.

Anglicans, of the sixteenth century and since, have not followed the early Martin Luther who, confronted by priests failing in pastoral duty as he understood it, stressed that the true priest is defined by functions performed. Hooker (*Laws* 5,77,2) unreservedly affirmed indelible character in ordination. The historic norms of the Church of England lay down that the minister of God's word and sacrament acts in the name of Christ. Influential Anglican theologians have said that when a priest consecrates, blesses or absolves, he does so not on his own authority but, in the apostle's phrase (2 Cor. 2.10), 'in the person of Christ'.

Finally, the Vatican welcomes ARCIC's eucharistic statement, acknowledging that in this respect the commission achieved the most notable progress towards consensus. What ARCIC has said about both sacrifice and presence is congenial and indeed even a matter for 'rejoicing'. The joy turns out to be tinged with a touch of regret that the affirmation of the true presence of Christ and his sacrifice is not cast in language more familiar to Roman Catholics, which would be achieved by defining the mode of change with the adverb 'substantially'. This adverbial form can be found in seventeenth-century Anglican divinity wishing to affirm the reality of the change by consecration as independent of the feelings of the worshipper, but also wishing to avoid the precise philosophy of substance. Whether something significant is added to ARCIC's statement by the Vatican's preferred wording is a matter deserving of prolonged study. At the time ARCIC gave considerable thought to the matter and concluded that the term 'transubstantiation', which the commission evaluated positively, did not add to the essential meaning of the text.

The implication of these observations is no doubt that the Vatican's difficulties are not barbed-wire fences that present insuperable hurdles. The questions belong among those derived and dependent affirmations which ARCIC saw as consequential matters arising from the initial eucharistic agreement, needing to be explored together.

The Vatican verdict concludes with the important concession or proviso that its remarks are not intended to diminish appreciation for the work of ARCIC. It is among the first rules of ecumenical dialogue that the integrity of partners to the conversation will be respected, and such positive words should not be treated as soft soap. The request is for further clarification and in some areas for further study. If the analysis in this comment on the Vatican response is roughly correct, it will be evident that some issues raised are not only intricate but points where Rome and Canterbury do not stand on opposite sides of a high defensive wall; they are questions which today every theologian has to wrestle with, and that struggle may better be carried out together rather than in separation.

From this inevitably brief and preliminary examination of the Vatican text it seems a reasonable deduction that the Roman response is not as cool as it has been represented. It is an invitation to continue, not a closing of the door. No one wants a false irenicism which cries 'Peace, peace' when there is no peace. A cry of 'War, war' when there is no sufficient ground for war would be even more undesirable. The Vatican verdict deserves to be wholly supported in its evident conviction that good ecumenism is more than polite co-existence in a state of permanent eucharistic separation.

A long series of past episodes and exchanges leads people to expect failure and disillusion. It is not easy for the historian to think of many instances where a break in eucharistic communion has been healed. But there are some. Success is necessarily excluded only when it is axiomatic that what the other partner in the dialogue can accept must, for that reason, be inadequate.

20
CHRISTOPHER HILL:
The Fundamental Question of Ecumenical Method (1992)

A Long-awaited Response

We have had to wait a long time for this official Roman Catholic Response to the Final Report of ARCIC I. Now that it has appeared, Anglicans of whatever school will at best be able to raise one cheer out of three. Some few Anglicans will be relieved at its implicit assumption that we are really Protestants, rather than reformed Catholics, whatever we say and however we worship. Others will say *sotto voce*, 'I told you so, let's get on with the main agenda without ecumenical diversion' – whatever that agenda will be. Yet others will be puzzled and saddened at the very uncertain signals Rome is sending to all engaged in ecumenical dialogue, not only Anglicans.

In these circumstances it is important for Anglicans and Roman Catholics to be as objective as possible in their assessment of the Response and to avoid snap judgments. To this end we need to ponder on the long delay.

In the spring of 1988 a first draft of a Response was being prepared in the Secretariat – now the Pontifical Council – for Promoting Christian Unity. While it was not anticipated that it would be published before the Lambeth Conference met in Canterbury that summer, when the Anglican bishops would formalise their own response, it was hoped to complete the Roman Response not too long after. That, at least, was the hope expressed. The draft was very much constructed from the responses to ARCIC I by conferences of Catholic bishops in many different lands. These had been requested by the Secretariat and were almost universally positive. But the Congregation for the Doctrine of the Faith did not like this draft.

So there began a prolonged discussion as to which Roman dicastery should be ultimately responsible for the text. Left to their own devices, either dicastery could have produced its response rather more expeditiously. The Congregation for the Doctrine of the Faith, it will be remembered, had already produced its *Observations* as a 'contribution to the continuation of this dialogue' in March 1982, only weeks after the publication of the Final Report itself. It comes as no surprise therefore that the cautious reservations the Congregation for the Doctrine of the Faith expressed then are now reiterated with more authority. In essence, what seems to have happened is that the Council for Promoting Christian Unity has persuaded the Congregation for the Doctrine of the Faith to accept a genuinely positive and ecumenical tone, while failing to persuade it to modify its substantive judgments.

It would be infantile to caricature the Congregation for the Doctrine of the Faith under Cardinal Joseph Ratzinger as 'traditionalist villains' and Cardinal Edward Cassidy and his Pontifical Council for Unity as 'ecumenical heroes'. The ecumenical debate is too complex to be helped by gross over-simplifications. All Churches rightly have their 'doctrinal watch dogs'. The Church of England invented its Faith and Order Advisory Group many years ago precisely to assist the bishops and the Church to make proper judgments about ecumenical documents. But there remain questions as to whether the Congregation for the Doctrine of the Faith really has the ecumenical experience and expertise to do this effectively or fairly. So many of the comments read as if drafted by those who have very little first hand experience of Anglican life and worship.

Who Decides?

When John XXIII convoked the Second Vatican Council he realised that the then Holy Office was not the appropriate instrument for dealing with other Christian Churches and communities. In consequence he set up a separate Secretariat under Cardinal Bea.[1] But the question of how Rome came to

---

[1] For a description of the origins of the Secretariat for Promoting Christian Unity, see Peter Hebblethwaite, *John XXIII: Pope of the Council* (Geoffrey Chapman, London, 1984); and the chapter by Tom Stransky in *Vatican II by those who were there*, ed. A. Stacpoole (Geoffrey Chapman, London, 1986).

ecumenical decision-making was neither envisaged nor resolved. That legacy remains. One dicastery knows the other Churches and fosters the dialogues but another makes the ultimate doctrinal decisions. This structural problem will adversely affect all the ecumenical dialogues in which Rome is engaged as they move to the crucial point where decisions have to be made.

This is not a negative judgment about particular Vatican personalities. Anglicans, too, know they have reached a point of inertia when it comes to ecumenical decision-making. In the case of the Church of England, differing emphases in the understanding of the ordained ministry were largely responsible for the failure of the Anglican–Methodist Scheme and the Covenanting Proposals. In the same way, the two relevant Roman dicasteries appear to have rather different ecumenical philosophies – and experiences. As a result, it is not hard to detect unresolved differences of ecumenical principle which will need to be consciously considered in the near future if the continuing dialogue (about which there is no doubt) is to be given direction, method and purpose. It is to those differences in method that I wish to draw particular attention as a matter of Anglican concern.

Method

Early in the Response there are no less than three nervous variants of a repeated refrain that there remain 'important differences regarding essential matters of Christian doctrine'. Yet the question asked of Rome was not 'Do the ARCIC statements conform to Catholic doctrine?' but, 'Are they consonant with Catholic *faith*?' The Response shows little evidence of the very important and celebrated distinction enunciated by Pope John XXIII at the opening of the Second Vatican Council: 'the substance of the ancient deposit of faith is one thing; and the way it is presented is another'. There was, of course, a certain nervousness about this distinction in Rome at the time, and in the *Acta Apostolicae Sedis* it became: 'For the deposit of faith itself, or the truths which are contained in our venerable doctrine, is one thing, and the way in which they are expressed is another, retaining however the same sense and meaning'. But the drift of the whole speech is clear enough and even the 'official' version makes clear that there is a distinction between the truths of faith and their expression in particular doctrines. This was a maxim often repeated by the late Bishop Christopher

Butler OSB in the sessions of ARCIC I and he saw it as an important achievement of post-conciliar Catholicism.[2] Further misunderstanding is revealed in the concluding section of the Response when 'consonance' with Catholic faith is interpreted as 'identity'. They are not the same.

One major consequence of asking simplistically for conformity to Catholic doctrine is the tendency to compare the Final Report to defined Roman Catholic teaching as found in the Councils of Trent and Vatican I. An example of this is found when the Response asks for an explication of the 'propitiatory' nature of the Eucharist. The word is an unhappy one. Many Anglicans (and Roman Catholics?) today would feel the imagery of propitiation to be inappropriate. Even at the Council of Trent the argument that the Mass placates an angry God was felt to be embarrassing; the 1552 draft was altered accordingly in 1562, though the words 'propitiation' and 'propitiatory' were retained. Though the language of propitiation is found at the heart of classical Anglican eucharistic rites, Anglicans have traditionally spoken of the Cross itself as propitiatory; the Eucharist being its sacramental representation.

My point here is not that Anglicans will totally reject the notion that the Eucharist has propitiatory significance – some, indeed (Waterland, for example), have affirmed this.

But many Anglicans will hear in this Tridentine language things that Rome is not actually intending to say, namely that Christ is being re-sacrificed. Here is the danger of using language from the Reformation and Counter-Reformation which ARCIC tried to avoid and which the Response seems determined to reintroduce.

The other major question of method raised by the Response concerns the doctrine of the Church. It lurks beneath a number of observations in the text; it surfaces explicitly when the Response alludes to inaccurate references to *Lumen Gentium* 8 and *Unitatis Redintegratio* 13. No details of misquotation or misrepresentation are offered. But the issue here is surely over the self-understanding of the Roman Catholic Church. The original draft of *Lumen Gentium* spoke of the exclusive identity of the Church of Christ with the (Roman) Catholic Church. But significantly *est* became *subsistit*. This was universally interpreted

---

[2] Bishop Butler gave the maxim in its original form in the hearing of the author at several ARCIC meetings; see also Peter Hebblethwaite's treatment of this speech in *John XXIII: Pope of the Council*, ch. 21 (see p.305 n.5).

by proponents and opponents at the time as a less exclusive ecclesiology and, therefore, positive for ecumenical dialogue. Since then the Congregation for the Doctrine of the Faith, in a criticism of Father Leonardo Boff, has said that *subsistit* was chosen 'exactly in order to make clear that the *one sole* subsistence of the true Church exists in the Roman Catholic Church' (emphasis mine). This interpretation has itself been publicly contested by Cardinal Willebrands and by Professor Francis Sullivan of the Gregorian.[3] It would seem that the Response is trying to say there is only one interpretation of *Lumen Gentium* and a narrow one at that. But is Rome really saying that the Orthodox Churches (leaving aside Anglicans for the moment) are not true Churches or part of the true Church of Christ? Such an interpretation of *Lumen Gentium* is in danger of stopping all ecumenical conversation.

Having raised these two central questions of ecumenical method, there remain a number of detailed points to which Anglicans may wish to respond.

Authority

Marian Dogmas

The Marian dogmas are specially singled out as an area where there is not yet a consensus. It would have been helpful if Rome had been more precise here, for ARCIC *did* record agreement on much of their content: in particular, that Mary, the Mother of God incarnate (*Theotokos*), was prepared by divine grace to be the mother of our Redeemer, by whom she was herself redeemed and received into glory. For Anglicans the problem is the sources of the dogmas as defined and their status as binding on all Christians rather than the truths the dogmas are intended to convey.

Petrine Ministry

In noting a number of Anglican reservations about the exercise of the Petrine ministry, the Response rightly calls for more

---

[3] See 'The Significance of Vatican II's decision to say of the Church of Christ not that it "is" but that it "subsists" in the Roman Catholic Church', *One in Christ*, 1986/2; and 'Vatican II's Ecclesiology of Communion', *One in Christ*, 1987/3.

discussion about the practical exercise of authority. But it must also gently be said that questions about the actual exercise of authority by Rome are surely not limited to Anglicans. To ask such questions about the manner of the present exercise of Roman authority is not to deny a proper Petrine ministry.

Assent of the Faithful

The Response asserts that ARCIC sees the 'assent of the faithful' as required for the recognition that a doctrinal decision of a pope or ecumenical council is immune from error. But the paragraphs cited (Authority II, paras. 27 and 31) do *not* speak of the 'assent of the faithful'. ARCIC I was very careful at this point not to fall foul of the *ex sese, non autem ex consensu* of *Pastor Aeternus*, IV. It speaks rather of the 'reception' of decision and rules out a quasi-democratic understanding by explicitly saying that 'it would be incorrect to suggest that in controversies of faith no conciliar or papal definition possesses a right to attentive sympathy and acceptance until it has been examined by every individual Christian and subjected to the scrutiny of his private judgment' (Authority II, para. 31).

Infallible Teaching

The Response is anxious that ARCIC has limited the authority of ecumenical councils to the 'central truths of salvation' or 'fundamental doctrines', whereas councils or the pope are able to teach definitively 'within the range of all truth revealed by God'. This objection accidentally tilts at a windmill. It is (so Anglicans have understood) a non-controversial axiom of Roman Catholic doctrine that there are important conditions for a definitive act of defined teaching. Vatican I made it clear that one of the conditions for an infallible act of defining is that it must determine a doctrine of faith or morals, that is to say a doctrine expressing divine revelation. This is precisely the meaning of the ARCIC phraseology. Vatican I also speaks explicitly of consonance with Holy Scripture and the Apostolic Tradition (*Pastor Aeternus*, IV). This, too, is echoed by ARCIC in *Authority: Elucidation*, 2. Vatican I's significant limitation of the scope of infallibility to that which has been revealed (in other words the central truths of salvation) is an important clue to ecumenical agreement on this most difficult of subjects.

Petrine Primacy

The Response insists that the primacy of the successors of Peter is something positively intended by God (so far ARCIC I and an increasing number of Anglicans are able to concur). It then adds that it is derived from the will and institution of Jesus Christ. By this it seems to mean by Jesus Christ during his time among us on earth, which ARCIC I did not interpret Vatican I as necessarily entailing. *Pastor Aeternus* speaks rather of Peter receiving the primacy 'immediately and directly' from Christ, and the bishops of Rome inheriting the primacy from Peter. The Response collapses this argument unhelpfully. Moreover, it places an unnecessarily tight interpretation upon Vatican I's *de jure divino* Petrine primacy. This would have important negative consequences for other aspects of Catholic theology. The Reformers, by and large, gave *de jure divino* a restrictive interpretation and so dismissed four (or five) of the sacraments as not instituted by Christ in the Scriptures. It is odd to find the Congregation for the Doctrine of the Faith endorsing such a narrow interpretation in one context while presumably rejecting it in another.

Having made some rather critical comments upon the section of the Response dealing with authority, I would stress that no Anglican believes that ARCIC I has solved all the problems. Rather (in the words of the Lambeth Conference), the work of ARCIC on authority is to be seen as a 'firm basis for the direction and agenda of the continuing dialogue'. In examining what the Response goes on to say about ARCIC on eucharist and ministry, I suspect those responsible for parts of the text have little direct experience of Anglicanism.

Eucharist

Eucharist as Sacrifice

The Response asks for a more explicit statement that in the eucharist the Church 'makes present the sacrifice of Calvary'. This might be done because it is uncontroversial amongst Anglicans that the Eucharist makes accessible the benefits of Christ's sacrifice. The traditional 1662 eucharistic rite prays that the Lord may grant us 'so to eat the flesh of thy dear Son Jesus Christ, and to drink his blood, that our sinful bodies may be made clean by his body and our souls washed through his most precious blood'. At the post-communion prayer it asks the Lord to accept our sacrifice, 'most humbly beseeching thee to grant that by the merits and death of thy Son Jesus Christ, and through faith in his blood, we and all thy whole Church may obtain remission of sins and all other benefits of his Passion'. Thus Anglicans would not naturally think of Calvary as absent from the eucharist. They would, however, wish (as do all Roman Catholics I have ever met) to avoid the suggestion that the sacrifice of Calvary is repeated.

Propitiation

I have already commented upon the desire to use 'propitiatory' language of the eucharist as this illustrates what I believe to be a misunderstanding of ecumenical method. Having registered this, it may be, paradoxically, that a proper understanding of the Council of Trent can help us see a way through. Though the doctrinal chapters and canons of the Council approved the offering of mass for the living and the dead, they deliberately avoided any particular theory of efficacy to explain this tradition.[4] The Tridentine theologians were not agreed about this, some favouring an efficacy *ex opere operato*, others favouring an efficacy *per modum suffragii*. The conciliar fathers adopted a generic and cautious way of speaking without closing the debate by offering a theoretical explanation of current practice. The Roman Catholic language of 'propitiation', as defined at the Council of Trent, could therefore be more open than it may sound to many Anglicans. The Lima text of the Faith and Order Commission of the World Council of Churches (endorsed by most Anglican Churches including the Church of England) goes as far as to say: 'It is in the light of the significance of the eucharist as intercession that reference to the eucharist in Catholic theology as "propitiatory sacrifice" may be understood'. There is no doubt that Anglicans have always seen the eucharist as the locus of intercession. An intercession is mandatory in both ancient and modern eucharistic rites. Moreover, there is explicit intercession immediately after communion that 'we *and all thy whole Church* may obtain remission of our sins, *and all other benefits of his Passion*' (emphasis mine). Moreover Anglicanism moved to a more

---

[4] Cf. Session XXII of 1562; and D. W. Power, *The Sacrifice We Offer: The Tridentine Dogma and its Reinterpretation* (T & T Clark, Edinburgh, 1987).

nuanced position on the question of the eucharistic sacrifice in the seventeenth century. One of the theologians who took most seriously that patristic and early medieval legacy, and who refused to say that at a certain point in history Christian tradition departed fatally from the truth, was the Caroline Divine, Bishop Jeremy Taylor, whose eucharistic theology has been recently studied in some detail by the former Anglican Co-Chairman of ARCIC, Archbishop McAdoo of Dublin. Taylor, basing himself upon the Christology of Hebrews 7, sees the Church's commemorative sacrifice as taken up into Christ's intercession in heaven.[5] At the end of the last century this theology found more official Anglican expression in the reply of the Archbishops of Canterbury and York to Leo XIII's Bull *Apostolicae Curae*. In their reply *Saepius Officio* of 1897 they spoke of the eucharist as a 'pleading' of Christ's sacrifice. In short, given the deliberate openness of the Council of Trent, and the totality of the Anglican tradition, the gap may not be as large as it looks.

Prayer for the Dead

The Response asks about prayer for the departed in the Eucharist. Prayer for the dead was included in the eucharistic prayer of the first Book of Common Prayer of 1549. This was omitted entirely from the more radical Prayer Book of 1552. But in 1662 a blessing of God for the departed was restored to the intercession. This passed from England into the wider Anglican tradition, though in Scotland and America the stronger tradition of the first Prayer Book was developed. In the Church of England today the authorised eucharistic rites all include a commemoration of the departed, and among liturgical options are included the traditional Roman proper preface for the dead and a freestanding collect adapted from the *commemoratio pro defunctis* of the traditional Roman *Canon Missae*.

Eucharistic Reservation/Adoration

On eucharistic reservation the question is not reservation as such but adoration. No doubt the Response is thinking of Trent's

---

[5] See H. R. McAdoo, *The Eucharistic Theology of Jeremy Taylor Today* (Canterbury Press, Norwich, 1988).

condemnation of those who say that in the Eucharist 'the only begotten Son of God is not to be adored with the worship of *latria*, also outwardly manifested'. No Anglican would deny *latria* to the only begotten Son of God. But it is true that a number of Anglicans find difficulty in the fully developed Counter-Reformation outward manifestation of eucharistic *latria* because this appears to them to be directed not to the inner reality of the sacrament of the eucharist – the body and blood of Christ – but to the outward sacramental signs divorced from sacramental reception in holy communion. Here a sideways glance at the eastern Orthodox tradition may be liberating. It is not in doubt (I take it) that Rome regards Constantinople as orthodox in eucharistic doctrine, in spite of the East never having received the later western cultus of the blessed sacrament. The sacrament is duly reserved on Orthodox altars. Yet no special or distinct veneration is given to the reserved sacrament, as such, which is not also offered to the altar, the sanctuary, and to the unconsecrated elements at the Great Entrance. Also relevant are the traditionally strict rubrics of the Prayer Book (and modern eucharistic rites) concerning the mandatory reverent consumption of all the consecrated species (other than that which is required for reservation for the sick or dying). These rubrics were, and are, directed *against* the notion that the consecrated elements revert to profane use after the end of the liturgy. Moreover a study of Anglican legal provision for the reservation of the sacrament by diocesan chancellors' courts (the faculty jurisdiction) would indicate something of contemporary Anglican concern for proper and reverent provision for the reservation of the blessed sacrament.

'Substantial' Change

Similarly, the Response asks for more clarity about the mode of Christ's real presence in the Eucharist. It asks for use of the language of 'substantial' change. Here again, Anglicans will want to ask whether this is also demanded of the Orthodox. Furthermore, can it really be wise so to 'canonise' the Aristotelian/Thomist philosophy of substance and accidents (without which the language of substantial change is either meaningless or dangerously close to physics) as if it were tantamount to revealed truth? Many Anglicans, when rightly understanding the language of substance and accidents in relation to the sacramental body and blood of Christ, well understand why the

Council of Trent described 'transubstantiation' as 'convenient and proper' and even as *aptissime*. But they go on to question whether what was 'most apt' then is necessarily most apt now and should be universally imposed ecumenically.

Ordination

'Sacramental Offering'

The Response asks Anglicans to affirm that the ordained priest, when celebrating the Eucharist, 'offers sacramentally the redemptive sacrifice of Christ'. Now ARCIC affirms unambiguously the legitimacy of speaking of the Eucharist as a 'sacramental sacrifice', with the proviso that this is not understood as a repetition of the historical sacrifice. What more is being asked here? Recent statements from the Roman magisterium have helpfully stressed that communion in the body and blood of Christ is a participation in the fruits of the sacrifice of our propitiation.[6] With this no Anglican will disagree. But there is also a growing suggestion of a distinction between the sacramental offering of the priest and the spiritual offering of the people. The point is made in the CDF's earlier *Observations* on ARCIC. But it can be argued that this goes beyond Trent. The Council spoke of Mass celebrated with the faithful, but without their sacramental participation in holy communion, a practice now happily much less frequent than at the time of Trent. In such a case, according to Trent, the people participate spiritually rather than sacramentally. But this is not to say when the faithful do receive communion that they do not participate in the sacrifice sacramentally.[7] If this novel distinction is being hinted at in the Response, Anglicans will want to consider its implications very carefully. Some Anglicans are more comfortable than others with the language of 'eucharistic sacrifice', but even those Anglicans would be cautious at any suggestion that *only* the ordained part of the Body of Christ is *sacramentally* joined to Christ's self-offering to the Father. Such an understanding seems to go against much of the best eucharistic theology of recent years. Moreover, it goes against the plain

---

[6] Cf. Pope John Paul II's Letter for Holy Thursday 1980, *Dominicae Cenae*; the full text in English translation, is in *Origins*, vol. 19, no. 41 (27 March 1980), pp. 653ff.

[7] Cf. Power, *The Sacrifice We Offer*.

meaning of the Latin liturgical texts which refer to a corporate sacramental offering.[8]

Priestly 'Character'

The Response asks for clarification of the fact that Christ 'instituted the sacrament of orders as the rite which confers the priesthood in the New Covenant'. Both Catholic and Anglican biblical scholars will not find that formulation of things easy, but an examination of the Anglican ordination rites (ancient and modern) would show exactly what Anglicans believe and practise as regards this question. Apparently the lack of the use of the term 'character' promoted this unease. ARCIC attempted to describe a commonly understood reality without using all the technical terms of the past. The term 'character' can, in English, be very easily misunderstood as denoting moral qualities, though this is not the intention of its use in the context of sacramental theology. However, the term 'character' is used officially in the Anglican tradition. It is enshrined in Church of England Canon Law that 'no person admitted to the order of bishop, priest or deacon can ever be divested of the character of his order', though he may, of course, be deprived or deposed of the exercise of his orders (C.1.2).

Since ARCIC drafted its *Elucidation* on the ordination of women, there has been much debate and development. Women priests have been ordained in a number of Anglican provinces. The Response is therefore correct to insist that the gender of subjects for ordination cannot be entirely separated from discussion about the nature of holy orders. If Anglicans and Roman Catholics have different practices with regard to the ordination of women to the priesthood (some Anglican provinces, that is) this clearly indicates important differences which must have implications for a total picture of the ordained ministry. The Response says nothing specifically about the diaconate. Does the official willingness of the Orthodox to readmit women to the diaconate weaken Catholic–Orthodox agreement about holy orders? Or the actual admission of women to the diaconate among the Oriental Orthodox, for example, the Armenian Apostolic Church?

---

[8] Including such a late text as the *Orate, Fratres*.

Apostolic Succession

The Response asks for more on the meaning of apostolic succession. Both an unbroken episcopal succession and an uninterrupted continuity in Christian doctrine (in communion with the college of bishops and its head) are seen as essential components of its meaning. *Lumen Gentium* 20 is cited as authority for this. *Lumen Gentium* 20 is by no means unacceptable to Anglicans with its careful historical reference to the fluidity and variety of ministries in the primitive Church and its important juxtaposition of a continuing Petrine ministry and a continuing apostolic ministry within the whole episcopate. But what the Response itself says seems to hint at a requirement that apostolic succession includes not only continuity of succession and teaching but also communion with the pope. If this is being said Anglicans would again ask about the Orthodox, for Vatican II certainly recognises apostolic succession in some Churches not in communion with Rome (*Unitatis Redintegratio*, 15).

Tradition

Finally, the Response turns to Scripture and the living tradition of the Church. Among the reasons for asking for further study of this question is the assertion in the Final Report than an infallible judgment would need to be 'manifestly a legitimate interpretation of biblical faith in line with orthodox tradition'. Is Rome really saying this need not be so? In which case what of Canon 749.3: 'No doctrine is understood to be infallibly defined unless this is manifestly demonstrated'? Having said this, no Anglican would wish to preclude further study of Scripture, Tradition and the authority of the living Church to teach. Indeed the Lambeth Conference of 1988 called for just such a continued exploration of 'the basis in Scripture and Tradition of the concept of a universal primacy, in conjunction with collegiality, as an instrument of unity'. Cardinal Ratzinger has stressed the importance of such a dialogue about Tradition and there is no doubt that this must be amongst the most important of matters for the continuing ARCIC agenda. Nevertheless, to this must be added the all important ecclesiological question: what is the status of Churches not in communion with Rome? If this question is not asked, and answered comparatively positively so that some ecclesiological value is accorded to such Churches, as I believe *Lumen Gentium* and

Unitatis Redintegratio intended, the scope and meaning of the living Tradition of the Church will be seriously attenuated.

Forgetting the Agreed Basis

Overall, I have the uneasy feeling that the drafters of much of the Response have forgotten the agreed basis for Anglican–Roman Catholic dialogue. I am reminded of John Henry Newman's visit to the Venerable English College, Rome, in 1833. Newman and Hurrell Froude called on the Rector, Nicholas Wiseman. They had two long talks with him at which Wiseman told them there was no hope for reunion without total acceptance of the Council of Trent.[9] Much of the Response, though not all, reads as if it were written from this simplistic perspective, with the addition of the definitions of the First Vatican Council and the Marian dogmas.

In their *Common Declaration* (1966) Pope Paul VI and Michael Ramsey consciously and explicitly spoke of a 'serious dialogue which, *founded upon the Gospels and on the ancient common traditions*, may lead to that unity in truth, for which Christ prayed' (emphasis mine). ARCIC consciously followed this mandate, which has been explicitly approved by Pope John Paul II. To test the results of ARCIC against definitions made since our separation is seriously to misunderstand the method of ARCIC, just as it is to set them up against traditional Anglican formularies. The Vatican Response will seem to many Anglicans to challenge the hitherto agreed method established and agreed by Paul VI and Michael Ramsey. This method has been further endorsed by the present Pope in Common Declarations with the Oriental Church in which even the definition of the Council of Chalcedon has proved to be expressible in other words.

The correspondence columns of *The Tablet* recently (26 October 1991) carried a long letter from Cardinal Ratzinger which touched on this crucial debate about ecumenical method. In it the Cardinal argued (from a personal point of view, I assume) that he had not gone back on his important statement of 1976 that 'Rome must not require a doctrine of primacy of the East other than what was formulated and experienced in the first millennium'. The Cardinal had on another occasion explained his understanding of this principle in relation to

9 I. Ker, *John Henry Newman: A Biography* (Oxford University Press, 1988), p. 69.

Anglicans.[10] He properly qualified it, if it is interpreted to mean the 'denial of the existence of the universal Church in the second millennium', with Tradition somehow becoming frozen at the end of the first.

But even with this important and wholly necessary ecclesiological qualification, it seems to me that much of the Response fails to take seriously the agreed method of ARCIC and fails to explore imaginatively the 'Ratzinger' principle: that is, how the Roman Catholic Church could agree ecumenically in faith with another Christian body *without* the imposition of definitions arrived at *in absentia* but with assurance that the essential content of faith is not denied. Moreover, there seem to be hints at the requiring of doctrine which goes beyond Trent on the eucharist, where Trent deliberately left options open.

I am not particularly surprised that Rome has felt bound to be so hesitant about ARCIC. Nor am I too depressed by this because I believe that its Response brings out into the open the clear need to discuss ecumenical method and an ecumenical ecclesiology, even before particular questions of authority. On the one hand there is the principle, upon which the Pontifical Council for Promoting Christian Unity works, of going behind definitions. On the other there is the traditional method of working of the Congregation for the Doctrine of the Faith in which any document is scrutinised for identity with current official teaching. And there is the fundamental question of where the living Tradition of the Church is to be found yesterday and today. If the Response ultimately provokes positive ecumenical decisions on these questions it will have done much good, in spite of its disappointing hesitations.

---

[10] For Cardinal Ratzinger's two statements, see the chapter 'Anglican–Catholic Dialogue: Its Problems and Hopes', in his *Church, Ecumenism and Politics* (St Paul Publications, Slough, 1987) (see also Chapter 22).

21
EDWARD YARNOLD:
Roman Catholic Responses to ARCIC I and ARCIC II (1993)[1]

Rome has now made three responses to the work of the two Anglican–Roman Catholic International Commissions. In 1982 the Congregation for the Doctrine of the Faith (CDF) published its *Observations* on the Final Report of ARCIC I [see Chapter 5]. Six years later the CDF produced a new set of *Observations* on ARCIC II's Agreed Statement *Salvation and the Church*. Finally in 1991, after a nine-year process in which all bishops' conferences throughout the world were consulted, the same Congregation was responsible for the definitive Roman Catholic Response to ARCIC I's Final Report.

In 1987 Rome passed judgment on another ecumenical agreement, the Faith and Order Commission's document *Baptism, Eucharist and Ministry* (BEM), which was published in 1982, a few months after ARCIC's Final Report. Since the subject-matter of the two reports partially coincides – both seek agreement over Eucharist and ministry – it may be illuminating to compare the responses made to ARCIC with those made to BEM. However, their scope differs in two important respects. First, while ARCIC was a bilateral dialogue, Faith and Order includes all the mainstream churches; secondly, while ARCIC sought to articulate an existing 'substantial agreement' of the two churches, BEM had the more modest aim of inviting the member churches to explore certain lines of 'convergence'.[2]

[1] This is a slightly modified extract from my article 'Roman Catholic Responses to ARCIC I and II', in *Reconciliation: Essays in Honour of Michael Hurley* (Columba Press, Dublin, 1993), pp. 32–52. I am grateful to the editor, Oliver Rafferty, for his permission to make use of it here.

[2] These documents have been published in many forms. For the two sets of *Observations* I shall be referring to the editions published by the Catholic Truth Society, London, 1982 and 1988 respectively; for the

1 The Status of the Responses

The *Observations* of 1982 begin with a note stating that they were formulated by the CDF 'at the request of the Holy Father'. The Congregation speaks in its own name (e.g. 'The Congregation finally has to note that . . .'); there is no claim that it is the Church's definitive judgment which is being expressed. As Cardinal Ratzinger explained in a letter to the Catholic Co-Chairman of ARCIC, Bishop Alan Clark, the *Observations* were intended as the CDF's 'contribution to the continuation of this dialogue'.

The corresponding *Observations* on the ARCIC II statement on salvation carry a higher degree of authority. Although, as with the previous document, the aim is said to be 'the furthering of the dialogue', it is now made clear that what is offered is not suggestions, but 'an authoritative doctrinal judgment', which carries 'the authority of a text approved by the Holy Father'. Evidently these second *Observations* constitute an act of the *magisterium*.

The 1991 Response to the Final Report is a document of still higher authority. Although not actually signed by Pope John Paul, it constitutes the Roman Catholic Church's formal judgment: the Pope referred to it as the 'Official' Response, given at a 'truly ecclesial' level.[3] The key section of the Response is a short 'General Evaluation' of four paragraphs, which explains its own authority as that of 'the Catholic Church's . . . definitive response to the results achieved by ARCIC I'. It is followed by an 'Explanatory Note' some ten pages long, which is described as 'the fruit of close collaboration between the Congregation for the Doctrine of the Faith and the Pontifical Council for Promoting Christian Unity'. This note puts forward the reasons which underlie the Response, without itself possessing the same definitive authority.

The BEM document was not judged to require a response of comparable authority. The response made no claims to provide a 'definitive judgment', being merely headed 'An Appraisal'. It

---

Response to ARCIC I I shall refer to the text in *Catholic International*, 3/3, 1–14 February, pp. 125–30, with its paragraph numbers; for the *Appraisal* of BEM, I shall refer to the edition in *Information Service*, Secretariat for Christian Unity, 65 (1988), pp. 121–39.

[3] Address to English bishops, which forms Chapter 13 in this collection.

was the work of the Secretariat (now the Council) for Promoting Christian Unity (CPCU). Instead of using such phrases as 'the Catholic Church judges', it is content more modestly to use expressions like 'we think', 'we believe', with the exception of statements of general encouragement, such as 'The Catholic Church sees in BEM a significant result of the ecumenical movement'.

2 Substantial Agreement?

ARCIC I's claim that 'substantial agreement' had been reached over the Eucharist and ordination and was possible even over authority caused much perplexity in Rome. The 1982 *Observations* made particularly heavy weather of the phrase, wondering whether 'substantial' was a synonym for 'real' or 'genuine', or whether it indicated 'a fundamental agreement about points which are truly essential'. If the latter, the CDF indicated that it was still not clear whether ARCIC judges that remaining differences concern only 'secondary points (for example, the structure of liturgical rites, theological opinion, ecclesiastical discipline, spirituality), or whether these are points which truly pertain to the faith'.

In reality ARCIC I attempted several times to explain the term 'substantial agreement'. The most explicit definition is given in the *Elucidation* to the Eucharist: 'unanimous agreement "on essential matters where it [the Commission] considers that doctrine admits no divergence" (Ministry, para. 17)' (Eucharistic Doctrine: *Elucidation*, para. 2). A somewhat different understanding of substantial agreement can be inferred from *Eucharistic Doctrine*, paragraph 12:

> We believe that we have reached substantial agreement on the doctrine of the eucharist. Although we are all conditioned by the traditional ways in which we have expressed and practised our eucharistic faith, we are convinced that if there are any remaining points of disagreement they can be resolved on the principles here established. . . . It is our hope that, in view of the agreement which we have reached on eucharistic faith, this doctrine will no longer constitute an obstacle to the unity we seek.

Substantial agreement therefore seems to imply that remaining points can be settled on the basis of the agreement reached and ought no longer to provide a reason for the churches to remain disunited.

It remains true however that ARCIC did not provide an answer to the CDF's question regarding the status of the secondary points over which agreement was not achieved. In discussing the objections which some Evangelicals feel against any form of adoration paid to the reserved sacrament, the *Elucidation* on the Eucharist indicates that such 'divergence in matters of practice and in theological judgements relating to them, without destroying a common eucharistic faith' exemplifies the meaning of substantial agreement (Eucharistic Doctrine: *Elucidation*, para. 9). It appears then that the remaining differences are not thought to relate to essential matters of faith. The earlier discussion of the question in the eucharistic statement, however, is not so clear (Eucharistic Doctrine, para. 12). Reference is made to 'a variety of theological approaches', but it is not stated whether all differences are of this kind. It is implied that agreement is substantial provided points of disagreement 'can be resolved on the principles here established', in which event 'this doctrine will no longer be an obstacle to the unity we seek'; but again it is not explained whether these points of disagreement may include matters of faith or only matters of practice or opinion. The 1991 Response clearly implies that the difference concerning reservation is one of faith: 'one remains with the conviction that this is an area in which real consensus between Anglicans and Roman Catholics is lacking' (para. 23).

The Secretariat (now Council) for Christian Unity worked out the following definition of substantial agreement for its own purposes in 1977:

> this relates to a basic nucleus without which the message of salvation is not transmitted in its integrity, while accepting that neither doctrinal elaborations nor practice correspond entirely among the partner churches. The essentials are assured, and there is the same shared intention of faith.[4]

In fact the distinction between matters of faith on the one hand, and expressions of doctrine and theological opinions on the other, is not free from difficulty. Even theological opinions

---

[4] Quoted in Y. Congar, *Diversity and Communion* (SCM, London, 1984), p. 140.

are attempts to express the implications of the faith. The bottom limit of substantial agreement is easy to define: if one church condemns another's doctrines as incompatible with Christian faith, there is no substantial agreement. More difficult to decide is the situation (the question of eucharistic adoration is a case in point) where one church is unable to endorse the doctrines of another church without however condemning them as heretical.

It would have been fair to ask ARCIC how it knew that remaining difficulties concerning the eucharist and ministry could be resolved on the grounds of the fundamental agreement that had been reached. One answer, which would be partly true, would be based on what Newman called a convergence of probabilities: an indefinable network of factors, arising from protracted discussion and the growth of intimate friendship, had enabled the participants to recognise their partners' faith as so close to their own that, as far as the doctrine in question was concerned, there no longer seemed any justification for their churches to remain apart. But in addition the essential areas of belief had long been identified; ARCIC judged these points to be truly fundamental, so that other connected issues must, almost by definition, be soluble on the agreed basis. Thirdly, there could be (as in Eucharistic Doctrine, para. 12) an appeal to the virtue of hope: the Holy Spirit that had taken them so far in agreement must be able to lead them on to solve remaining problems.

3 Consonance

When the Final Report was sent to the two churches, each church was asked whether it was in agreement with the contents of the report. The question however was asked not in terms of substantial agreement but of consonance: each church was asked whether the Final Report was 'consonant in substance with [its] faith'. As is well known, the answers which the two churches gave are very different in tone.

On the Anglican side, each of the twenty-nine autonomous churches gave its answer to the question, before an answer was given for the whole Anglican Communion at the Lambeth Conference of 1988. A booklet entitled *Towards a Church of England Response to BEM and ARCIC* was compiled by the Faith and Order Advisory Group of the Church of England to provide material on which the Church of England's response was based.[5] It was explained that:

> Minor discrepancies are of no hindrance, and it may be presupposed that the language of the ARCIC statements is not simply identical with the language of the Anglican tradition itself. . . . To express an opinion on whether the statements are 'consonant in substance with the faith of Anglicans' is to make a judgement, in the matters of which the statements treat, about whether they are compatible not with any formulary of the past but with the living faith of Anglicans.[6]

On the Eucharist the verdict was:

> We believe that we can say with the Commission 'this is the Christian faith of the Eucharist'. Moreover we believe the Final Report on the Eucharist to be 'consonant in substance with the faith of Anglicans'.[7]

The judgment passed on ministry was similar, although it was admitted that the question of the ordination of women was a matter of 'fundamental . . . doctrine': 'We agree that we can recognise our own faith in the text; it is consonant with the faith of Anglicans'.[8]

The eventual judgment of the Church of England followed the guidance of the FOAG booklet. In similar terms the Lambeth Conference, representing the whole Anglican Communion, resolved that the Agreed Statements on Eucharist and Ministry were 'consonant in substance with the faith of Anglicans', even though an Explanatory Note indicates that this verdict was not unqualified:

> The Provinces gave a clear 'yes' to the statement on *Eucharistic Doctrine*. . . . Some Provinces asked for clarification about the meaning of *anamnesis* and bread and wine 'becoming' the body and blood of Christ. But no Province rejected the Statement and many were extremely positive. . . . While we respect continuing anxieties of some Anglicans in the area

---

[5] The judgment of the other provinces of the Anglican Communion are summarised in *The Emmaus Report: A Report of the Anglican Ecumenical Consultation of 1987* (Church House Publishing, London, 1987).

[6] *Towards a Church of England Response to BEM and ARCIC* (CIO Publishing, London, 1985), p. 67 [not in our extract].

[7] *Towards a Church of England Response to BEM and ARCIC*, p. 74 [p.118].

[8] *Towards a Church of England Response to BEM and ARCIC*, pp. 79–80 [p.126].

of 'sacrifice' and 'presence', they do not appear to reflect the common mind of the Provincial responses. . . . Both are areas of 'mystery' which ultimately defy definition. But the Agreed Statement on the Eucharist *sufficiently* expresses Anglican understanding . . .[9]

The provinces had given a similar 'yes' to the Statement on ministry, though problems concerning, for example, language and style, and the meaning of priesthood are acknowledged. It is admitted that 'an ambivalent reply came from one Province which has traditionally experienced a difficult relationship with the Roman Catholic Church'. The note recognises that such difficulties may be due to non-theological reasons: 'this seems to reflect the need for developing deeper links of trust and friendship as ecumenical dialogue goes forward'.[10] It is evident then that Lambeth, like the Church of England's FOAG, did not believe consonance required identity of language or even compatibility with past formulas.

It seems in fact that there is a whole range of possible understandings of consonance. At the lowest end of the scale one would place compatibility or non-contradiction: in this sense one could say that the proposition that the moon is made of green cheese is consonant (i.e. compatible) with the faith of Anglicans (or Roman Catholics). At the other extreme one would find identity of meaning, even if not of verbal expression. The Anglican understanding of consonance evidently falls somewhere between these two extremes. This is especially evident in the FOAG booklet, which rejects the use of past formularies as a standard (even of compatibility!) and speaks instead of 'the living faith of Anglicans'. The Roman Catholic CPCU's understanding of substantial agreement, quoted above, which speaks of 'the same shared intention of faith' with the preservation of essentials, also seems to fall into the middle of the range.

The 1991 Roman Response, however, comes to the upper limit of the scale. It is, of course, inevitable that the Catholic understanding of consonance should be more rigorous than the Anglican, for the simple reason that Anglicans do not grant such normative status to post-patristic classical formulas of

[9] *The Truth Shall Make You Free 1988* (Church House Publishing, London, 1988), pp. 210–11 [pp. 154–5].
[10] *The Truth Shall Make You Free 1988*, p. 212 [p. 155].

belief as Catholics do. Although the creeds and the definitions of the first four (or seven) councils do constitute for Anglicans binding statements of faith, the same cannot be said of later formulas. This is evident in the Declaration of Assent and its Preface in the rite for the ordination of a bishop in the Church of England's Alternative Service Book of 1980, in which the Archbishop is to state that the Church of England

> professes the faith uniquely revealed in the holy Scriptures and set forth in the catholic creeds, which faith the Church is called upon to proclaim afresh in each generation. Led by the Holy Spirit, it has borne witness to Christian truth in its historic formularies, the Thirty-nine Articles of Religion, the Book of Common Prayer, and the Ordering of Bishops, Priests, and Deacons.

In reply the bishop-elect affirms his 'belief in the faith which is revealed in the holy Scriptures and set forth in the catholic creeds and to which the historic formularies of the Church of England bear witness'. In other words, the 'historic formularies' of the Church of England do not have the same authority as the scriptures and the creeds. Scripture and creeds are the unique vehicles or expressions of revelation; the other formularies are witnesses to that revelation, and are therefore normative only in so far as their witness is accurate. Consequently what Anglicans will require of ecumenical documents is that they be faithful to the revelation contained in scripture and set forth in creeds; a document will not necessarily be deficient if it is not consonant with everything contained in the witnesses to revelation.

For Catholics, on the other hand, the definitions of all the ecumenical councils and papal *ex-cathedra* pronouncements are normative. The ARCIC Report will have to pass the test of consonance with them. But what does such consonance involve? Although neither the *Observations* of 1982 nor those of 1988 speak expressly of 'consonance', the Response of 1991 makes its understanding of the term very clear:

> . . . the Roman Catholic Church was asked to give a clear answer to the question: are the agreements contained in this Report consonant with the faith of the Catholic Church? What was asked for was not a simple evaluation of an ecumenical study, but an official response as to the *identity* [italics mine] of the various statements with the faith of the Church.

In the light of this understanding of consonance as equivalent to identity, the Response states that certain doctrines need 'greater clarification *from the Catholic point of view*', that 'the *faith of the Catholic Church* would be even more clearly reflected' if certain further points were made, that certain statements need 'further clarification *from the Catholic perspective*' (italics mine).

Now neither the Response nor the earlier *Observations* demand that agreed formulas should be *verbally* identical with those of the Roman Catholic Church. Such a demand would have been inconsistent with Pope John Paul II's address to ARCIC I in 1980, in which he seemed to commend the commission's method:

> Your method has been to go behind the habit of thought and expression born and nourished in enmity and controversy, to scrutinise together the great common treasure, to clothe it in a language at once traditional and expressive of the insights of an age which no longer glories in strife but seeks to come together in listening to the quiet voice of the Spirit.

The 1988 *Observations* give the clearest statement of what is wanted, though without using the term 'consonance':

> Without disavowing anything in a method which has produced incontestable results, one could still ask if it would not be opportune to perfect the procedure in such a way as to permit a more precise determination of the doctrinal content of the formulas employed to express a common faith.

The CDF characterises the language of the ARCIC agreement on salvation as 'symbolic', and would perhaps pass the same judgment on the language of the Final Report. The danger it sees in such a method is that it makes it difficult to construct a 'truly univocal agreement'. What is wanted is 'more rigorous doctrinal formulations', which would permit 'a rigorous comparison between the respective positions'. Such formulations need not be 'scholastic ones': the CDF does not disapprove on principle of ARCIC's attempt to find a new language untainted with polemical associations.[11]

If then the identity that Rome is requiring between the ARCIC statements and Roman Catholic faith is not a verbal

[11] *Observations* (1988), p. 16.

identity, what is it? What it seems to envisage is an agreement which, in rigorous language which is incapable of misinterpretation, expresses the Roman Catholic faith with the full precision and the full detail in which it has been officially defined. Thus it is not sufficient to affirm the sacrificial nature of the Eucharist: one must also state that 'the Church . . . makes present the sacrifice of Calvary', and that the eucharistic sacrifice has a 'propitiatory nature . . . which can be applied also to the deceased' (Response, para. 21). It is not sufficient to affirm that the Eucharist is Christ's gift of himself to the Church in which the bread and wine become the body and blood of Christ: one must also state that Christ 'makes himself present sacramentally and substantially when under the species of bread and wine these earthly realities are changed into the reality of his Body and Blood, Soul and Divinity' (para. 22).

Commentators on the Response have wondered whether this demand for identity contradicts some very high level directives which ARCIC had been given. In 1966 Pope Paul VI and Archbishop Michael Ramsey, in their Common Declaration which led to the setting up of ARCIC, announced their intention of setting up a 'serious dialogue . . . founded on the Gospels and on the ancient common traditions' which would lead to 'unity in truth'. Pope John Paul II's 1980 address to ARCIC I developed this idea: 'We have a common treasure, which we must recover and in the fullness of which we must share, not losing certain characteristic qualities and gifts which have been ours even in our divided state.'

If the dialogue was to be based on the ancient common traditions, the Report could not be required to include agreement about all post-reformation developments of the basic common faith. Unless the Church was deficient in its faith for fifteen hundred years, the ancient traditions up to the reformation must include all that is essential.

Once more we are back with the question of substantial agreement. Can one separate the essentials of a doctrine which must be included in the common tradition and treasure, and which any genuine agreement must contain, from the more elaborate conceptions of the doctrine (the 'characteristic qualities' of which Pope John Paul spoke), which have taken time to develop, but are still expressions of the same essential faith? An affirmative answer can claim the support of the Vatican II 'hierarchy of truths', according to which doctrines 'vary in their connection with the foundation of the Christian faith'.[12] The 1982 *Observations* expressly excludes the appeal to this concept, but does not justify its attitude.[13]

4 Freedom from Ambiguity

There is another side to the Response's insistence on identity, namely the requirement that all possible ambiguity must be removed. This demand is already explicit in the first set of *Observations*:

> Certain formulations in the Report are not sufficiently explicit and hence can lend themselves to a twofold interpretation, in which both parties can find unchanged the expression of their own position. . . . In effect, if a formulation which has received the agreement of the experts can be diversely interpreted, how could it serve as a basis for reconciliation on the level of church life and practice?[14]

The 1988 *Observations* quote this passage *in extenso*; it is in this context that they raise their doubts about the capacity of 'symbolic' language to formulate a 'truly univocal agreement'. So too the Response 'looks for certain clarifications which will assure that these [common] affirmations are understood in a way that conforms to Catholic doctrine'.[15]

The Secretariat for Unity also found BEM to be insufficiently unambiguous at certain points. Thus what BEM says about the Eucharist as the 'sacrament of the unique sacrifice of Christ' is criticised for not saying 'unambiguously that the eucharist is in itself a real sacrifice, the memorial of the sacrifice of Christ on the cross'.[16]

I have written elsewhere that 'the search for perfectly unambiguous formulas as a prelude to reunion is a wild-goose chase'.[17] This is true for at least two reasons. First, the truth about God and his gracious dealings with the human race is too vast to be captured in any single theological formula or

[12] *Unitatis Redintegratio*, 11.
[13] *Observations* (1982), A.2(ii).
[14] *Observations*, A.2 (iii).
[15] Response, Explanatory Note.
[16] Response to BEM, III.B.2.
[17] 'Response to the Response: I', *The Tablet*, 7 December 1991, p. 1525.

system. Consequently there needs to be a diversity of expressions of the faith if our conceptions are not to be impoverished. It also follows that any statement about God that is not trivial is likely to be capable of more than one interpretation. Secondly, since terms acquire new associations when they are used in new cultural contexts and translated into different languages, it will be impossible to ensure that ideas from one theological tradition are grasped in the identical sense by another tradition. A certain ambiguity is therefore of the nature of ecumenical agreements. It is harmful only if it conceals fundamental differences; it is benign if it allows each side to bring its characteristic religious experience to the interpretation of the same fundamental faith.

But how can one tell that there is the same fundamental faith? The criterion is not to be found in verbal formulas alone. As I wrote in the article quoted in the last paragraph:

> Subscription to common dogmatic formulas is only one of many strands that bind the members of a Church together in a common faith. Common scriptures, a mutually acceptable standard of Christian life, shared worship, particularly shared holy Communion, a common ministry, and a single universal primacy are other bonds of faith. . . . If reunion is to be achieved it will come only at the end of a courtship during which the two churches have grown together in faith, life, worship and mission.

Expert Opinion

22

CARDINAL JOSEF RATZINGER:
Anglican–Catholic Dialogue – Its Problems and Hopes (1983)

Introduction: Agreed Statements and the Position of the Roman Congregation for the Faith

In a series of sessions between January 1970 and September 1981 the Anglican–Roman Catholic International Commission drew up statements on the Eucharist, Ministry and Ordination, and Authority in the Church. The aim of the Commission was to prepare a way for the restoration of intercommunion between the two Churches. There was no intention of solving *all* controversial issues, but it was hoped under these headings to get to grips with the major causes of division. Even here no claim was made to have achieved complete agreement in every detail[1] but conviction was expressed that the statements provided a fundamental common approach to these questions which might be termed 'substantial agreement', since fundamental principles were developed in them, whereby any remaining

[1] *Anglican-Roman Catholic International Commission, The Final Report*: Windsor, September 1981 (CTS/SPCK, London, 1982). The admitted limitation of the document with regard to achieved consensus is clearly expressed especially in *Authority II*, section *Jurisdiction*, paras. 16–33. Also in other places, e.g. *Elucidation* to *Eucharistic Doctrine*, paras. 8 and 9, certain limitations are mentioned.

particular disagreements in these areas might be resolved.[2] The
document accordingly concludes with the confident assertion
that now – in 1981 – it is more than evident that 'under the
Holy Spirit, our Churches have grown closer together in faith
and charity. There are high expectations that significant initiatives will be boldly undertaken to deepen our reconciliation
and lead us forward in the quest for full communion'.[3]

At the same time the Commission was fully aware that the
ultimate decision as to the ecclesiastical relevance of its findings did not rest with itself. All along it had intended, according
to the ecclesiastical mandate which had called it into being, to
submit its statements to the 'respective authorities'. Since its
purpose was not merely academic but focused on ecclesiastical
reality, the statements had to go through an official ecclesiastical
process of examination and judgement.[4] This took place when
the sessions came to an end in September 1981. It was also
clear that, since ecclesiastical authority is structured differently
in each case, examination and decision making would also have
to be conducted on quite different lines by the respective
authorities. Perhaps one should remark at this point that any
presentation of the theme 'Authority in the Church' which was
really intended to lead to unity, would have to take into
account in a much more concrete way the actual form of
authority in order to do justice to the question. For if there was
surprise afterwards at the fact that the Roman Catholic Church
can give an authoritative answer more immediately than
Anglican structures allow for, this is surely an indication that
too little attention had been paid to the actual functioning of
authority. It was probably not made clear enough that the pope
– especially since Vatican II – has a special authentic teaching
function for the whole Church: it is not indeed infallible but
does make authoritative decisions.[5] On the other hand the text
left one completely in the dark as to the concrete structure of
authority in the Anglican community. Those well acquainted
with Anglicanism know that the Lambeth Conference, originally
instituted in 1867, was not due to meet for several years,

---

[2] Cf. *Eucharistic Doctrine*, para. 12: 'We believe we have reached substantial agreement on the doctrine of the eucharist . . . if there are any
remaining points of disagreement they can be resolved on the principles here established . . .'

[3] Conclusion, p. 99.

[4] E.g. *Authority I*, para. 26 (Conclusion).

[5] Cf. *Lumen Gentium*, 12, 22; especially in this context, 25.

according to its regular timing, and that no authoritative pronouncement could be made before that date. But ought not the text to have mentioned this structure in order to give a true explanation of the problem of authority without stopping short of the concrete reality? Would not the right and indeed necessary thing have been to explain what sort of teaching authority and jurisdiction belongs or does not belong to this assembly of bishops? Should one not also have gone into the question of the relation between political and ecclesiastical authority in the Church which first touches the nerve-point of the question of the Catholicity of the Church or the relation between local and universal Church? In 1640 Parliament decided as follows: 'Convocation has no power to enact canons or constitutions concerning matters of doctrine or discipline, or in any other way to bind clergy or religious without the consent of Parliament.' That may be obsolete, but it came to mind again in 1927 when on two occasions a version of the Book of Common Prayer was rejected by Parliament.[6] However that may be, these concrete questions should have been clarified and answered, if a viable agreement about 'Authority in the Church' was the aim in view. For it is of the essence of authority to be concrete, consequently one can only do justice to the theme by naming the actual authorities and clarifying their relative position on both sides instead of just theorizing about authority.

But to go back to our starting point: this parenthesis was only inserted because, after there had been theoretical substantial agreement about authority in the Church, the actual intervention of authority resulted in misunderstanding and bad feeling. What had happened? According to the express intention of ARCIC, the Congregation for the Faith, commissioned by the pope as central organ of ecclesiastical authority, had set to work examining the texts as soon as they were completed, and then on 29 March 1982 promulgated a detailed statement of their opinion. This was first despatched to the

---

[6] Th. Schnitker, *The American Book of Common Prayer* (Th Rev 78, 1982, 265–72) points out that as a result of 'Church of England (Worship and Doctrine) Measure 1974', the Church of England itself, without ratification from Parliament, can make decisions about its liturgical books. With Schedule 2 of this document the Act of Uniformity 1662, like almost all liturgical enactments of state controlled churches, has become invalid (a.a.O., Note 3, col. 266f).

Bishops' Conference as a 'Contribution to the current dialogue', and then on 6 May 1982 published in the *Osservatore Romano*.[7] Pursuing the matter further, one can say that this was an example of the functioning of precisely that structure of authority sketched out by Vatican II. One can clearly recognise three characteristic elements of that structure – the office of Peter's successor, the worldwide college of bishops, and relation in dialogue to other Christian Churches and denominations. In this case we see ecumenical dialogue raised from the sphere of particular groups – which are not yet authoritative, however important and well authorised they may be – and transferred to the level of matters concerning the whole Church in a universal and obligatory way. Then the See of Peter speaks through one of its central organs, not indeed in a definitive manner, yet with an authority which carries more weight in the Church than a merely academic publication about the question would. Based on the teaching of the Church, the document provides guidelines for further development of the dialogue. And finally the whole college of bishops, as successors of the apostles, are drawn into the dialogue in their capacity of responsibility for the whole Church.

The Fundamental Problem of the Dialogue: The Authority of Tradition, and the Central Organs of Unity

1 Preliminary Note on the Situation of the Discussion

The above statements have already brought us right to the heart of the problem with which Anglican–Catholic dialogue is concerned. A first reading of the ARCIC documents might well convey the impression that nothing but Vatican I's teaching about papal primacy, and the more recent Marian dogmas, stood in the way of complete agreement. The reaction of the media, which are always bound to be on the look-out for something striking and quickly grasped, intensified this impression which only too easily turned into the opinion that reconciliation was held up only by particular nineteenth century dogmas on the part of Rome. Were this the case, it would certainly be

[7] The essential content of the text was pre-announced in a letter, published on 31 March 1982 in the *Osservatore Romano*, from the Prefect of the Congregation for the Faith, to the Catholic Chairman of ARCIC, Bishop Clark.

hard to understand why Rome laid so much stress on such recent, particular doctrinal developments, apparently even wishing to raise them to a touchstone of ecumenism. In point of fact, both the aforesaid dogmas are only the most tangible symptoms of the overall problem of authority in the Church. The way one views the structure of Christianity will necessarily affect in some measure, great or small, one's attitude to various particular matters contained within the whole. For this reason I do not wish here to go into the particular points which surfaced in the dialogue between Catholics and Anglicans, and which have already been dealt with in the ARCIC Report as well as in the comments of the Congregation for the Faith. I would prefer to approach one single point from various aspects – the point which has already emerged from a simple account of the course of events as the core of the problem, namely the question of authority. This is identical with the question of tradition and cannot be separated from that of the relation between the universal Church and a particular Church. Even this problem cannot receive comprehensive, systematic treatment here. Within the limits of this short essay it would seem more to the point to dispense with systematic procedure and simply juxtapose a series of observations which will nevertheless, each in its own way, reflect something of the whole.

But first it would seem fitting to comment briefly on the general nature of the statement of the Congregation for the Faith and of the Agreed Statements of ARCIC which underlie it. Almost everywhere newspapers and reports tell how the communication from the Roman Congregation begins with a few short, meaningless and florid compliments, and that everything is merely negative and critical, so that by the end of it one is left with a discouraging impression. Such an assertion could only be the result of a very superficial reading of the text. In the relatively short first section, dealing with the subject as a whole, the positive side is stated first and then followed up by criticism. This pattern is retained throughout the sections dealing with particular subjects. Attention is first drawn to the important steps forward that have been made in dealing with the particular questions, and then guidelines are laid down to show the way ahead if a really viable basic 'substantial agreement' is to be reached. Actually it is impossible to read through the ARCIC statements without feeling a great sense of gratitude, for they show how far theological thought has matured in the last decade as regards shared insight. Recourse to scripture and the Fathers has brought to light the common foundations of diverging confessional developments, and so opened up that perspective in which apparently irreconcilable elements can be fused together into the wholeness of the one truth. The desire for unity is plain: one might say that the hermeneutics of unity have made a new understanding of the sources possible, and conversely, recourse to the sources has evoked hermeneutics of unity. All this is indisputable and makes the ARCIC documents so outstanding that they could be, and had to be, transferred from the sphere of private preparatory work into the forum of the Church's public dialogue. But all this must serve too to justify the courage needed to face the questions squarely and fully both in statement and deliberation. Approbation and criticism are not mutually exclusive: each demands the other. It is only when both are joined together that we get an authentic vehicle for true dialogue. This will be taken for granted as I proceed now to deal with the most urgent questions.

2 *The Authority of Tradition*

The complex of questions we are concerned with here cannot possibly be contained within the single concept 'primacy'. It includes, over and above, determining the co-ordination of scripture–tradition–councils–episcopate–reception. The last two ideas refer to the respective roles of bishops and laity in the formation of Christian doctrine. It is a universal tenet amongst Christians that scripture is the basic standard of Christian faith, the central authority through which Christ himself exercises his authority over the Church and within it. For this reason all teaching in the Church is ultimately exposition of scripture, just as scripture in its turn is exposition of the living word of Jesus Christ: but the ultimate value of all is not what is written but the life which our Lord transmitted to his Church, within which scripture itself lives and is life. Vatican II formulated these mutual relations very beautifully: 'Through tradition the complete canon of sacred books is made known to the Church. Within her the Holy Scriptures are themselves understood at greater depth and ceaselessly put into action. So it is that God who spoke of old, never ceases to converse with the Bride of his beloved Son, and the Holy Spirit – through whom the living voice of the Gospel resounds in the Church and through her in the world beyond – leads the faithful into all truth and causes the word of Christ to dwell amongst them in full measure' (cf. Col. 3.16).[8] There is a priority of scriptures as witness and a priority of the Church as the vital environment for such witness, but both are linked together in constantly alternating relationships, so that neither can be imagined without the other. This relative priority of the Church to scripture obviously presupposes also the existence of the Universal Church as a concrete and active reality, for only the whole Church can be the locus of scripture in this sense. So the question of defining the relation between a particular Church and the universal Church has obviously already claimed a place amongst the fundamental problems.

The mutual dependence of a community living the Bible, and of the Bible in which the community finds the inward standard of its being, is first represented as a subtle spiritual reality, but it becomes a very practical issue with the question: How is scripture recognised in the Church? Who decides whether what you say is in accord with scripture or not? It is rather ambiguous when ARCIC says: 'Neither general councils nor universal primates are invariably preserved from error even in official declarations'.[9] It is still more emphatic in another place: 'The Commission is very far from implying that general councils cannot err and is well aware that they sometimes have erred'.[10] The Synods of Ariminum and of Seleucia are quoted as examples of this. Then it goes on to say: 'Article 21 (i.e. of the Anglican Articles of Religion) affirms that general councils have authority only when their judgements "may be declared that they be taken out of Holy Scripture".' The ARCIC text adds that according to the argument of the Statement also, 'only those judgements of general councils are guaranteed to exclude what is erroneous or are protected from error which have as their content fundamental matters of faith, which formulate central truths of salvation and which are faithful to Scripture and consistent with Tradition'.[11] Moreover there is need for reception; about this it says in what seems a rather

---

[8] *Dei Verbum*, 8.
[9] *Authority II*, para. 27.
[10] *Authority: Elucidation*, para. 3.
[11] *Authority: Elucidation*, para. 3., 'which have as their content, "fundamental matters of faith"'.

dialectical way that 'reception does not create truth nor legitimize the decision', the authority of a council is not derived
entirely from reception on the part of the faithful; on the other
hand it also teaches that a council is 'not so evidently self-
sufficient that its definitions owe nothing to reception'.[12] Another
passage is even more explicit: 'If the definition proposed for
assent were not manifestly a legitimate interpretation of
biblical faith and in line with orthodox tradition, Anglicans
would think it a duty to reserve the reception of the definition
for study and discussion'.[13]

The phrase 'manifestly a legitimate interpretation of biblical
faith' catches one's attention. The dogmas of the pre-Reformation
Church are quite certainly not 'manifestly legitimate' in the
sense in which 'manifest' is used in modern exegesis. If there
were such a thing as the 'manifestly legitimate', obvious enough
to stand in its own right out of range of reasonable discussion,
there would be no need at all for councils and ecclesiastical
teaching authority. On this point questions raised by the continental European Reformation are fully present amongst the
Anglicans. It is true they are modified by the fact that the
survival of the episcopate retains the fundamental structure of
the pre-Reformation Church as the form of life within the
ecclesiastical community to this day. This assures a fundamentally
positive attitude to the doctrinal tenets of the pre-Reformation
Church. Originally this was the intention also of the continental
denominations, but the pull away from tradition was much
stronger in their communities, so that there was far less ability
to hold fast. This modification of the principle of 'scripture
only' has, however, long been more on the level of fact than
of principle; it is true that fact could facilitate the step down
to the fundamental level. This should not be too difficult,
considering the actual authority of tradition. In any case
further dialogue must get to grips in real earnest with this
fundamental issue.

3 The Universal Church and Its Central Organs as the Condition of Tradition

But to return once again to our starting point in the analysis of
the text. Nothing 'manifest' can be derived from intellectual

[12] *Authority: Elucidation*, para. 3.
[13] *Authority II*, para. 29.

discussion or from the mere fact of general opinion in the Church. Ultimately we come up against an anthropological question here; beyond what is purely objective, nothing is 'manifest' to anyone save that he lives. For that reason interpretation is always a question of the whole complex of life.[14] To transfer authority in this way to what is 'manifest', as is done in the passage already quoted, means linking up faith with the authority of historians, i.e. exposing it to conflicting hypotheses. Quite the contrary – keeping in view the faith testified to in the New Testament itself and the life of the early Church, we must hold fast to the conviction that there can be no second sifting through of what the universal Church teaches as universal Church. Who would presume to undertake such a task? One can read greater depth into a pronouncement of the universal Church; one can improve on it linguistically; one can develop it further by focusing on the centre of the faith and on new perspectives opening up a way forward, but one cannot 'discuss' it in the ordinary sense of the word.

At this point it becomes clear what the episcopal office means and what exactly 'tradition' is in the Church. According to the Catholic way of thinking, a bishop is someone who can express the voice of the universal Church in his teaching, or to put it another way: the episcopate is the supreme court in the Church as regards both teaching and decision, because it is the living voice of the universal Church. An individual bishop has full authority as pastor of a particular Church because, and in so far as, he represents the universal Church.

'Apostolic succession' is the sacramental form of the unifying presence of tradition.[15] For this reason the universal Church is not a mere external amplification, contributing nothing to the essential nature of Church in the local Churches, but it extends into that very nature itself. Here it is necessary to contradict the ARCIC Report where it says 'The Second Vatican Council allows it to be said that a Church out of communion with the Roman See may lack nothing from the viewpoint of the Roman

---

[14] Cf. especially the important essays from J. Pieper, *Buchstabierübungen* (München, 1980), pp. 11–30; E. Coreth, *Grundfragen der Hermeneutik* (Freiburg, 1969); H. Anton, 'Interpretation', in J. Ritter-K. Gründer, *Historiches Wörterbuch der Philosophie*, IV (1976), pp. 514–17.

[15] J. Ratzinger, *Theologische Prinzipienlehre* (München, 1982), pp. 251–63, and 300–14.

Catholic Church except that it does not belong to the visible manifestation of full Christian communion'.[16] With such an assertion wrongly claiming the support of Vatican II, Church Unity is debased to an unnecessary, if desirable, externality, and the character of the universal Church is reduced to mere outward representation, of little significance in constituting what is ecclesial. This romantic idea of provincial Churches, which is supposed to restore the structure of the early Church, is really contradicting the historical reality of the early Church as well as the concrete experiences of history, to which one must certainly not turn a blind eye in considerations of this sort. The early Church did indeed know nothing of Roman primacy in practice, in the sense of Roman Catholic theology of the second millennium, but it was well acquainted with living forms of unity in the universal Church which were constitutive of the essence of provincial Churches. Understood in this sense, the priority of the universal Church always preceded that of particular Churches.

I will just instance here three well known phenomena: letters of communion, which bound Churches together; the symbolism

[16] *Authority II*, para. 12. The text of *Lumen Gentium*, 8, quoted here in support, is far from expressing such a conviction. The text runs: 'Haec est unica Christi Ecclesia, quam in Symbolo unam, sanctam, catholicam et apostolicam confitemur . . . Haec Ecclesia, in hoc mundo ut societas constituta et ordinata, subsistit in Ecclesia catholica, a successore Petri et episcopis in eius communione gubernata, licet extra eius compaginem elementa plura sanctificationis et veritatis inveniuntur, quae ut dona Ecclesiae Christi propria, ad unitatem catholicam impellunt.' (This is the unique Church of Christ which in the Creed we avow as one, holy, catholic and apostolic . . . this Church, constituted and organised in the world as a society, subsists in the Catholic Church, which is governed by the successor of Peter and by the bishops in union with that successor, although many elements of sanctification and truth can be found outside of her visible structure. These elements, however, as gifts properly belong to the Church of Christ, possess an inner dynamism towards Catholic unity.) Neither does *Unitatis Redintegratio*, 13, quoted in the same context, say anything of the kind. It gives a typology of *divisions*, and ends the description of communities resulting from sixteenth-century divisions with the sentence: 'Inter eas, in quibus traditiones et structurae catholicae ex parte subsistere pergunt, locum specialem tenet Communio anglicana.' (Among those in which some Catholic traditions and institutions continue to exist, the Anglican Communion occupies a special place.)

of collegiality at the consecration of a bishop. This ceremony was always linked up with living tradition by cross-questioning and acceptance of the Creed, while the imprint of the universal Church was manifest in the fact that bishops of prominent sees were represented: mere neighbourly recognition would not suffice; it had to be made clear that the prominent sees were in communion with each other, as it fell to them to guarantee the character of the universal Church in the case of this particular one. Finally one should include here what people today like to call the conciliarity of the Church, though they often have romantically simplified ideas about it. For it is a known fact that conciliarity has never functioned simply of its own accord by the pure and spontaneous harmony of plurality, as many present day statements would seem to suggest. Actually the authority of the emperor was necessary to summon a council. Take away the person of the emperor, and you can no longer discuss the conciliar reality of the medieval Church but only a theological fiction. Closer consideration shows that the participation of Rome, the See centred on the place where SS. Peter and Paul died, was of great significance for the full validity of a council, even if this factor is less in evidence than the position of the emperor. All the same, Vincent Twomey has already shown in a very well documented piece of research, that already in the contest at Nicaea two opposed options stand out clearly: the Eusebian and the Athanasian, i.e. the idea of an imperial universal Church as against a really theological conception in which it is not the emperor but Rome which plays the decisive role.[17] However that may be, the imperial Church

---

[17] V. Twomey, *Apostolikos Thronos. The Primacy of Rome as reflected in the Church History of Eusebius and the historico-apologetic writings of St Athanasius the great* (Münster, 1982). This extremely thorough work (to my mind) marks a turning point in the approach to this subject in dogmatic history. Here perhaps for the first time it is again brought to light how profoundly imbued the pre-Reformation Church was with the Petrine idea and its connection with the See of Rome, and also how soon the conception of a state church began to break away from it. A recently published book by St Horn, *Petrou Kathedra* (Paderborn, 1982), throws similar light on the fifth century. Now that both these books have appeared, the commonplace judgements of the present day on the subject will have to be thoroughly re-examined and possibly revised. Cf. also by St Horn, 'La "Sedes Apostolica": Theological outlook of the East at the beginning of the sixth century', *Istina*, 1975, pp. 435–56.

has vanished, and with it the emperor too: Thank God, we may say. Meanwhile, if one wants to discuss the conciliarity of the Church in a way that is realistic and meaningful, the question inevitably arises: what office is important enough from a theological point of view to replace and sustain the function fulfilled by the emperor?[18]

At this point the question about the later development of history must inevitably be faced as a theological issue; a mere return to the medieval Church is no solution even from a theological point of view. Jean Meyendorff has recently tackled the whole subject with an uninhibited realism which might well serve as a model for research with an eye to the future. He shows how, once the central organs of unity, founded on a theological basis, were given up after the break up of the old imperial Church, this led in fact with compulsive inward logic to state churches springing up everywhere. These did not correspond at all to the medieval idea of local Church or parish, though an attempt was made to justify them theologically in that way. Instead, they brought in their train a tendency to particularise Christianity, contrary to the essential idea of 'Church' in the New Testament and pre-Reformation Church.[19] Once the universal Church had disappeared from view as a concrete reality actually leaving its mark on the local Church, and a link had been forged with some political or ethnic reality as a framework for the latter, the whole pattern of ecclesiastical government changed – including the evaluation of episcopal office, and so involving alteration in the structure of the Church. It was not only an outward 'manifestation' which fell away but a power which had influenced from within. It is in this context that Meyendorff wonders whether it would not actually be better to devote more attention to the idea of development in the Church, and use that as an approach to the theological content of primacy.

---

[18] The same objection applies especially to the Catholic–Orthodox joint statement, *Le mystère de l'Eglise et de l'Eucharistie à la lumiere du mystère de la Sainte Trinité*.

[19] J. Meyendorff, *Kirchlicher Regionalismus: Strukturen der Gemeinschaft oder Vorwand des Separatismus?*, in G. Alberigo, Y. Congar and H. J. Pottmeyer, *Kirche im Wandel. Eine kritische Zwischenbilanz nach dem Zweiten Vatikanum* (Dusseldorf, 1982), pp. 303–18; cf., e.g., p. 311: 'one can see how modern nationalism has deformed legitimate ecclesiastical provincialism and turned it into a cloak for ethnic separatism.'

The latter is offset by the negative legalism which resulted from the tendency to particularise and was in evidence after the break up of the old empire wherever the link with the unifying function of the papacy had been severed.[20]

Reflections like these must on no account lead to one sided assertion of the 'Roman' point of view. They do point towards the principle of a unifying office, but they also call for self criticism on the part of Roman Catholic theology. Without a doubt there have been misguided developments in both theology and practice where the primacy is concerned, and these must be brought to light with the same perspicacity and frankness that Meyendorff has shown with regard to misguided developments in a theology and practice geared simply to the local Church. By this means the theological core could really be brought to view and be seen as acceptable. The principle of the primatial office in the universal Church, in my opinion, must not be weakened to the extent of being reduced to mere manifestation, while the reality of the universal Church is theologically dissolved. On the other hand the outward ways of putting the office into practice are subject to alteration and must always be tested afresh by the principle. The consequences of this for the Catholic–Anglican dialogue became evident to us rather as a side-result of the introductory report on its last phases. In order to reach a viable unity, the form of authority in the Anglican Church must be spelt out with complete realism, and there must be no shirking the question of the relationship between episcopal and political authority, for that was after all the start of the separation. The fact that since then the Anglican community has spread all over the world, has anyway led automatically to modifications of the original pattern, so that history itself has helped to rectify history. Parallel to these considerations, most careful thought must be given to variations in practice, potentially contained in the principle of primacy.

4 Tradition and Belief

With all that has been said, it should have become clear that the question of the universal Church and of the primacy as its

[20] Meyendorff, *Kirchlicher Regionalismus: Strukturen der Gemeinschaft oder Vorwand des Separatismus?*, in G. Alberigo, Y. Congar and H. J. Pottmeyer, *Kirche im Wandel. Eine kritische Zwischenbilanz nach dem Zweiten Vatikanum*, pp. 316ff.

real central organ is not simply a matter of an isolated Roman problem, of varying significance to different people. It is at heart a question of the most powerful and communal presence of the Word of God in the Church, and as we have said, this question includes that of the universal Church and its authority as well as the official instruments of this authority. To put it in a different way: it is a question of what one actually means by 'tradition'. In this connection I think a comment on terminology might bring us further. In quite a number of places in the ARCIC papers the two dialoguing parties – Anglican and Catholic – are referred to as 'our two traditions'.[21] 'Tradition' has become a key-word in recent ecumenism and is used in theological classification of the difference between various churches and denominations: they are referred to as 'our traditions'. This terminology expresses a quite definite idea about the degree of separation and the way to restore Church Unity. The different forms of the reality 'Church' are according to this 'traditions' in which the heritage of the New Testament has found manifold realisation. This means that divisions are regarded theologically as of secondary importance, even when historically seen as venerable and noteworthy realisations of common Christianity. One might say that in the most recent publications about dialogue 'tradition' is the new name for 'confession', which certainly means that a fundamental change of model has taken place in the vision of Church and faith. Wherever 'tradition' is substituted for 'confession' the question of truth is resolved into reconciling concern for what history has brought about.

One more thought comes to mind which will take us back to the theological question from which we started. If two such different subjects as the Catholic Church and the Anglican Church are grouped together under the common term 'our two traditions', the profound difference in estimation of the phenomenon 'tradition' – such a hallmark of the identity of each – is obliterated. But unfortunately one searches in vain through the ARCIC texts for an analysis of what 'tradition' means to each. Roughly speaking one might summarise it like this: in the Catholic Church the principle of 'tradition' refers, not only and not even in the first place, to the permanency of

---

[21] Cf. *Ministry and Ordination: Elucidation*, para. 3: 'both traditions'; *Authority I*, para. 18: 'both our traditions' so also ibid., para. 9; ibid., para. 25: 'our two traditions', and *Authority II*, para. 8; ibid., para. 15: 'both our traditions'.

ancient doctrines or texts which have been handed down, but to a certain way of co-ordinating the living word of the Church and the decisive written word of scripture. Here 'tradition' means above all, that the Church, living in the form of the apostolic succession with the Petrine office at its centre, is the place in which the Bible is lived and interpreted in a way that binds. This interpretation forms a historical continuity, setting fixed standards but never itself reaching a final point at which it belongs only to the past. 'Revelation' is closed but interpretation which binds is not.[22] There can be no appeal against the ultimate binding force of interpretation. So tradition is essentially marked by the 'living voice' – i.e. by the obligatory nature of the teaching of the universal Church.

If, on the other hand, one consults the Articles of Religion or the 'Lambeth Quadrilateral' of 1888, the difference strikes one immediately. The similarity of Article 19 on the Church with Article 8 of the Augsburg Confession hits one in the eye in the same way as the similarity of Article 20 on Authority in the Church with the corresponding Article 15 of the Confessio Augustana. Now both the Confessio Augustana and the Articles of Religion assume that Creed and dogmas are taken over from the pre-Reformation Church. One cannot strictly speaking apply *sola scriptura* here in the face of a fundamental recognition of tradition. But for all that, the tendency is to regard tradition as a recognised heritage of texts from the past. At the same time the right of the living voice of the Church is minimised in theology by the demand for testing against scripture, while in practice it is reduced to the sphere of mere discipline, which is thereby cut off from its true foundations. This restriction is to a certain extent projected into the past in the Articles of Religion, in so far as it is expressly stated that just as the Church of Jerusalem, Alexandria and Antioch erred, so also the Church of Rome has erred in matters of faith, and general councils too (Articles 19 and 21).

5 Tradition Can Never Be Closed

At this point another omission in the ARCIC documents should be noted: it has to do with the concrete realities of each Church. It is true that ARCIC defends itself against accusation

---

[22] Cf. My own contributions in K. Rahner and J. Ratzinger, *Offenbarung und Überlieferung* (Freiburg, 1965).

that it has contradicted Article 21 of the Articles of Religion.[23]
But it does not explain anywhere what force these Articles and
the Book of Common Prayer actually have. In this case too, as
in the question of authority, one can only grasp the concrete
situation by investigating these matters, for obviously we are
touching here on what an Anglican would regard as 'tradition'.
In the discussion about the texts it was evident that both the
Articles of Religion and the Book of Common Prayer have great
influence as standards. It seems to me all the more strange that
from the reverse point of view the Catholic ecumenical paper
Irénikon felt obliged to criticise the Congregation for the Faith
severely in an editorial because in its analysis of the Agreed
Statements it had brought in definitions promulgated in the
Catholic Church since the separation. *Irénikon* speaks (in a
quite unirenic way) of the 'painful' impression that the Congregation has made. With finger raised in reproach it continues:
'If this attitude has already had consequences in dialogue with
the Anglicans, one can imagine how it would block the
way towards restoring canonical and sacramental communion
with the Orthodox Church'.[24]

A kind of ecumenical dogma seems to be developing here
which needs some attention. Quite likely it began with this
train of thought: for intercommunion with the Orthodox, the
Catholic Church need not necessarily insist on acceptance of
the dogmas of the second millennium. It was presumed that
the Eastern Churches have retained in the traditional form of
the first millennium, which in itself is legitimate and, if rightly
understood, contains no contradiction to further developments.
The latter after all only unfolded what was already there in
principle in the time of the undivided Church. I myself have
already taken part in attempts to work things out like this,[25] but
meanwhile they have grown out of hand to the point at which
councils and the dogmatic decisions of the second millennium
are supposed not to be regarded as ecumenical but as particular
developments in the Latin Church, constituting its private
property in the sense of 'our two traditions'. But this distorts
the first attempt to think things out into a completely new thesis
with far-reaching consequences. For this way of looking at it

[23] *Authority in the Church: Elucidation.*
[24] *Irénikon,* 55 (1982), pp. 161f, quotation p. 162.
[25] Cf. *Theologische Prinzipienlehre,* (München, 1982), pp. 109–211 (text
from 1976).

actually implies denial of the existence of the Universal Church in the second millennium, while tradition as a living, truth-giving power is frozen at the end of the first. This strikes at the very heart of the idea of Church and tradition, because ultimately such an age test dissolves the full authority of the Church, which is then left without a voice at the present day. Moreover one might well ask in reply to such an assertion, with what right consciences, in such a particular Church as the Latin Church would then be, could be bound by such pronouncements. What once appeared as truth would have to be reduced to mere custom. The great age-long claim to truth would be disqualified as an abuse.

All this means that a far-reaching thesis, the princples and consequences of which have not been thought out, has been raised to the level of a self-evident axiom. To belittle it is to incur ungracious censure. But this very self-evidence which convinced *Irénikon* that it was its duty to pass censure from its lofty look-out on the Congregation for the Faith, demands decisive response. To my mind the central truth of what they are trying to get at is this: unity is a fundamental, hermeneutic principle of all theology, and we must learn to read the documents which have been handed down to us, according to the hermeneutics of unity, which show up much that is new and open doors where only bolts were visible before. Such hermeneutics of unity will entail reading the statements of both parties in the context of the whole tradition and with a deeper understanding of scripture. This will include investigating how far decisions since the separation have been stamped with a certain particularisation both as to language and thought – something that might well be transcended without doing violence to the content of the statements. For hermeneutics are not a skilful device for escaping from burdensome authorities by a change of verbal function (though this abuse has often occurred), but rather apprehending the word with an understanding which at the same time discovers in it new possibilities.

Ecumenical dialogue does not mean opting out of living, Christian reality, but advancing by means of the hermeneutics of unity. To opt out and cut oneself off means artificial withdrawal into a past beyond recall; it means restricting tradition to the past. But that is to transfer ecumenism into an artificial world while one goes on practising particularisation by fencing off one's own thing. Since this preserve is regarded as immune from dialogue but is still clung to, it is lowered from the realm of truth into the sphere of mere custom. Finally the question arises as to whether it is a matter of truth at all, or just of comparing different customs and finding a way of reconciling them. In any case, the remark that the introduction of dogmatic decisions passed since the separation should not be regarded as the high point of the dialogue denotes a flight into the artificial which should be firmly resisted.

6 Tradition and Eucharist

Now to get back to the ARCIC document after this detour. Everything said so far has revolved round the question of authority and tradition. I have tried to show that here and nowhere else really lies the fundamental problem. To solve it would be decisive for the question of unity. It would not be hard to show that this question affects also the particular areas in which full agreement has not yet been reached, and which were noted in the communication from the Congregation for the Faith: eucharist with emphasis on sacrifice, transubstantiation and, according to circumstances, adoration of the consecrated species; sacramental nature and content of the priesthood (with the question in the background of the institution of the sacraments and of their actual number); theological substantiation and concrete ecclesiastical content of the Petrine office. It is not possible to deal with all these things here. But let me just add one remark about the question of the eucharist. The great reformed denominations and the Anglican community accepted the ancient creeds as part of their own belief, and so the Trinitarian and Christological faith defined in the councils of the early Church has been kept out of the debate. Side by sde with scripture and combined with it, this is the actual nucleus of the unity which binds us together and gives us hope of complete reconciliation.

For this reason we must for the sake of unity strenuously resist any attempt to break up this central ecclesial deposit or to discard as outmoded the practice based on it of reading scripture together. A mere fundamentalist approach to the Bible, adopted these days by quite a number of people, would not bring us together but would soon break up the Bible itself. Without this centre the Bible would cease to be one book and would lose its authority.

So, although unity remained in the Creeds, the break in the form of eucharistic liturgy had its full effect. But in point of fact, in spite of all textual and ritual differences, the consistent unity of structure and understanding of the eucharistic liturgy in the pre-Reformation Church (together with the baptismal liturgy) was the vital habitat in which the Christian dogma of that Church was rooted. The authority of tradition in the case of the eucharistic model carries no less weight than in the case of councils and their creeds, even though it is differently expressed – through constant living enactment instead of by conciliar decree. It is really only possible to make an artificial separation between the two: in both cases it is the one basic form of the pre-Reformation Church expressing itself. Unfortunately this connection was no longer easily recognisable in the late medieval Church and its celebration of Mass. But all the same one can imagine what it would mean for ecumenism if the inseparability of this union were again both manifest and recognised. If we had today to 'prove' the Trinitarian dogma and Christological faith from scripture in the same controversial way as the sacrificial character of the eucharist, our endeavour to reach common conclusions would certainly be no less arduous. On the other hand, if the basic form of the liturgy of the early Church were accepted as a lasting heritage, ranking with conciliar creeds, this would provide unifying hermeneutics which would render many points of contention superfluous. The Church's liturgy being the original interpretation of the biblical heritage has no need to justify itself before historical reconstructions: it is rather itself the standard, sprung from what is living, which directs research back to the initial stages.[26]

I do not think that this sort of consideration is merely an intellectual game. Fundamentally it again points to the question of mere history and the significance of its content (*Geschichte*), of growth and life, i.e. the problem of authority and tradition which has occupied our minds throughout these ruminations. It is essential to have the most accurate knowledge possible of what the Bible says from an historical point of view. Progressive deepening of such knowledge can always serve to purify and enrich tradition. But what is merely historical remains ambiguous. It belongs to the realm of hypothesis,

[26] Cf. J. Ratzinger, *Das Fest des Glaubens* (Einsieden, 1981).

whose certainty is intellectual, not certainty by which to live.[27]
To live by faith and die for faith is possible, only because the
power of the living community, which it created and still
creates, opens up the significance of history and renders it
unequivocal, in a way that no amount of mere reasoning could
do. The two levels we are referring to can be well illustrated by
a formula in the ARCIC documents. As the authors unfold
their theological vision, they repeatedly use the phrase 'we
believe'.[28] If I understand them aright, what it actually means is
'it is our opinion': it is expressing the opinions of theologians.
But it is only when 'we believe' is transformed from 'this is our
opinion' to 'this is our faith' by what has been thought out
theologically that it is caught up into the full life stream of the
Church; only in this way can unity be achieved. The task that
lies before us is to find a way to effect this transition. The document from the Congregation for the Faith was intended as a
contribution towards this.

Conclusion – Prospect for the Future

This brings me to my conclusion. Perhaps what I have said
sounds in places rather depressing. It may have given the
impression that there are far more problems than signs of

[27] Cf. R. Spaemann, *Die christliche Religion und das Ende des modernen
Bewusstseins*, in the international Catholic periodical *Communio*, 8
(1979), pp. 251–70, especially pp. 264–8.
[28] To give just some examples, though the meaning of the word is perhaps
not exactly the same in each case: *Ministry and Ordination*, para. 6: 'we
believe'; *Elucidation* to it, para. 6 (para. 2): 'The Commission believes';
Co-Chairmen's Preface to *Authority I*, para. 4: 'we believe'; *Authority I*,
para. 25: 'we believe'. I find it difficult to answer the question as to the
exact force of the claim made for the contexts, especially because for
the actual teaching of the Church a terminology is used that is very similar to those expressions of the Commission in the aforementioned texts,
cf., e.g., *Authority II*, para. 27: 'The welfare of the *koinonia* does not
require that all the statements of those who speak authoritatively on
behalf of the Church should be considered permanent expressions of
the truth. But situations may occur where serious divisions of opinion
on crucial issues of pastoral urgency call for more definitive judgement.
Any such statement would be intended as an expression of the mind of
the Church . . .' This inevitably gives rise to the question as to how the
mind of the Church and faith of the Church relate to each other, which
means that the respective levels of faith and theology must be further
clarified.

hope. But here too it is true that the problems belong to the realm of thought, the hopeful signs to the realm of life. The pope's visit was a clear indication of this: because it was a lived event, it was also a gesture of hope. Of course thought and life belong together; to separate them would destroy both. The hopes of all in our days have come from those who have lived the faith and suffered for it. Hope has directed thought along new ways and made unifying hermeneutics possible. In this sense Catholic theology can and must agree to the idea of reception. Unity can grow only if particular communities live out their faith with unity as their goal. There must always be interplay between thought and life, ministry and community. Although at times things have been held up, there is much that is hopeful, precisely with regard to the fundamental problem of the authority of living tradition and its central organs in the universal Church, and also in what concerns the intimate mutual relationship between the universal Church and each particular Church. The fact that most of the communities which were once national or state churches have transcended the frontiers of countries and continents means that there is a new openness to the meaning of 'catholicity' in the original sense of the word. In the same way actual experience of lived ecclesial community has moderated exaggerated fundamental-ist notions with regard to scripture and facilitated new under-standing of the meaning of tradition and of doctrinal authority on a sacramental basis. In both cases contact with the Orthodox Church has proved stimulating. The Eastern Church has enabled reformed communities to experience a form of Catholicity free from the burden of Western history; and on the other hand, thanks to their common structure, it has enabled the Catholic Church of the West to detect a number of its own exaggerations and prejudices and helped it to differ-entiate better between what is essential to its character and what is merely accidental. Much is on the move, and the ARCIC papers are part of an endeavour to seize the opportunity of the moment, follow the way opened up for us and carry possibility through to actuality. No one can predict when convergence will end in unity, just as no one could have fore-seen the ways which have brought us so far. History shows us that a superficial unity which jumps the gun without inward preparation through actual living could only prove harmful. Greater unity is really to be found in the fact that the separated communities are passionately seeking the truth together with the firm intention of imposing nothing which does not come from the Lord on the other party, and of losing nothing entrusted to us by him. In this way our lives advance towards each other because they are directed towards Christ. Perhaps institutional separation has some share in the significance of salvation history which St Paul attributes to the division between Israel and the Gentiles – namely that they should make 'each other envious', vying with each other in coming closer to the Lord (Rom. 11.11).

As regards practical measures for the future progress of affairs between Anglicans and the Catholic Church, the Pope and Archbishop Runcie in their joint declaration at Canterbury on 29 May 1982 announced the next step to be taken: 'We are agreed that it is now time to set up a new international Commission. Its task will be to continue the work already begun: to examine, *especially in the light of our respective judgements on the Final Report*, the outstanding doctrinal differences which still separate us, with a view towards their final resolution; to study all that hinders the mutual recognition of the ministries of our Communions; and to recommend what practical steps will be necessary when, on the basis of our unity in faith, we are able to proceed to the restoration of full communion'.[29]

That is a modest statement as well as a hopeful one. The task it sets before us cannot be accomplished by a commission alone; it needs the prayerful support of the whole Church, which in the last resort is always the inspiration of any hope of unity.

Postscript

Reflections on the Debate Aroused by My Article

There was an extraordinarily lively reaction to these reflections on the Anglican–Catholic dialogue that were first published in 1983. They appeared in the recently founded journal *Insight,*

---

[29] *Acta Apostolicae Sedis*, 74 (1982), 8, p. 925. The above mentioned Editorial of *Irénikon* (see note 24) when naming the first task significantly omits the phrase 'especially in the light of our respective judgements on the Final Report'; it contradicted too obviously the polarity suggested by the said article between the text of the Congregation of the Faith and the utterances of the Pope – not a very fair way of conveying information to the reader.

and this devoted a whole issue to the debate. Among those taking part were such important representatives of the Church of England as Christopher Hill and the Bishop of London, Graham Leonard, while among Catholic contributors were Cecily Boulding OP, Alberic Stacpoole OSB, and Edward Yarnold SJ. Finally there was an impressive contribution from a representative of the Catholic wing of the Church of England, William Ledwich.[1] Jean Tillard OP, one of the outstanding Catholic theologians on ARCIC, took the dialogue up in *The Tablet*, and a wealth of material was provided by the founder and editor of *Insight*, Martin Dudley.[2]

The debate focused on three key areas: the question of authority in the Church; tradition and traditions; and the relationship between the local and the universal Church. My impression was that the debate on the first of these subjects, the question of authority, was the most productive. Christopher Hill emphasized that it would in fact be nonsense to suppose that the Church in the second millennium has lost its voice. He also established that 'tradition' could not simply consist of bits and pieces that had been handed down. He saw the answer to this problem in the Lambeth Quadrilateral of 1888, which points to an internal interaction of scripture, the creeds, the sacraments and the historic episcopate. In his view these in their mutual internal relationship guarantee both the link between the Church and its origin and the contemporary relevance of its voice. To see the present nature of the Word in its totality one would need to go further and understand this 'quadrilateral' against the background of the consensus of the faithful, which for him expresses the participation of the whole Church in the life and continuity of the faith.[3] Martin Dudley went into even greater detail on this question. He carefully worked out the individual elements of the concept of authority from recent statements of the Anglican Communion in order then to evaluate their position theologically within the Christian

---

[1] All these contributions are to be found in *Insight: A Journal for Church and Community*, vol. I no. 4 (December 1983), 'Authority – Tradition – Unity; The Response to Cardinal Ratzinger'.

[2] J. Tillard, 'Dialogue with Cardinal Ratzinger: Tradition and Authority' and 'Christian Communion', in *The Tablet*, 7 and 14 January 1984, pp. 15–17 and 39–40; Martin Dudley, 'Waiting on the Common Mind: Authority in Anglicanism', in *One in Christ*, 1984/1, pp. 62–77.

[3] Christopher Hill, 'Reflections on Cardinal Ratzinger's article', *Insight*, vol. I, no. 4 (December 1983), pp. 5–13; the reference is to p. 12.

ecumenical scene on the basis of the classical concept of the *via media*. In this Dudley went back to Newman's ideas before his conversion. According to these the Anglican *via media* would be represented as follows: Protestantism limited the external means (of making the word of God present) to the text of the Bible, the interpretation of which was left to private judgement or simple reason. The Roman Church pushed reason, scripture and antiquity to one side and thus staked everything on the authority of the Church as it exists now. The Anglican Communion by contrast held reason, scripture, antiquity and catholicity in balance with an emphasis on the authority of antiquity, but where this was silent on the voice of the present Church.[4] Dudley then for his part tries to fill out these somewhat schematic ideas and at the same time to deepen them. For him, as for Christopher Hill, the interaction of a variety of factors is important. Authority is distributed among scripture, tradition, the creeds, the ministry of the word and the sacraments, the witness of the saints and the *consensus fidelium*, 'which is the continuing experience of the Holy Spirit through his faithful people in the Church'. In Anglicanism we have what is a dispersed rather than a centralized authority, 'having many elements which combine, interact with and check each other'. They are organized in a process of mutually supporting and checking each other[5] and thus form a 'system of checks and balances (in which) the truth of God makes itself known and accepted in a consensus or common mind'.[6] The system may seem complicated but is in fact very simple in its fundamental idea, the expression of God's multiform loving provision against the temptations to tyranny and the dangers of unchecked power.[7]

These important and pregnant statements are however powerfully confronted by the passionate questions raised by William Ledwich in his article 'With Authority, not as the Scribes'. Ledwich too traces a line from Newman to the present, but in contrast to Dudley he does not confine himself to Newman's attempt to defend the Anglican principle of the *via media* but puts the whole Tractarian dispute in relation to the struggles of the present day. It is impossible in a few lines to

[4] Dudley, 'Waiting on the Common Mind', p. 71.
[5] Dudley, p. 77.
[6] Dudley, p. 76.
[7] Dudley, pp. 76 and 77.

give an idea of the dramatic picture that emerges. I would therefore like briefly merely to indicate what I feel is the decisive point. In Newman's day every kind of interpretation of the Thirty-nine Articles was permitted except for an explicitly Catholic one.[8] Conversion became imperative for Newman once the Anglican hierarchy had explicitly rejected as unacceptable his attempt at a Catholic interpretation.[9] No doubt it is progress that in contrast today a Catholic interpretation has become possible. But in Ledwich's eyes this progress is very relative if one considers the manner in which Catholicism can now occupy a place within Anglicanism: 'That Catholicism is a party within Anglicanism no one can realistically deny . . . But it remains true that Jesus did not found a Catholic party in a cosmopolitan debating society, but a Catholic Church to which he promised the fulness of truth . . . A body which reduces its catholics to a party within a religious parliament can hardly deserve to be called a branch of the Catholic Church, but a national religion, dominated by and structured on the principles of liberal tolerance, in which the authority of revelation is subordinate to democracy and private opinion.'[10] I do not presume to give any judgement on this depiction. Certainly it would not be right to want to see in Ledwich the sole and final word on the Anglican Communion of today. But it would be equally wrong simply to leave on one side as disruptive this voice marked by personal experience, by passion and by passionate love both for the Anglican Church and for Catholic truth. It remains that the debate has produced important exemplifications of detail and has illuminated the question of authority a good bit more. But it also remains that the problem has not been solved but continues to form the chief question of the Catholic–Anglican dialogue. However one may judge in detail Ledwich's findings, it will be difficult to contradict his central contention. The question that is really at issue in the Church today has remained precisely the same as in the days of the Tractarians: the place of authority and the value of dogma as opposed to private judgement.[11]

8 William Ledwich, 'With Authority, not as the Scribes', *Insight*, loc. cit. pp. 14–23; the reference is to p. 16. (Translator's note: Rev. William Ledwich left the Church of England in the summer of 1984 over the Bishop of Durham affair to join the Orthodox Church.)

9 Cf. C. S. Dessain, *John Henry Newman*, London, 1966, p. 75.

10 Ledwich, p. 21.

11 Ledwich, p. 17.

*Two Fundamental Elements of Modern Ecumenical
Theology and the Problems Connected With Them*

While the debate on authority in the Church was abundantly
fruitful precisely in its differences, the outcome on the two
other points – tradition (traditions) and the relationship between
the local and the universal Church – strikes me rather as meagre.
Much of what was said rests on misunderstandings, while much
also overlooked the heart of the matter. What disappointed me
above all was what was said in response to my remarks about
tradition. It was not a question here of terminological quarrels,
as could be deduced from the reactions. Rather I had maintained that lurking behind the new concept of tradition was the
elimination of the question of truth. The difference between
the Churches is reduced to a difference of 'traditions' (customs).
This puts the ecumenical dispute on a completely new track: it
is no longer man's great struggle for the truth but the search
for compromise in the matter of tradition, for a balancing out
of different customs. I had expected so large a claim to be
bound to evoke a passionate debate: instead I was reminded
that talk of 'our traditions' had been customary in ecumenical
circles for some decades. Since for the past forty years I have
been trying to share in theological activity I was of course
aware of this. This does not mean that I want to dispute that
on these points some interesting and important things were
said on matters of detail, but it would not seem to me appropriate to bother the reader with learned details of a controversy
that is now already several years old. Instead I would like to
choose a simpler and, I think, more fruitful way by trying,
independently of the preceding debate, briefly to state my
position on two fundamental elements of ecumenical theology
which are often presupposed without being questioned but
which in reality contain a host of unsolved problems.

The 'conciliarity' of the Church
Today the model of the Church's 'conciliarity' increasingly
surfaces in order to clarify the relationship between the universal Church and the particular Church. From two points of view
this strikes me as a mistake. In my book *Das neue Volk Gottes*
I was able, on the basis of detailed philological analysis, to
demonstrate the profound semantic and factual difference
which in the language and thought of the early Church separated

the concepts of *communio* and *concilium* from each other.[12] While *communio* can virtually act as an equivalent for Church and indicates its essential nature, its mode of life and also its constitutional form, the same does not in any way apply to the concept *concilium*. In contrast to communion, to union in and with the body of Christ, council is not the act of living of the Church itself but a particular and important act within it which has its own great but circumscribed sgnificance but which can never express the life of the Church as a whole. To put it another way, the Church is not a council. A council happens in the Church but it is not the Church. A council serves the Church but not *vice versa*. From the point of view of the Fathers of the Church it is completely nonsensical and unthinkable to describe the whole Church as some kind of permanent council. A council discusses and decides but then comes to an end. The Church, however, is not there to discuss the gospel but to live it. Hence a council presupposes the constitution of the Church but is not itself that constitution. The idea of a perpetual conciliarity of the Church as the basic form of its unity, of its existence as a unity, springs rather from the idea, to use Ledwich's polemical description, of a 'cosmopolitan debating society'[13] than from the thought of scripture and the Fathers.

But even the inner idea of the council presupposed in the slogan of 'conciliarity' is wrong. What is assumed here is that the council, the harmony of all the local Churches, is at the same time the only form of expression of the universal Church *qua* universal Church, its only constitutional organ. I have already pointed out in the preceding contribution on the Anglican–Catholic dialogue that one cannot see how under such conditions a universal council could come into being at all. The difficulties which the Eastern Church is facing on the road to a pan-Orthodox synod provide a quite concrete verification of this problem. In fact the Church of the Fathers never saw itself as a pure combination of particular Churches with equal rights. One can roughly distinguish in it three basic ideas of the constitution of the universal Church, though admittedly these were slow to take on their specific forms and become separated from each other. The East knew two fundamental models: one was the pentarchy, a fourth-century expansion of

[12] Joseph Ratzinger, *Das neue Volk Gottes*, Düsseldorf, 1969, pp. 151–63.
[13] Ledwich, p. 21.

the three primatial sees of the Council of Nicaea in which a foundation of Petrine theology was united with practical political aims. Rome and Antioch are Petrine sees: Alexandria in the shape of St Mark is also able to claim a Petrine origin for itself. If originally Jerusalem was excluded from the authoritative sees on the basis of the idea of its mission being translated to Rome, it now returns among their circle as the place of the origin of the faith: at the same time the recent *translatio imperii* from Rome to Constantinople, the imperial city on the Bosphorus, made it possible for the latter to be included among the primatial sees. The reference to Andrew then became a kind of theological variant of the idea of translation and the idea included in it of the brotherly equality of the two cities. Be that as it may, the early episcopal Church was aware of itself against the background of the Petrine idea and its historical variations as a pentarchy, but not as a general conciliarity or as a 'federation of love' (as *sobornost*).[14] The mixed theological and political model of the pentarchy, which was not in any way seen as the fruit of mere historical accidents or political expediency, was then admittedly increasingly overlaid by the imperial model of the state Church in which the functions of the Petrine ministry devolve upon the emperor: the emperor becomes the actual executive organ of the universal Church.[15] In keeping with this the pentarchy in the Byzantine state Church markedly regressed to become the monarchy of the Ecumenical Patriarch. If we should regard this connection between the monarchy of the emperor and that of the Ecumenical Patriarch as a second model, then finally the idea of the succession of Peter at Rome – in no way restricted to the city itself and its immediate sphere of influence – must be classed as the third model. For this model the single successor of Peter, the bishop of Rome, is the properly biblically based executive organ of the universal Church, without at first the pentarchy and the position of the emperor being seen as totally incompatible with it.

My conclusion from the whole of this is that the model of conciliarity is unsuitable for the oneness of the universal Church in and from the particular Churches and should be given up. The dialogue should be conducted much more

[14] Cf. E. von Ivánka, *Romäerreich und Gottesvolk*, Freiburg/Munich, 1968, p. 146.
[15] Cf. the examples in A. Grillmeier, *Mit ihm und in ihm. Christologische Forschungen und Perspektiven*, Freiburg, 1975, pp. 386–419, especially p. 407.

explicitly against the background of the actual history of the Church and the experiences it has undergone, as Meyendorff has expressly indicated. Then my conviction is that the indispensability of the Petrine principle would come to light and at the same time we would also see the breadth of its possible forms of realization.

Traditionibus or *sola scriptura*? A new ecumenical formal principle

Anyone who reads attentively the ever growing number of ecumenical agreed statements gets ever more clearly the impression that the classic criterion of *sola scriptura* is hardly ever still applied but that in place of this a new formal principle seems to be developing that I would tentatively like to describe by the label *traditionibus*. This seems to me to be most clearly the case in what is called the Lima text on Baptism, Eucharist, Ministry, which appeared in 1982. What is meant by this? The impression arises that scripture – torn to pieces by the disputes of different confessions and different exegetes – is regarded as too insecure for one really to be able to base oneself on it. But what is available are the 'traditions', i.e. the actual forms of Christian life in which individual confessions live. These are 'traditions'. This factual datum thus becomes the starting-point and also the inner standard of the ecumenical dialogue. The 'traditions' are there, and because they are there one must come to terms with them. Ecumenical irenism excludes simply rejecting actual historical interpretations of Christianity. The effort must rather be directed at bringing them into a relationship of amicable tolerance. In this it is completely unimportant to ask when and how a tradition arose. The fact that it could and can sustain Church life gives it its right in the ecumenical quest. Thus what is factual – the existence and persistence of a practice – obtains a hitherto unknown weight.

A few examples may make this clear. In Africa, we are told by BEM (the Lima document), there are communities which baptize only by the laying on of hands, without water.[16] The consequence? One must study the relationship of this practice to baptism with water. In some 'traditions' it is the custom to give children merely a blessing in order to link them to the

---

[16] BEM, Baptism, Commentary 21b. In view of the ease with which they can be tracked down there is no need to list individually the references to the various instances quoted.

Church: only when they can make a confession of faith themselves are they baptized. Other communities baptize their children, who then later, when they are mature enough, make
their own confession of faith. What should one do? See both
'traditions' as fundamentally of the same kind. Some Churches
have started ordaining women while others refuse to do so.
What follows from this? The blessing that clearly lies on the
ordination of women also justifies it, but not everyone has to
adopt it. The sacramental understanding of the ministry in the
threefold form of diaconate, presbyterate and episcopate is
ancient and proper to the entire Catholic form of the Church.
In general it is not recognized by the Churches of the Reformation. What should one do? The Churches of the Reformation
should seriously consider entering the form of ministry of the
apostolic succession, but at the same time both forms of ministry should be recognized as completely valid, and entry into
the sacramental ministry should take place in a non-sacramental
form, for example by means of a certificate. These examples
may suffice to make clear the nature of the new formal principle:
'traditions' are simply to be accepted as such at first; they are
the reality with which the ecumenical scene has to deal. The
task of ecumenical dialogue is then to seek fairly the necessary
compromises between the different traditions, compromises
that do not destroy anyone's identity but make it possible for
everyone to recognize each other.

This is no longer Luther's or Calvin's principle of scripture;
we do not have to waste any words over that. But it is also
something quite other than the Catholic (or Orthodox) principle
of tradition. In the latter it was a case of 'apostolic traditions'
which were 'of divine right'; in other words, traditions which
rested on revelation without their being explicitly recorded as
such in scripture. Purely 'human traditions', the existence of
which nobody disputed, could demand respect but could not
be brought up to the level of revelation. Today, however, the
crisis of exegesis seems to mean that the idea of a real origin
from Jesus (institution) and thus of a real quality of revelation
has become so uncertain that recourse is hardly still had to it.
What is certain are the 'traditions', and now it no longer counts
for very much whether they arose in the first, in the tenth, in
the sixteenth or in the twentieth century, nor in what way
they arose. Once again we must be cautious about making a
judgement. Even classic doctrine had established that even in

scripture there were traditions that could be purely of human right (for example the obligation on women to cover their heads) and that on the other hand what had belonged to the essential nature of the whole from the start without having been stated explicitly could become visible in the living tradition of the Church as the agent of tradition. But in this there always remained the requirement that this kind of context of development must exist and thus an inner connection with the origin and that to this extent a certain justification in the light of the original sources was needed. But where the common agent of tradition disappears, the idea of development thereby becomes untenable and actual traditions become the sole bearers of Christian reality, one finds oneself on a different plane which is neither that of the Reformers nor that of the Catholic Church.

This kind of openness to factual data certainly has its positive side. Old prejudices lose their power; a new impartiality arises that is able to see and to understand others' ideas. So in the event realizations became possible that could only with difficulty have been imagined under the domination of the old principles. In this climate precious rapprochements have succeeded precisely in the concept of ministry and in the understanding of sacrifice, two apparently insuperable focuses of controversy. To this extent one can grant this principle a heuristic intermediate function that is helpful. But in no way can it or should it mean anything more. For if one were to agree completely on regarding all the different confessions simply as traditions, then one would have cut oneself completely loose from the question of truth, and theology would now be merely a form of diplomacy, of politics. Our quarrelling ancestors were in reality much closer to each other when in all their disputes they still knew that they could only be servants of one truth which must be acknowledged as being as great and as pure as it has been intended for us by God.[17]

Anyone who wants to see in these remarks an attack on recent ecumenical work has understood nothing of what I am

---

[17] I refrain from adding here another separate section on the local Church and the universal Church: the most important aspect of this is at least hinted at in the first part of this book [*Church, Ecumenism and Politics*]. I should also refer to the section 'Kommunion – Kommunität – Sendung' in my book *Schauen auf den Durchbohrten*, Einsiedeln, 1984, pp. 60–84. It

concerned about. What has been achieved in the way of agreements is precious and must not be lost but must be deepened
and extended. But we must see to it that in this we do not
silently make ourselves the absolute rulers of our faith and thus
by pressing on thoughtlessly destroy the living thing that we
cannot create but can only cherish. It is good that the traditions have entered into the ecumenical scene. But if we cannot
link them with scripture in a single principle we have lost the
ground from under our feet. Every hope bears its own danger
within it. It only remains hope if we do not refuse to face up to
the danger.

---

would also be important to take more notice once again of the important exegetical work of recent decades. To cite just one example, I refer
to O. Michel's book that appeared in expanded form in 1983, *Das
Zeugnis des Neuen Testamentes von der Gemeinde*, and recall H. Schlier's
major commentary on Ephesians (Düsseldorf, 1958).

23
Executive Committee of the Evangelical Fellowship of the Anglican Communion – An Extract from an Open Letter to the Anglican Communion (1988)

A Introduction

1 An Open letter, signed by 125 Anglican evangelical leaders, was addressed in June 1977 to the Anglican episcopate. It concerned relations between the Anglican Churches and the Roman Catholic, Eastern Orthodox, Old Catholic and Ancient Oriental Churches.

Over 10 years later, with the agenda of the 1988 Lambeth Conference in mind, 511 Anglican evangelical leaders from 35 countries address this Open Letter to the worldwide Anglican episcopate. It focuses entirely on the ARCIC enterprise.

2 The Bishops at the 1978 Lambeth Conference described the first three ARCIC statements as 'a solid achievement'. Taking them as a whole, we agree with this judgment. We also venture to echo the appreciation expressed in 1982 by the Archbishop of Canterbury and the Pope for the 'dedication, scholarship and integrity' of the Commission's members.

3 We are aware of the 'ecumenical impatience' of some who regard our church leaders as unnecessarily dragging their feet, and of others who dismiss our continuing separation as a sixteenth century European squabble which need not inhibit them. At the same time, the Anglican provinces which have so far responded to the Anglican Consultative Council's questions about ARCIC, while seeking generally to be positive, have expressed important reservations, anxieties, criticisms, and requests for clarification and elaboration, many of which we share (see *Emmaus Report*, 1987).

4 We ourselves are strongly committed to the quest for both the unity and the purity of the church, indeed for 'that unity in truth for which Christ prayed', as Pope Paul VI and Archbishop Michael Ramsey put it in their Common Declaration of March 1966. So we are grateful that ARCIC has said from the beginning that there are some 'essential matters where it considers that doctrine admits of no divergence' (Ministry, para. 17) and that 'the achievement of doctrinal agreement . . . is central to our reconciliation' (Final Report, Conclusion, p. 99).

5 A crucial question, therefore, is how we are to distinguish between these 'essential matters', on which there must be unity, and those 'matters indifferent' (*adiaphora*), in which we should give each other liberty. For we look neither for a rigid uniformity in all matters, nor for an unlimited pluralism, but for a principled comprehensiveness. And must we not add that the 'principle' or criterion of a true comprehensiveness is Holy Scripture, since those doctrines which are demonstrably taught by Scripture (and only those) must be regarded as primary and essential? Our Anglican formularies unequivocally affirm this. We also note the Roman Catholic bishops' acceptance at the Second Vatican Council of 'two streams' of revelation in place of Trent's 'two source' view. We understand this to imply that tradition, being the church's developing interpretation of Scripture, always stands in dependence upon it. If so, is this not a significant move towards the recognition that Scripture has a normative authority over tradition?

6 It is because the ARCIC documents do not express this perspective with sufficient clarity that we believe it necessary to press the question we asked in the 1977 Open Letter, namely whether both churches 'are yet sufficiently ready to test all their traditions of teaching and practice by Holy Scripture, as we know we are bound to test ours, in order to correct what the theology of the Bible will not justify'. The supremacy of Scripture was the formative principle of the Reformation. We could never ourselves surrender it. We are convinced that its unambiguous acknowledgment by our two churches would both express our loyalty to Christ (who himself subordinated tradition to Scripture) and greatly accelerate our progress towards an acceptable unity.

7 We seriously wonder, therefore, whether the right question has been put to the churches, namely whether the first four

ARCIC statements are on the one hand 'consonant in substance with the faith of Anglicans' and on the other 'consonant
in substance with the faith of the Catholic Church'. For the two
churches can reply only by comparing ARCIC's work with their
own foundation documents (especially the 39 Articles and the
decrees of the Council of Trent). But to do this is surely to contradict ARCIC's basic methodology, which is to go *behind* the
sixteenth century debates and definitions, and to re-examine
earlier teaching, and especially that of Scripture. The Commission
followed this principle most notably in its fresh evaluation of
the Petrine texts. *Observations*, however, did not. This document,
the critique of the Final Report issued in 1982 by the Sacred
Congregation for the Doctrine of the Faith in Rome, declared
ARCIC's teaching in certain crucial areas to be incompatible
with Catholic dogma as defined by earlier Councils like Trent
and Vatican I. We respectfully ask, therefore, what is the status
of *Observations*? Cardinal Willebrands has explained, in his
essay *Anglicans, Roman Catholics and Authority* (1987), quoting
what he had said in 1983, that it had been decided both that
the ARCIC Report should be sent to the episcopal conferences
and that the Sacred Congregation for the Doctrine of the Faith
should be asked to send its experts' observations 'as a contribution to the dialogue and as a help to Catholics in reading the
document with discernment'. Although *Observations* is here called
no more than 'a contribution', and although the response of the
Bishops' Conferences has been more positive than the Sacred
Congregation's, it was nonetheless officially commissioned, so
that we need to be told how much authority it has in the
Roman Catholic Church's evaluation of the Final Report.

More important, what is the status, in regard to the work of
ARCIC, of those documents which helped to define our two
churches' identities? It is well known that Anglican Evangelicals
value the 39 Articles, the Book of Common Prayer and the
Ordinal, because they seem to us to enshrine biblical truth,
especially in relation to such vital doctrines as salvation, the
church and the sacraments. We do not regard these formularies
as infallible, however. Insofar as biblical truth may be expressed
more clearly, we are ready to see them improved and even
replaced. We wonder whether Roman Catholics can say something comparable about Trent and Vatican I?

8 Our main criticism of the ARCIC I statements, therefore, is
that they are not radical enough. That is, they do not subject

our Anglican and Roman inheritance to a sufficiently rigorous *biblical* scrutiny. They betray a reluctance to allow the Spirit of God through the Word of God to challenge beliefs and practices which have been hallowed by centuries of tradition. But must we remain for ever prisoners of our past? Only Scripture can set us free.

9 As we venture to share with our bishops some of the conscientious problems which we have with the ARCIC documents, we wish to clarify our aims and motives. We have tried to write, as we hope we will be read, in a spirit of Christian humility and charity. We are far from claiming that our judgments are always right; we are open to correction. We also recognise the integrity of those who, having wrestled with the same issues, have reached different conclusions. So there is a need and room for further discussion. We know that eucharistic hospitality between our two churches is already in some situations being practised. But closer union must surely depend on closer agreement. And we are convinced that the Holy Spirit of truth and love is able to bring us to this. We plead, therefore, against premature decisions and for more time in which the dialogue may develop.

B The Five ARCIC Statements

B.I Eucharistic Doctrine

1 There is much in ARCIC I's first Agreed Statement which we welcome. We are particularly thankful for the unequivocal statement in para. 5 that 'Christ's death on the cross . . . was the one, perfect and sufficient sacrifice for the sins of the world' and that 'there can be no repetition of or addition to what was then accomplished once for all by Christ'.

2 We agree that ARCIC's understanding of *anamnesis* or 'memorial' ('the making effective in the present of an event in the past', para. 5) does not necessarily compromise the once-for-all nature of Christ's atoning sacrifice (*Elucidation*, paras. 3 and 5), for it draws a clear distinction between the historical event and sacramental action. At the same time we share the misgivings expressed by some provinces. For the Commission's use of the word is controversial; it is made to bear a weight which is not justified by Scripture.

3 We have two grave problems with the text.

The first concerns the relationship between Christ's sacrifice and the eucharist. We agree that the eucharist is 'no mere calling to mind of a past event or of its significance' (para. 5), for it is also a proclamation of, and indeed a participation in, Christ's sacrifice. In what sense, however, do we participate? The ARCIC phrase is that we both participate in the benefits of his passion and 'enter into the movement of his self-offering' (last sentence of para. 5, repeated in *Elucidation*, para. 5). To us, however, there is a serious confusion here between two kinds of participation, which seem to be mutually incompatible. We do indeed share in the benefits of Christ's sacrifice (1 Cor. 10.16), and offer ourselves to him in gratitude for it; but we cannot share in the offering of it, or even be drawn up into the movement of it. For we cannot see how the offering of ourselves, being a response to Christ's self-offering, can be simultaneous with it or part of it.

4 We understand the desire to 'identify' with Christ, for by God's grace we are 'in Christ', united to him and drawing our life from him, like branches in the vine and limbs in the body. In consequence of this identification, we are said to 'share in his sufferings', enduring for his sake the world's opposition, as a condition of sharing in his glory (e.g. Rom. 8.17; 2 Cor. 1.5; Col. 1.24; Heb. 13.12f; 1 Pet. 1.20f; 4.12ff; Rev. 1.9).

Never, however, does the New Testament speak either of us offering ourselves 'in Christ' or of Christ uniting us with himself in his own self-offering. Instead, it portrays him both as our example, so that we are to give ourselves in love *like* Christ, who loved us and gave himself up for us (Eph. 5.2), and as our mediator, so that *through* him we should continually offer to God our sacrifice of praise (Heb. 13.15). Indeed, it is only through his perfect self-offering that ours becomes acceptable. But to offer ourselves to God *like* Christ, *through* Christ and *in response to* Christ is not to do so *in* him or *with* him in his own sacrifice. That language does exactly what ARCIC agrees we must never do: it obscures the fundamental fact of the uniqueness of Christ's sacrifice (para. 5). According to *Observations,* ARCIC's formula is not definite enough, for it does not clearly express 'a participation of the Church, the Body of Christ, in the sacramental act of her Lord, so that she offers sacramentally in him and with him his sacrifice' (B.I.1). We believe it is essential for ARCIC to disassociate itself from this interpretation.

Talk of 'identification with' Christ in his self-offering or of 'participation in' the movement of it is at least confusing, at worst pelagian. For the sake of theological clarity and spiritual health we urge that the distinction between Christ's sacrifice and ours must be preserved, lest the perfect and the tainted, the atoning and the eucharistic, the divine initiative and the human response be confounded with one another.

5   Our second problem concerns the real presence of Christ. We ourselves strongly affirm that at every Eucharist Jesus Christ is himself personally and objectively present, ready to make himself known to us through the breaking of bread and to give himself to us so that we may 'feed on him in our hearts by faith'. But we reject any notion of substantial change in the elements themselves, and we affirm that such a change is not necessary for the full reception of Christ. Even though the word 'transubstantiation' is relegated to a footnote (n. 2), what the word has stood for is still retained, namely 'a change in the inner reality of the elements'. The *Elucidation* clarifies both that the change envisaged is not a material one, and that Christ's presence is not limited to the elements (para. 6). Nevertheless, we cannot accept the simple, unexplained statement that before the eucharistic prayer there is merely 'bread', while afterwards there is 'truly the body of Christ' (p. 26). What we can accept is what Hugh Latimer said at his last trial: 'that which before was bread now has the dignity to exhibit Christ's body. And yet the bread is still bread, and the wine is still wine, for the change is not in the nature but in the dignity'. This has been called 'trans-signification' (not least by some Roman Catholic theologians), as distinct from 'transubstantiation'.

We also believe that Christ's body and blood are 'verily and indeed taken and received by the faithful in the Lord's Supper' (Catechism), that 'the means whereby the body of Christ is received and eaten in the Supper is faith' (Article XXVIII), that those lacking 'a lively faith . . . in no wise are . . . partakers of Christ' (Article XXIX) and that therefore 'the real presence of Christ's most blessed body and blood is not to be sought for in the sacrament, but in the worthy receiver of the sacrament' (Hooker's *Ecclesiatical Polity* V 67.6).

One of the reasons why we oppose the notion of a substantial change is that such teaching lays itself open to the cultus related to the consecrated elements, especially Adoration and Benediction, whose absence *Observations* notes, declaring that 'the adoration rendered to the Blessed Sacrament is the object of a dogmatic definition in the Catholic Church' (B.I.3). Respectfully but firmly we reject this, as also ARCIC's attempt to defend it in *Elucidation*, paras. 8 and 9. We are greatly disturbed by the cultus relating to the reserved sacrament, in whatever form and in whatever church it is practised.

B.II Ministry and Ordination

1 We are glad that ARCIC I's second Agreed Statement begins with 'the life and self-offering of Christ' as the perfect model of ministry (para. 3), recognizes the uniqueness of the ministry of the apostles (para. 4), acknowledges the Holy Spirit as the source of the diversity of ministries evident in the New Testament (para. 5), and declares some form of oversight 'an essential part' of the church's life from the beginning, with a threefold pastoral ministry emerging clearly in the post-apostolic period (para. 6).

2 We agree with those critics, however, to whom this statement has seemed to have 'too clerical an emphasis' (*Elucidation*, para. 1). The priesthood of all believers is acknowledged (para. 7), but not their ministry. Moreover, in so far as the ministry of the laity is mentioned, it seems to be exercised in the church; the ministry of God's people as servants and witnesses in the world is overlooked.

3 It is conceded that the New Testament uses a variety of images to describe ministerial function (para. 8), but never calls ministers 'priests' (para. 13). Yet the Commission did not face the implications of this fact, namely that no special priesthood attaches to ordained ministers which is not also shared by lay ministers, except when 'priest' is being used in its etymological sense of 'presbyter', the only sense in which the Anglican Reformers retained it. Instead, the Commission defend their concept of ministerial priesthood on the ground that 'Christians came to see the priestly role of Christ reflected in these [ordained] ministers and used priestly terms in describing them' (para. 13). The reason for this was eucharistic, namely that the presiding minister, reciting Christ's words and distributing Christ's gifts, 'is seen to stand in a sacramental relation to what Christ himself did in offering his own sacrifice' (para. 13). We regret that we cannot accept this reasoning: it originated in

the third century and lacks any biblical warrant. We disagree that 'the essential nature of the Christian ministry . . .' is 'most clearly seen in' the eucharistic celebration (para. 13, cf. *Elucidation*, para. 2), and we entirely reject the statement of *Observations* that 'the priestly nature of the ordained minister depends upon the sacrificial character of the Eucharist' (B. II.1). To be sure, the public worship of the people of God was from the earliest sub-apostolic period led by the bishop or presbyter, who could therefore be regarded as their representative. Yet in this common praise he was not exercising a priestly function which they did not share; he and they belonged equally to the 'holy priesthood offering spiritual sacrifices acceptable to God through Jesus Christ' (1 Pet. 2.5). Instead, the distinctive nature of the ordained ministry, according to the New Testament, is surely pastoral oversight, which is mainly exercised by the ministry of the word, to which the ministry of the sacraments also belongs. The primary movement of ministry is not towards God (in offering) but towards human beings (in proclamation and service), because that is the primary movement of the word and sacraments.

4 We note the statement that Christian ministers, particularly in presiding at the eucharist, are 'representative of the whole church in the fulfilment of its priestly vocation', but do not understand the corollary that 'their ministry is not an extension of the common Christian priesthood, but belongs to another realm of gifts of the Spirit'. We ask for clarification.

5 There could, of course, be no reunion between Rome and Canterbury without a mutual recognition of ministries, and that is not possible until Pope Leo XIII's bull *Apostolicae Curae* (1896), which declares Anglican ordinations 'completely null and void', is revoked. This papal judgment rested on two alleged 'defects' in Anglican ministers, the first of 'intention' (the bishop did not intend to ordain priests who would offer the sacrifice of the mass) and the second of 'form' (the Ordinal of 1552 contained no reference to eucharistic sacrifice). ARCIC I expressed the view, however, that the whole issue had been put in 'a new context' by its 'agreement on the essentials of eucharistic faith with regard to the sacramental presence of Christ and the sacrificial dimension of the eucharist, and on the nature and purpose of priesthood, ordination and apostolic succession' (Ministry and Ordination, para. 17; *Elucidation*,

para. 6). Cardinal Willebrands commented favourably on this in his letter to the Co-Chairmen of ARCIC II (13 July 1985), and added that what the Roman Catholic Church sees as the two defects of intention and form could possibly be removed if ARCIC I's doctrines of eucharist and priesthood are both accepted by the two churches and seen to be expressed in the Anglican Ordinal (*Anglican Orders in a New Context*). But it is precisely in these areas of eucharistic presence, sacrifice and priesthood that full agreement continues to elude us.

6 Related to the question of priesthood is the debate on the full ordination of women, which the Co-Chairmen of ARCIC II in their reply to Cardinal Willebrands (14 January 1986) called 'a fresh and grave obstacle to reconciliation of ministries'. We have to confess that we evangelicals are as divided on this issue as other Anglicans. We are glad to hear that ARCIC II has been requested to study it.

B.III *Authority in the Church I*

1 It is particularly welcome to us that the first Statement on *Authority in the Church* begins with the clear confession that Jesus Christ is Lord, to whom God has given all authority, and further affirms that 'the Holy Spirit keeps the Church under the Lordship of Christ' (Authority I, para. 7).

2 We regret, however, that the Statement proceeds at once to the topics of 'Christian Authority' and 'Authority in the Church'. For the essential New Testament corollary to the authority of Christ is not the authority, but rather the humility, of his people, as exemplified by him in his incarnation and ministry. It seems to us a serious omission that the Statement nowhere refers to the warnings of Jesus against the abuse of authority (e.g. Mark 10.42ff; Matt. 23.1ff); such behaviour belongs to the world, he said, adding 'not so with you'. In his kingdom greatness is to be measured by service not rule, by slavery not authority. We know, of course, that other passages in the New Testament allude to the place of authority (e.g. 1 Thess. 5.12f; Heb. 13.7, 17, 24). Yet this has to be seen in the light of the new and modest style of leadership which Jesus introduced.

3 When we come to the question how Christ exercises his authority in the church, we find an inconsistency in the Statement, which it seems to us urgent to resolve. At times Scripture is accorded the supreme place which it has in our historic Anglican formularies, and which we believe Rome also now recognizes, or is very close to recognizing. Thus the church may 'translate' or 'restate' the faith, and 'make judgments' in times of crisis, but only if these are 'consonant with the apostolic witness recorded in the Scriptures', that is, 'consonant with Scripture' itself (paras. 15 and 19). The *Elucidation* emphasizes this, although here 'the primary norm' is said to be Jesus Christ as 'set forth and interpreted in the New Testament writings' (para. 2). At other times, however, Scripture is toppled from its supremacy into being only 'a normative record' (para. 2), and bracketed with other authorities, so that in both our traditions, it is said, 'the appeal to Scripture, to the creeds, to the Fathers, and to the definitions of the councils of the early Church is regarded as basic and normative' (para. 18). But we must insist that this is not Anglican, nor (at least since Vatican II) does it seem to us to be truly Roman. Tradition is exceedingly important for the interpretation of Scripture, but an appeal may always be made from tradition back to the Scripture it claims to interpret. Can we not agree that it is first and foremost by his word that Christ rules his church? We do not see any possibility of the reformation and reunion of our churches unless they are both ready to test their traditions by Scripture and, if Scripture requires it, to modify and even abandon them.

Of course Paul wrote of his teaching as 'tradition' (*paradosis*), which he had himself received and in his turn passed on to the churches (e.g. 1 Cor. 15.3ff; 2 Thess. 2.15; 3.6; cf. 2 Tim. 2.2; 1 John 2.24; 2 John 9ff). But, as Oscar Cullmann has argued, a clear line has to be drawn between apostolic and post-apostolic traditions. The former are the foundation, the latter the super-structure. Hence the need, which the early church perceived, to determine the New Testament canon. What the ARCIC statement means by tradition is the church's post-apostolic teaching, and it is in this sense that we too are using the word.

4 The two views of tradition, which the *Elucidation* describes and declares to be not necessarily contradictory (para. 2), seem

mutually incompatible to us, unless the 'revelation' mentioned three times in relation to the second view refers to the biblical revelation. Apart from this, what needs to be clarified is that, *however tradition is viewed*, it must be made subordinate to Scripture. The failure of the Commission to grasp the nettle of the Marian dogmas is a case in point, those of her Immaculate Conception (1854) and of her Bodily Assumption (1950). It is acknowledged that they 'raise a special problem for those Anglicans who do not consider that the precise definitions given by these dogmas are sufficiently supported by Scripture' (Authority II, para. 30). When the dogma of the bodily assumption was promulgated in 1950, however, Archbishops Geoffrey Fisher and Cyril Garbett were much more outspoken in the statement they issued: 'The Church of England renders honour and reverence to the Mother of our Lord Jesus Christ. But there is not the smallest evidence in the Scriptures or in the teaching of the early church of belief in the doctrine of her bodily assumption. The Church of England refuses to regard as requisite for a saving faith any doctrines or opinions which are not plainly contained in the Scriptures' (17 August 1950).

5 Further clarification is needed of the Commission's Statement and *Elucidation* on the authority of general councils. Although we ourselves believe in God's continuing, providential care of his church, we do not conclude from this that its decisions, when it meets in ecumenical council, 'exclude what is erroneous' (para. 19). Rather we confess (with our Anglican forefathers) that councils 'may err, and sometimes have erred', since not all their members are 'governed with the Spirit and Word of God' (Article XXI). Indeed, according to its *Elucidation*, the Commission seems to agree. It is neither declaring that councils cannot err, it says, nor denying that some have (para. 3). Their judgments are inerrant only if they (a) relate to 'fundamental matters of the faith', (b) are clarifications of Scripture, not additions to it, and (c) are 'faithful to Scripture and consistent with Tradition'. If these second and third qualifications indicate the priority of Scripture over tradition, as they appear to, then the inerrancy of councils has become a phantom. For now their decisions exclude what it erroneous only if, by being biblical, they exclude what is erroneous. So we hope the Commission is saying that the decisions of councils

are open to correction by Scripture, and that they have no binding authority 'unless it may be declared that they be taken out of holy Scripture' (Article XXI).

6 Similarly, the claim to papal infallibility must surely be subject to the supreme authority of Scripture. For if the two supposed infallibilities (of church and pope) were unqualified, they would be among the most important truths of Christianity. But Scripture says nothing about either. Its silence is eloquent.

B.IV *Authority in the Church II*

1 The fourth report of ARCIC I (*Authority in the Church II*), in which the delicate subject of papal primacy is considered, contains much that we applaud. To begin with, there is a fresh and courageous re-examination of the Petrine texts, on which the claim to papal primacy has traditionally been based. As a result, the honest admissions are made that, although Jesus gave Peter a position of special importance, it was 'a leadership of service', it did not isolate him from the other apostles (para. 5), 'the New Testament contains no explicit record of a transmission of Peter's leadership' (para. 6), and it offers 'no sufficient basis' for a universal primacy of the bishop of Rome, even if it is held that this is God's purpose and not contrary to the New Testament (para. 7). We welcome the candour of these statements. We also note, however, that they are unacceptable to the Sacred Congregation for the Doctrine of the Faith, who insist on the assertion of Vatican I that 'the apostle Peter . . . received immediately and directly from Jesus Christ our Lord a true and proper primacy of jurisdiction' (*Observations*, B.III.1).

2 Two particular questions concern us. The first relates to the ground on which an acceptance of Roman primacy might be based, and the second to the form which such a primacy, if accepted, might take.

First, the basis. Having conceded that the Petrine texts are insufficient, the Commission resorts to historical and pragmatic alternatives. It is, of course, a fact of history that gradually the primacy of the Roman see developed, and that this came to be seen by many as the guidance of the Spirit and 'a gift of divine providence' (para. 13). This could never be proved, however, for some church history (not least, the history of the papacy) has exemplified a deviation from God's will, rather than a conformity to it. The Commissioners' other argument is that 'like any human community the Church requires a focus of leadership and unity' (Ministry and Ordination, para. 7); it is 'needed' to safeguard the church's faith and unity. But is this not the reasoning rather of secular than of Christian minds? The church as the divine society is not 'like any human community' that it should model itself on the patterns of the world. The oversight of the local church is different; it is God's plainly revealed purpose and provision (e.g. Acts 14.23; 20.28; Eph. 4.11ff; 1 Tim. 3.1ff; Titus 1.5ff). But nothing similar is envisaged in the New Testament for the world-wide church. On the contrary, the church's supreme head is Christ himself, to whom universal authority has been given, and who rules his people by his word and Spirit. We are not at all convinced that an earthly pastor with universal oversight is desirable, let alone necessary.

3 Supposing, however, for the sake of argument, that these scruples could be overcome, and that the Anglican Communion were to recognize the papal primacy, what form might it take? It can be maintained that already Vatican I's declaration of infallibility and universal jurisdiction has been modified by Vatican II's emphasis on collegiality, and that – at least in theory – the primatial authority is intended to 'support', not 'override', the ministry of the bishops (Authority I, para. 12). Nevertheless, the Commission is right to voice Anglican fears of both Vatican centralization and papal autocracy (para. 19). At the beginning of any realistic consideration of papal primacy, Anglicans would want to secure explicit assurances that it would involve neither 'the suppression of . . . traditions which they value' nor 'the imposition of wholly alien traditions' (para. 22).

4 Although we do not believe that the New Testament envisages any visible, human authority figure as head of the church, what we could contemplate, as not incompatible with the New Testament, would be a leadership somewhat similar to the role exercised by the Archbishop of Canterbury in the world-wide Anglican Communion, expressing historical continuity, visible unity, personal affection and a ministry of brotherly support, but not infallibility or universal jurisdiction. Similarly, within the fellowship of autonomous Orthodox Churches the

Ecumenical Patriarch possesses neither infallibility, nor universal jurisdiction, nor even 'primacy', but rather a certain 'seniority' which 'is to be understood in terms not of coercion but of pastoral service' (*Anglican–Orthodox Dialogue*, the Dublin Agreed Statement 1984, paras. 21–30). As a first step towards such a servant-image, which is already expressed in the title 'servant of the servants of God', we dare to hope that the Pope will renounce such other traditional titles as 'the Vicar of Jesus Christ, the successor of the Prince of the Apostles, the Supreme Pontiff of the Universal Church'. We would welcome such a gesture; it would reassure us that a reformed and remodelled primacy might be possible and acceptable. But *Observations* gives us little hope. Instead, it asserts the Pope's intrinsic power of jurisdiction, and quotes Vatican II's reference to his 'full, supreme and universal authority over the whole Church' (B.III.2).

[Section BV, which examined ARCIC II's statement *Salvation and the Church*, has been omitted here.]

C Conclusion

1 We are glad that the ARCIC enterprise is an ongoing process, and we urge patient perseverance, until 'real and tested theological agreement' is reached (*Open Letter* 1977, para. 3). We anticipate that ARCIC II will review ARCIC I's four statements in the light of the responses of both churches to them, and we hope that at the same time they will find a way to incorporate into the main text of each statement the material now contained in its *Elucidation*. We are also grateful that they have invited, in relation to *Salvation and the Church*, 'observations and criticisms made in a constructive and fraternal spirit'. We request that in their task of revising all five statements, they will be asked to take the contents of this Open Letter into consideration.

2 We also consider it essential that ARCIC II will make a statement about the form which any official relationship between the Anglican Communion and the Roman Catholic Church might take. What is in mind when the expression 'full visible communion' is used (Final Report, Introduction, para. 9)? How could the Anglican Communion be 'united not absorbed', as

Cardinal Mercier put it in 1925? And what are the limits of acceptable diversity in such a union without absorption, as Archbishop Runcie asked in 1981? We hope ARCIC II will explore the possibility of something similar to the 1931 Bonn Agreement between Anglicans and Old Catholics, which based full communion on agreement in primary doctrines, while tolerating disagreement in secondary matters. This would seem to be compatible with ARCIC's own principle of unity in those essentials which can admit no divergence.

3 The possible reunion between the Roman Catholic and Anglican Churches is rightly described as a 'reconciliation'. But reconciliation between two parties previously at enmity demands repentance on both sides. Such repentance should begin with profound regret over attitudes of pride, intolerance and rancour which have exacerbated our differences, and in which we admit with shame we have ourselves shared. Do we not need, however, to repent of some past (and continuing) opinions, teachings and statements, as well as of past attitudes and actions? Do we not have to confess that in some areas 'we were wrong'? Can our two churches bring themselves to say this? There can be no genuine reunion without reformation, no reconciliation without repentance.

24

FRANCIS SULLIVAN:
The Vatican Response to
ARCIC I (1992)

The Final Report of the First Anglican–Roman Catholic International Commission (ARCIC I) was completed in 1981, and released early in 1982. In March, 1982, the Congregation for the Doctrine of the Faith published its critical *Observations* on that Report.[1] Shortly thereafter, copies of the Final Report were sent to the episcopal conferences of the Catholic Church, with the request that they send to the Holy See their responses to it. Some of those responses were published, prior to the directive of the Holy See that they were not to be released to the press. Finally, ten years later, we now have 'the Catholic Church's definitive response to the results achieved by ARCIC I'.[2] There is no reference at all in this Vatican document to any contribution which the responses received from the episcopal conferences might have made to it. This seems regrettable, especially in view of the fact that several of those responses were prepared by bishops whose close contacts with churches of the Anglican Communion made them better judges of the achievement of this dialogue than others might be who had little or no first hand experience of Anglican life and worship.

This 'definitive response' describes itself as 'the fruit of a close collaboration between the Congregation for the Doctrine

[1] AAS 74 (1982), pp. 1063–74.
[2] *Origins,* 21/28 (19 December, 1991), pp. 441–7. The number in parentheses following quotations from this Response indicates the page in *Origins.* It should be noted that there are two rather serious misprints in the text as given in *Origins,* both on p. 446. In the first column, 'These sacraments stand in need' should read: 'These statements stand in need'; in the second column, 'those who were appointed bishops and apostles' should read: 'those who were appointed bishops by the apostles.'

298

of the Faith and the Pontifical Council for Promoting Christian Unity'. I think it is important to note that this is not a case of collaboration between equal partners. The Apostolic Constitution *Pastor Bonus* of 1988, which established the competence of the various dicasteries of the Holy See, gives the CDF the last word on any document coming from the other dicasteries, if it deals with matters of faith.[3] *Pastor Bonus* explicitly states that the PCPCU must work in close collaboration with the CDF in the preparation of any document that it wishes to publish.[4]

I think an expert in source-criticism would not have much trouble deciding which elements of the Response are due primarily to the CDF, and which are the contributions of the PCPCU. It would be simple enough to compare the definitive Response with the *Observations* published by the CDF back in 1982. This comparison shows that practically every critical observation made by the CDF then, appears again in the final Response. From this fact one could safely conclude that the critical elements in the Response are the work of the CDF. The major difference between the 1982 *Observations* and the 1991 Response is the presence in the latter of some positive statements of commendation for the work done by ARCIC I. I think it not unlikely that these can mainly be attributed to the collaboration of the PCPCU. It might be worthwhile at this point to quote a few of these positive remarks:

> The Report . . . witnesses to the achievement of points of convergence and even of agreement which many would not have thought possible before the Commission began its work. As such, it constitutes a significant milestone not only in relations between the Catholic Church and the Anglican Communion but in the ecumenical movement as a whole.
>
> It is in respect of Eucharistic Doctrine that the members of the Commission were able to achieve the most notable progress toward a consensus. . . . The Catholic Church rejoices that such common affirmations have become possible.
>
> On both the eucharist and the ordained ministry, the sacramental understanding of the Church is affirmed, to the exclusion of any purely 'congregational' presentation of

---

[3] AAS 80 (1988), p. 873 (art. 48), p. 874 (art. 54).
[4] AAS 80 (1988), p. 896 (art. 137).

Christianity. The members of the Commission are seen as speaking together out of a continuum of faith and practice which has its roots in the New Testament and has developed under the guidance of the Holy Spirit throughout Christian history.

(On the questions of authority and primacy) One can rejoice in the fact that centuries of antagonism have given way to reasoned dialogue and theological reflection undertaken together.

While we must be grateful for these positive statements, we have to recognize the fact that they are outweighed by the predominantly negative judgment which this Vatican Response has expressed on the achievement of ARCIC I. The negative character of the Response is evident from a comparison between what ARCIC I claimed to have achieved, and what the Response grants that it has achieved.

ARCIC I claimed to have reached: (1) substantial agreement on eucharist, ministry and ordination; (2) consensus on basic principles of authority and primacy; (3) convergence on questions concerning papal primacy and infallibility where consensus had not been reached. In judging the achievement of ARCIC I it is essential to keep in mind the different degrees of agreement which it claimed to have reached. It is important also to note carefully what ARCIC I did not claim to have achieved.

What, then, does the Vatican Response say to the claims made by ARCIC I?

The first question I would ask is whether the authors of the Response fully understood the exact nature and limits of the claims made by ARCIC I.[5] I could not help asking myself this

---

[5] One could also ask how carefully the authors of the Response read the text of the Final Report. Certainly they did not always quote it accurately. I have found no less than seventeen inaccuracies in the quotations which the Response gives from the Final Report. The most serious of these are the following. On p. 443, col. 2: the words 'the provision of' are omitted from the phrase 'we believe that the provision of a ministry of this kind . . .' The reference is given to MOE, 4; it should read MO, 6. The following reference is given as MOE, 12; it should read MOE, 2. On p. 444, col. 1: the word 'wholly' is omitted from the phrase: 'can be known to be wholly assured'; the word 'all' is omitted from the phrase 'When it is plain that all these conditions have been fulfilled'; and the words 'of the truth' are omitted from the phrase: 'Anglicans can agree in much of the truth that the dogmas . . .'.

question, when I found such statements as the following in the Response:

'It is not possible to state that substantial agreement has been reached on all the questions studied by the Commission.' But ARCIC I did not claim that it had reached substantial agreement on *all* the questions it had studied.

'There still remain between Anglicans and Catholics important differences regarding essential matters of Catholic doctrine.' ARCIC I did not deny this. It clearly acknowledged the fact that important differences remain regarding the dogma and exercise of papal infallibility.

'There are still areas that are essential to Catholic doctrine on which complete agreement . . . has eluded the Anglican–Roman Catholic Commission.' ARCIC I did not claim to have reached *complete* agreement in any area. Even where it claimed to have reached substantial agreement, it admitted that points of disagreement could remain, but it believed that these could be resolved on the basis of the principles that had been agreed on.[6]

'Differences or ambiguities remain which seriously hinder the restoration of full communion in faith and in the sacramental life.' ARCIC I did not claim that its agreements would justify the restoration of full communion in faith or sacramental life. The last sentence of the Final Report expressed 'high expectations that significant initiatives will be boldly undertaken to deepen our reconciliation and lead us forward in the quest for the full communion to which we have been committed, in obedience to God, from the beginning of our dialogue.'

It would seem correct to say, in the light of the points just made, that at least to some extent the negative character of the Vatican Response is due to the fact that it criticizes ARCIC I for not achieving results which the Commission itself did not claim to have achieved.

We now come to the Vatican verdict regarding the results which the Commission did claim to have achieved.

ARCIC I claimed to have reached substantial agreement in the areas of Eucharist and Ordained Ministry. However, the following statement of the Response seems to deny that ARCIC I has achieved substantial agreement in this area: 'Before setting forth for further study those areas of the Final

---

6 *Eucharistic Doctrine: Elucidation*, para. 2.

Report which do not satisfy fully certain elements of Catholic doctrine and which thereby prevent our speaking of the attainment of substantial agreement, it seems only right and just to mention some other areas in which notable progress has been achieved . . .' In what follows we see that while on some questions regarding Eucharist and Ordained Ministry 'notable progress has been made,' there still remain 'certain statements and formulations in respect of these doctrines that would need greater clarification from the Catholic point of view.' The final word on this matter is: 'Further clarification or study is required before it can be said that the statements made in the Final Report correspond fully to Catholic doctrine on the Eucharist and on Ordained Ministry.' It is clear that for the Vatican, ARCIC will not have achieved 'substantial agreement' on Eucharist and Ordained Ministry until its statements 'fully satisfy' and 'fully correspond' to Catholic doctrine.

It was the claim of ARCIC I that it had reached consensus on basic principles of authority in the church. The verdict of the Vatican Response is as follows: 'When it comes to the question of Authority in the Church, it must be noted that the Final Report makes no claim to substantial agreement. The most that has been achieved is a certain convergence, which is but a first step along the path that seeks consensus as a prelude to unity.' (443) So where ARCIC had claimed consensus on basic principles, the Response can see only convergence as a first step on the way to consensus.

ARCIC I admitted that it had not reached agreement on several questions regarding the nature and exercise of papal primacy, including especially the question of papal infallibility, and its exercise in the definition of two Marian dogmas. But it did claim that where it had not achieved consensus, it had at least registered a degree of convergence. The Vatican Response would seem to deny that ARCIC had even reached convergence on these issues, saying: 'There are still other areas that are essential to Catholic doctrine on which complete agreement or even at times convergence has eluded the Anglican–Roman Catholic Commission. In fact the Report itself acknowledges that there are such matters, and this is particularly true in respect of the Catholic dogma of papal infallibility.' The Response then goes on to spell out the lack of agreement on papal infallibility and the Marian dogmas.

Given the fact that ARCIC I clearly admitted that it had not achieved a consensus on these issues, it seems unduly to heighten the negative tone of the Response to put such emphasis on the fact that ARCIC I did not reach agreement on them. This emphasis is seen in the fact that when the Response comes to point out remaining areas of disagreement, it immediately devotes four long paragraphs to the lack of agreement on papal infallibility and its exercise in defining the Marian dogmas, and twice quotes the statement which expresses Anglican reservations regarding the dogma of papal infallibility. In any case, what the Response demonstrates is only what ARCIC admitted: that it had not reached a consensus on these issues. I do not believe that the Response has refuted ARCIC's claim to have achieved at least a certain convergence in their regard.

The authors of the Vatican Response were evidently aware that their judgment on the achievement of ARCIC I would be seen as a negative one. Toward the end of the document they justify themselves by saying: 'It must be remembered that the Roman Catholic Church was asked to give a clear answer to the question: are the agreements contained in this Report consonant with the faith of the Catholic Church? What was asked for was not a simple evaluation of an ecumenical study, but an official response as to the identity of the various statements with the faith of the Church.'

The terms used here shed some light on what I see as the basic question raised by this Response, namely: what were the criteria on which the Vatican has based its judgment on the work of ARCIC I? A comparison of the two sentences we have just quoted shows that for the authors of this Response, to say that an agreed ecumenical statement is *consonant* with the faith of the Catholic Church, means that it must be *identical* with that faith. Further examination of the Response shows that an agreed dialogue statement will not be seen as identical with Catholic *faith*, unless it corresponds fully with Catholic *doctrine*, and indeed with the official Catholic formulation of that doctrine. It must furthermore be expressed in such a way as to exclude all ambiguity; and the Vatican document seems to know no way to exclude such ambiguity except to use the precise formulas by which the Catholic Church is accustomed to express its faith.

At any rate, this is how I would interpret the particular judgments on which the Response has based its verdict that

ARCIC I has not reached substantial agreement on any of the issues which it has treated. It is not my intention here to discuss these particular issues in detail. What I think sufficient to substantiate my interpretation of the Response, is to quote a number of the statements in which the Vatican has expressed its dissatisfaction with various elements of the ARCIC Final Report. I believe that these critical remarks bear out my contention that what the Vatican would require of an agreed dialogue statement is that it fully correspond to the language of official Catholic doctrine.

After noting some 'common affirmations' that ARCIC I made concerning the Eucharist, the Response adds: 'The Catholic Church rejoices that such common affirmations have become possible. Still, as will be indicated further on, it looks for certain clarifications which will assure that these affirmations are understood in a way that conforms to Catholic doctrine.' Later on, we see what specific 'clarifications' the Vatican would require concerning the Eucharist. One of these is that the 'propitiatory character of the Mass' be explicitly affirmed, since this 'is part of the Catholic faith.' Another is that because to say that in the Eucharist the bread and wine 'become' the body and blood of Christ is 'insufficient to remove all ambiguity regarding the mode of the real presence,' it must be said that this 'is due to a substantial change in the elements.' In other words, to remove all ambiguity and correspond fully with Catholic doctrine regarding the Eucharist, one would have to use the language of Trent about 'propitiatory sacrifice' and 'substantial change'.

With regard to the ordained ministry, the Response finds the ARCIC agreed statement defective in that it does not refer to the 'character' imparted by priestly ordination. The reasons given suggest that in the view of the authors of the Response, if one did not employ the language of 'priestly character', one would not be able adequately to maintain the distinction between the ministerial priesthood and the common priesthood of the baptized, or the recognition of Holy Orders as a sacrament instituted by Christ. These would seem rather drastic consequences to be drawn from the choice not to employ a particular theological concept in an agreed ecumenical statement.

After quoting the passage in which ARCIC I sets out what it describes as 'the essential features of what is meant in our two traditions by ordination in the apostolic succession,' the Vatican

Response says: 'These statements stand in need of further clarification from the Catholic perspective.' One of these clarifications would be to recognize in the apostolic succession an 'unbroken line of episcopal ordination from Christ through the apostles down through the centuries to the bishops of today.' (446) Here again the needed clarification would seem to call for using official Catholic language: in this instance, that of *Lumen Gentium* 20, from which the Response then gives a lengthy quotation.

The conclusion I come to after studying this Response to ARCIC I is that what the CDF would require of an agreed dialogue statement is that it fully correspond to Catholic doctrine, and that, to do so, it must use the language in which the Roman Catholic Church has expressed that doctrine. The question, then, is whether these are appropriate criteria by which the Catholic Church should answer the question whether agreed statements issuing from its dialogue with the Anglican Communion, are consonant with the Catholic faith.

There are several reasons for giving a negative answer to this question. The first is based on the statement which Pope John XXIII made in his opening address to the Second Vatican Council on October 11, 1962: 'The substance of the ancient doctrine of the deposit of faith is one thing, and the way in which it is presented is another.'[7] The Council referred to this

---

[7] W. M. Abbott, SJ, *The Documents of Vatican II* (Geoffrey Chapman, London, 1965), p. 715. The sentence which we have quoted corresponds perfectly to the Italian version of Pope John's opening speech, which was published in *L'Osservatore Romano*, 12 October 1962, p. 3, and in *La Civiltà Cattolica*, n. 2697 (3 November 1962), pp. 209–17, here p. 214. A. Belloni has shown that the Italian version of this sentence is faithful to the manuscript which John XXIII had prepared for his opening address. (See A. Melloni, 'Sinossi critica dell'allocuzione di apertura del Concilio Vaticano II *Gaudet Mater Ecclesia* di Giovanni XXIII,' in G. Alberigo *et al.*, *Fede Tradizione Profezia* (Paideia Editrice, Brescia, 1984), p. 269.) However, the same issue of *L'Osservatore Romano*, pp. 1–2, gives the official Latin text of the Pope's address, which has an expanded version of this sentence, which could be translated: 'For the deposit of faith, or the truths which are contained in our venerable doctrine, are one thing, and the way they are expressed is another, with, however, the same sense and the same meaning' (p. 2, col. 5). While it was this Latin version that Pope John read at the opening session of the Council, he evidently preferred his Italian original, for on a subsequent occasion when he returned to this idea, he expressed it with the same terms he had used in his manuscript (cf. *Discorsi Messaggi Colloqui del Santo Padre Giovanni XXIII*, V, 13).

statement when it invited theologians 'to seek continually for more suitable ways of communicating doctrine to the men of their times,'[8] and applied its truth when it spoke of the differences between the Eastern and Western Churches in the theological expression of their doctrine. Its statement on this latter point is of fundamental significance for determining the appropriate method of ecumenical dialogue:

> In the investigation of revealed truth, East and West have used different methods and approaches in understanding and proclaiming divine things. It is hardly surprising then, if sometimes one tradition has come nearer than the other to an apt appreciation of certain aspects of a revealed mystery, or has expressed them in a clearer manner. As a result, these various theological formulations are often to be considered as complementary rather than conflicting.[9]

There is surely a legitimate application of such ideas to the differences of doctrinal formulation between the various Western Churches, as well as between East and West. In fact we can see an application of such ideas in the terms used by Pope Paul VI and Archbishop Michael Ramsey in their *Common Declaration* of March 24, 1966, in which they expressed their intention 'to inaugurate between the Roman Catholic Church and the Anglican Communion a serious dialogue which, founded on the Gospels and on the ancient common traditions, may lead to that unity in truth, for which Christ prayed.'[10] If a dialogue is founded on the Gospels and on the ancient common tradition, it hardly seems correct to judge its results on the standard of one church's subsequent formulation of its faith.

Finally, we have the important statement which the present Holy Father, John Paul II, made in the audience which he gave to the members of ARCIC I in 1980. With obvious approval of the method which they had adopted in their dialogue, he said:

> Your method has been to go behind the habit of thought and expression born and nourished in enmity and controversy, to scrutinise together the great common treasure, to clothe it in a language at once traditional and expressive of the

---

[8] *Gaudium et Spes*, 62.
[9] *Unitatis Redintegratio*, 17.
[10] The Final Report (CTS/SPCK, London, 1982), p. 118.

insights of an age which no longer glories in strife but seeks to come together in listening to the quiet voice of the Spirit.[11]

These statements of John XXIII, Paul VI, John Paul II and the Second Vatican Council, suggest the appropriate criteria by which the Roman Catholic Church ought to judge whether the agreed statements produced by ecumenical dialogues in which it is engaged, are consonant with Catholic faith. I would further suggest that we can find a good example of the kind of judgment that could be made on the basis of these criteria, in the Response to ARCIC I produced by the Conference of Bishops of England and Wales.[12] These Catholic bishops had good reason to say: 'Our Response will have particular significance in the continuation of this dialogue between our two communions, especially in this land in which the Anglican communion finds its centre . . .'[13] They expressed themselves as conscious of bearing a special responsibility in this process of consultation, and of their role both to judge how far the statements of ARCIC I are in harmony with the Catholic faith, and to point out anything which they considered to be inadequate in its treatment or expression.

However, before entering into their judgment on the agreed statements, they first made it clear that they understood and approved of the methodology which ARCIC I had employed. They said:

> Since Vatican II it is increasingly recognised that the truth of revelation can be expressed in a variety of ways. The substantial agreement achieved by ARCIC I has been possible because of the particular methodology adopted by the commission. This has been described as one of its most striking features. It was commended by Pope John Paul II when he said to the members of the commission . . . [they then quote the passage we have cited above, and continue]: We too welcome the emergence of this methodology. It is characterised by a joint endeavour to explore our 'common tradition', and achieves an understanding of the context in which concepts arose, how this coloured their meaning and

[11] Address of Pope John Paul II to the members of ARCIC I at Castelgandolfo, 4 September 1980, in *One in Christ*, 16 (1980), pp. 341–2; here p. 341.
[12] *One in Christ*, 21 (1985), pp. 167–80 (see Chapter 7).
[13] *One in Christ*, 21 (1985), p. 168.

what remains open to further development. It brings about a shared understanding of revelation as expressed in histori-cally conditioned formulae. We commend this methodology, as entailing a serious attempt to develop patterns of thought and language which give profound and precise expression to our shared faith.[14]

The Bishops of England and Wales believed that their response to the Final Report of ARCIC I would have particular significance in the continuation of this dialogue. It certainly deserved to do so, and I believe it would have, if their under-standing of the methodology employed by the International Commission, and of the criteria that would be appropriate in judging its achievement, had been adopted by the consultors of the Congregation of the Faith. On the other hand, if the Vatican is going to continue to apply the criteria which it has used in judging the work of ARCIC I, then I fear that the ecumenical dialogues in which the Catholic Church is involved have a rather unpromising future ahead of them.

25

JOS VERCRUYSSE:
Ordained Ministry in the Catholic Response to ARCIC (1992)

In December 1991 the Catholic Church published its long expected official Response to the Final Report, published in 1982 by the Anglican–Roman Catholic International Commission (ARCIC), consisting of the statements worked out by the commission since 1973. The Response is – the text says – 'the

[14] *One in Christ*, 21 (1985), pp. 168–9.

fruit of a close collaboration between the Congregation for the Doctrine of the Faith and the Pontifical Council for Promoting Christian Unity' (para. 3).[1] Because of its official status the note is a significant and authoritative contribution to the dialogue between the Anglican Communion and the Roman Catholic Church. Definitive and fully committed as it is, though, it doesn't intend to slow down the dialogue. On the contrary, the drafters hope:

> that its definitive response . . . will serve as an impetus to further study, in the same fraternal spirit that has characterized this dialogue in the past, of the points of divergences remaining, as well as of those other questions which must be taken into account if the unity willed by Christ for his disciples is to be restored (para. 4).

The same hopeful appreciation is to be found in the concluding paragraph, where we read:

> The above observations are not intended in any way to diminish appreciation for the important work done by ARCIC I, but rather to illustrate areas within the matters dealt with by the Final Report about which further clarification or study is required before it can be said that the statements made in the Final Report correspond fully to Catholic doctrine on the eucharist and on ordained ministry.

In our contribution we will deal with the questions regarding ordained ministry. We will try thus to assess the Response and to understand the core of its critical remarks.

1 The Canterbury Statement on *Ministry and Ordination*

Because the Response asks for clarifications only about some particular aspects of the text it is appropriate to recall briefly the concern and the content of the statement on *Ministry and Ordination*, that was published in 1973 by the International Commission after its meeting in Canterbury. It is important to keep in mind that the statement chose to present a global approach to ministry. One should not forget either that ARCIC intends to look at the particular questions in the light of an overall ecclesiological perspective summarized with the term *koinonia*. As the Co-Chairmen had stated already in the preface

---

[1] The text is published in *Catholic International*, 3, pp. 125-30.

to the Canterbury Statement, they wanted to look at the doctrine of ministry, and specifically at the understanding of the ordained ministry and its place in the life of the Church. This specific concern is summarized in the introduction to the Final Report:

> In the statement *Ministry and Ordination* it is made clear that *episcope* exists only to serve *koinonia*. The ordained minister presiding at the eucharist is a sign of Christ gathering his people and giving them his body and blood. The Gospel he preaches is the Gospel of unity. Through the ministry of word and sacrament the Holy Spirit is given for the building up of the body of Christ. It is the responsibility of those exercising *episcope* to enable all the people to use the gifts of the Spirit which they have received for the enrichment of the Church's common life. It is also their responsibility to keep the community under the law of Christ in mutual love and in concern for others; for the reconciled community of the Church has been given the ministry of reconciliation (2 Cor. 5.18).[2]

The document does not deal first of all with the *priestly* aspect of ministry. When speaking of this aspect, it does it in 'the wider context of our common convictions about the ministry' (Ministry and Ordination, para. 1), adding subsequently that 'the ordained ministry can only be rightly understood within this broader context of various ministries, all of which are the work of one and the same Spirit' (Ministry and Ordination, para. 2).

The statement describes in a first section the role of all ministry in the life of the Church, both ordained and not ordained. Their purpose is to build up the community and to minister reconciliation in it: 'All ministries are used by the Holy Spirit for the building up of the Church to be his reconciling community for the glory of God and the salvation of men' (Ministry and Ordination, para. 5). The apostolic character of ministry and its New Testament features are treated in this wider context (Ministry and Ordination, para. 4). 'The New Testament shows that ministerial office played an essential part in the life of the Church in the first century, and we believe that the provision of a ministry of this kind is part of God's design for his people' (Ministry and Ordination, para.

---

[2] Final Report (CTS/SPCK, London, 1982), Introduction, para. 6.

6). Out of a considerable diversity in the structure of pastoral ministry during the first century, emerged in the second half of the second century the threefold ministry of bishop, presbyter and deacon that became universal in the Church.

The second section of the statement examines the threefold structure of the ordained ministry. As a priestly community, the whole community has its own purpose: 'The Christian community exists to give glory to God through the fulfilment of the Father's purpose,' i.e. by their life of prayer and surrender to divine grace, and by their careful attention to the needs of all human beings. Ordained ministry must be seen in that perspective: 'The goal of the ordained ministry is to serve this priesthood of all the faithful' (Ministry and Ordination, para. 7). The Church too requires a focus of leadership and unity. The functions of the ministers are described in the New Testament with a variety of images. But it is crucial for the development of the statement to see that 'an essential element in the ordained ministry is its responsibility for "oversight" (*episcope*)' (Ministry and Ordination, para. 9). It characterizes all ordained ministry in its own way, presbyters and deacons as well as bishops. A few paragraphs develop some particular features of the exercise of ordained ministry, viz. the ministry of the word, the celebration of the sacraments, the proclamation of reconciliation and especially the celebration of the eucharist, as the central act of worship. 'He who has oversight in the church and is the focus of its unity should preside at the celebration of the eucharist' (Ministry and Ordination, para. 12). It is especially regarding these two paragraphs that the official answer of the Catholic Church asks for clarification.

The last section of the Canterbury Statement deals with the entry into ordained ministry by the act of ordination, seen again in the larger context of *koinonia*: 'Ordination denotes entry into this apostolic and God-given ministry, which serves and signifies the unity of the local churches in themselves and with one another. Every individual act of ordination is therefore an expression of the continuing apostolicity and catholicity of the whole Church' (Ministry and Ordination, para. 14). Paragraph 15, describing ordination as a *sacramental act*, has been welcomed by the Response asking however for further clarification. As it does also for the next paragraph dealing with the meaning of the rite of episcopal ordination as expressing the essential features of what is meant by ordination in the apostolic succession.

In the concluding paragraph the members of the commission state their conviction that the text 'represents the consensus of the Commission on essential matters where it considers that doctrine admits no divergence' (Ministry and Ordination, para. 17).

In 1979 the ARCIC published some *Elucidations* to the text dealing with the meaning of priesthood, the sacramentality of ordination, the origins and the development of the ordained ministry, the ordination of women and the validity of Anglican Orders.

It is necessary to have in mind this global and systematic development of the Canterbury Statement, leading from the general to the particular, in order to give the correct weight to the particular and specific questions asked in the official Response of the Catholic Church.

2 The Official Response: Positive Assessment of the Final Report

When looking now at the Explanatory Note of the Catholic Response one must admit that the positive remarks are kept rather brief. The Response does not expand on the general development of the Canterbury Statement, which proceeds – as we have seen – in a deductive way from a general consideration to a more particular exposition of ordained ministry. The Response has nothing to say on this because in doing so the Canterbury Statement is in full agreement with the conciliar decree on the Church, *Lumen Gentium*, and with several other ecumenical texts on ministry, such as *Baptism, Eucharist, Ministry* of the Faith and Order Commission. What was said in the official Catholic response to the BEM document could well have been repeated here. That response appreciated among other things,

> the embodiment of the ordained ministry within the wider theological and ecclesiological horizon of God's salvific work through Christ and his church, in which diverse and complementary gifts are bestowed upon the community and the individual members of the whole people.[3]

---

[3] *Churches Respond to BEM*, vol. VI (Faith and Order Paper 144) (WCC, Geneva, 1988), p. 26.

Among the matters of significant consensus the Response to
the Final Report singles out a few points that have to do directly
with the 'priestly' character of the ordained ministry, as dealt
with more particularly in paragraphs 13 and 14 of the Canterbury Statement and in the second of the following *Elucidations*.

First, there is an explicit acknowledgment of the distinction
between the priesthood common to all the baptized and the
ordained priesthood. These are two distinct realities and
belong to another realm of the gifts of the Spirit (Ministry and
Ordination, para. 13; Ministry and Ordination: *Elucidation*,
para. 2). These statements correspond, although in a less
scholastic terminology, to the doctrine expressed in *Lumen
Gentium* that the common priesthood of the faithful and the
ministerial priesthood differ 'essentially and not only in
degree.'[4] Both are however linked with the fundamental priesthood of Christ and related to one another: 'The goal of the
ordained ministry is to serve this priesthood of the faithful'
(Ministry and Ordination, para. 7).

Second, the answer mentions with approval the fact that
ordination is described as a 'sacramental act' (Ministry and
Ordination, para. 15). This statement has been clarified in the
Elucidations by giving a kind of definition of what is meant by
a 'sacramental act' and how it can be applied to ordination:
'Both traditions agree that a sacramental rite is a visible sign
through which the grace of God is given by the Holy Spirit in
the Church' (Ministry and Ordination: *Elucidation*, para. 3).

Third, the Response also approves the statement that
ordained ministry is an essential element of the Church. It
quotes therefore paragraph 6 of *Ministry and Ordination*: 'The
New Testament shows that the ministerial office played an
essential part in the life of the Church in the first century and
we believe that the provision of a ministry of this kind is part
of God's design for his people.'[5] The statement is explained
further in *Elucidation* paragraph 4, leading to the conclusion:
'It was recognized that such ministry must be in continuity not
only with the apostolic faith but also with the commission
given to the apostles.' The assertion implies a reference to
Christ giving such a commission. One has to keep in mind the
method used by the ARCIC commission. By giving the historic

---

[4] *Lumen Gentium* 10.
[5] The Response para. 7, refers to *Elucidation*, para. 2 of *Ministry and
Ordination*, para. 6, leaving out 'the provision of . . .'

evidence of the emergence of a threefold ministry and of its responsibility for *oversight* in the Church, it intends to refer to the tradition, using the historic evidence thus as a theological argument that is relevant for today's doctrine and practice. The original context points to the *ordained ministry* in a larger understanding than only the priestly ministry, whereas the criticisms of the Response are actually specifically addressed to the issue of the *priestly* ministry.

A fourth point of consensus is the affirmation that only the ordained minister presides at the eucharist (Ministry and Ordination: *Elucidation*, para. 2). The statement should be seen though in relation to paragraphs 12 and 13 of the Canterbury Statement, speaking of the link between the role of the bishop as responsible for oversight and the celebration of the eucharist: 'Hence it is right that he who has oversight in the church and is the focus of unity should preside at the celebration of the eucharist' (Ministry and Ordination, para. 12). In a particular paragraph referring to both the statements on the *Eucharistic Doctrine* and on *Ministry and Ordination* the Response appreciates that 'the sacramental understanding of the Church is affirmed, to the exclusion of any purely "congregational" presentation of Christianity' (para. 8). The point is not so much the questionable allusion to 'congregationalism', but the acknowledgment of the commonality in a sacramental understanding of the Church. The document does not only use a 'sacramental' terminology but considers in ministry clearly its acting 'in the name of Christ' (Ministry and Ordination: *Elucidation*, para. 2). This sacramental view is clearly present in the description of what ministry means for the *koinonia*: 'The ordained minister presiding at the eucharist is a sign of Christ gathering his people and giving them his body and blood.'[6]

3 The Core of the Critical Remarks

Differently from the comments to *Authority in the Church*, in which differences and disagreements are clearly stated – as is done indeed in the ARCIC statement itself – the explanatory note asks only for clarification from a Catholic point of view with regard to ministry and ordination.[7] Without going into

[6] Final Report, Introduction, para. 6.
[7] See expressions as 'would need greater clarification from the Catholic point of view . . .', para. 20; 'more clearly reflected . . .', para. 21; 'made clearer . . .', para. 24.

detail on the direction such clarifications should take, the Response indicates concerns. Further dialogue will have to ask how they are to be dealt with in relation to Catholic theology.

3.1 Priesthood – Sacrifice – 'In Persona Christi'

If I have correctly understood, there is a central concern in the observations, even a certain suspicion that the *sacrificial character of the eucharist* together with its relation to a priestly conception of the ministry is not clearly enough affirmed. We may see here a connection with a quite traditional point in the controversy between Catholicism and Anglicanism, that should be properly cleared up in the ongoing dialogue. It must be examined also in the light of the more general ecumenical debate on eucharist and sacrifice as explained for example in *Baptism, Eucharist and Ministry* and in the report of the Joint Roman Catholic–Lutheran Commission on the eucharist.[8] The Windsor Statement and the *Elucidations* to *Eucharistic Doctrine* have declared unambiguously 'that the eucharist is a sacrifice in the sacramental sense, provided that it is made clear that this is not a repetition of the historical sacrifice' (Eucharistic Doctrine: *Elucidation*, para. 5). This assertion is appreciated in the Response as 'the most notable progress toward a consensus' (para. 6). Both texts, the statement and the *Elucidations*, make great efforts to underline the 'sacramental' character of the *anamnesis*/memorial, expressing a strong conviction of sacramental realism (Eucharistic Doctrine: *Elucidation*, para. 5):

> The notion of *memorial* as understood in the passover celebration at the time of Christ – i.e. the making effective in the present of an event in the past – has opened the way to a clearer understanding of the relationship between Christ's sacrifice and the eucharist. The eucharistic memorial is no mere calling to mind of a past event or of its significance, but the Church's effectual proclamation of God's mighty acts (Eucharistic Doctrine, para. 5).

The sacrificial character of the eucharist is described as entering into the movement of Christ's self-offering (ibid., para. 5, also Eucharistic Doctrine: *Elucidation*, para. 5). It is an identification with the will of Christ who has offered himself

---

[8] *Growth in Agreement*, ed. Harding Meyer and Lukas Vischer (New York, Geneva, 1984), especially paras. 34–7.

to the Father on behalf of all mankind (Eucharistic Doctrine: *Elucidation,* para. 5). One has to keep in mind such explicit affirmations about the sacrificial character of the eucharist expressed though in a more global and relational way than classic Catholic theology is accustomed to.

Here I see the context of the questions asked by the Response. The Windsor Statement does not speak *explicitly* of the specific role of the minister and his ordination when treating of the sacrificial character of the eucharist, although the *Elucidations* assert without hesitation that the celebration of the eucharist presupposes a validly ordained minister (Ministry and Ordination, para. 2). In fact, the Response had already asked with regard to the Windsor Statement, that it should be clearly affirmed 'that in the eucharist, the Church, doing what Christ commanded his Apostles to do at the Last Supper, makes present the sacrifice of Calvary' (para. 21), and next 'that the sacrifice of Christ is made present with all its effects, thus affirming the propitiatory nature of the eucharistic sacrifice, . . .' (para. 21). This is expressed also in the first question for clarification with regard to *Ministry and Ordination,* which states, quoting largely *Elucidation,* para. 2:

> He [the priest who, in the person of Christ, brings into being the sacrament of the eucharist] not only recites the narrative of the institution of the Last Supper, pronouncing the words of consecration and imploring the Father to send the Holy Spirit to effect through them the transformation of the gifts, but in so doing offers sacramentally the redemptive sacrifice of Christ (para. 24).

A modification and an addition however qualify the text. Where the *Elucidation* spoke of acting 'in the name of Christ,' the Response speaks in a more *sacramental* way of 'in the person of Christ.' The addition stresses at the same time the *sacramental* and the *sacrificial* character of what the priest does *in persona Christi* when celebrating the eucharist. Acting *in persona Christi* expresses a more intimate and personal link between Christ and the minister than the one expressed by 'acting in the name of.' The sacramental realism of the sacrifice is thus stressed: 'in so doing [he] offers sacramentally the redemptive sacrifice of Christ,' accepting fully that *anamnetic* actualization does not mean however 'repetition.' Indeed such language does not imply any negation of the once-for-all sacrifice of Christ by any addition or repetition (Ministry and Ordination, para. 13).

The Canterbury Statement declares 'that in the eucharist the ordained minister "is seen to stand in sacramental relation to what Christ himself did in offering his own sacrifice".' Nevertheless, the Explanatory Note asks that the text should refer more explicitly to the fact that Christ himself instituted the sacrament of orders as the rite which confers the priesthood of the New Covenant (para. 24). But the point of the criticism seems to be the fact that the Canterbury Statement apparently does not refer to the *sacramental character* of priestly ordination. Without explaining at length what is meant by the sacramental character and without any intention of entering into a theological discussion about its content the Response asserts its importance for the right comprehension of what priestly ministry is. It is central to the Catholic understanding of the distinction between the ministerial priesthood of Christ and the common priesthood of the baptized, the text says. Even if one could hardly deny that the priesthood of the baptized is rooted in the sacramental character of baptism, 'it belongs to another realm of the gifts of the Spirit' (Ministry and Ordination, para. 13). The character has moreover a link with the recognition of the institution of Holy Orders by Christ. However for the Response the 'character' expresses more than merely the *unrepeatability* of the ordination, as the Council of Trent stated in its decree on the sacrament of order.[9] It 'implies a *configuration to the priesthood of Christ*.' The remark may be interpreted in the light of the conciliar decree on the Church, *Lumen Gentium*, describing the character of episcopacy: 'a sacred character is impressed in such wise that bishops, in an eminent and visible manner, take up the part of Christ himself, teacher, shepherd and priest, and act as his representatives (*in eius persona*).'[10] The interpretation of the character expresses thus what has been said in the previous paragraph about the acting in the person of Christ and qualifies in a personalizing way what is meant by the particular

---

[9] *Sessio XXIII*, de Sacramento Ordinis, cap IV and can. 4 (DS 1767, 1774). *Conciliorum Oecumenicorum Decreta* (Bologna, 1991), pp. 742 and 744.

[10] *Lumen Gentium*, para. 21; 'et sacrum characterem ita imprimi ut episcopi, eminenti ac adspectabili modo, ipsius Christi magistri, pastoris et pontificis partes sustineant et in eius persona agant.'

sacramental relationship between the priestly ministry and Christ as High Priest (Ministry and Ordination: *Elucidation,* para. 2). The Response qualifies *Ministry and Ordination* para. 15. It agrees with what is said, stressing however that the gift of God bestowed and the promise of divine grace – that are irrevocable – mark the receiver personally as *shalish* and representative of Christ's ministry and priesthood. At the same time however the minister is called to correspond to the best of his possibilities to the seal that has been put upon him.

3.2 Ordination of Women

It is understandable that the Response deals with the developments within the Anglican communion with regard to the ordination of women. It takes up the assertion of the *Elucidation* to *Ministry and Ordination* saying 'that the principles upon which its doctrinal agreement rests are not affected by such ordinations; for it was concerned with the origin and nature of the ordained ministry and not with the question who can or who cannot be ordained' (Ministry and Ordination: *Elucidation,* para. 5). The Response questions the assertion and finds that the problem is dismissed too swiftly. It declares that 'differences in this connection (i.e. with regard to the ordination of women) must therefore affect the agreement reached on ministry and ordination' (para. 25). The exchange of correspondence between Pope John Paul II and Cardinal Johannes Willebrands and the Archbishop of Canterbury Robert Runcie in November 1985 and June 1986 is referred to. To understand the affirmations of the Response one has to look at the theological content of the exchange of letters.[11] The Archbishop of Canterbury writes that the decision to open ordination to women rests upon serious theological reflection. The positive reason for such a development is seen in the application of a fundamental principle of the Christian economy of salvation, namely the inclusive character of the humanity of Christ, to the representative nature of the ministerial priesthood.

> They [some Anglicans] would argue that priestly character lies precisely in the fact that the priest is commissioned by the church in ordination to represent the priestly nature of the whole body and also – especially in the presidency of the

[11] *SPCU-Information Service* (1986), n. 61, pp. 106–11.

eucharist – to stand in a special sacramental relationship with Christ as High Priest in whom complete humanity is redeemed and who ever lives to make intercession for us at the right hand of the Father. Because the humanity of Christ our High Priest includes male and female it is thus urged that the ministerial priesthood should now be opened to women in order the more perfectly to represent Christ's inclusive High Priesthood.[12]

The reply of Cardinal Willebrands states that neither the Catholic Church nor the Orthodox Church consider themselves competent to alter the unbroken Tradition to ordain only men to the presbyterate and episcopate. The cardinal develops also a theological reason for it. In this regard the document recalls the declaration *Inter Insigniores*, published by the Sacred Congregation for the Doctrine of the Faith. The letter stresses especially the wider but appropriate connection with sacramental theology and ecclesiology: 'The practice of only ordaining men to the priesthood has to be seen in the context of an ecclesiology in which the priesthood is an integral and essential aspect of the reality of the Church.'[13] The 'real continuity between the redemptive work of Christ and the priestly office' can also be admitted by the holders of the legitimacy of ordination of women because of the indicated inclusive humanity of Christ. But the imagery and symbolism used by the Scriptures is also to be considered as indicative for the pattern of ministry:

> The picture of human redemption that is put before us in the Scripture is of a God who is powerful to save and of a people who receive salvation as a free gift. Feminine imagery is used to reveal the place of the human family in God's plan of salvation. . . . In its tradition, the Church has understood itself in terms of this feminine imagery and symbolism as the Body which received the Word of God, and which is fruitful in virtue of that which has been received. . . . It is precisely in this perspective that the representative role of the ministerial priesthood is to be understood.[14]

Because of the biblical symbolism of bridegroom and bride 'the male identity is an inherent feature of the economy of

12 *SPCU-Information Service* (1986), p. 108.
13 *SPCU-Information Service* (1986), p. 111.
14 *SPCU-Information Service* (1986), p. 111.

salvation, revealed in the Scriptures and pondered in the Church.'[15] It reflects itself in the theology of the ministry:

> The ordination only of men to the priesthood has to be understood in terms of the intimate relationship between Christ the Redeemer and those who, in a unique way, cooperate in Christ's redemptive work. The priest represents Christ in His saving relationship with His Body the Church.[16]

In the correspondence of 1985/1986 appears also the key word of the Response to the Final Report, '*in persona Christi*':

> However unworthy, the priest stands in *persona Christi*, Christ's saving sacrifice is made present in the world as a sacramental reality in and through the ministry of priests. And the sacramental ordination of man takes on force and significance precisely within this context of the Church's experience of its own identity, of the power and significance of the person of Jesus Christ and of the symbolic and iconic role of those who represent Him in the eucharist.[17]

Against this background the statement of the Response 'that the question of the subject of ordination is linked with the nature of the sacrament of holy orders' becomes understandable (para. 25). However, the age old and more fundamental discussion of what the significance of symbols, icons and allegories as theological arguments are, will remain on the table.

3.3 Apostolic Succession

The observation about apostolic succession may appear somewhat out of proportion in a response to a dialogue between partners for whom an historic episcopate is not precisely a matter of controversy: 'We both maintain' – say the *Elucidations* to the Canterbury Statement – 'that *episcope* must be exercised by ministers in the apostolic succession' (Ministry and Ordination: *Elucidation*, para. 4).

The link between the apostolic character of teaching and mission and the apostolic succession in ministry is expressed in *Ministry and Ordination*, para. 16.

---

[15] *SPCU-Information Service* (1986), p. 111.

[16] *SPCU-Information Service* (1986)

[17] *SPCU-Information Service* (1986)

Because they [the ordaining bishops] are entrusted with the oversight of other churches, this participation in his ordination signifies that this new bishop and his church are within the communion of churches. Moreover, because they are representative of their churches in fidelity to the teaching and mission of the apostles and are members of the episcopal college, their participation also ensures the historical continuity of this church with the apostolic Church and of its bishop with the original apostolic ministry. The communion of the churches in mission, faith and holiness, through time and space, is thus symbolized and maintained in the bishop. Here are comprised the essential features of what is meant in our two traditions by ordination in the apostolic succession (Ministry and Ordination, para. 16).

The Response asks in a rather dense paragraph (para. 27) for further reflection upon the link or 'the causal relationship' between the two elements in the understanding of the apostolic succession, viz. the historic succession in ministry through episcopal ordination and the uninterrupted continuity in Christian doctrine and teaching in union with the college of bishops and its head, the Successor of Peter. Except for the specific role of the Successor of Peter – that has to be treated in a specific study – Roman Catholics and Anglicans could as the documents of ARCIC show come to a large agreement about the two aspects. The problem of the reciprocal link and the 'causal relationship' – which is not so explicitly expressed in the original Latin text of *Lumen Gentium* 20 – as the English translation the Response uses, seems to suggest – shows interestingly enough the distinctive concern of the Response and points again to the 'sacramental' dimension of ministry. This is also evident from the examples given, when showing that the question stands at the heart of the ecumenical discussion. In fact it mentions next to the nature of the Roman primacy, the reality of the eucharist and the sacramentality of the ministerial priesthood.

4 The Validity of Anglican Ordinations

In the last paragraph of *Ministry and Ordination* the Anglican–Roman Catholic Commission states with regard to the judgement on the validity of Anglican Orders:

We are fully aware of the issues raised by the judgement of the Roman Catholic Church on Anglican Orders. The development of the thinking in our two communions regarding the nature of the Church and of the ordained ministry, as represented in our Statement, has, we consider, put these issues in a new context. Agreement on the nature of ministry is prior to the consideration of the mutual recognition of ministries (Ministry and Ordination, para. 17).

That new context was specified in the *Elucidation*:

It believes that our agreement on the essentials of eucharistic faith with regard to the sacramental presence of Christ and the sacrificial dimension of the eucharist, and on the nature and purpose of priesthood, ordination, and apostolic succession, is the new context in which the questions should now be discussed (Ministry and Ordination, *Elucidation*, para. 6).

These statements have been echoed in a letter from Cardinal Johannes Willebrands to the co-presidents of ARCIC II of July 13, 1985, in which the position of the Catholic Church with regard to Anglican ordinations is explained.[18] The letter recognizes that important developments have occurred since the Bull *Apostolicae Curae* in the field of liturgical renewal and in the relations between both communions. So the letter concludes saying, 'This is to say that, if both Communions were so clearly at one in their faith concerning the Eucharist and the Ministry, the context of this discussion would indeed be changed.'[19] Recently the Anglican–Roman Catholic Consultation in the United States examined the new situation in a survey report published under the title, 'Anglican Orders: A Report on the Evolving Context of their Evaluation in the Roman Catholic Church.'[20] In the Response however we do not find any word about this rather delicate but unresolved matter. Though conscious of the delicacy of the topic, the drafters of the Response probably did not want to enter into the matter because the Response itself with its request for clarification and its declaration 'that it is not yet possible to state that substantial agreement has been reached' (para. 2), casts a shadow upon the rather optimistic view of the ARCIC document. The

[18] *SPCU-Information Service* (1986), n. 60, pp. 23–4.
[19] *SPCU-Information Service* (1986), p. 24.
[20] *Origins*, 20 (1990), pp. 136–46; *One in Christ*, 26 (1990), pp. 256–79.

Response makes clear that according to the Catholic authorities, both communions are in fact not yet fully at one in their faith concerning the eucharist and the ministry. It remains however true that a theological clarification about the nature of ministry and ordination with the acceptance of the consequences in the practice of the Church are relevant elements that 'put the issue in a new context.' It cannot be denied that the topic will remain in some way on the agenda of the relations between both confessions.

5 Conclusion

Admittedly, the official response of the Catholic Church has already been experienced by many as a rather cold shower and continues to be received with mixed feelings. Nevertheless, it has to be received for what it claims to be, a quite critical 'impetus to further study' (para. 4). With regard to ministry and ordination the text invites us to deepen the *understanding of the sacramental nature of the ordination and of the ordained himself.* By their ordination priest and bishop become in some way in their person sacramentally marked to act *in persona Christi.* This emphasis is evident in a Catholic approach. The official response of the Catholic Church brings the dialogue also back to one of the crucial topics of the larger ecumenical discussion today: the better understanding both of the nature of the human mediation in the achievement of salvation and of the sacramental dimension of the Church.

26
JOHN McHUGH:
Marginal Notes on the Response to ARCIC I

(The following notes were originally written, as my personal comments, at the request of, and for the private use of, Bishop Clark, and therefore take much for granted. That first version made liberal use of technical terms, and all quotations were given, naturally, in Latin. To revise it for publication was not easy. On the one hand, since the comments were now to be addressed to the responsible authorities in Rome, it would have been nonsensical to present the Latin texts only in a necessarily imperfect translation, or to sacrifice the precision and clarity engendered by the use of the theological short-hand so customary in Rome. On the other hand, to make the text intelligible to a general readership unfamiliar with the technical terms, it was necessary to rewrite certain paragraphs; and it was also necessary to supply translations of certain passages, for the benefit of the increasingly large number of those who are not at home in Latin. The text, however, remains simply 'Marginal Notes', and is not intended as a general assessment of the document. This version was completed in May 1992.)

In the General Evaluation paragraph 2, the phrase 'regarding essential matters of Catholic doctrine' and in the Explanatory Note paragraph 5, the phrase 'certain elements of Catholic doctrine' would profit from clarification. The Latin term *doctrina catholica* (meaning literally 'Catholic teaching') is exceedingly common in schools of Catholic theology, and nowhere more than in Rome. It has, however, when used in a technical sense, two quite distinct meanings. It is sometimes used generically, in a broad sense, to denote everything that the universal Church presents as its official and authoritative teaching, whether it is put forward with infallible authority or not. But in technical works of Catholic theology, this term *doctrina catholica* is much more commonly employed in a very strict sense, as a term used to designate specifically those areas of doctrine which the universal Church teaches officially, and with authority, but without in any way claiming that the charism of infallibility guarantees the truth of every statement there made, i.e. while allowing for the possibility that this teaching might contain error. In this sense, 'Catholic doctrine' designates all that area of official teaching which is not 'dogma', or inseparably connected with dogma. Exactitude of terminology has always been an exemplary characteristic of the Roman schools, and the document would have gained in clarity and precision had the customary language of dogma, *de fide*, 'theologically certain', *doctrina catholica*, 'common opinion of theologians' etc. been employed.[1]

But the Response does not use this terminology, in a laudable endeavour to be intelligible to those unacquainted with such arcane distinctions. Unfortunately, this leads it into the very dangers which those distinctions were specifically designed to preclude. So, for example, when the Response mentions 'Catholic doctrine', one cannot always tell for certain (a) whether the phrase is being used in a non-technical sense, to refer to matters that are for the Catholic articles of faith (what is technically known as 'dogma'), or (b) whether it refers to teaching that is merely authoritative, but not definitive (i.e. not

---

[1] The definitions just given of 'Catholic doctrine' in the two technical senses of the term are taken, of set purpose, from a widely used, and very conservative, manual of theology published by the Spanish Jesuits forty years ago, *Sacrae Theologiae Summa* I, Tract. III, *De Ecclesia*, by Ioachim Salaverri, paras. 892-3, p. 784 (Biblioteca de Autores Cristianos, 2nd edition, Madrid, 1952). The mentioning of the exactitude of terminology in the Roman schools is also deliberate, the word 'Roman' being here used to designate those schools of theology which are situated in the city of Rome. The reference comes from John Henry Newman's words in his defence of the papal magisterium against Mr Gladstone. 'At Rome the rules of interpreting authoritative documents are known with a perfection which at this time is scarcely to be found elsewhere. Some of these rules, indeed, are known to all priests, but even this general knowledge is not possessed by laymen, much less by Protestants, however able and experienced in their own several lines of study or profession' ('A Letter to the Duke of Norfolk', in *Difficulties of Anglicans*, vol. 2: in the standard edition by Longmans, Green and Co., London, various dates, p. 294).

'dogma'), or (c) whether it is intended to embrace both. The second paragraph on *authority in the church* (para. 10) supplies a good example: it distinguishes between some 'questions that are of great importance for the faith of the Catholic Church' where there is agreement or convergence, and 'other areas that are essential to Catholic doctrine', where there is not. An Anglican might well inquire what is the exact meaning of, and the precise difference between, these two categories, and whether the Anglican Communion is being asked to assent to propositions which are taught, officially indeed, but not as indispensable articles of the faith, by the Magisterium of the Roman Communion.

So when we come to the section on the *magisterial authority of the Church* (para. 15) the sharp-cut distinction there drawn between the importance of (a) the assent of the faithful and (b) 'the authoritative definition itself on the part of the authentic teachers' seems to reflect the opinion of one school of theology within the Roman Communion which would give greater weight to the visible and external magisterium than to the invisible and internal teaching of the Holy Spirit. Yet the Second Vatican Council solemnly assures us that, when all the faithful 'from the bishops to the very last of the faithful laity' (St Augustine) exhibit a worldwide consensus on matters of faith or morality, they cannot be mistaken in their belief. And the reason for this statement is that since God's faithful people have all received an anointing from the Holy One, an anointing which abides within them and teaches them all things (1 John 2.20-1, 27), this invisible and internal witness of the Holy Spirit must, does, and always will, bear clear witness to what is true (*Lumen Gentium* 12). Hence it is surely permissible for a loyal Catholic to maintain that the invisible witness of the Spirit in the hearts of the Christian faithful has been, throughout the centuries, at least as important as the historically conditioned utterances of the Magisterium, whether from bishops or from theologians, in preserving purity of doctrine; and to believe that God always uses both these internal and external witnesses to protect his Church from irreparable error.

The rejection of the ARCIC statement about the interpretation of the First Vatican Council (para. 18) is puzzling. The Response rejects the idea that this Council's words *ius divinum*, 'need not be taken to imply the universal primacy as a permanent institution was directly founded by Jesus during his life on earth'. Three comments may be made:

(1) *Pastor Aeternus*[2] affirms, in chapter 1, that 'uni Simoni Petro contulit Iesus *post suam resurrectionem* summi pastoris et rectoris iurisdictionem' (DS 3053),[3] so that the conferring of the primacy is clearly placed *after* the mortal life of Jesus was over. It is unusual to designate events which are placed after the resurrection as taking place during the earthly life of Jesus.

(2) Chapter 1 also affirms 'primatum iurisdictionis in universam Dei Ecclesiam immediate et directe beato Petro Apostolo promissum atque collatum a Christo Domino fuisse' (DS 3053).[4] Chapter 2 then proceeds to the solemn declaration and definition that this primacy is 'by the will and authority of Christ' (*eodem auctore*) to continue for all time, and that the bishop of Rome succeeds to this universal primacy (DS 3056–8); but in this second chapter (by contrast with the first) the words *immediate et directe* ('immediately and directly') are nowhere to be found. Nor do they occur in the text of its canon. This reads: 'Si quis ergo dixerit, non esse ex ipsius Christi Domini institutione seu iure divino, ut beatus Petrus in primatu super universam Ecclesiam habeat perpetuos successores: aut Romanum Pontificem non esse beati Petri in eodem primatu successorem: anathema sit' (DS 3058).[5] No Catholic therefore may deny that the permanence of the primacy results from the institution of Jesus Christ, or that it belongs to the divine constitution of the Church; but the wording of chapter 2 does not appear to decide irrevocably the question whether 'the universal primacy as a permanent institution was *directly* founded by Jesus *during his life on earth*'.

---

[2] *Pastor Aeternus* is the title of the document issued by the First Vatican Council in 1870 defining the scope of papal primacy and infallibility.

[3] That is, in English, 'on Simon Peter alone, Jesus, *after his resurrection*, conferred the role of highest shepherd and ruler, with jurisdiction'. The reference DS denotes the *Enchiridion Symbolorum Definitionum et Declarationum de rebus fidei et morum*, originally compiled by H. Denzinger in 1854, its 32nd edition being edited in 1963 by A. Schönmetzer (Freiburg-im-Breisgau, Herder). Each paragraph is numbered, and the book is always cited by the number given in the margin.

[4] '. . . that primacy of jurisdiction over the whole Church of God was promised to and conferred upon blessed Peter the Apostle immediately and directly by Christ the Lord.'

[5] 'Should anyone say that it is not by the institution of Christ the Lord himself, in other words, by divine constitution, that blessed Peter should have successors for ever in the primacy over the entire Church; or alternatively, that the Bishop of Rome is not the successor of Peter in that same primacy: that person is to be considered a heretic.'

(3) In fact, the absence of the words *immediate et directe* from chapter 2 would appear to leave a Catholic theologian free to maintain that the permanent continuation of Peter's primacy might by the will of God have been the fruit of the guidance of the Holy Spirit, so that it would indeed have been 'in accordance with the institution of Christ' (*secundum Christi ipsius institutionem*, DS 3057), even if the need to secure a succession in this primacy had been perceived only after Jesus' final departure from this earth. For according to St John's Gospel, Jesus promised Peter and the other apostles that the Holy Spirit would teach them all things (John 14.26, cf. 15.26), and would guide them in the path of all truth (16.13–14). On the basis of these texts, it would seem permissible for a Catholic to hold that whatever Peter and the apostles subsequently judged to be permanently necessary for the constitution of the Church (e.g. freedom from observance of the Mosaic Law, Acts 15.23–9) was ultimately *ex ipsius Christi Domini institutione seu iure divino*[6] (cf. Matt. 28.18–20). Indeed, this would be the most perfect manifestation imaginable that Peter as leader of, and in company with, the others, had in truth received that *plenitudo potestatis*, that 'fullness of power' within the Church on earth, upon which *Pastor Aeternus* is centred.

But the most disturbing sentence is found under the heading *Eucharist* (para. 22), where we read that 'these earthly realities are changed into the reality of his body and blood, soul and divinity'. However, what at first reading appears to be an egregious heresy is in fact quite obviously the result of mere human error in the word-processing of the final text! No Catholic has ever suggested that the bread and wine are changed into the soul and divinity of the Lord. Clearly, what has happened is that an original draft speaking of the Real Presence of Christ in the Holy Eucharist, in his 'body, blood, soul and divinity',[7] has been combined with another statement speaking of the sacramental and substantial change in the earthly elements, and someone has overlooked the need to delete from the final text the words 'soul and divinity'. Anyone who uses a word-processor will be only too ready to forgive the error we have all made.

---

[6] i.e. 'by the institution of Christ the Lord himself, in other words, by divine constitution'.

[7] The wording is based on the decree of the Council of Trent, Session XIII, canon 1 (DS 1651), and is very familiar to elderly English Catholics from the old Catechism.

The next paragraph (para. 23) on the adoration of the reserved sacrament will be very hard indeed for Anglicans to understand. For here the Response asserts that ARCIC's statement 'creates concern from the Roman Catholic point of view'. This statement, taken together with the abrupt introduction of the term *Roman* Catholic (twice in this paragraph), as distinct from Catholic *tout court* (which has hitherto been used nearly everywhere), will be interpreted by many, and certainly by the Orthodox and virtually all the Eastern Churches, as confirming, albeit inadvertently, their conviction that in the eyes of some members of the Roman Curia only the devotional practices of the Latin Rites really do justice to the perduring Sacramental Presence in the Holy Eucharist.

The following paragraph (para. 24, sub-section 2) on the *ordained ministry* seems strained, when it asks 'that the institution of the sacrament of Orders by Christ himself be made clearer.' The wording of Trent XXIII runs: 'Si quis dixerit, ordinem sive sacram ordinationem non esse vere et proprie sacramentum a Christo Domino institutum, vel esse quoddam humanum, excogitatum a viris rerum ecclesiasticarum imperitis, aut esse tantum ritum quemdam eligendi ministros verbi Dei et sacramentorum: an. s.' (DS 1773, cf. 1764).[8] Thus Trent defined nothing concerning the time or manner of the institution of this Sacrament, and does not affirm that it was *directe vel immediate a Christo Domino institutum*. Indeed, it was fully aware that the subdiaconate and the minor orders were of ecclesiastical institution, and almost certainly regarded the institution of deacons (cf. Acts 6), and the introduction of a hierarchical distinction between *episcopi* and *presbyteri*, as being of apostolic rather than dominical origin. This would consort well with the remarks made above about the *plenitudo potestatis* (in the first paragraph on p. 328).

Paragraphs 27–8 on the *interpretation of Scripture* are genuinely embarrassing. Paragraph 27 reads: 'As is well known, the Catholic doctrine affirms that the historico-critical method is not sufficient for the interpretation of Scripture', and the next sentence begins (para. 28) with the words 'The Final

---

[8] 'Should anyone say that Order – in other words, sacred ordination – is not in a true and proper sense a sacrament instituted by Christ the Lord, or is something human thought up by men unskilled in church affairs, or alternatively, that it is merely a rite for choosing ministers of God's word and of the sacraments: that person is to be considered a heretic.'

Report seems to ignore this when dealing with the interpretation of the Petrine texts of the New Testament, for it states that they "do not offer sufficient basis" on which to establish the primacy of the bishop of Rome'. Anyone who reads these two consecutive sentences of the Response might be pardoned for concluding from them that paragraph 28 is criticizing ARCIC's Final Report for attempting to discern the meaning of Holy Scripture by relying on the historico-critical method alone.

But the passage in question (Authority II, paras. 6–7) is in fact concerned with the *interpretation* of the Petrine texts by the Fathers and doctors of the early Church, and therefore can in no way be considered as advocating the view that the historico-critical method on its own is sufficient for the interpretation of Scripture. The ARCIC document merely states first, that 'the New Testament contains no explicit record of a transmission of Peter's leadership' (para. 6), and secondly, that 'it is possible to think that a primacy of the bishop of Rome is not contrary to the New Testament, and is part of God's purpose regarding the Church's unity and catholicity, while admitting that the New Testament texts offer no sufficient basis for this' (para. 7).

The Response is here not entirely fair in its criticism of ARCIC, for anyone who reads paragraph 28 without checking these references (as I myself did at first) could easily be misled. Indeed, at that first reading, I thought the Response was here criticizing the Final Report for appealing, as it were, to a theology of the type formerly used by (for example) St Robert Bellarmine, and found also in many manuals written for students in the first half of this century, in which the authors sought to resolve the problems involved in the Catholic teaching about the primacy of Peter by resorting to a 'proof from Scripture alone', without invoking the witness of tradition. This is, as the above references show, quite untrue, but the English of the Response is so worded that it might very easily be misunderstood by anyone who did not look up the references; and they will assuredly be the majority of readers.

Another rather awkward juxtaposition is found in paragraph 9 on *authority in the church*, where the second sentence states a point negatively ('The most that has been achieved is a certain convergence, which is but a first step along the path that seeks consensus as a prelude to unity'), and the third makes the same point positively ('Yet even in this respect, there are certain signs of convergence that do indeed open the way to further progress in the future'). It would have been easy to construct one sentence containing both ideas, and without relegating either to a concessive clause. '. . . the Final Report makes no claim to substantial agreement. Yet there is evidence of a convergence of positions which opens the way to further progress in the future'.

The general impression is that the final revision may have been entrusted to a sub-committee or a secretary charged with putting together a comprehensive response, but without authority to make more than minor modifications to proposed drafts of various sections of the document. This would account for those judgments which are juxtaposed, but which do not sit well with the neighbouring sentence.

A purely literary examination of the document seems to point inexorably to this conclusion, but it was only when the above text had been written that I learned that this Response was issued without any protocol, either at the beginning or at the end. This is most unusual in a document from the Holy See, which has throughout history been so meticulous, indeed exemplary, in diplomatics. It is being said that the Response emanates jointly from the Sacred Congregation for the Doctrine of the Faith and the Pontifical Council for Christian Unity; but the text itself does not say by whose authority it is issued. Indeed, the text itself carries the signature neither of Cardinal Ratzinger nor of Cardinal Cassidy, nor of any official attached to either office. I am informed, however, that Cardinal Cassidy has written a letter to accompany the Response, and it would obviously be quite absurd to suggest that the Response, merely because it is devoid of protocol, lacks the stamp of authority. On the other hand, the reader, especially any reader accustomed to the traditional practices, usages and style of the Roman Curia, is left at the end genuinely perplexed concerning the precise degree of authority ascribed by the Holy See to the Response, and therefore to some of the statements which it contains.

Conclusion

27
CHRISTOPHER HILL:
Summary–Where We Are Now

The first thing to say in an assessment of our present position is that significant developments, both positive and negative, have taken place beyond the theological boundaries of the first ARCIC. The second Commission has, for example, published important Agreed Statements on justification and ecclesiology (*Salvation and the Church*, CTS/Church House Publishing, London, 1987), on the mystery of the visible communion of the Church (*Church and Communion*, CTS/Church House Publishing, London, 1991); and now, breaking entirely new ecumenical ground, on morals, communion, and the Church (*Life in Christ*, CTS/Church House Publishing, London, 1994). Moreover, the growing unity between our two Churches is not confined to the work of international bodies. There is increasing trust, affection, collaboration, common worship, and joint witness in many places and at all levels.

Less happily, the ordination of women to the priesthood continues to be a contentious issue between us (and among Anglicans). Major Anglican Provinces have now ordained women to both the priesthood and episcopate, and an official Roman Catholic negative has been strongly expressed by Pope John Paul II in his letter to the Catholic bishops of 13 May 1994. This confirms the earlier declaration of the Congregation for the Doctrine of the Faith (*Inter Insigniores*) of 1976, and the correspondence between successive Popes and Archbishops of Canterbury since 1975. Yet the obstacle of the ordination of women is, it is largely agreed on all sides, *primarily* a matter of authority. For Rome, whatever 'illustrations' are offered to confirm current practice, the heart of the matter is the Roman conviction that the Catholic Church does not have the authority to make this development.

While this discussion about *authority* continues within and between the two Communions, we would do well to do all we can to resolve the older problem of orders that still lies before us. If we are sufficiently agreed about the meaning of the eucharist and the ordained ministry, the classical obstacle of 'Anglican orders' is resolvable.[1] Are we, therefore, sufficiently agreed?

As far as Anglicans are concerned, the actual decision of the last Lambeth Conference is clear. It was reached *after* synodical decisions upon the Agreed Statements over the Anglican Communion. All the Provinces were asked the same questions about *Eucharistic Doctrine* and *Ministry and Ordination* and their *Elucidations*. The Lambeth Conference echoed the positive response of the Provinces by declaring that the two Statements (and their *Elucidations*) were 'consonant in substance with the faith of Anglicans'.

It is, however, fair to ask what was actually meant by this decision. Some have asked whether, for Anglicans, 'consonant in substance' means no more than that a statement falls within an agreed comprehensive spectrum of Anglican doctrines. Against this minimalistic interpretation, it must be said, first, that never before in Anglican history has such an elaborate procedure been established for the examination of a doctrinal question. Each Province was asked to give an official reply; the replies were officially collated and summarized by an international consultation that published its findings for the Conference to consider. This procedure was itself officially established for the Conference by the Anglican Consultative Council (Newcastle, 1981). The Council had asked how it was 'possible for a Communion of autonomous Provincial Churches to come to a common acceptance of an ecumenical agreement'. It was clear that this must involve the 'formal

---

[1] This is the import of the significant letter to the Co-Chairman of the ARCIC II of 1985, signed by Cardinal Willebrands, the President of the (then) Pontifical Secretariet for Unity, see p. 181. The full text can be found in E. Yarnold's *Anglican Orders–A New Context* (CTS, London, 1986).

acceptance' of the Provincial Synods. However, it was to the bishops of the Lambeth Conference that the Council looked, after the judicial decisions of the Synods, to 'discern and pronounce a consensus'.[2] This is exactly what the Lambeth Conference thought it was doing. The Explanatory Note to the Resolution indicates that the Conference was aware that some Anglicans had continued anxieties about *Eucharistic Doctrine* and *Ministry and Ordination*. Nevertheless, it noted a 'clear "yes"' to the Statements from the Provinces, and spoke of them as 'sufficiently' expressing Anglican belief (cf. p. 155).

Second, the word 'consonant' was suggested by ARCIC I through its Co-Chairman in a letter to their representative authorities (September 1981). It means 'in agreement', 'accordance', or 'harmony with'. The term does not imply identity, but means much more than compatibility (cf. Chapter 21, pp. 241–247).

Third, the sharp, even fierce, debate in Synods throughout the Anglican Communion and at the Lambeth Conference itself is a clear indication that what was to be passed or rejected was important. Both Anglicans in favour, and the minority who were critical of the ARCIC Statements, believed that the questions they were being asked mattered vitally. Permissive acceptance would not have generated such passion. What was decided was close to the heart of Anglican identity.

The Roman Catholic response has complications of a different order. The initial response of the Congregation for the Doctrine of the Faith of 1982 (Chapter 5) was in many ways very cautious; but it was not definitive, and was described by Cardinal Ratzinger himself as 'its contribution to the continuation of this dialogue' (Chapter 6). The published responses from the various Episcopal Conferences (invited by the then Vatican Secretariat for Promoting Christian Unity at the same time as Anglican response was being elicited from the Provinces) were much more positive, e.g. England and Wales (Chapter 7). The official Roman Catholic *Response* (Chapter 10) displayed *both* these characteristics. Some parts were highly positive; other parts were not so much negative as confusing, because of the difficulty in fully accepting the ARCIC method.

Reflection on the Vatican *Response* elicited the conviction by members of both ARCIC I and II that while the dialogue on

---

[2] For a fuller discussion of the process leading up to the Lambeth Conference, see Chapter 16, pp. 187–190.

authority still had a large agenda to complete, although having begun promisingly, the problems of eucharistic doctrine and ministry and ordination were closer to solution (excepting the ordination of women to the priesthood). Some members of ARCIC I were invited to draft a *Clarification* for ARCIC II to consider and adopt (Chapter 17). This was then considered by the Vatican, because it was the Vatican *Response* that had called for it. Cardinal Cassidy, President of the Council for Christian Unity, wrote to the Co-Chairman of ARCIC, basically accepting the *Clarifications* on behalf of 'the appropriate dicasteries of the Holy See' (Chapter 18). In other words, this important letter comes not only in the name of the Council for Unity, but also the Congregation for the Doctrine of the Faith. The Cardinal's letter speaks of 'new light on the questions concerning Eucharist and Ministry . . . for which further study had been requested'. It also affirms that 'the agreement reached on Eucharist and Ministry by ARCIC I is thus greatly strengthened and no further study would seem to be required at this stage'.

The Co-Chairmen of ARCIC II have commented upon Cardinal Cassidy's letter. They describe the *Clarifications* and the Letter as constituting 'a very important element in the reception of ARCIC's agreements on Eucharist and the under-standing of Ministry' and 'an important stage in our growth towards fuller communion'. They describe the agreement on these two areas as 'now more definitive'.[3] The *Clarifications* seem, therefore, to have changed the Vatican *Response* (on the eucharist and on the ordained ministry) into something con-siderably less hesitant. Indeed, the criticism (direct or indirect) of the *Response* by Roman Catholic theologians and even Episcopal Conferences (cf. Chapters 11, 14, 21, 24, 25, and 26) seem to have been heeded. Even if acceptance of defined Roman Catholic teaching is still preferred by the Congregation for the Doctrine of the Faith as avoiding all ambiguity, there seems now to be a recognition that the *Clarifications* do give us sufficient assurance of real agreement. We can truly recognize our own faith in them. It is important at a time of some pes-simism about our relationship that this significant recognition is noticed and appreciated by Anglicans and Roman Catholics alike.

[3] A Statement by the Co–Chairmen of ARCIC II on the publication of the *Clarifications* and Cardinal Cassidy's letter (CTS/Church House Publishing, London, 1994).

28

EDWARD YARNOLD:
Conclusion – What Next?

While the process of the reception of ARCIC I was unfolding, a new Commission (ARCIC II), established by Pope John Paul II and Archbishop Robert Runcie, began a new stage of the work in 1983. The task that the two primates formulated for it in their *Common Declaration* of 1982 was:

> to examine, especially in the light of our respective judgments on the Final Report, the outstanding doctrinal differences which still separate us, with a view towards their eventual resolution, to study all that hinders the mutual recognition of the ministries of our communions, and to recommend what practical steps will be necessary when, on the basis of our unity in faith, we are able to proceed to the restoration of full communion.

So far ARCIC II has published two Agreed Statements in accordance with the first item of this agenda: *Salvation and the Church* (1987), and *The Church as Communion* (1991). Its present work is on the Church's moral teaching, a subject of study which had been recommended as early as the Malta Report (para. 23). Some preliminary consideration has also been given to the second item on recognition of ministries; that study has become more urgent in view of the growing number of Anglican churches, including the Church of England, that have decided to ordain women to the priesthood.

The third item on ARCIC II's agenda concerns 'practical steps'. This is in accordance with ARCIC's charter, the *Common Declaration* of Pope Paul VI and Archbishop Michael Ramsey, which, as we saw in the Introduction to this book (p. 11), determined that the dialogue should include 'matters of practical difficulty'. The Final Report in its Conclusion looked forward to the tackling of such matters:

The convergence reflected in our Final Report would appear to call for the establishing of a new relationship between our Churches as a next stage in the journey towards Christian unity. . . . There are high expectations that significant initiatives will be boldly undertaken to deepen our reconciliation and lead us forward in the quest for the full communion to which we have been committed, in obedience to God, from the beginning of our dialogue (Conclusion, pp. 76–100).

In the light of the difficulties that have been encountered in the years since the publication of the Final Report, it is scarcely possible to read these brave words without a poignant sense of disappointed hopes.

It is true that the agenda that the Pope and the Archbishop set the new Commission in 1982 envisaged the practical steps that would need to be taken at the *end* of the process 'when, on the basis of our unity in faith, we are able to proceed to the restoration of full communion'. Nevertheless, the difficulties into which relations between the two Churches have run seem to call urgently for such practical steps in order to prove that progress can be made, not yet leading indeed to the restoration of full communion, but to a deepening of that 'certain yet imperfect communion' which, according to Pope John Paul and Archbishop Robert Runcie, the two Churches already share (*Common Declaration*, 2 October 1989).

Such a strategy would be in accordance with the aim that ARCIC has always set itself of seeking 'unity by stages'.[1] It would also conform to the principle that Pope John Paul II proposed in Constantinople in 1979 with regard to Roman Catholic relations with the Orthodox:

We must not be afraid to reconsider, on both sides, and in consultation with one another, canonical rules established when our awareness of our communion . . . was still dimmed, rules which, perhaps, no longer correspond to the

---

[1] Final Report, Authority I, para. 26. The concept of achieving 'unity by stages' was first formulated in the discussions of the Anglican–Roman Catholic Preparatory Commission. It was then worked out in detail in two papers written for the Preparatory Commission respectively by Bishop (later Archbishop) Henry McAdoo, who was later to become Co-Chairman of ARCIC I, and Bishop Christopher Butler. See *Anglican–Roman Catholic Dialogue: The Work of the Preparatory Commission*, ed. A. C. Clark and C. Davey (London, 1974), pp. 21, 84–106.

results of the dialogue of charity and to possibilities they have opened. It is important in order that the faithful on both sides may realise the progress that has been made; and it is to be hoped that those who are in dialogue will be concerned to draw out the consequences of coming progress for the life of the faithful (AAS 71 (1979), p. 1602).

One might judge that the present is not a fruitful moment to make such institutional changes in the relations between the Anglican Communion and the Roman Catholic Church at the world level. Time is needed to assess the implications of the Roman Catholic response to ARCIC and the recent decision of the Church of England to ordain women to the priesthood, both of which developments appear discouraging. This does not however mean that no new stage in our relationships is possible. What it does appear to mean is that, while ARCIC II continues the dialogue, for the time being new practical initiatives will most fruitfully be sought at the national, diocesan and parochial level, rather than the universal level. Such was the recommendation of ARCIC II, which believed that awareness of 'the extent of the communion already existing between our two churches . . . should encourage Anglicans and Roman Catholics *locally* [our italics] to search for further steps by which concrete expression can be given to this communion which we share' (*Church as Communion*, para. 58).

Although many of these initiatives will be pursued in conjunction with other churches, in Britain – under the auspices of the Churches Together movement – the 'special place' that Vatican II accorded the Anglican Communion[2] suggests that a closer relationship between Roman Catholics and Anglicans will continue to be appropriate. Many of the recommendations of the 1968 Malta Report could still be implemented. In particular, steps might be taken to 'alleviate some of the difficulties caused by mixed marriages, to indicate acceptable changes in Church regulations [concerning such marriages], and to provide safeguards against the dangers which threaten to undermine family life in our time' (para. 16). The fruitful co-operation between the two Churches in running shared schools might be extended. The occasional worship that is celebrated in common by the two Churches could be placed on a formal basis, even though shared communion cannot yet be approved.

In the early promise of his pontificate during the Second

Vatican Council, Pope Paul VI addressed the observers from other churches with these words:

> As for us, like the watchman of whom Isaiah spoke – 'Watchman, what of the night?' (Isa. 21.11) – we are on the alert, craning to see, and happy each time we do, those signs in the heart of the night heralding the dawn. By this we mean signs that some progress has been made in the dialogue that has been started on, some step forward towards a *rapprochement* with those who are sustained by the same gospel and who hear resounding in the depths of their souls the same glorious appeal of St Paul to the Ephesians: 'One Lord, one faith, one baptism, one God and Father of all, who is above all, and through all, and in all' (Eph. 4.4–6).

In every diocese, in every parish, there is something that can be done to hasten this dawn.

Sources

Some of the documents contained in this collection were published earlier as follows:

The Common Declaration and the Final Report (CTS/SPCK, London, 1982).

Cardinal Ratzinger's Letter in *The Tablet*, 3 April 1982, p. 350; his article 'Anglican–Catholic Dialogue', *Insight*, 1 (1983), pp. 2–11, and in J. Ratzinger, *Church, Ecumenism and Politics* (St Paul Publications, Slough, 1988).

The Response of the Roman Catholic Bishops of England and Wales to ARCIC I (CTS, 1985).

The comments of the Faith and Order Advisory Group, in *Towards a Church of England Response to BEM & ARCIC I* (CIO Publishing, London, 1985).

The Lambeth Conference Resolutions, in *The Truth Shall Make You Free* (Church House Publishing, London, 1988).

The Official Response of the Holy See (CTS, 1991).

The 1991 Statement of the Roman Catholic Bishops of England and Wales (CTS, 1991).

Archbishop George Carey's Comments on the Holy See's Response, in *Anglican and Roman Catholic Response to the Work of ARCIC I* (General Synod of the Church of England, London, 1992).

Pope John Paul II's Address to a Group of English Bishops, *Catholic International*, 3 (1992), p. 455.

French Episcopal Commission's statement, an original translation by V. Bywater, R. Greenacre and E. J. Yarnold.

The account of the meeting between the Pope and the Archbishop, *Compassrose*, 67 (1992), p. 1.

343

ARCIC II, Requested *Clarifications* and Cardinal Cassidy's Letter (CTS, 1994).

H. Chadwick, 'Unfinished Business', *The Tablet*, 1 and 8 February 1992.

C. Hill, 'The Fundamental Question', in *One in Christ*, 28 (1992/2), pp. 136–47.

E. J. Yarnold, 'Roman Catholic Responses', *Reconciliation: Essays in Honour of Michael Hurley*, ed. O. Rafferty (Columba Press, Dublin, 1993), pp. 32–52.

The Open Letter of the Executive Committee of the Evangelical Fellowship (Grove Publications, Bramcote, 1988).

F. A. Sullivan, 'The Vatican Response', *Gregorianum*, 73 (1992), pp. 489–98.

J. Vercruysse, 'Ordained Ministry', *Ecumenical Trends*, 21 (1992), pp. 149/1–163/15.

The following chapters were written specially for this volume: C. Hill, 'The Scope of this Book' and 'Summary'; E. J. Yarnold, 'The History of ARCIC I' and 'What Next?'; and J. McHugh, 'Marginal Notes on the Response to ARCIC I'.

We are grateful to the authors and original publishers.

© C. Hill, E . J. Yarnold, H. R. McAdoo, A. C. Clark, J. Ratzinger, Faith and Order Advisory Group, the General Secretary of the Anglican Consultative Council, the Bishops' Conferences of England and Wales and of France, *Compassrose*, M. Santer, C. Murphy-O'Connor, H. Chadwick, Grove Books, F. A. Sullivan, J. Vercruysse, and J. McHugh.